Ex Libris

GREAT TRUE STORIES OF
CRIME
MYSTERY
&
DETECTION

FROM THE READER'S DIGEST

The Reader's Digest Association Pty. Ltd.—Sydney • Wellington

Drawings by

Sam Dion

Marvin Friedman

Tony Kokinos

Fred Mason

Bruce Johnson

Printed in Canada

CONTENTS

Murder at Harvard

By Stewart H. Holbrook

UNTIL the gray and melancholy twenty-third of November, the people of Boston, like most Americans, had been talking all through 1849 of nothing but the great California gold rush. But on that Friday, Boston had something nearer home to occupy its attention. Dr. George Parkman had disappeared in broad daylight. It was as incredible as if Bunker Hill Monument had sunk into the bowels of the earth. A Boston Parkman simply did not, could not, disappear and leave no trace. The police went to work, and so did hundreds of citizens, spurred by a reward of $3000 for the doctor, alive or dead.

That day the eminent doctor had left his Beacon Hill home about noon. He had gone to the Merchants' Bank. From there he had called at a greengrocer's to leave an order. Later he had been seen walking rapidly toward Harvard Medical College. At or near the college, it appeared, he had walked straight into Valhalla.

It was Dr. Parkman who had given the very land on which the then new Medical College stood. Moreover, he had endowed the Parkman Chair of Anatomy, occupied by Dr. Oliver Wendell Holmes. The Parkmans had been prominent from what, even by Boston standards, were ancient times. All the Parkmans were well-to-do; the doctor was so wealthy that his son, who never earned a penny in his life, was able to leave $5,000,000 for the improvement of Boston Common. The usually staid Boston press went into a dither and police arrested scores of persons.

Professor John White Webster made a call on the missing man's brother, and said that he had had an interview with the doctor in the Medical College on Friday afternoon, at which time he had paid Dr. Parkman $483. Dr. Parkman had then left the college, said the professor.

Webster, a graduate of Harvard Medical, had taught chemistry at Harvard for more than twenty years. With their four pretty daughters, the Websters were noted for the hospitality they lavished on the faculty. His professor's salary of $1200 annually was wholly inadequate. While it was known that Webster owed the doctor money and that the doctor had gone to collect it, the professor was not under suspicion. Who could suspect a faculty member of Harvard? It began to look as if some thug had waylaid the doctor, done away with him and made off with the $483 which Webster said he had paid Parkman.

Apparently nobody suspected Webster—except a morose and obscure man named Ephraim Littlefield, a janitor at Harvard Medical College. It appears to have been a generous act of Webster's that set Littlefield on his trail like a hound of hell. On the Tuesday following Parkman's disappearance, Webster presented a thumping big turkey to Littlefield—the first gift the janitor had received in seven years of work at the college. Littlefield not only brooded over the gift, but he was troubled because talk on the street had it that "they'll sure find Dr. Parkman's body somewhere in the Medical College." Medical col-

leges in those days were held to be notorious receivers of the products of professional body snatchers.

"I got tired," said Littlefield in explaining his next move, "of all that talk." Accordingly, into his dismal basement apartment at the college he lugged drills, hammers, chisels, crowbars. He told his startled wife that he was going to dig through the brick vault under Professor Webster's laboratory room. Mrs. Littlefield was dreadfully frightened; suspicion of a Harvard professor was an act against nature, perhaps even against God.

A few days before Parkman's disappearance, the janitor explained to her, he was helping Webster in his laboratory. Suddenly Dr. Parkman appeared before them. "Dr. Webster," he cried, "are you ready for me tonight?" Webster replied: "No, I am not ready tonight." Parkman shook his cane. "Dr. Webster," he said savagely, "something must be accomplished tomorrow." Then he left.

For the next several days, Littlefield had brooded and wondered whether on the next call Professor Webster *had* been ready. "And *now*," said the janitor to his wife, "what do you think?"

So on Thanksgiving Day, while the turkey sputtered in the oven, he hammered and drilled his way into the solid brick wall. Progress was slow, but Littlefield was as determined as he was suspicious. At noon he refreshed himself with the great bird and cranberries, then returned to his labors. He continued his work on Friday, after his regular duties, and that night broke through. "I held my light forward," he related, "and the first thing I saw was the pelvis of a man and two parts of a leg. I knew," he added darkly, "this was no place for such things."

Littlefield called the police. Within a short time Webster was in a cell of the city jail. Next day the press and the town went delirious. "Horrible Suspicions!!" screamed the normally sedate *Transcript*. "Arrest of Professor J. W. Webster!" Harvard College and Beacon Hill seemed about to tumble into the Charles River.

Professor Webster was put on trial on the nineteenth of March, 1850. The state's star witness, janitor Littlefield, took the stand and his testimony was bad indeed for the professor. The defense presented a long and distinguished array of character and other witnesses. President Sparks of Harvard thought Webster "kind and humane." Nathaniel Bowditch, son of the celebrated mathematician, believed Webster to be "irritable though kindhearted." Oliver Wendell Holmes testified both for the defense and the state. For the latter, he said that whoever had cut up the body alleged to be that of Dr. Parkman had certainly been handy with surgical knives.

The state was attempting to prove that the remnants of

human mortality discovered in the vault—and in the laboratory stove—were those of Dr. Parkman; and the defense was doing its best to prove the fragments to have been almost anybody but Dr. Parkman. Day after day the trial continued and much of Boston sought to get into the courtroom. The marshal cleared the visitors' gallery every ten minutes, thus permitting thousands of persons to witness portions of the event of the century.

Slowly the coils closed around Professor Webster; and late on the eleventh day the jury was charged by Chief Justice Lemuel Shaw in an address which is still considered by lawyers to be one of the great expositions of all time on the subject of circumstantial evidence. Three hours later the jury returned a verdict of guilty.

Long before Professor Webster was hanged on August 30, 1850, he made a confession. On that fatal Friday, Parkman had called Webster a scoundrel and furiously shaken his cane in the professor's face. Then, said Webster, "I felt nothing but the sting of his words, and in my fury I seized a stick of wood and dealt him a blow with all the force that passion could give it." One blow was enough. Parkman fell, bleeding at the mouth. Webster bolted the doors, stripped the dead man, hoisted him into the sink and then dismembered him with the deft professional strokes that had been admired by Dr. Holmes.

The painful celebrity that came to Harvard has been dissipated in the century that has intervened, but more than one member of the faculty long felt the blight cast by Professor Webster. Bliss Perry once related how his mother, at Williamstown, Massachusetts, refused to entertain a Harvard professor who had come there, some twenty years after the crime, as a delegate to a convention of New England college officials. Mrs. Perry vowed firmly that she could not sleep "if one of those Harvard professors was in the house." The professor who had to find quarters elsewhere was James Russell Lowell.

Another incident concerns the lawyer (later the Union general) Ben Butler, to whom Harvard had somehow neglected to grant an LL.D. While he was cross-examining a witness in court, and treating him rather roughly, the judge intervened to remind Butler that the witness was no less than a Harvard professor. "Yes, I know, Your Honor," said Ben. "We hanged one the other day."

Professor Webster's fame is secure. He remains the only Harvard professor to have performed lethally while a member of the faculty, and the sole college professor to gain entrance to the chaste pages of the *Dictionary of American Biography* on the strength of his stout right arm.

Bachelor Michael Norton accumulated a sizable fortune and clung to it. Suddenly, without a word to any of his relatives, he dropped out of sight. After ten years passed in silence, Michael's relatives divided his estate under a state law providing that a person is presumed dead if absent without an explanation for ten years or more. Just as they were about to enjoy their newly acquired wealth, however, Michael popped up, as hale and hearty as ever. He explained that he had been "seeing the world." Told he was declared dead, he roared with laughter—until his relatives refused to return his estate. Then he sued.

"That law isn't worth the paper it's written on," Michael snorted. "It's clearly unconstitutional. You can't take away a person's property just like that."

The Supreme Court held that any state could dispose of the property of a missing person after a proper lapse of time. So Michael lost. As to letting the missing person reclaim his property if he reappeared the court said: "Now and then an extraordinary case may turn up, but constitutional law, like other mortal contrivances, must take some chances, and in the majority of instances, no doubt, justice will be done." (Based on a 1911 decision of the Supreme Court of the United States.)

—*Bruce M. Jones*

Four Months
in a Haunted House

By Harlan Jacobs

NOTE: *The name signed to this article is not the author's real name. At the time of this incident he occupied an important position in a leading university, and his editor vouches for this as a true account of his experiences.*

FOR FOUR MONTHS I once lived in a haunted house, or at least in a house that offered every evidence of being haunted.

The place in question is a lonely little cottage on Cape Cod. Though it had been built nine years before, it had never been occupied until we took it for the summer; so Helen and I were the first persons who ever spent a day or night in it.

On the night of our arrival Helen had gone to bed early while I was sitting up at work over a manuscript. The upper floor of the house consisted of two fairly large bedrooms, with a sizable foyer between them. Helen was asleep in the front bedroom, and I was writing at a table in the rear one. The night was warmish, and all the inner doors were therefore open. I was naturally trying to be as quiet as I could, but in a little while I knew that Helen had awakened.

"Was it you," she called, "who made that tapping noise?"

"Maybe it was," I replied. "Is this the noise you mean?" And I gave a few little jogs to my writing table.

"No, no!" called Helen. "That's not the sound at all. What I heard was a tapping that seemed to come from the brick walk in front of the door downstairs. It was like somebody tapping on the bricks with a cane. Didn't you hear it?" I wandered into her room and said a few words about dreaming, but very unsuccessfully. Still, neither of us took the matter seriously, and after a few moments we let it rest.

The next night we were in the living room downstairs. About ten o'clock the taps came, on the brick walk just outside the door—or about ten feet from where I sat. There were about a dozen taps, possibly a second apart, which sounded just like the impact of a cane upon the brick. "That's what I heard last night," cried Helen, while I snatched up a flashlight from the mantel and made for the door. Just before I flung it open the tapping ceased. An instant later I was outside, with my flash playing all around the place. There was no one to be seen— not a sign of man or animal, or of anything to break the silence of the night.

Now the same thing happened, in exactly the same way, many times in the course of the summer—I should say about fifty in all. It always came in the night, and three times out of four at about ten o'clock; the details were always just the same. Of course we did everything in our power to find the cause. Over and over we scrutinized the walk in the daylight, brick by brick. A dozen nights I took my station by the door as the hour of ten drew near; but if the tapping came, it ceased the moment I sprang out and left no vestige of a cause behind it. At last we gave it up, for greater mysteries had come upon us.

Before I come to those I must mention several minor marvels, for I am giving all events in the order of their occurrence. The next three happened to me alone. They came on three successive nights of our second week in the house, and each of them within a minute or two after I had gone to bed.

Barely had I put my head upon the pillow when I heard a sound as of a box of matches falling from the chiffonier and striking flat on the floor. I could almost have sworn it was a box of matches. But at any rate I had heard *something* fall and, since there was no reason for it, I arose and turned on the light, wondering. There was not an object on the floor. I looked all over the room, under the chairs and chiffonier, in the closet. There was nothing to see. Not a thing had fallen.

The next night it was a sheet of newspaper that swished across the floor through the whole length of the room. Again the sound would be a hard one to mistake. But there was no such paper in the room, nor was there any breath of a breeze to set one in motion. By this time, however, I was hardly surprised to find no sort of paper in my room, or anywhere on the whole upper floor, which I searched at once.

The third night brought a louder noise and a more peculiar one. Once more I had hardly got to bed when something like a rolling pin seemed to fall flat on the floor and then roll across the room, *ker-lump, ker-lump, ker-lump,* until it clattered against the wall and came to rest. I bounded out of bed and pulled the string for the light, but there was not a thing to be seen on the floor. Nor was there any object in the room, or any other room, which showed the slightest sign of disturbance.

At this point my reader may possibly be muttering "Rats!"

Every one of the few persons who so far have heard my story has sooner or later put in a word about rats or mice. But I have had plenty of experience with rats—and their sisters and their cousins and their aunts. These were not rats or animals of any kind.

Even the next phenomenon was not a big one, though it was a very frequent one. Together or apart, Helen and I both heard it several hundred times during the summer. We heard it at any hour of the day or night, in every room of the house, and literally in every wall and partition. It was so omnipresent that we gave it the playful name of the "Universal Click."

I now come to something more startling. If my reader has been waiting to hear about footfalls in our cottage he is not going to be disappointed. There were footfalls to be heard all over the little house. They began in our third week in the place and they continued at irregular intervals all through our stay. Sometimes we would hear them three or four times in a given day or night, though sometimes a whole week would pass without our hearing them at all. First and last, I think we must have heard them at least forty times during the season.

They were very audible indeed. No one need imagine I am speaking of any muffled sound in some far corner of the cottage. I am speaking of a steady *tramp*, *tramp*, *tramp* as of a person with good leather heels walking on the floor of the room right over our heads, or almost as often on the floor downstairs when we happened to be on the upper story. It sounded like the natural gait of a grown man. There were *never* any muffled steps; no rational person who heard the noise could have had the slightest doubt at first that there was someone walking about the house.

In evidence of this I may recount a single incident out of a good many I could furnish. In our colony there was a young woman—let us call her Mary Smith—who was so familiar with us that she would often stroll through our open door without troubling to knock. Now one day when Helen was alone at work upstairs, she heard someone step through the door below and walk around a little. Thinking it might be Mary, she called down, but received no answer. Then she started down the stairway. The footsteps below ceased as she descended, and when she reached the lower floor she found it empty.

By the time of this incident, for which I have gone ahead in my story, we had long been familiar with all the ways of the Thing which we had now come to call our "ghost." So it was no surprise for Helen to find an empty room where she had just heard somebody walking—she had known the same thing to happen too many times before. She merely muttered something about the old ghost at his usual tricks and went back up to her work. Instantly the Thing walked in and around the lower room again, just as before. This time Helen stole noiselessly down the steps. Again the footsteps ceased, again the room was bare; and once more, after a good look about the yard, Helen went back upstairs.

Hardly was she back at work above when it all began again. Again the feet came over the threshold and walked about the lower floor. But this time Helen stayed where she was. There was no use in creeping downstairs any more—we had both tried it so many times before. And then in a moment came a call:

"Very busy up there?" It was the cheery voice of Mary Smith. And now Helen knew that there was no difference in her ear between the footsteps of the Thing and the footsteps of Mary Smith.

The grandest of our various demonstrations, and the most terrific, was a noise that could easily have been heard for a mile. We call it our Grand Piano Smash, for we have no better way to tell what it was like.

This came on us first about the middle of the summer. In the living room one night we heard a crash from the garage which was enough to deafen our ears and to set the whole house quivering. It was just as if a grand piano had suddenly lost its legs and crashed to the floor. There was no piece of furniture in the entire house that could have made any such uproar in toppling. But we took no time to wonder about the cause of the din. We plunged for the garage to look at the catastrophe, and we probably got there within three seconds after the crash had resounded.

There was not a hint of anything wrong. We were using the garage as a storage space for books, but not even a book on a shelf had fallen. All was in perfect order. Of course we went all over the house and all around the grounds—only to find everything exactly as it should be. There was not a trace of a reason for the terrific crash we had heard. The same thing happened at least twice again, and probably three times. The reason for possible doubt about the last occasion will be apparent in a moment.

Except for Mary Smith, we had hardly had a visitor all summer, for our work was absorbing. But at the end of September three of our friends came for a weekend. They were my lawyer, who was drawing up an intricate contract for me, and his wife and daughter, a sophomore at Vassar. My lawyer is about the toughest-minded skeptic in all my acquaintance, and his wife and daughter are anything but giddy or nervous. All the same, I thought it best to give the man a word of warning. Into his unbelieving ears, therefore, I poured a good part of the story I am telling now. It was a total waste of breath. My whole story was scouted.

"And for my part," concluded the legal rationalist, "I wish to heaven I could hear a little from your precious ghost!"

That night the ladies went out to an amateur play while the lawyer and I stayed at home to grapple with our contract. We were deep in the complicated figures when all of a sudden came a crisp little click in the wall right behind my friend's head.

"Your friend the Universal Click?" he inquired.

"Yes."

"Some little snap in the drying wood, no doubt," he remarked, as he eyed the board.

I went on with my list. "Whatever happens," I silently resolved, "I shall simply ignore it. I shall read right on — and leave it to him!"

In about twenty minutes the familiar footfalls sounded, directly over our heads. With all the composure at my command I went on reading; and I did not raise my eyes till my companion had shot up out of his chair.

"What on earth is that?" he cried.

"Only the ghost," I answered.

"Ghost your grandmother! There's a man upstairs. Come on!"

In a moment we were upstairs, but of course there was nothing to be seen; and I exulted as I watched my hard-boiled friend search in amazement for what I knew he would never find. I will say for him that he made a thorough hunt. He ransacked rooms and attic, he pried and prodded into closets. He tiptoed on the railing of an upper balcony and scanned the roof with a flashlight. But he had to give up. "Sarah and Dorothy had better not know," he cautioned.

We did not do any more work that night. We talked about the Thing until the ladies came in, and then we changed the topic. Soon we all went to bed.

Our house was so small that all three of our visitors insisted on sleeping in one room—the front bedroom upstairs which was normally Helen's. The husband and wife took the big bed and the daughter a cot by the wall. Helen fell heir to my single bedroom, and I camped out on a sofa downstairs. Shortly after I went to bed I heard our visitors above get up and walk around a little, and I heard also their muffled voices. Thereafter all was silent for the night.

My first glance at them next morning told me they had met with excitement.

"What was that awful crash last night?" was their first inquiry.

"Crash? What crash?"

"That fearful crash just after we went to bed—it sounded like the ceiling falling in the garage!"

I sought Helen's eyes with a glance full of meaning. "Did you hear a crash?" I asked.

"Not a sound," she replied.

"Neither did I," I continued. "Tell us what you heard."

And they told us. They gave us an accurate description of the Grand Piano Smash just as we had heard it three times before—and as we did *not* hear it, for some unfathomable reason, the fourth time. I could not have described the Smash more truthfully. And they acknowledged that they had been terrified—so terrified that they had got up and taken their daughter into the bed between them! And here my story comes to an end.

Without an exception the few persons who have heard our tale have said a good deal about the creaking of the planks in wooden houses and a good deal about mice. But we have lived in many a wooden house, old and new, and we know all the noises that boards are likely to make. We heard many a creak in this house, but we were never tempted to confuse one of them with any noise such as I have described. We have also lived on close terms with mice and are familiar with their ways. There were plenty of them in the cottage when we first moved in, but we set four traps and caught them all within a week; and even before then they had never twirled a rolling pin or upset a grand piano. When skeptics bring up creaking boards and scampering mice, we manage a weary smile.

I ought to say too that we are not the kind of couple who would naturally keep open house for ghosts. We are very plain citizens, of later middle age, and we have never had a shadow of belief in spectral visitants.

To this day I have no better notion of what our "ghost" was than of what lies at the bottom of the ocean. I should certainly like to know, but I gravely doubt whether I ever shall. *Something* strange was loose in that house, and I wish I could discover what it was.

I once spent the night at the cabin of an old Kentucky mountaineer who was a firm believer in ghosts, and we mulled over this interesting subject until bedtime.

During the night I was awakened by a dry, rustling sound, as if something were moving slowly across the floor. The old man heard it too; He struck a match and peered cautiously about into every part of the room.

"What is it?" I asked.

"Nothin' much," said the old fellow disgustedly, crawling back into bed. "Thought it mighta bin a real spirit, but t'weren't nothin' but a common old rattlesnake." —*Phil C. Holmes*

The Shadow of a Doubt

By Fulton Oursler

EARLY in this century an Omaha gambler was put on trial, accused of trying to blow his worst enemy into smithereens. The result was an astonishing courtroom upset—a classic of criminal defense and of legal resourcefulness when the case seemed lost.

On Monday, May 23, 1910, John O. Yeiser, an Omaha attorney, read in his morning paper of an attempt on the life of the town's most powerful politician. Let us call him Jack Plenister. Once a frontier gambling operator, he was now master of a political ring and was said to collect a percentage from every game of chance within five hundred miles of Omaha.

At precisely 2:50 p.m. on the day before, Jack Plenister, coming back from a walk, saw a suitcase on the front porch of his house. About to pick it up, he spied a white string running from the keyhole of the bag to the porch railing. Plenister telephoned for the police. Detectives cut away the lid and exposed a revolver, the string tied to its trigger, nesting in a stack of dynamite sticks.

Reading the news report, John Yeiser was dubious.

Why such an easily seen rig as a white string stretched across the porch? The lawyer's doubts deepened when the afternoon papers said that a suspect was already behind bars. Who was the dynamite plotter and what was his motive? The prisoner was Frank Erdman, a small-time hanger-on in the local gambling crowd. Recently he had quarreled with Plenister and the gang had kicked him out. "A disgruntled henchman, out for revenge," was the police theory of the crime.

That night John Yeiser appeared at the county jail and offered his services to Erdman free of charge. But Erdman shook his head morosely. "It's no use. Everything is against me. Sure, I hate Jack Plenister. What's more, I've got no alibi; I stayed in my room until late yesterday afternoon—but nobody saw me there. I've got no friends, no witnesses, no bail money. This is a frame-up to put me away. Better not waste time on me."

Nevertheless, John Yeiser became Erdman's counsel, and as the case came to trial he told his client he felt sure he could at least deadlock the jury. "They haven't enough evidence to prove you guilty 'beyond the shadow of a doubt,'" he declared. Equally confident he remained, even when seven witnesses, one after the other, swore they had seen Erdman near Plenister's house just before the suitcase was found. In his cross-examination, Yeiser forced each of the seven witnesses to admit that he was connected with the gambling syndicate and therefore had an interest in the case.

Then the prosecutor called his star witnesses—two young sisters. Everybody in the courtroom had been wondering about these girls, because all seven witnesses had mentioned seeing two girls in white dresses walking past the Plenister house. The story the sisters told was simple, direct and utterly damning.

May 22 had been their confirmation Sunday. After services in church they had strolled home, going by the Plenister house at 2:15 p.m. They were precise about the time and emphatic in their declarations; they had seen Erdman entering an alley behind the house, they remembered his limp, his checked suit and cap.

Across the courtroom sat the prisoner, wearing a checked suit. When asked to come nearer to the bench, he walked with a limp. When they clamped a checked cap on his head, he admitted it was his. With heavy heart, Yeiser faced the older girl. The most any counsel could do with such an obviously truthful witness was to grope and probe for contradictions, hoping to shake the jury's confidence in her accuracy.

"What did you and your sister do when you came out of church?"

"We had our picture taken."

"And where did you go for that?"

"We did not go anywhere. The minister's wife took it; we just stood on the church steps."

"Have you the picture?"

"Yes, Mr. Yeiser. Right in my purse."

At this point the judge declared a two-hour recess. Carrying the snapshot in his pocket, John Yeiser walked into a cafeteria. At a solitary table he sat brooding over his lunch. The testimony of the two girls had made the state's case invulnerable. There was the photograph showing the church steps, on which stood, in long white confirmation dresses, the two sister witnesses. Nothing there to give him any hope. Or was there? Then an indefinable hunch stirred in Yeiser's subconscious. What was it that seemed to be jogging his mind—some unnoticed clue or overlooked detail? Could it be the shadow? There *was* a shadow on the snapshot. It covered a large area on

the right side, an irregularly shaped blotch. Exasperating to have something bobbing up and down on his mind, but still eluding him!

Suddenly an idea struck him. He left his unfinished meal and presently was standing in front of the church. Above him loomed the belfry tower, whose clock now struck one brazen note. He quickly found a taxi, and in fifteen minutes he got out at the observatory of Creighton University. Knocking on the door, he said to an attendant: "I would like to see the astronomer."

Next morning the courtroom was jammed. Word had flown about town that John Yeiser was going to spring a surprise—he had obtained an adjournment the previous afternoon on the ground that he had new evidence.

The first defense witness was a small man in the garb of a Jesuit priest, the Reverend William Rigge, who sat on the stand with his square ecclesiastical hat on his lap.

"You are the professor of astronomy at Creighton?"

"I am."

"I show you a snapshot. Is it possible, by looking at this photograph, for you to tell at what time the picture was taken?"

"Yes," answered the priest. "I can tell you the time within one minute."

"How can you be sure?"

"By the angle cast by the shadow of the steeple on the picture."

"What time was it taken?"

"At 3:20 o'clock in the afternoon of May 22."

The significance of the statement astounded the judge and jury and dumfounded the district attorney. Here was expert evidence that cast doubt on the tales of seven witnesses and the memories of the two girls in white. If they had really seen Frank Erdman, it must have been fully half an hour after the suitcase had been found.

The case against Erdman began to crumble. Cross-examination could not shake the calculations of the astronomer. All night he had toiled over his figures, and in the morning he had worked with surveyors on the scene, spurred on by the possibility of saving an innocent man from imprisonment.

Even though the supreme court of the state set Erdman free, there were doubters. No one, skeptics declared, could fix time just by a shadow on a snapshot. But one year later, and again two years later, to the very day and hour, the chief of detectives, the astronomer and others connected with the case held a reunion on the church steps and had their picture taken there. And when the print was made, the shadow of the steeple fell across them at exactly the same angle as in the original snapshot.

How We Trapped Capone

By Frank J. Wilson,
former Chief, U.S. Secret Service,
as told to Howard Whitman

W HEN my wife and I left Baltimore for Chicago in 1928, all I said was, "Judith, I'm after a fellow named Curly Brown." If I'd told her that Curly Brown was an alias of Scarface Al Capone, she'd have turned the car around then and there and made me take up some respectable trade like piano tuning. My assignment was to find clear proof of income-tax evasion by Capone. In previous years he had filed no tax return or had reported insignificant income.

Art Madden, our Chicago agent-in-charge, told me that hanging an income-tax rap on Alphonse Capone would be as easy as hanging a foreclosure sign on the moon. The Grand Panjandrum of the checkered suits and diamond belts had Cook County in the palm of his hand. He did all his business anonymously, through front men. To discourage meddlers, his production department was turning out fifty corpses a year.

For a base of operations the government gave me and my three assistants an overgrown closet in the old Post Office Building, with a cracked glass at the door, no win-

dows, a double flat-topped desk and peeling walls. I spent
months in fruitless investigation through banks, credit
agencies and newspaper files.

I prowled the crummy streets of Cicero but could get
no clue to show that a dollar from the big gambling
places, the horse parlors, the brothels or the bootleg joints
ever reached Scarface Al Capone. Jake Lingle, a Chicago
Tribune reporter, had been seen with Capone in Chicago
and Miami and, from the tips I got, he wasn't just writing interviews. So I saw the *Tribune* boss, Robert R.
McCormick, and told him Jake Lingle's help would be
appreciated by the United States government. "I'll get
word to Lingle to go all the way with you," said the
colonel. Lingle was assassinated next day in a subway,
right in the busiest part of the city.

I was stuck, bogged down. Sixteen frustrating months
dragged by. Capone was all over the front pages every
day. It was common talk that he got a cut on every case of
whiskey brought into Cook County; that he ran a thousand speakeasies, a thousand bookie joints, fifteen gambling houses, a string of brothels; that he controlled half a
dozen breweries. He had bought a Florida palace on
Palm Island and was spending $1000 a week on banquets.
He tore around in sixteen-cylinder limousines, slept in
fifty-dollar pajamas and ordered fifteen suits at a time at
$135 each. His personal armed forces numbered seven
hundred, equipped with automatic weapons and armored
automobiles. But evidence of lavish living wasn't enough.
The courts had to see *income*.

One night, in a desperate mood, I decided to check over
all the data which my three assistants and I had piled up.
By one o'clock in the morning I was bleary-eyed, and
while gathering up my papers I accidentally bumped into
our filing cabinet. It clicked shut. I couldn't find the

key anywhere. "Now where'll I put this stuff?" I wondered. Just outside, in a neighboring storeroom, I found an old filing cabinet full of dusty envelopes. "I can lay this old junk on the table," I thought to myself. "I'll put my own stuff in overnight."

In the back of the cabinet was a heavy package tied in brown paper. Just out of curiosity I snipped the string and found three ledgers, one a "special column cashbook." My eye leaped over the column headings: "Bird cage," "21," "Craps," "Faro," "Roulette," "Horse bets." Here was the diary of a large operation, with a take of from $20,000 to $30,000 a day. Net profits for only eighteen months (the books were dated 1925–26) were over half a million dollars.

"Who could have run a mill that size?" I asked myself. The answer hit me like a baseball bat: only three people— Frankie Lake, Terry Druggan or Al Capone! But I had already cleaned up the Druggan-Lake case. Two from three leaves one.

The ledgers had been picked up in a raid after the murder of Assistant State's Attorney William McSwiggin in 1926. They came from one of the biggest gambling palaces in Cicero, The Ship, where diamond-studded crowds from Chicago laid down $3,000,000 a year in wagers. Here was a record of *income*. If I could hang it around the neck of Al Capone, we'd have a case at last.

Scarface must have found out that we were closing in. On the inside of the gang I had planted one of the best undercover men I have ever known, Eddie O'Hare. One afternoon word reached me that Eddie wanted to see me at once. When we met, he was red-faced and excited. "You've got to move out of your hotel, Frank. The big fellow has brought in four killers from New York to get you. They know where you keep your automobile and

what time you come in and go out. You've got to get out
this afternoon!''

"Thanks for tipping me off, Eddie," I replied. So I
phoned Judith I had a surprise for her—we were moving
to the Palmer House, where she had once said she'd like to
live. I left word at my hotel we were going to Kansas and
drove to the Union Station—but right on through and
around to the Palmer. Judith was completely confused
and I hoped Al's torpedoes were, too.

Later Eddie met me with another report: "The big
fellow's offering $25,000 reward to anybody who bumps
you off!" When the story broke in the papers that Capone
had put a price on my head, Judith took it with amazing
calm. She simply said, "We're going straight home to
Baltimore!" I finally won her over by promising she could
be with me as much as possible. Women always think
they're bulletproof.

Meanwhile I was working on the handwriting in the
ledgers of The Ship. I think we must have collected handwriting samples of every hoodlum in Chicago—from voting registers, savings accounts, police courts. The painful
process of elimination finally left me with a character
named Lou Shumway, whose writing on a bank deposit
slip was a dead twin to that in the ledgers. I heard from
a tipster that Shumway was in Miami, probably working at Hialeah or the dog tracks. All I had to go on was
a description: "Shumway is a perfect little gentleman,
refined, slight, harmless—not a racetrack sport at all."

In February 1931, I stood by the rail at Hialeah looking at the man I had been stalking for nearly three years.
Scarface Al Capone sat in a box with a jeweled moll on
either side of him, smoking a long cigar, greeting a parade of fawning sycophants who came to shake his hand.
I looked upon his pudgy olive face, his thick pursed lips,

the rolls of fat descending from his chin—and the scar,
like a heavy pencil line across his cheek. When a country
constable wants a man, I thought, he just walks up and
says, "You're pinched." Here I was, with the whole U.S.
government behind me, as powerless as a canary.

Two nights later, I spotted the "perfect little gentleman" my tipster had described, working at a dog track.
I tailed him home, and picked him up next morning as
he was having breakfast with his wife. He turned pale
green. When I got him to the Federal Building, I said
cold-turkey: "I am investigating the income-tax liability
of one Alphonse Capone."

Gentleman Lou turned greener yet, but he pulled himself together and said, "Oh, you're mistaken. I don't know Al Capone."

I put my hand on his shoulder. "Lou," I said, "you have only two choices: If you refuse to play ball with me, I will send a deputy marshal to look for you at the track, ask for you by name and serve a summons on you. You get the point, Lou. As soon as the gang knows the government has located you, they will probably decide to bump you off so you can't testify.

"If you don't like that idea, Lou, come clean. Tell the truth about these ledgers. You were bookkeeper at The Ship. You can identify every entry in these books—and you can tell who your boss was. I'll guarantee to keep it secret until the day of the trial that you are playing ball with me. You will be guarded day and night, and I'll guarantee that Mrs. Shumway will not become a widow." Lou quivered like a harp string but finally gave in. I spirited him out of Miami and hid him in California.

But we still had to show that *income* actually reached the pockets of Al Capone. A painstaking checkup on all the recorded money transactions in Cicero finally showed that one "J. C. Dunbar" had brought gunnysacks full of cash to the Pinkert State Bank and bought $300,000 in cashier's checks.

Agent Nels Tessem and I caught up with "Dunbar," whose real name was Fred Ries, in St. Louis. We tailed a messenger boy with a special-delivery letter and slapped a subpoena in Ries's palm. He was annoyed, especially since the letter was from Capone's headquarters telling him to flee to Mexico. He wouldn't talk at first. But after a week in a special vermin-ridden cell in a jail we picked out for him—we knew he had a pathological fear of bugs—Ries cried uncle. We sneaked him before a Chicago grand jury in the middle of the night. His testimony put the profits of The Ship squarely in the pockets of Scarface Al! I packed my scowling little treasure off to South America with government agents to guard him until we should need him in court.

In the autumn of 1931, two weeks before the Capone trial, Eddie O'Hare reported to me: "Capone's boys have a complete list of the prospective jurors. They're fixing them one by one—passing out thousand-dollar bills, promising political jobs, giving donations to churches. They're using muscle, too, Frank." Eddie handed me a list of ten names and addresses. "They're right off the jury list—names 30 to 39!"

Next morning I went with U.S. Attorney George E. Q. Johnson to the chambers of Federal Judge James H. Wilkerson, who was to sit in the Capone trial. The judge was reassuring—somehow he seemed like a match for Scarface Al. Sure enough, the ten names Eddie had given me tallied with the judge's list. But the judge didn't seem ruffled. He said calmly, "Bring your case into court as planned, gentlemen. Leave the rest to me."

The day the trial started, I fought my way through reporters, photographers and sob sisters. Al Capone came into the courtroom in a mustard-colored suit and sat down at the counsel table just a few feet from me. Phil D'Andrea, Al's favorite bodyguard, sat beside him, sneering at the crowd. As Judge Wilkerson entered in his black robe, Capone, behind the mask of his moon-face, seemed to be snickering over the jury of new-found friends and intimidees who would soon send him back to the overlordship of Chicago.

Judge Wilkerson called his bailiff to the bench. He said in crisp, low tones, "Judge Edwards has another trial commencing today. Go to his courtroom and bring me his entire panel of jurors. Take my entire panel to

Judge Edwards." The switch was so smooth, so simple.
Capone's face clouded with the black despair of a gambler who had made his final raise—and lost.

The trial marched on. My gems, Gentleman Lou
Shumway and the bug-bedeviled Ries, stood their ground
on the witness stand, though Capone and Phil D'Andrea
were staring holes through them the entire time. I kept
my eyes on D'Andrea. When he got up to stretch during
a recess I could have sworn I saw a bulge in his right hip
pocket. But no, I thought, there wasn't a crumb in the
world who would dare to bring a gun into federal court.
I saw him stretch again. I had the boys send in word that
a reporter wanted to see him. I followed him out of the
courtroom. Nels Tessem and Jay Sullivan, my colleagues,
led him down the corridor. As we passed Judge Wilkerson's chambers I shoved him inside. "Give me that gun!"
I snapped. D'Andrea handed it over. "Give me those
bullets!" He ladled out a handful of ammunition.

Judge Wilkerson interrupted the trial to cite D'Andrea
for contempt and send him away for six months. Capone
growled, "I don't care what happens to D'Andrea. He's
a damn fool. I don't care if he gets ten years." Al was
cracking.

The trial wound up in mid-October. As the jury returned I felt sure we had won. "Gentlemen," intoned
Judge Wilkerson, "what is your verdict?"

"Guilty!" The courtroom broke up like a circus after
the last performance. Reporters ran out of court. Lawyers ran. Mobsters ran. Everybody seemed to be running but Scarface Al Capone. He slumped forward as if
a blackjack had hit him.

When I got home, Judith cried, "You did it! I knew
you were going to do it all the time!" Then she sighed.
"Now can we go back to Baltimore?"

Counsel Assigned

Condensed from the book of the same title
By Mary Raymond Shipman Andrews

A VERY OLD MAN told the story years ago. He was a
splendid old fellow, straight and tall, with brilliant
eyes. He had met his companion, an American, casually
in a Bermuda hotel, and the two fell to talking. The older
man told of events, travels, adventures. But his main
enthusiasm was for his profession, the law. The dark eyes
flashed as he spoke of great lawyers.

"It's nonsense"—the big, thin, scholarly fist banged the
chair arm—"this theory that the law tends to make men
sordid, that lawyers are created merely to keep an eye on
their clients' purses. I am a very old man; I have seen
many fine deeds done by physicians and parsons, but one
of the finest was the performance of a lawyer acting in his
professional capacity." With that he told this story:

The chairman of the county committee stopped at the
open door of the office. The nominee for Congress was
deep in a letter. The chairman, waiting, regarded at
leisure the face frowning over the paper. It was like a
mountain cliff—rocky, impregnable, lonely and grim, yet
lovely with gentle things that bloom.

The candidate folded the letter and swung about in his chair. "Sorry to keep you waiting, Tom. I was trying to figure out how a man can be in two places at once. It looks as if I can't make the speech here Friday."

"Can't make—your speech! You must be joking."

The man in the chair shook his head. "Not a bit of it." He got up and began to stride about the room with long, lounging steps. The chairman excitedly flung remonstrances after him. "Cartwright might beat us yet, you know; it won't do to waste a chance—election's too near."

The large figure stopped short, and a queer smile twisted the big mouth and shone in the keen, visionary eyes. "I can't tell you why, Tom," he said, "and I'd rather not be asked, but I can't make that speech here Friday." And the issue was concluded.

Friday morning at daybreak the candidate's tall figure stepped through the silent streets of the Western city before the earliest risers were about. Traveling afoot, he swung along into the open country, moving rapidly and with tireless ease. Nine o'clock found him in a straggling town, twenty miles from his starting point. The court-house door stood wide to the summer morning. Court was already in session, and the place was crowded. The Congressional candidate, unnoticed, sat down in the last row.

It was a crude interior of white walls, of unpainted woodwork and wooden benches. The newcomer glanced about as if familiar with such a setting. A larceny case was being tried. He listened closely and seemed to study lawyers and judge; he missed no word of the comments of the people near him. The case being ended, the district attorney rose and moved the trial of John Wilson for murder. There was a stir through the courtroom. In the doorway appeared the sheriff leading a childish figure, a boy of fifteen, dressed in poor, home-made clothes, with a conspicuous bright head of golden hair. He was pale, desperately frightened. The judge, a young man, faced the criminal, paused pityingly, then steadied himself.

"Have you a lawyer?" he asked.

The lad shook his unkempt yellow head. "No. I dunno—anybody. I hain't got—money—to pay."

"Do you wish the court to assign you counsel?" In the stillness a boot scraped the floor. The man in the back seat rose, slouched forward, stood before the judge.

"May it please Your Honor," he said, "I am a lawyer. I should be glad to act as counsel for the defense."

The judge looked for a moment at the loose-hung, towering figure. "What is your name?" he asked.

The man answered quietly: "Abraham Lincoln."

A few men here and there glanced at the big lawyer again; this was the candidate for Congress. That was all they thought. None of the frontier farmers and backwoodsmen in homespun jeans or the women in calico and sunbonnets who heard the name spoken dreamed that it was to fill one of the great places in history.

"I know your name, Mr. Lincoln; I shall be glad to assign you to defend the prisoner," the judge answered. The jury was drawn. Man after man came under the scrutiny of Lincoln's deep eyes; but he challenged no one. The hard-faced audience began to glance at him impatiently. The feeling was against the prisoner, yet they wished to see some fight made for him.

The district attorney opened the case for the People. He told with few words the story of the murder. The prisoner had worked on the farm of one Amos Berry the autumn before, in 1845. On this farm was an Irishman, Shaughnessy by name. He amused himself by worrying the boy, and the boy came to hate him. On the twenty-eighth of October the boy was driving a wagonload of hay to the next farm. At the barnyard gate he met Shaughnessy, with Berry and two other men. The boy asked Berry to open the gate, and Berry was about to do so when Shaughnessy spoke. The boy was lazy, he said—let him get down and open the gate himself. The Irishman caught the pitchfork which the lad held, pricked him with it and ordered him to get down. The lad sprang forward, then, snatching back the pitchfork, flew at the Irishman and ran one of the prongs into his skull. The man died in an hour. This was the story.

By now it was the dinner hour—twelve o'clock. The court adjourned and the judge and the lawyers went across the street to the tavern. One lawyer was missing. Nobody noticed the big man as he passed down the shady street with a little woman in shabby clothes who had sat in a corner of the courtroom crying silently.

"That's the prisoner's mother," a woman whispered when court opened again and the defendant's lawyer seated her carefully before he went forward to his own place. The district attorney called and examined eyewitnesses. There appeared to be no doubt of the criminal's guilt. The lad sat huddled, colorless from his months in jail, sunk in apathy—a murderer at fifteen.

The afternoon wore on. The district attorney's nasal voice rose and fell, examining witnesses. But the big lawyer sitting there did not make one objection, even to statements very damaging to his client. He scrutinized the judge and the jury; one might have said that he was studying the character of each man. At length the district attorney said: "The People rest," and court adjourned for supper.

It was commonly said that the boy was doomed; no lawyer, even a "smart" man, could get him off after such testimony, and the current opinion was that the big hulking fellow could not be a good lawyer or he would have put a spoke in the wheel for his client before this.

Court reopened at 7:30. Not a seat was empty. The small woman in her worn calico dress sat close to the bar this time, near her son. The judge entered. And then Abraham Lincoln stalked slowly up through the silent benches. He laid a big hand on the prisoner's thin shoulder, and the lad started nervously. Lincoln bent down.

"Don't be scared, Sonny," he said, quietly, yet everyone heard every word. "I'm going to pull you out of this hole. Try to be plucky for your mother's sake."

The boy glanced over at the shabby woman, and when she met his look with a difficult smile, he tried to smile back. The audience saw the effort of each for the other, the judge saw it, and the jury—and Lincoln's keen eyes, watching ever under the heavy brows, caught a spasm of pity in more than one face. He took off his coat and stood in his shirt sleeves.

"Gentlemen of the jury," began Abraham Lincoln, "I am going to try this case in a manner not customary in courts. I shall not call witnesses; the little prisoner over there is all the witness I want. I shall not argue. All I'm going to do is tell you a story, and then leave the case in your hands." There was a stir through the courtroom. The voice, rasping, unpleasant at first, went on:

"You, Jim Beck—you, Jack Armstrong—" The stranger's huge knotted forefinger singled out two in the jury. "You two can remember—yes, and you as well, Luke Green—fifteen years back, in 1831, when a long, lank fellow in God-forsaken clothes came into this country from Indiana. His appearance, I dare to say, was so striking that those who saw him haven't forgotten him. He was dressed in homespun jeans, with the breeches stuffed into rawhide boots. Gentlemen of the jury, I think some of you will remember that young man. His name was Abraham Lincoln." The gaunt speaker paused and pushed up his sleeves a bit, and the jurymen saw the muscles of hand and forearm. Yes, some of them remembered the young giant who had been champion in everything that meant physical strength. They sat tense.

"The better part of a man's life consists of his friendships," the strong voice went on, and the eyes softened as if looking back over a long road traveled. "There are good friends to be found in these parts; that young fellow in blue jeans had a few. It is about a family who befriended him that I am going to tell you.

"The boy Abraham Lincoln left home at twenty-two to shift for himself, and in those pinching times he could not always get work. Late one fall afternoon, when he had walked miles looking for a chance, he heard an axe ring and came upon a cabin. It was a poor cabin even as settlers' cabins go. There was cloth over the windows instead of glass; there was only one room, and a loft above. Abraham strode up to the cabin hopefully and asked for shelter." Again the voice paused and a smile flashed in pleasant memory. "Gentlemen of the jury, no king ever met with a finer welcome. Everything he had, the owner of that cabin told Abraham, was his. The man brought the tired boy inside. Two small children played on the floor, and a little woman was singing the baby to sleep by the fire. The visitor climbed up a ladder to the loft after supper.

"Next morning he did a few chores to help, then asked if there were jobs to be got. The man said yes; if he could chop and split rails, there was enough to do.

"'Do you like to work?' the woodsman asked. Abraham had to tell him that he wasn't a hand to pitch into work like killing snakes, but yet—well, the outcome of it was

that he stayed and proved that he could do a man's job.
For five weeks Abraham lived in the cabin. He chopped
with the father, did housework with the mother and
romped with Sonny, the golden-haired, laughing baby,
many a time. No part of his life has ever been more light-
hearted or happier."

The lawyer picked up his coat and, while every eye in
the courtroom watched him, he fumbled in a pocket and
brought out a letter. "The young man who had come
under so large a weight of obligation prospered in later
life. By good fortune, by the blessing of God, he made for
himself a certain place in the community. As much as
might be, he has—I have—kept in touch with those old
friends, yet in the stress of a very busy life I have not of
late years heard from them. Till last Monday morning
this"—he held up the letter—"this came to me in
Springfield. It is a letter from the mother who welcomed
a tired youth to her humble cabin. Her husband died
years ago; the two older children followed him. The
mother who sang to her baby that afternoon"—he swept
about and pointed to the meek, small woman shrinking
on the front seat—"the mother is there." The arm
dropped; his luminous eyes shone on the boy criminal's
golden head; in the courtroom there was no one who did
not hear each low syllable of the sentence which followed.

"The baby is the prisoner at the bar."

In the hot, crowded place one caught a gasp; one heard
a woman's dress rustle and a man clear his throat. Then
silence, and the counsel for the defense let it alone to do
his work. It shaped the minds before him as words could
not. All over the room men and women were shuffling,
sighing, distressed with the ferment of that silence. The
frayed ends of the nerves of the audience were gathered
up as the driver of a four-in-hand gathers up the reins of

his fractious horses. The voice of the defendant's lawyer sounded over the throng.

"Many times," he spoke as if reflecting aloud, "many times I have remembered those weeks of unfailing kindness from those poor people, and have prayed God to give me a chance to show my gratefulness. When the letter came last Monday calling for help, I knew that God had answered. An answer to prayer comes sometimes with a demand for sacrifice. It was so. The culminating moment of years of ambition for me was to have been tonight. I was to have made tonight a speech which bore, it is likely, success or failure in a contest. I lay that ambition, that failure, if the event so prove it, gladly on the altar of this boy's safety. It is for you"—his strong glance swept the jury—"to give him that safety.

"Gentlemen of the jury, I said when I began that I should try this case in a manner not customary. I said I had no argument to set before you. I have told the story; you know that at an age when this boy's hands should have held schoolbooks or fishing rod they held the man's tool which was his undoing; you know how the child was goaded by a grown man till in desperation he used that tool at hand. You know these things as well as I do. All I ask is that you deal with the little fellow as you would have other men deal in such a case with little fellows of your own at home. I trust his life to that test. Gentlemen of the jury, I rest my case."

Abraham Lincoln sat down.

A little later the jury filed out. Half an hour passed; then there was a bustle, and people who had left the courtroom crowded back. The small woman in the front row clasped her hands tightly together. The jury filed in and sat down. "Gentlemen of the jury," the clerk's voice spoke monotonously, "have you agreed upon a verdict?"

"We have," the foreman answered.

"What is your verdict, guilty or not guilty?" For a second, perhaps, no one breathed in all that packed mass. The small woman stared palely at the foreman; every eye watched him. Only the boy, sitting with his golden head down, seemed not to listen.

"Not guilty," said the foreman.

With that there was pandemonium. Men shouted, stamped, waved, tossed up their hats; women sobbed; one or two screamed with wild joy. Abraham Lincoln saw the slim body of the prisoner fall forward; with two strides he had caught him up in his great arms and passed him across the bar into the arms of the woman, who rocked him, kissed him. The whole room surged toward her, but Lincoln stood guard and pushed off the crowd.

"The boy's fainted," he said loudly. "Give him air." And then, with a smile, "She's got her baby—it's all right, friends. But somebody bring a drink of water for Sonny."

The old man's story was ended. After a moment's silence, he spoke again, as if answering objections. "Of course such a thing could not happen today. It could not have happened then in Eastern courts. Only a Lincoln could have carried it off anywhere, it may be. But he knew his audience and jury, and he measured the character of the judge. It happened. It is a fact."

The listener glanced curiously at the old man. "May I ask how you came by the story? You told it with a touch of intimacy, almost as if you had been there. Is it possible that you were in that courtroom?"

The bright, dark eyes of the old man flashed; he smiled with an odd expression, as if smiling back half a century to faces long ago dust. "I was the judge," he said.

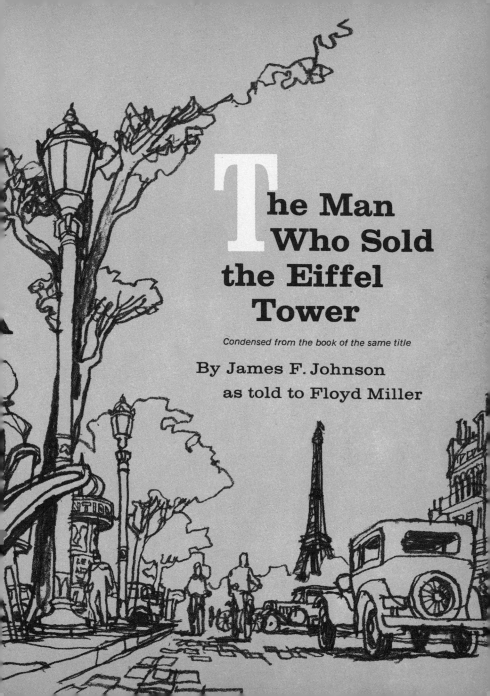

The Man Who Sold the Eiffel Tower

Condensed from the book of the same title

By James F. Johnson
as told to Floyd Miller

*In all the annals of crime there has never been another felon quite
like Victor Lustig. His unique arsenal of talents—the polish of a
diplomat, the theatrical instinct of a master showman, the morals
of a tiger shark—enabled him to baffle the police of two continents for twenty-odd years. James F. Johnson, then an agent of the
U.S. Secret Service, played a central role in the case which finally
brought the master criminal to justice. In this absorbing narrative
he has recaptured all the drama, surprise and suspense which were
the essential elements of his quarry's near-incredible career.*

THE VETERAN confidence man who called himself
Count Victor Lustig (among twenty-three other aliases) seemed to possess uncanny immunity to the law.
Operating with hypnotic charm, he mercilessly fleeced
victim after victim, but forty-six arrests resulted in not a
single conviction. It was the U.S. Secret Service that
finally put Lustig permanently behind bars. As an operative in that relentless and formidably single-minded
organization (from which I have recently retired), it was
my privilege to help make the crucial forty-seventh arrest—the one which was his undoing.

But years before we were assigned to that exciting manhunt, Victor Lustig obligingly brought his person, and
his spotted record, to the attention of the Secret Service.
It happened because of a swindle he hatched in the flamboyant, star-struck atmosphere of Hollywood. For what it
illustrates about the man and his profession, the story is
worth telling from the beginning.

The party was raucous and uninhibited. A woman was
dancing the Charleston on top of a grand piano; the air
was thick with smoke and empty chatter. Amid the crush
of people were perhaps a dozen beautiful young girls who
were pushing, posing, smiling, hoping a producer would

see them and give them their big break in pictures. The gathering was a carnival of vulgarity typical of Hollywood in the mid-twenties. Among all the guests, one man seemed oddly out of place. Dignified and reserved, with a square, handsome face, he was dressed in the most conservative English manner. Before long he approached one of the hopeful starlets. Bowing from the waist, he introduced himself as Count Victor Lustig.

The girl's eyes opened wide at the mention of his title, and wider still when Lustig identified himself as a producer. She was only eighteen, and her professional credits were limited to a single walk-on in a B picture. Understandably, when the impressive stranger told her that she seemed to him "a girl of luminous talent," and that he was going to make her a Broadway star, she was completely taken in. Shortly thereafter she accompanied him to Havana, where they lodged in a suite at one of the leading hotels.

For Lustig, this part of the swindle was merely stage-setting; he needed a pretty girl to lend credibility to his role of "producer." Now the plot could proceed in earnest, the next step being an intensive search for a likely "mark," or victim.

For the next few days Lustig and his unwitting accomplice, Estelle Sweeney (stage-named "Stellar Swan"), did a little sight-seeing, gambled occasionally, let themselves be seen. Soon Lustig's attention focused on a big, blond, middle-aged American who evidenced a certain flair for self-dramatization. Had he once been bitten by the theater bug? If so, Lustig knew this was precisely the mark he was seeking. It was simple enough to maneuver an introduction. The American, a wealthy farm-implement salesman named Ronald Dodge, was evidently im-

pressed by Lustig's spurious title. But as the talk turned
to Lustig's beautiful companion, the confidence man
knew that his grift sense had been unerring. For when he
dropped the term "leading lady," Dodge fairly snapped
at the lure.

"You know something?" he said enthusiastically.
"Your being a Broadway producer impresses me more
than your title. I've been interested in the theater all my
life!" Dodge described the college theatricals in which he
had starred, the little-theater groups he had abortively
tried to organize in his hometown. Ruefully he confessed
that he had been successful on many levels, but not on
the one where he had set his heart—the theater. Lustig
listened sympathetically and then, having whetted his
victim's curiosity, politely terminated the conversation.

As he had expected, Dodge began to pursue him all
over Havana, pitifully eager to share vicariously in the
magic life of a producer. With infinite calculation, Lustig
led his man on, alternating tempting hints about the
play he planned to produce with maddening periods
when he seemed willing to discourse on any subject *but*
the theater. By the end of a week of this, Dodge was
mesmerized. The time was ripe to introduce the question
of money.

The only thing holding up rehearsals, Lustig told
Dodge confidentially, was that he still lacked $50,000 of
the estimated $70,000 production costs. Of course, no in-
dividual would be allowed to put up more than 49 percent of the total, for Lustig insisted on retaining a controlling interest. . . .

"You've got a deal!" Dodge cried. "I'll put up the
$34,000."

Lustig hesitated. "Ronald," he said, "you're a friend,
and I dislike taking money from friends—especially on a

gamble as hazardous as this. If we have a flop, we lose every cent. Honestly, I wouldn't advise you to invest in any Broadway production." Dodge was crestfallen. He began to argue vehemently with Lustig, assuring him that as a devotee of the theater he was more than willing to assume the risks involved.

At last Lustig capitulated. He agreed to call upon Dodge in the latter's hometown, Providence, Rhode Island, to settle the final details as soon as he had raised the remainder of his own share. Not until then, Lustig insisted, could the deal be consummated. For three weeks Lustig let Dodge "tighten up"—worry that somehow this once-in-a-lifetime opportunity might slip through his fingers. Then, curtly dismissing Stellar's tearful pleas that she be allowed to accompany him on his "business trip," Lustig left for Providence.

Dodge was overjoyed when he called. An hour later, in Lustig's hotel room, the "count" stacked up thirty-six thousand-dollar bills before Dodge's eyes, and Dodge in turn produced his $34,000 share in cash. Lustig locked the two stacks of bills in his suitcase and placed it on a shelf in the closet. Then the partners agreed to celebrate with a drink at a nearby speakeasy. Shortly they were interrupted by a bellboy from the hotel; there was a telephone call for Count Lustig from London. "Probably about the English rights," Lustig said cheerily. "I'll be right back. Wish us luck!"

Dodge did. But after thirty minutes he grew fidgety and strolled back to Lustig's hotel room. It was empty. There were no clothes, no suitcases—no money. Lustig had vanished.

Livid with fury, Ronald Dodge immediately called the police. And here it became evident that Lustig had made a basic mistake. One of the principles of a con game is to

offer the victim a chance of quick money in a slightly
crooked manner—via a fixed horse race, an illegal "inside tip," or the like—thus leaving him reluctant to go to
the police. But there was nothing remotely illegitimate in
this deal; Ronald Dodge's ambition to become a Broadway angel was above reproach. Dodge summoned the
authorities so fast that they almost caught Lustig at the
Providence railroad station; he barely made good his
escape by stealing a car and driving on back roads to
Montreal, where he hid out with underworld acquaintances.

But Dodge was not through yet. Pursuing Lustig on
his own, he retraced his steps to Havana, where he
found Stellar Swan in pathetic circumstances. Lustig had
abandoned her with the unpaid hotel bill, and, unable to
speak a word of Spanish, she had been forced to take a
job in the chorus line of an obscene strip joint. She was
broken in spirit and ashamed. Dodge gave her $200 and
advised her to go home.

And now his feeling toward Lustig changed. Whereas
before he had been angered and outraged, after seeing
what had happened to Stellar Swan he felt a deep personal hatred. Once home again in Providence he raised
such a ruckus that Lustig decided even Montreal wasn't
safe enough, and under cover of a forged passport he embarked on a freighter for France. From there, his trail led
straight to the New York office of the Secret Service.

Brooding in exile, Lustig concentrated on the problem
of how to get back into America, the land of lushest pick-
ings for a man of his talents. The major ports of entry, he
knew, would be closely watched, for the fervor of Dodge's
crusade had by now stirred up the police of half a dozen
states. But by May 1927 Lustig had contrived a char-

acteristically bold solution. In the first week of that month he confidently boarded the *Mauretania*, bound for New York. On the second day at sea Lustig penned a cable in the ship's radio room. Directed to the New York resident agent of the U.S. Secret Service, it read: "Have extremely important information for you. Will dock aboard the *Mauretania* Wednesday. Count Victor Lustig." For the rest of the voyage he relaxed and allowed himself to be lionized by the passengers at the captain's table.

As Lustig knew, the Secret Service is charged by law with two specific responsibilities: guarding the President and apprehending counterfeiters. Our New York operatives, assuming that Lustig had information about a counterfeiting scheme, dispatched two agents in a pilot boat to board the *Mauretania* before she docked. Lustig received them in a first-class cabin, exuding his well-rehearsed air of nobility.

"I won't be able to talk now," he said. "I'm packing and saying good-bye to friends. But the moment we land I shall be glad to come to your office. However," he continued, "there may be one slight difficulty. I've been involved in a little misunderstanding in Providence, and the police may be waiting to question me. I might even have to return to Rhode Island."

Agent Peter Rubano answered bluntly, "If you have information about counterfeiting or a threat to the President, that takes top priority. Anything else can wait."

"I leave it to you gentlemen," Lustig replied innocently.

As Lustig had foreseen, a New York detective was waiting to take him into custody when the ship docked. But Rubano, flashing his Secret Service shield, intervened, explaining the federal government's jurisdiction. The detective shrugged. "If you guys got a case on him, I guess he's yours," he said, and walked off.

At the New York office of the Secret Service, Lustig was most coöperative. He talked a great deal but remarkably little information of use came out of him. Rubano ordered lunch sent in, then returned to the interrogation, determined to pin the confidence man down to hard facts. As the fourth hour passed, and the fifth, and the sixth, Lustig showed no signs of fatigue or even of resentment when the questions became sharp and personal.

"Unfortunately," Lustig apologized, "a few dates and names have slipped my mind, but with your assistance I'm sure I'll recall them. I came voluntarily, and I'll gladly work right around the clock with you if necessary. Now, what was that last question again?" Rubano couldn't get angry with a man who was trying so hard to be helpful. Finally at midnight, his nerves frazzled, his senses reeling under the torrential flow of Lustig's words, Rubano gave up. Momentarily forgetting that Lustig was wanted elsewhere, he waved a limp hand toward the door and said, "Good night." Lustig walked into the darkened streets of New York, a free man.

And so he evaded Dodge's sentinels precisely as he had planned. But the Service never forgot his brazen deception and, when he later became involved in a bona fide counterfeiting operation, we went after him with missionary zeal. It was then that I began to trace his past in earnest.

The more I learned about him, the more he fascinated me. Had all the fabulous exploits attributed to him actually happened? I set out to retrace his steps on two continents, interviewing his victims, checking police records, following every available scrap of evidence. Eventually I managed to piece together the whole story of his amazing career.

Lustig served his criminal apprenticeship aboard the transatlantic liners which, prior to the First World War, were the favorite habitat of the wealthy international set. He had run away from his respectable home in what is now Czechoslovakia while still in his teens, spent some time as a petty thief in Paris and soon concluded that gambling promised much greater rewards with far less risk. Where better to find partners for a "friendly game" than among the jaded, temporarily captive millionaires in the salons of the era's "floating palaces"? As soon as he had mastered the basic skills of card-sharping, Lustig set sail on the Atlantic.

During his third voyage Lustig noticed another professional working the same ship—a tall, lean fellow whose delicate fingers could palm a card so skillfully that even Lustig wasn't sure it had been done. Upon introducing himself, Lustig learned that he had been watching Nicky Arnstein, one of the most accomplished gamblers of the day. Throughout the rest of the year they worked the boats together, and the partnership provided Lustig with an invaluable postgraduate course in the psychology of the sucker.

A brilliant practitioner of the indirect approach, Arnstein insisted on the importance of making the victim suggest the game. "You make yourself available, and friendly, and then wait for *him* to get the idea," he explained in one of their shipboard conversations. "And when he does, you must be a little reluctant." Lustig was dubious. It didn't seem to him that many games would develop that way.

"Perhaps not," Arnstein said. "But the important ones

do. Let me give you a little demonstration. Did you notice the man I was speaking with when you came in? His
name is Henry Dixon. He's rich and he's bored. He
hasn't suggested cards yet, but he will. When he does,
I'll confess to him what I am, and he'll still be hooked.
You watch."

Arnstein drifted back to the bar and resumed his conversation with Dixon. By the second drink, Dixon suggested a game of cards. Arnstein thought for a moment.
Then he said, "I don't think so, Mr. Dixon. I'd like to
keep your friendship."

Dixon bristled. "You think I'd be a poor loser?"

"Not at all," Arnstein replied. "But you wouldn't have
a chance. You see, I'm a professional gambler."

"Well I'll be damned!" Dixon declared.

Watching the amazing dialogue from a nearby table,
Lustig was convinced that Arnstein had gone too far. But
he was wrong. By the time Dixon and Arnstein met the
next day at cocktails the mark was eager. "I've never
played with a professional gambler," he said. "I'd like to
try it. Who knows? I might win."

"Who knows?" Arnstein replied, but still he refused to
play. He refused again on the following day, and the
next. Only on the very last night out of New York did he
allow himself to be forced to play with Henry Dixon. And
he took him for $30,000. Lustig never forgot the basic
lesson: make the mark *want* to give his money. It was on
this bedrock rule that he built all his later success.

When World War I choked off transatlantic travel,
Lustig temporarily returned to his old Parisian haunts.
But as soon as the war was over he made directly for
America. The Roaring Twenties were about to unfold:
everyone was getting rich in the stock market; everyone
was breaking the law by toting a hip flask. It was, in

short, the perfect setting for Lustig's maturing talents.

On his arrival in New York he looked up Nicky Arnstein and through him gained entrée to the American underworld. But Lustig was essentially a loner, and though he hung out on the fringes of the organized mobs, he never became deeply involved with them. He did, however, come into possession of $25,000 in hijacked Liberty Bonds as a result of his friendship with Arnstein. Precisely how he acquired them no one knows, but they became a basic prop of his trade. Genuine bonds, they would be honored at any bank. And that was exactly how Lustig first made use of them.

Tormut Green, president of the American Savings Bank in Salina, Kansas, often wondered what malevolent fate had saddled him with the Marsten farm. He had been forced to foreclose on it a few years back, and now the buildings were crumbling, taxes had to be paid and there was no purchaser in sight. Nor was there likely to be. Everybody knew the place was no good. Then one soft spring day in 1924 a most unusual caller appeared in Green's office. People in Kansas didn't dress in striped pants and spats, as this fellow did; nor was the banker's ear accustomed to the cultured, slightly foreign-sounding accents in which the man spoke. Somewhat uncomfortably, Green identified himself and inquired, "What can I do for you?"

"My name is Count Victor Lustig," the visitor said. "I want to buy a farm."

"A farm?" Green said, suddenly coming alive.

"Yes," Lustig replied as he took a seat. "You see before you, monsieur, a refugee from the Old World. Our peasants in the East Tyrol have risen in revolt and seized everything. Our vineyards and herds which have been passed from father to son for generations are gone. I must start all over again."

"Yes . . . of course," Green said.

"I've been looking around the country here," Lustig went on, "and I have found a place I like. I believe it is called the Marsten farm. Do you know who owns it?"

"I . . . we own it," Green said weakly. He felt as if he were in a dream. "It is for sale—at the proper price."

Lustig put on a rueful expression. "I was able to escape from Austria with very little of the family wealth." From an inside pocket he withdrew an envelope and handed it to the banker. "When I reached New York, I converted the family jewels into these. Will they be enough?"

Green opened the envelope and out spilled $25,000 in Liberty Bonds. Barely able to contain himself, he managed to say, "Why, yes, I believe we could let it go for this amount." Lustig carefully repocketed his bonds, and then Green and John Rose, a bank vice-president, took him on a tour of the Marsten property. Its poverty made the bankers apologetic at first, but Lustig, apparently not at all discouraged, spoke glowingly of what the place would look like in a few years. When he had completed his inspection, he suggested that the two bankers meet him next day in his hotel room to complete the sale.

"There is one more thing," Lustig then said. "It will be a number of years before the farm begins to pay, and I will need operating capital. I have another $25,000 in Liberty Bonds. Would it be possible to cash them?"

"Nothing could be easier," Green assured him.

The following day when the two bankers arrived at Lustig's room, they brought $25,000 in cash and the deed to the Marsten farm. Lustig took a brown-paper package from a dresser drawer and opened one end to reveal a stack of bonds. "Fifty thousand dollars' worth," he said, and then dropped the envelope back into the drawer and closed it. From another drawer he removed a bottle of whiskey. "In Austria," he said urbanely, "we have a small ceremony that accompanies the purchase of land."

The bankers were more than ready to participate in the old Austrian ceremony; in fact, they participated several times. Then Lustig handed them the package of bonds in return for the $25,000 cash, plus the deed. There were handshakes all around, and Green and Rose returned to the bank to inspect the bonds. What they found turned them cold sober. They raced back to the hotel, but Lustig was gone. His room was empty, and they stood in the middle of it, whey-faced, clutching a package that contained nothing but old newspapers.

Lustig, convinced that most men would cut their losses and try to forget the whole thing, made no effort to cover his tracks. This time he was wrong. A few days later he found himself on his way back to Kansas, handcuffed, sharing a compartment with a detective and the bank's lawyer, a gentleman named Ray Alston. During most of the eighteen hours it took to reach Chicago, Lustig seemed completely unruffled by the situation. He talked, casually, discursively, with no apparent object. But slowly a pattern began to emerge. He was impressing on Alston the fact that it was to his clients' disadvantage to bring him to trial. The trial would be humiliating for the bankers, Lustig pointed out. If confidence men are considered immoral, people who have dealings with them are usually assumed to share in that immorality. And, after all, was it an honorable thing to ask $25,000 for the Marsten place?

"But the worst thing," Lustig continued, "will be the run on the bank. As soon as the depositors learn how

easily their officers were bilked, they'll lose confidence in
them. The bank will be ruined. If, on the other hand, you
release me, I'll pay back all of the money. There will be
no loss and no disgrace."

Lustig's proposal was contrary to all of Alston's instincts, and yet there was a logic to it, and a magic sort
of simplicity. When they reached Chicago the lawyer
placed a call to Salina and talked long and earnestly
with the bankers. In the end they agreed to release the
confidence man on condition that he pay back the money.
Lustig agreed. Then, in a sharper tone, he said, "Mr.
Alston, you've caused me a great deal of inconvenience
and humiliation. You've handcuffed me and taken me
away from my New York bank. I have no money. I am
aggrieved, and I require $1000 in compensation."

"I'll see you in hell first," Alston stormed.

"If you don't compensate me," Lustig said, "you'll see
me in court testifying against your clients."

And so he got the $1000. Of course, he had no intention
of paying back the money, and he well knew that, trial
or no, the story would leak out in Salina. He was right in
predicting a loss of public confidence: the American
Savings Bank was forced to close its doors, and Rose and
Green were ruined.

It was in Montreal that Lustig met his next major
mark. As usual, he had checked into the best hotel in
town. Soon the appearance of an incongruous couple in
the hotel dining room intrigued him. The man was
elderly, distinguished-looking; his companion was much
younger, pretty and slightly blowzy. The bell captain, in
response to discreet inquiries, revealed that the man was
Linus Merton, a small-town Vermont banker who often
spent vacations in Montreal with his "wife." The wife,

however, was a different woman each visit. Lustig concluded that Merton was made to order for a grift.

In his opening move, Lustig displayed his unfailing
ingenuity. He hired the best pickpocket in the city to
spirit Merton's wallet out of his pocket, warning his agent
not so much as to look at its contents. Merton was so overjoyed when Lustig then returned the "lost" billfold—
which contained $500 in addition to his personal papers—
that he offered Lustig a substantial reward. With chill
hauteur, Lustig disdained the gesture.

Two days later Lustig had a bottle of wine delivered
to the banker and his "wife" at dinner. Delighted at
being forgiven the gaucherie of offering a nobleman a
reward, Merton insisted that the count share the bottle
with them. A warm friendship rapidly developed. Inevitably, Merton became curious as to how his new friend
made his money, for he seemed to have a great deal of it.
The count was reticent at first, but, pressed, he brought
out his usual story of ancient lands lost to rebellious
peasants. "I was not trained to work for money," he
said, "and I have had to improvise."

"You seem to have done quite well," the banker said.
"How *do* you earn a living?"

"On the horses," Lustig said.

"You're a gambler?" Merton exclaimed.

"Hardly a gambler, Linus. I bet on sure things."

He had a cousin Emil, he explained, who was a telegraph operator. As U.S. race results came into Montreal,
it was Emil's job to relay them to various betting parlors.
But now and then Emil was able to delay sending the
reports just long enough to telephone them to the count,
who then bet on the known winner. "It's really quite
simple," Lustig said. "I'll place a small bet for you today
with my own money. One hundred dollars. If you win,

it's yours. If you lose, which is impossible, you can take
me to dinner."

That afternoon he casually counted $1000 into Mer-
ton's hands. "The horse paid ten to one," he said with a
smile. "There, now you have my secret. Let's say no
more about it." But of course the banker wanted to learn
a great deal more about it. "Count," he asked, "could I
bet this money again tomorrow? Could I go with you
and place it myself?" Lustig shrugged dubiously; he
couldn't take anyone else in without Emil's approval.
But, since Merton was a friend, he would see.

The next morning the two men met Emil at the telegraph office. Emil (played by the pickpocket who had
stolen Merton's wallet) at first demurred but finally, in
deference to Lustig's warm endorsement of the banker,
agreed to let Merton in. That afternoon Lustig took
Merton to a betting parlor where prosperous-looking
men—actually members of the Montreal underworld
who had been carefully rehearsed by Lustig—were standing before a teller's cage, calmly wagering amounts of
$10,000, $20,000, $30,000. The blood rushed to Merton's
head. He began to see the way to make a fortune overnight.

Lustig looked at his watch and nudged the banker. It
was time for Cousin Emil to call. They went to a phone
at the front of the establishment and, when it rang,
Lustig let Merton take it.

"Hindquarter is the winner in the fourth race," came
Emil's voice. Then the phone clicked dead. And sure
enough, Hindquarter paid off six to one.

Merton couldn't bring himself to bet very much at
first, but when the wires closed that afternoon he had
won $2500. By the end of the second day's play, he had

$5000, and he was becoming greedier by the hour. Lustig decided it was time to take him.

The following morning the two men met as usual with Cousin Emil to give him his share of the winnings. But Emil had a long face, and even the money did not cheer him up. Finally he blurted out, "I'm quitting my job."

There was a moment of stunned silence. Then Lustig asked, "What's the matter, cousin?"

"It's my wife. She's been ill for some time, and now the doctors have diagnosed tuberculosis. I must move her out of this climate immediately."

"But, good Lord, man," Merton exploded, "won't you wait awhile? I mean, just as we've got this thing going. . ."

"You think money means more to me than my wife?" Emil yelled in outraged tones. "Well, it doesn't. I'm quitting immediately." Lustig stepped between the two men. "Of course, of course," he said soothingly. "Elsa's health is more important than anything." Then, turning to the banker, he said, "I'm sorry, Linus, but I agree with my cousin. And after all, you've made a few dollars."

"Can't we play just once more?" the banker pleaded. "We could make a killing!"

"It would take a lot of money to make a killing," Lustig said. "Unless we could pool our funds. I can raise about $30,000, but that's not really enough. Could you match it, Linus?"

"I . . . I guess so," Merton stammered.

Lustig turned to his cousin. "How about it, Emil? Shall we have one more play?" The sad-faced man nodded. "I'll do it for Elsa's sake. I'd like her to live out her remaining years in luxury." As he walked back to the hotel, Lustig was in high spirits, babbling small talk to prevent the banker from having any second thoughts. When they neared the hotel, Lustig said, "We must tell

your wife about our plans. Really, you ought to promise
her half the winnings."

"Half!" the banker croaked. "What in the world for?"
Lustig gave him a conspiratorial grin. "There is a way
of doing things, old chap. You needn't tell her how *much*
you win. Give her a thousand or so. It is the gesture that
counts."

When they returned to Merton's room, Lustig insisted
he tell his "wife" the good news, and the banker could
not refuse. "Daddy!" the woman squealed, throwing her
arms around Merton's neck. Lustig suppressed a smile.

The next day Lustig steered Merton, nervously clutching close to $70,000 in his damp hands, back to the
bookie parlor. At the appointed time the phone rang.
Cousin Emil's voice said, "Place it on Hilda's Way in
the sixth."

Merton had just time to make the bet before the caller
shouted, "They're off," and the cage closed. The race
was reported at each quarter-pole; it was a duel between
Hilda's Way and My Man. They came down the stretch
neck and neck . . . and the winner . . . My Man! Hilda's
Way was second.

Linus Merton went ashen; Lustig had to help him out
of the wire room. "What happened?" he mumbled over
and over. "What went wrong?" Lustig appeared equally
distraught. "We must find Cousin Emil. Are you sure
you understood him?" They found Emil just as he was
leaving the telegraph office, and when he heard the news
he turned on the banker in a rage. "You stupid idiot!"
he cried. "I said, *place* it on Hilda's Way. Don't you know
that 'place' means to run second? You've ruined me!
My poor Elsa . . ."

"We'll have another play tomorrow," Lustig said.

"We can't," Emil groaned. "I've quit. My boss will

never hire me back." Lustig soothed his cousin, offering to lend him the money to move his wife. Then he led the dazed banker back to his room, assuring him in farewell that they would get in touch with him when they set up the play again in a few months.

Lustig was already packed; all he had to do was pay off the "actors" in the wire room and leave town. He was almost certain Merton would keep his mouth shut, but he wanted to take no chances. And so he loitered in the hotel lobby until the banker's "wife" came bustling in from a shopping tour. "Congratulations, my dear," he said to her, bowing gallantly. "You are now a wealthy woman." With a cry of delight she ran for the elevator. Lustig smiled, picked up his suitcase and departed. Merton could not convince her that he was telling the truth when he said he had lost the bet. She followed him all the way back to Vermont and threatened to tell his wife the full story unless he paid her. Merton could not raise the money, and when the threat was carried out his wife left him.

The quality that set Lustig above all other confidence men was his ability to improvise audaciously. Never was this better illustrated than when he concocted one of the most fantastic swindles of all time on the basis of a single newspaper article. Lustig had departed for Paris after defrauding Merton and had passed an entire week in apparent idleness, sipping vermouth at sidewalk cafés, leisurely scanning the daily papers. With him during this period was "Dapper Dan" Collins, a small-time grifter whom Lustig was currently representing as his "private secretary." Just as Dapper Dan began to despair of Lustig's ever getting down to business, the count suddenly folded his paper and placed it before his partner.

"I know what our mark is," he said. "I don't know *who* we'll take, but he is in the iron-salvage business. He has recently made a couple of good deals, and now he has an appetite for bigger things. Read this." He pointed to a short item reporting that needed repairs on the Eiffel Tower would cost thousands of francs. The government was investigating the possibility that it might be cheaper to tear it down than to maintain it.

Dapper Dan's eyes flashed in disbelief. "Are you crazy?" he said. "You can't . . ."

"I think we can. The newspaper has already done the hard work for us. We'll need government credentials and a few letterheads, but I have a friend who can supply those. Let's get to work."

Some days later five men received a personal letter from the deputy director-general of the bureau which had jurisdiction over the Eiffel Tower, inviting them to meet and discuss the placement of a government contract. The time was 3 p.m. Friday at the deputy's suite in the Crillon Hotel. On the appointed day Lustig called the meeting to order. "Messieurs, your attention, please. I am about to share with you a government secret known only to me, the Premier and the President." He paused dramatically. "The government is going to scrap the Eiffel Tower." There was a moment of silence. This was indeed something big.

"No doubt this is a shock to you," Lustig said, "but we must face the facts." They had read about the high cost of repairing the tower? Yes, they had. "It was originally built only as an attraction for the Paris Exposition of 1889, and it was never intended to be a permanent part of the city. Even from the first it outraged the esthetic sensibilities of all men of taste. You must look at it in that light." The count's guests, thinking of the profits involved, were quite willing to see it in that light.

Lustig then escorted the party through an inspection of the tower. It had cost more than 7,000,000 francs to build, he explained, and the salvageable high-grade iron would come to seven thousand tons. In businesslike fashion he described the number, size and weight of the girders. When he had finished, he requested that the dealers send sealed bids to his hotel by the following Wednesday. "And remember," he concluded, "you are in possession of a state secret. I trust your discretion."

Lustig had already selected the most promising mark in the group: André Poisson. The man was of peasant origin, and socially he was ill at ease. Almost desperately, he wanted to achieve greater and greater financial success to compensate for this failing.

The bids arrived promptly, and next day Dapper Dan called on André Poisson to inform him that his was the successful one. By the following week Poisson had raised the money, and Dapper Dan called again to arrange a final meeting in Lustig's suite. When he returned, Collins told Lustig, "The mark is nervous. He asked why we were using the hotel rather than the Bureau offices."

"Then we must prove to him," said Lustig, "that we really are government officials. I think I know the way."

The mark arrived as arranged. "Monsieur Poisson," Lustig said warmly, "congratulations. We must drink a toast to your success."

"The deal isn't completed yet," Poisson grunted.

"Ah, to be sure. Then to business before the toast." Turning to Collins, Lustig said, "You may return to the Bureau. I shall be at my desk at three."

The moment Collins was gone, Lustig's air of bureaucratic arrogance fell away. "Monsieur," he said with a trace of humility, "we have one more bit of negotiation.

The life of a government official is not an easy one. We must entertain handsomely, we must dress in the height of fashion—yet for all this we are paid pitifully small wages. So, in the letting of government contracts, it is customary for the official in charge to receive—"

"A bribe?" the mark interrupted.

"Monsieur, you are blunt."

"And that is why we meet here, rather than at the Bureau?"

"Discretion." Lustig smiled.

Poisson threw back his head and brayed, feeling suddenly superior to this public official. "I am not a country bumpkin," he said. "I know how things are done." From one pocket he took a certified check, from the other a wallet bulging with bank notes. Smiling his apologies, Lustig headed toward the bar to pour the toast of celebration. Within an hour he had cashed Poisson's check and entrained for Austria.

Lustig and Collins indulged themselves lavishly at one of Vienna's best hotels for a month, during which Lustig unfailingly read all the Paris daily newspapers. Then he said to Collins, "The mark has still not gone to the police. That can mean only one thing: he is too embarrassed to admit his gullibility, too afraid that it would make him the laughingstock of Paris. He has decided to carry our secret to the grave. And since he hasn't taken possession of the tower, I think we can safely sell it again." And sell it again they did. Surely only their second victim's screams of outrage when he discovered he'd been taken prevented a third sale.

On his return to the United States, Lustig gravitated almost instinctively to Palm Beach, then the favorite playground of America's wealthiest set. But even among those cosmopolitan millionaires Lustig's entrance created a sensation. He drew up to the most exclusive hotel in the city in a glittering Rolls-Royce chauffeured by a liveried Japanese. Dowagers in ranks on the hotel porch craned their necks for a glimpse of this monocled aristocrat, but for two days thereafter he secluded himself in his room, while their curiosity mounted.

When he finally did appear, he settled himself on the beach with book and umbrella, at some distance from the others. Shortly his chauffeur came down the beach at a dogtrot, clutching a cablegram. The count received it with a bored sigh, glanced at it and said he did not wish to reply. Within an hour the chauffeur was back with another; again no reply. This happened again and again, and all the next day, until by the third afternoon the beach population had focused its entire attention on the count and the endless parade of urgent but unanswered messages. No one, of course, guessed that the cablegrams were blank.

Toward the end of the week the count came out of his splendid and mysterious isolation. The cablegrams, he let it be known, were from European financiers desiring his backing or advice on various projects. But since he was not interested in making more money than he had, the messages went unanswered.

He had accomplished his first objective: he was socially accepted, even sought after. But Lustig was not interested in the established upper class; he had staged this elaborate playlet to impress someone less sophisticated, someone who didn't belong and desperately wished to—who it would be, Lustig did not yet know.

When a newcomer named Herman Loller arrived in a forty-foot cabin cruiser, wearing a yachting costume but obviously an amateurish seaman, Lustig decided to keep

an eye on him. In the next few days, as he watched
Loller overtip, heard him laugh too loudly, observed his
failures to ingratiate himself with the Beach's social
leaders, he knew he had found his mark. It was not
difficult to strike up a conversation with a man whom
everyone was assiduously ignoring. Lustig asked a question of him one day at the cigar stand, and they were soon
conversing easily. A warm friendship ensued.

Lustig hadn't known at first just how to take Loller,
but as the days passed he decided the man's naïveté indicated the Rumanian Box, a piece of equipment he always
carried with him. In the hands of most confidence men
this money-making device was a crude affair that was
supposed to alter paper currency, changing fives to tens,
or tens to twenties. But nothing was crude in Lustig's
hands, and he had refined both the box and the pitch.

One afternoon as the two men were lounging on the
afterdeck of Loller's boat, they began discussing money
matters. Loller ventured to express his envy of Lustig, a
rich nobleman who apparently did not have to work to
earn a living. Lustig launched into his story of peasant
revolt and lost lands; times had been difficult for him,
too. But, he said, he had eventually found a way out of
his troubles.

"I have a machine which by a chemical process can
duplicate any paper currency of any denomination with
complete accuracy. I insert a thousand-dollar bill and
out come two bills—identical."

Loller looked at him incredulously. "You're kidding,"
he said.

"Not at all. You've heard of Emil DuBray? No? A
chemical engineer, a genius," and here he launched into
an elaborate tale of international skulduggery, the upshot
of which was that he had come into possession of the only

model of the money-making machine invented by the now-dead "genius."

"But what if you get caught?" Loller asked. "I mean . . . counterfeiting . . ."

"I'm not counterfeiting, my dear fellow. I reproduce genuine currency, indistinguishable from the original. All the banks accept it. Would you like to watch me run off a thousand-dollar bill this afternoon?"

Loller would indeed. He accompanied Lustig to his room. From a closet shelf Lustig removed a small box. There was a narrow slot at either end, and along one side a series of gleaming brass knobs and dials. It was so beautifully crafted that its very appearance bespoke extraordinary properties.

Lustig now took a thousand-dollar bill, which he allowed Loller to examine, and inserted it in one slot. Then he placed a piece of paper cut exactly to money size in another slit and delicately adjusted a series of knobs. "The bill and the blank are now immersed in a chemical bath which transfers the images of one to the other without damaging the original," he explained. "The process takes six hours."

In exactly six hours the two men returned to Lustig's hotel room. The count carefully readjusted all the knobs, turned the ejector lever, and out came two wet thousand-dollar bills. As he held them up for inspection, he could see that Loller still didn't really believe it. "Why don't you take each one to a different bank for examination, so as not to excite curiosity about our little secret?" he suggested.

Loller returned from his expedition convinced, as Lustig knew he would, for he had concealed the second bill in the machine before Loller ever stepped into the room. Both were quite genuine—except that Lustig had skillfully altered the threes and eights so that their serial numbers matched.

"Count," Loller asked, "is this the only machine in existence?"

"Why, yes." He watched Loller's crestfallen expression, then added, "Of course, I know all the specifications."

Loller moistened his lips. "Would you sell me this one? I'll pay you $25,000—all I have at the moment. I know it's a great favor to ask, but you can make yourself another one. . . ." The next day Lustig checked out with Loller's $25,000. Since it took six hours for the machine to operate, he figured he had at least that long to make his getaway.

As it turned out, he had a great deal more time than that. A stubborn man, Herman Loller did not give up his illusions easily. When the machine did not work, he

assumed he had operated it incorrectly and started over again. This continued for days, for weeks, during which he completely ignored his faltering business.

Finally one day his wife smashed the box with a hammer. "Look, you fool," she cried. "There's nothing inside but a few rollers and an empty pan!"

Loller stared fixedly at the pan. "Yes," he said at last, "that's the trouble. The chemical formula has dried up. When I see the count again, I'll get some more. Then we'll be rich."

"You're crazy," his wife said. "You're plumb crazy." And, in a way, he was.

Lustig next defrauded Ronald Dodge, and after using the Secret Service to evade the police, he moved on to Oklahoma. But here he slipped: he was caught trying to sell phony bonds and was jailed. Lustig knew that he couldn't be convicted—there had been no witnesses to the swindle attempt—but he also realized that, when news of his arrest reached police departments in the East, he would be in for serious trouble from Dodge. He had, he estimated, about forty-eight hours to escape before he would be extradited.

The jail was a small one-room affair, and Lustig soon struck up a conversation with the sheriff, S. R. Richards. Lustig regaled his fascinated custodian with lurid stories of high life in foreign capitals and, as the hours slipped by, Richards felt the need to boast of his own big parties, principally extended binges on New Orleans' Bourbon Street. Before long, prisoner and keeper were seated together at the sheriff's desk, sipping whiskey recently confiscated from a bootleg still. As the drinks took effect, the sheriff's confidences slowly became more intimate. At last he revealed that he had been dipping into public

funds (he was also county treasurer) to finance his night
life. The accounts were now short $25,000, and he was
desperate.

Lustig poured the sheriff another drink and shook his
head in commiseration. But he couldn't help observing,
with a small smile, that $25,000 wasn't very much money.
"I've made that much in an afternoon," he said with a
shrug.

"You have? How?" the sheriff wanted to know.

"I have a machine that duplicates currency," said
Lustig. Then he went on to describe the Rumanian Box
in detail. Lustig offered to demonstrate it—if only the
sheriff would get the machine from his suitcase. The
demonstration produced the desired effect. Next morning
Lustig had both his freedom and $10,000—which the
sheriff took from county funds, confident that the money
machine he had purchased with it could easily repay
everything.

This happened in March. The following November,
Lustig was relaxing over breakfast in a Chicago hotel
when there was a sharp knock at the door. He opened it
and looked into the muzzle of a gun behind which
loomed the apoplectic face of Sheriff S. R. Richards.

"It took me eight months to find you," Richards cried.
"Now I'm going to kill you."

"Why, what in the world is the matter, Sheriff?"
Lustig asked calmly.

"The box doesn't work."

Amazement and disbelief spread over Lustig's face.
"That's impossible," he said.

"Don't give me that," the sheriff interrupted. "I
worked on it for a month after you left. I tried everything
and I didn't get a single bill out of it."

"Did you turn the sequential knob twice to the right

and then back to point-ten on the left? Then move the additive switch ten seconds later? Exactly ten seconds, not nine or eleven? Then did you set the three-stage inductive knob *before* you turned the compressor?"

The sheriff's gun began to waver. "I don't know—all I know is it won't work," he said.

Lustig sighed. "I can see you're not manually dexterous enough to operate the machine. The only thing for me to do is to come down there and operate it for you. Unfortunately, I'm tied up in some important business deals right now."

The gun steadied again.

"But," Lustig hastened on, "in the meantime I'll give you back your $10,000." Extracting his billfold, Lustig counted out the money in crisp hundred-dollar bills. The sheriff, numb with amazement, put his gun in his pocket. "This is mighty sporting of you," he mumbled.

"Not at all," Lustig assured him, easing him toward the door. "When I come down to fix the machine you can pay me again." He put his arm around Richards' shoulders. "You've had a bad few months, but now that everything is cleared up, I think you deserve a little celebration. Why don't you use some of that money to live it up for a couple of weeks?"

"Say, that's an idea," the sheriff said. He departed almost jovially.

Each morning after that, Lustig bought all the New Orleans papers. On the fourth day he found what he sought. Sheriff S. R. Richards of Remsen County, Oklahoma, had been arrested, following a three-day spree on Bourbon Street, for passing counterfeit hundred-dollar bills. He was subsequently tried, convicted and sent to a federal penitentiary.

By this time Ronald Dodge's one-man crusade was

making life miserable for Lustig. His name, face and
aliases were circularized to police departments all over
the country, and he began to find himself arrested frequently. Although he always beat the rap one way or
another, he eventually decided to give up the con game
for a few years and lie low in Mexico, in the hope that
the police would forget him. But when he returned, the
Great Depression was on, and the day of easy money was
over. Lustig now seemingly faded from the criminal
scene. In fact, however, he had carefully considered the
situation and then settled on the biggest mark in sight—
Uncle Sam.

Our first faint inkling of the operation came in 1934,
when sixteen Secret Service men, including myself, were
summoned to New York from all parts of the country to
form a special squad. We didn't know why we were
there, but we knew it had to be something important.
Robert Godby, our boss on this assignment, came right
to the point as soon as we were all assembled.

"The New York clearinghouses," he announced, "are
picking up queer at the rate of $100,000 a month." A
low whistle went around the table. That was a record
amount of counterfeit, we knew, and if $100,000 a month
was being picked up, the chances were that twice as
much was being printed.

Godby opened an envelope and removed a hundred-
dollar bill. "Have a look at this," he said. Again we were
surprised. The bill would have fooled anyone but an
expert; it was the best we had ever seen. We began asking
questions. Were there any leads? Where did the paper
come from? The ink? The copper plate? Any clues on the
identity of the engraver? Where was he operating? To
all our questions Godby shook his head. There were no
leads, no clues, absolutely nothing. All we knew for cer-

tain was that somewhere in this country our quarry was in a room with a printing press, paper, ink and the best set of counterfeit plates of American currency ever made. Where was that room?

"That's our assignment," Godby said. "And it's round-the-clock for all of us." He tapped the counterfeit bill with a blunt finger. "We've got to find those plates."

My first step was to contact my sources—my stoolies. But I learned nothing from them. Next we went to paper suppliers to check on unusual sales of high-rag-content paper; we visited manufacturers of copper plate and high-grade printing ink. But all this checking led us nowhere. Then one morning Godby called us together to announce the first break in the case. "We know who the engraver is," he said. We all jerked erect in our seats. "His name is William Watts," Godby went on. "He made a counterfeit note about seven years ago. It didn't get much circulation, but the Bureau in Washington has compared a sample with the new note. They're sure Watts is our man."

Godby passed around a picture of Watts. "We don't know much else," he said. "Watts is a graduate pharmacist, and in the twenties he ran a drugstore in Omaha. About 1925 he popped up in Chicago, counterfeiting whiskey labels for Al Capone. He was a quiet type who didn't make many friends, and for the last seven years he hasn't been seen around. There's only one man who ever seemed to get close to him . . . Victor Lustig."

"But Lustig's too smart to get involved in counterfeiting," I objected.

"I didn't say he was involved. Watts and he were good friends, and he may be able to lead us to him. It's a slim lead, but it's all we have. Let's find Lustig."

We were more than happy to have a legitimate excuse

for apprehending Lustig, but inquiry after inquiry to the police departments of major cities throughout the world failed to develop any substantial leads. Only one slender link to the confidence man emerged from all our efforts. We followed it up simply because we had nothing else to go on. Lustig had recently come to the attention of the Pittsburgh police, not because they had any charge against him but solely because of his association with one Hanna Smith, a madam who ran a call-girl operation. A jealous brawl between two of her girls had resulted in mayhem, and Hanna had hastily left town.

"Now what?" someone glumly asked Godby. The information hardly seemed white-hot.

"Once a madam, always a madam," Godby replied grimly. "We check on every call-girl operation in the country, if necessary."

We seemed to be getting further and further away from counterfeiting as the weeks passed with no trace of Hanna Smith, Lustig or anyone else conceivably involved in the case. But then one day the New York vice squad tipped us off that they were about to close in on a madam working calls from an apartment off Park Avenue. At our request, they agreed to postpone the arrest until we could case the place. We had a pretty fair photograph of Hanna, so we staked out the apartment building and waited, for four, eight, twelve hours. At last the woman in the picture came out. It was Hanna Smith, no question about it.

We immediately spliced in a tap to Hanna's wire, and since we had learned that she introduced Lustig to her friends as "Mr. Frank," we added that name to his other aliases and settled in to listen.

After several weeks we still had nothing to show for our time but reams of racy dialogue. Then late one afternoon I heard the rising excitement in Godby's voice as he took a call from the agent on duty at the tap. He slammed down the receiver and turned to me. "Mr. Frank just called Hanna. He's coming to her apartment within the hour. You and Seckler stake out the place. Don't approach him. Just identify him if you can, and phone back for orders." Seckler and I grabbed our hats and moved out on the double.

After two hours of waiting outside Hanna Smith's apartment building, we began to think that we had somehow missed "Mr. Frank." The only picture we had of Lustig was six years old; he could have changed a lot in that time. I checked with headquarters, but there was no new information from the tap.

I had just returned from phoning when Seckler grabbed my arm and pointed across the street. A well-dressed man had just come out of the apartment building. Was it Lustig? As we followed him, one of us on each side of the street, I studied his walk. Most Americans walk purposefully, whereas Europeans tend to saunter. This man sauntered.

Before we could get a close look at him, he turned a corner and entered a drugstore. I rejoined Seckler. "He's shadow-conscious," Seckler said. "I don't think he's spotted us yet, but we'll have to handle him carefully." I slipped into the drugstore and dialed Godby from the phone booth. While I was waiting for the connection, the man we were following turned from the counter and for a moment I saw his face clearly. I recognized him at once.

"Yes?" Godby snapped on the phone.

" 'Mr. Frank' is Lustig all right," I said. "I'm looking at him right now."

"Stay with him," Godby said.

"Look, chief," I replied, "this guy is very tough to work on the street. He's extremely shadow-conscious. If we want him, I suggest we take him now."

"I'll have to call Washington for instructions," Godby said. "Meanwhile, keep on his tail, and call back in an hour."

As I hung up, Lustig left the drugstore. I met Seckler outside, and he nodded toward the south. Just then Lustig stepped into a car at the curb. A driver was at the wheel, the motor was running and the car moved speedily into the traffic.

"Quick!" Seckler called, grabbing my arm. Luckily we were nearly opposite our own car. I dived behind the wheel, and we roared off, but in a sudden influx of rush-hour traffic we lost him. I tried circling back through several streets in the area in the hope that we might catch a glimpse of him before he got too far away, but it was hopeless. Finally, with a sick feeling, I turned back downtown. Godby and four other agents were waiting for us near Hanna Smith's apartment, and as I climbed out of the car he said, "Washington says it's okay to pick him up."

"We're not going to pick him up today," I said shamefacedly. "I lost him."

We gave him the details and Godby pondered. As his voice ran on, speculating, planning our next move, I stood silent and depressed. Then a vision floated slowly before my eyes. It was Lustig's car, and in it sat the confidence man talking animatedly to the driver. I blinked my eyes and looked again. It was no vision—it was real! There was his car, moving slowly in the traffic.

"It's him," I croaked. "It's Lustig!"

We all turned to look, and before our eyes the car pulled in to the curb and parked a half block away.

Godby turned to me and snapped, "Johnson, you take him. Smith, get the driver. Rubano and Seckler, cover them. Play it safe; they may be armed. Let's go."

I loosened my gun in my shoulder holster and walked quickly down the street. Lustig and the driver were still talking. When I came opposite the car, I turned suddenly, jerked open the door and grabbed Lustig by the arm. "Secret Service," I said. I pulled him from the car and frisked him, but he had no gun. Smith brought the driver around to the street, and then the rest of the squad moved in.

"What's this all about?" Lustig asked, his eyes wide with innocence. Then he looked around the circle of men, saw Rubano and said, "Oh, I remember you."

Rubano, with some feeling, replied, "And I remember you and that twelve hours of double-talk you gave me."

"All right," Godby said. "Let's go downtown."

We spent the next twenty-four hours questioning Lustig. He spoke of his exploits, rackets and deals with complete candor, as if he were entertaining guests at dinner. But, because he knew it was the only charge on which we could book him, he never once mentioned counterfeiting. We learned that he was just on the verge of completing his latest grift and was to meet the mark that evening. As it grew later, he boldly suggested that we release him so that he could keep his "business appointment." He promised to return.

"Are you kidding?" Godby asked in amazement. "You expect me to release you so you can commit a crime?"

"The gentleman I am going to see *wants* to give me $10,000," Lustig said smoothly. "It seems a pity to deny him that pleasure."

Godby sent a man to inform Lustig's mark that he had almost been swindled. When he returned, the agent told us the mark was sore as a boil—but not at Lustig. "The chump thinks we loused him up on a chance to make some easy money, and he's furious at *us*," he said. "I swear, Lustig had him hypnotized."

We kept after Lustig hour after hour, firing the questions so rapidly that he did not have time to launch into any of his dazzling fables. Gradually, a series of small admissions began to accumulate. First Lustig acknowledged that he had known Watts in Chicago. Then he admitted seeing Watts from time to time in the East.

"Where in the East?" Godby demanded.

"Various places," Lustig replied. "Mainly in a Jersey bar."

"Do you know where he lives?"

Lustig insisted that Watts was extremely evasive on this score and that he had no idea where Watts's house was. Godby kept hammering at the theme, until finally Lustig blurted out: "He assured me he had a comfortable room. He said he could look out his window at the Hudson River and watch the ships dock. And that he had morning sunlight, which is good to have when you work on plates."

It was out! Watts *was* working on plates, and Lustig knew he was. But after this, we learned nothing more. Lustig swore that that was all he knew, and he stoutly maintained that he himself had nothing to do with counterfeiting.

The moment had come, we decided, to make a deal with him. Whatever his other crimes, they were not in our jurisdiction; our sole responsibility was to get those plates. And so we implied, without making any promises, that if Lustig would help us, we would not be ungrateful. He got the point. "I might be able to lay my hands on those plates," he said at last. "I'm not certain, but I think I can. I'll need some help from a friend, however."

The "friend" turned out to be Dapper Dan Collins. We let them converse privately for a few minutes, and then Dan left, promising to return that afternoon. He did, promptly, bringing us the key to a baggage locker in a Times Square subway station. We would find what we were looking for, he announced, in the locker. Two agents went to examine the cache. They returned with a package containing three sets of plates and $51,000 in counterfeit currency. Lustig stood up, bowed, smiled and made as if to leave.

But this time he didn't get away with it. We held him, arraigned him on charges of conspiracy and possession of counterfeit money, and asked the judge to set bail at $50,000. Lustig screamed "double-cross" every step of the way to the Federal House of Detention. But it wasn't a double-cross on our part.

Lustig, we'd found, had tried to con us again. The plates Dapper Dan had led us to weren't the near-perfect Watts plates at all. They were, in fact, hardly worth the metal they were scratched on.

As soon as Lustig went to prison the flow of Watts's counterfeit notes began to dry up, so we knew we had half the team. And while his trial pended, Lustig would get an unpalatable taste of prison life, after which we'd squeeze him again. He'd talk eventually, we were sure. And then an incredible thing happened: Lustig broke out of the Federal House of Detention, located in the heart of Manhattan and supposedly escapeproof.

After hours of interviewing everybody in the jail, we were able to reconstruct the break. At noon the prisoners were always taken to the roof for exercise. Lustig, pleading illness, was allowed to remain in his cell. The corridors were deserted, half the guards being on the roof, the other half at lunch. From under his mattress Lustig removed a rope of sheets which he had collected by withholding one sheet from the laundry pickup each week. He unlocked his cell door—how he got the key we never discovered—and walked down the hall to the washroom. Then, with a pair of wire cutters he had got hold of—somehow—he clipped the heavy screen on the window and stepped out on the ledge. Several pedestrians looked up at him, but he pretended to be washing the window. Suddenly the sheet rope snaked to the ground, and down Lustig came. He bowed to the circle of bystanders, walked quickly around the corner and disappeared.

The escape created a furor. Henry Morgenthau, Secretary of the Treasury and head of the Secret Service, read us the riot act; Governor Herbert Lehman of New York lashed at the police for their inefficiency; the press, learning of the "deal" we had made with Lustig, simultaneously damned us for proposing it and for not honoring it. We were under fire from all directions. Worse, we had reached a dead end in our search for those crucial plates. Hanna Smith refused to talk. Dapper Dan Collins had merely played the role of errand boy in securing the fake plates for Lustig. All we had left was Watts's name and a vague hint concerning his possible hideout.

From what Lustig had said, we knew only that it must have been somewhere along the lower New Jersey Palisades, overlooking the Hudson. I went with another member of the special squad one morning to a pier in Manhattan from which we could look across the river at the thousands of windows gleaming in the forenoon sun. Was Watts still behind one of those myriad reflections? Or had he fled when the uproar over Lustig's escape reached the headlines? There was only one way to find out. All that long, hot summer I visited one house along the Palisades after another, asking for a roomer who lived alone, a mild-mannered man who didn't go out much. This went on through July, August, and into September. I lost count of how many doorbells we rang, how many landlords we questioned.

And then, in September, Secret Service men, working with the FBI, recaptured Lustig in Pittsburgh. Momentarily, we were cheered by the news. We talked excitedly as if our case was finished—until we realized that tomorrow we would be back ringing doorbells in New Jersey.

A few weeks later when we met in the office for our evening rundown, agent George Pears said, "I've got a possible." He referred to his notes. "Large rooming house, Union City. Overlooks the Hudson and gets the morning light. He's a Mr. John Ramsey, mousy type, no visible means of support, no friends, no wife. When he rented the room he gave a reference in Omaha, Nebraska."

"That's where Watts had his drugstore!" I exclaimed.

"Yeah," Pears said glumly. "That's what puts me off. Watts would never have given a genuine reference."

"Maybe," Rubano said, "but we'll have to check it out."

The next morning six agents gathered at the door of Ramsey's room. "Milkman," Pears called. "Did you want to pay me this morning?"

Everyone poured in as the door opened. A little, frightened man staggered backward before the rush, blinking, his mouth open. On a table by the window were a copper plate and a set of etching tools. Hidden in the room were the near-perfect plates for that hundred-dollar bill, along with plates for several other denominations and about $50,000 in counterfeit currency. We had our man.

Watts, alias Ramsey, made no attempt to conceal anything. He had been alarmed by Lustig's arrest, escape and recapture, but he was afraid he would attract attention by running, so he sat tight.

On December 5, 1935, Lustig and Watts stood trial. Watts turned state's evidence and recounted in full detail the partnership between them. Together they had created and distributed $1,340,000 in counterfeit currency. Gone was Lustig the *bon vivant*, the debonair man of the world. On December 7·he stopped the trial by mumbling a plea of guilty. He was sentenced to twenty years.

But even now he was not free of his own sordid past. "Do you know what prison Sheriff Richards is in?" he inquired when I talked with him shortly after the sentencing.

"You mean the one you framed with the counterfeit money? Lewisburg, I think."

"Can you fix it so I don't go there?" he pleaded. "I don't care where I go, except there." His quavering tone was a far cry from the confident accents we had come to expect of the old Lustig.

As it turned out, he was sent to Alcatraz. In 1947 he died. Ironically, the death certificate listed his occupation as "apprentice salesman." To the man who sold the Eiffel Tower twice, this would surely have seemed the unkindest cut of all.

When a coal-mine operator in Canon City, Colorado, found that the combination on his office safe had jammed, he telephoned the warden of Colorado State Prison and asked whether any of his inmates would know how to open it. Twenty minutes later a convict and a prison guard showed up. The inmate twiddled the dials a few moments, then calmly opened the door. "What do you figure I owe you?" asked the mine operator.

"Well," said the convict, "last time I opened a safe, I got $1800!"
       —*W. T. Little*

The Case of Lord Dufferin

By Louis K. Anspacher

THIS IS the story of a mysterious and ghostly warning which saved the life of no less a person than the famous Lord Dufferin, at the time England's ambassador to France. Formerly he had distinguished himself as governor-general of Canada, ambassador to Italy and governor-general of India. The details of this story have been carefully investigated by the well-known French psychologist de Maratray, who brought them to the attention of the British Society for Psychical Research.

Lord Dufferin has accepted an invitation from an old friend, Sir Henry B——, to visit him in Ireland. It's a fine moonlight night. Everything is calm and serene. Lord Dufferin undresses slowly, goes to bed and soon falls asleep. But for no reason at all he suddenly awakens. The whole atmosphere of the room is strangely changed— charged with something electric! Dufferin feels something ominous and foreboding around him that he can't explain.

The ghostly moonlight falls full into his room. He lights the light. This gets rid of the fantastic shadows. He shakes himself to be sure that he's awake. He lights a cigarette and tries to compose himself. His senses are strangely alert, but he can't discover anything to explain the queer feeling of premonition.

"Well, well—" thinks Dufferin, "I'm getting foolish and moonstruck like a credulous girl. All these old places in Ireland are supposed to be haunted anyway. Perhaps a ghost or a banshee is wandering tonight."

He doesn't really believe any of that nonsense. These superstitions mean nothing to the practical man of affairs, and that's that.

His windows are open. What are these sounds? Why—a late bird is fluttering. And there are the crickets and tree toads—yes. . . . But that long, low moaning—what is it? There's not a breeze stirring. It can't be the soughing of the trees outside nor the whisper of the curtains in his room. Why, an owl of course—everything sounds strange on a moonlit night.

But wait. There it is again! It sounds like something human panting and moaning! Perhaps somebody's hurt. Dufferin jumps out of bed again and goes quickly to the windows.

They are large French windows opening down to the floor and giving on a lawn shaded by majestic old trees. The sounds seem to come from the huge shadow cast by the trees. Dufferin stands peering into the shadows, when suddenly something begins to move. The moaning and panting continue. A figure comes out of the dark into the full light of the moon. It's a man staggering under an enormous weight that he's carrying on his shoulders. This black, boxlike thing hides his face from Dufferin.

Both of them are in the full moonlight now, and Dufferin sees that the man is bearing a huge coffin. Is somebody making away with a body? Dufferin crosses the

lawn to overtake the man and says: "Look here! What
have you got there?"

At this challenge the man lifts his head from under his
burden. Dufferin sees a face of such ghoulish, baleful ugli-
ness, so terribly repulsive, that he falls back a step. It
is a face of such hateful and contorted vileness that it
burns itself indelibly on Dufferin's mind.

He now nerves himself and cries out: "Where are you
taking that?" And as he approaches the man with the
coffin to stop him, the man disappears before his eyes.
Dufferin has walked right *through* him and the coffin!
There are no footprints in the dewy grass. Nothing but
the mocking moonlight and the eerie noises of the night.

Dufferin goes gooseflesh all over, but he doesn't want
to arouse the house and he returns to his room. There he
writes down every detail of this strange occurrence in his
diary. Promptly after breakfast, he questions Sir Henry.
He finds that there has been no death or recent burial in
the village, nor can anyone recognize his description of
the man with the coffin.

There the mystery stood. And, if there were no sequel,
this story might have remained just one of those bewil-
dering events that by degrees become a legend.

Some years afterward, Lord Dufferin is appointed ambassador to France and, in the course of his official duties,
attends a diplomatic reception at the Grand Hotel in
Paris. The foyer of the hotel is crowded with representa-
tives of many countries. His private secretary conducts
Dufferin to one of the elevators, before which several
state officials are standing. They wait respectfully for
Dufferin. England's ambassador has precedence. Dufferin, passing through them, bows graciously.

The door to the elevator is opened. Dufferin is about
to enter—when his eye suddenly falls upon the man who

operates the lift. Dufferin recoils with a start of horror!
He puts out his hand and stops his secretary from entering. What's the matter?

He sees before him the very same face that branded itself upon his memory years before in Ireland! He gazes
at the man in terror. Yes, there are the same ghoulish
leer, the same contorted features. But how can that surly
and malicious face and that unforgettable squat body
have transported itself over the years from a lonely,
moonlit moor to appear suddenly in the elevator of the
Grand Hotel in Paris? These thoughts pass through his
mind as quickly as a drowning man sees the whole
panorama of his life in a brief cinema-flash.

Dufferin is a man of great self-control. From an observer's viewpoint, it merely looks as if the British ambassador has changed his mind. He utters a few conventional excuses and asks the other officials not to wait for him. He leaves his secretary standing there.

Some of the officials enter the lift. The door closes and the elevator ascends. Dufferin rushes to the office of the hotel manager. He is just asking about the man running the elevator and where he came from. But before the manager can answer, a terrible crash is heard. Cries of anguish fill the corridors. Dufferin's secretary appears with his eyes starting out of his head. There has been a terrible accident. The very elevator that Dufferin recoiled from entering—run by the very man he had seen years before in Ireland—rose to the fifth floor, when suddenly the cable broke and the car crashed down the shaft, crushing and mutilating all those inside of it!

The accident is historic. The newspapers of the time were full of it. The mysterious elevator man was killed with those he was taking up in the lift. No one could say who he was. With all the resources at his command, Lord Dufferin was never able to find out anything further.

Now, my friends, the facts are there. The evidence is incontrovertible. But nobody has been able to explain the facts. We only know that in this mysterious way Lord Dufferin's life was saved. I don't pretend to know how these things happen. I only tell you the story as it occurred.

A prospective guest from Erie, Pennsylvania, wrote the manager of New York's Hotel Taft:

"Dear Sir, I regret to inform you that due to an untimely murder in our family, I must cancel our reservations." —*Hy Gardner*

Detective's Holiday

By Octavus Roy Cohen

Hank Granger sought my advice because he heard that I was supposed to know all about hunting and fishing in the sparsely settled country where I lived. Hank was almost six feet tall and compactly built. His card informed me that he was a member of the Boston Police Department. From the first I liked him.

He had come a long way because he had heard our region was rich in game and fish. "With my annual vacation and accumulated days off, I've got nearly a month— and I'm going to have fun!" he told me.

He had been unable to get a room at the one small hotel in our village, and asked me if there might be a home where he could board. He also wanted to hire a guide who owned a good bird dog. I suggested that he drive with me to Amos Watkins'.

Amos was a farmer and hunter who knew every inch of the country; he had a comfortable home; a wife and three children, Doug, Pete and Sally; and an assortment of hunting dogs. Since Amos wasn't busy on his farm at this time of year, he agreed to take Hank as a boarder and act as his guide. Marion Watkins was considerably younger than her husband and obviously devoted to him. She was slim and blonde and pretty, and also unmistakably competent. After an enormous lunch I drove Hank Granger back to town to get his luggage.

"Mrs. Watkins doesn't look old enough to be the mother of those children," he said.

"She's not," I explained. "Amos' first wife died several years ago. He met Marion on a trip to the state capital and fell in love with her. At first we all thought it might prove to be a wrong match, but you've never seen such a happy couple."

A client was waiting in my law office, so I asked a friend of mine to take Hank back to Amos'. Hank thanked me profusely and said, "I'm glad you didn't tell them I'm a detective. I'd be pleased if you wouldn't tell anybody. When peaceful folks find out you're a detective they think you're different from other people. And I'm certainly not."

Several days later I ran into Hank and Amos in the general store, buying supplies. They obviously were getting along fine. Amos asked me to come out for dinner the following night. I didn't need much urging, for I knew Marion's cooking.

It was an enjoyable evening. Marion played a few simple melodies on an ancient organ and Amos got out his guitar. But several times during the evening I caught Hank looking at Marion with a steady, searching gaze.

The following Tuesday Amos came to my office. He looked worried. "Hank's sick," he said. "The doc thinks he's got pneumonia."

I drove out to the Watkins home. If Amos himself had been ill, the household couldn't have been more efficiently adjusted to his needs. Amos had rigged up a buzzer from Hank's bedside to the kitchen. The kids were in the parlor, playing quietly, as though reluctant to disturb the stranger whom they affectionately called "Uncle Hank."

Doc Stewart was taking care of Hank, but from the way Marion handled things in the sickroom, I could tell that she had once been a nurse. Amos told me that Hank had insisted on going to the county hospital but that Marion had vetoed the idea. "They're short of nurses. He needs constant attention and Marion is able to give it to him."

Considering the seriousness of his illness, Hank recovered rapidly. He was granted sick leave to add to his vacation time.

As Hank's convalescence progressed I sensed a certain tension in the Watkins household. I couldn't explain it, and it worried me. One day, after Hank had recovered enough to take walks around the farm, he said he wanted to have a talk with me. We went to a bench near the spring house and sat down.

Hank said, "This is confidential. There's a warrant outstanding for Marion, under her maiden name. The first time I saw her I thought I'd seen her photograph at headquarters. When I got sick and she nursed me I knew for sure, because the girl who has been wanted for several years by the police was a nurse. And her description checks."

"What did she do?"

"Two young fellows were caught one evening while they were robbing a store, and she was in their car. She may or may not have been the lookout. Anyhow, my duty is to take her back to Boston. But it's a tough decision for me—she pulled me through."

I understood the struggle going on inside the man. I

thought of Amos and the three kids and of the warm, happy home Marion had made for them. "Does Marion know that you know?"

"We haven't spoken about it, but I'm sure she does."

I said, "The warrant is under another name. You could be wrong."

"No, a trained detective sees a photograph and it sticks in his mind. It's like something you file away in a drawer, ready to pull out when the time comes."

I said, "You tell me that Marion wasn't actually a participant in the robbery. She was a young girl. Since then she has done all the reforming that any correctional institution could desire. And she's already had her punishment—knowing you suspected her, knowing you might take her back and break up that happy family."

"Don't you suppose I've been over all this a hundred times?" he exclaimed angrily. "Do you think I *want* to hurt Marion and Amos and the kids?" His anger departed as suddenly as it had come, and in its stead were misery and bewilderment.

I said, "You're not on duty, you're on vacation."

"A policeman is a policeman twenty-four hours a day. Nothing relieves you from your duty." I decided not to argue any more. This was Hank Granger's problem, and the answer had to be Hank's. I left him and drove home.

Long, anxious days passed, during which I hoped that Hank would see that white was not always white nor black always totally black. Time was running out: his decision could not be indefinitely postponed.

There came a Saturday morning ugly with the portent of storm. Amos phoned and asked me to come out that afternoon—they wanted to have an important talk with me. I reached the Watkins house shortly after four o'clock in the midst of a windstorm. Hank and Amos and Marion

led me into the parlor. The children were sent to their
playroom upstairs. The rain came then—a sudden deluge
which pounded on the roof and against the windows.
Amos said to me, "I wanted you in on this. Hank says
he's already discussed the matter with you." I nodded.

"Before Marion consented to marry me, she told me
about what happened long ago in Boston," Amos continued. "Last night Hank let us know who he really is.
Neither Marion nor I attempted to influence his decision.
If Hank wants to take Marion back to Boston I will go
with them and leave the children with neighbors. I want
you to know that we understand Hank's position. He
must do what he feels is right."

A broken branch, caught up by the gale, smashed
against the house. None of us moved, nobody said anything. Marion was looking at the floor, her cheeks
drained of color, her expression one of utter misery.
Hank stared at his knuckles. He too looked miserable.
There seemed to be nothing more to say. And then,
suddenly, terrifyingly, came a sound like a thunderclap
as a great pine tree beside the house toppled and crashed
on the roof. Just above the kids' room there was a rending
and ripping of beams and timbers. We all dashed for
the stairway.

Doug, Pete and Sally were running toward us, frightened but unhurt. When they reached the foot of the
stairs they stood uncertainly for a moment and then they
rushed to Hank Granger. Pete threw his arms around
Hank's leg, and Sally and Doug each grabbed one of
Hank's hands. Sally was crying, and Doug and Pete were
trying manfully not to. Hank picked the little girl up in
his arms.

"You're all right now, Sally," he said softly. "Everything is okay."

Sally whimpered, "Uncle Hank, I was so scared!"
"You're not scared now, are you?" said Hank.

Doug answered, "No. You wouldn't let anything hurt us, would you, Uncle Hank?"

"No," the big man answered. "I sure wouldn't." Hank Granger straightened; his eyes, as bright and clear as his conscience, looked straight at Amos. I knew then that Hank had reached his decision.

Amos and Marion were silent. The gratitude they felt could not be put into words. The storm still raged outside, but it seemed less fierce. And inside the house fear vanished. The ordeal was over. I felt like applauding. I had watched a fine man doing the thing he believed was right.

Away from my small hometown for the first time, I invited a new girl acquaintance to dinner in Washington, D.C., suggesting that she choose the place. That night we entered the magnificent dining room of an exclusive hotel; most of the guests wore evening dress and at a circular table was a large group of bemedaled men and their furred and bejeweled ladies. I was greatly impressed—and greatly worried, for I had only $14 with me.

When the check came, one glance confirmed my fears: I was short two dollars. Chatting cheerfully while I pondered my problem and quaked within, I noticed a tall, distinguished man in full evening dress standing by the entrance, watching the group at the circular table. I excused myself and approached him, unobserved by my guest. "Are you the headwaiter?" I asked.

He looked at me sharply, then smiled. Hurriedly I told him my problem.

"It happens to the best of us," he said, and took out a wallet. "Will ten help?"

I stammered my thanks. "Think nothing of it," he said, and handed me a card. "Mail it to me when you can."

Later I looked at the card. Under his name were the words "Federal Bureau of Investigation." —*Robert Jordan*

A Stranger in the Car

By Gerald L. Moore

August 16, 1957, dawned hot in Trenton, New Jersey. I was a traffic officer then, and I went on duty at 7 a.m. At about 9:30 I parked my three-wheel motorcycle at the corner of Warren and State streets, where the shade of a building was a welcome relief as I watched the flow of traffic through the intersection. Suddenly a man got out of a car and came running toward me.

"Officer," he shouted excitedly, "there's a blue Chevrolet west-bound on Fifth with a hand sticking out of the trunk! The car has a South Carolina license."

Here is the drama in the middle of which I found myself—as its details were unfolded later.

AT ABOUT 2:30 a.m. that day twenty-two-year-old Sergeant Samuel Tanner and his twenty-year-old wife, Sally, were driving north on Highway 1 from Alexandria, Virginia. Tanner had been home in South Carolina on a fifteen-day leave, and was returning to duty at McGuire Air Force Base, Fort Dix, New Jersey. His headlights picked up a young-appearing hitchhiker, dressed neatly in checkered sports shirt and gray slacks. "Shall we give him a lift, honey?" Tanner asked his wife.

"I don't know, Sam. It might be all right," she replied.

"He looks okay," said Tanner. "He may be another serviceman." He stopped, shouted, "How far you going, buddy?"

"New York," the man answered.

"We can take you as far as Trenton, New Jersey," said Tanner. "That's where we live."

"Okay," the man answered, clambering into the back seat of the two-door Chevrolet sedan.

The airman wondered at the hitchhiker's reluctance to enter into conversation. As minutes passed, he remembered things he had read about hitchhikers and began to worry mildly. He could see that Sally, who was expecting their first child, was worried, too.

But miles rolled by and nothing happened, so Sam and his wife began to relax. The man in the back seat, who looked older than he had first appeared to be, had fallen asleep. Had the Tanners known they had befriended a convicted killer, they would not have been so complacent as they drove through the night toward Trenton.

George Denwhite Roberts, thirty-six, had been released from an Indiana reformatory after serving a three-year sentence in 1943. In 1944 he began a one-to-five-year penitentiary term in Missouri. In 1948, convicted of first-degree murder in Kansas City, he started a life sentence in the Kansas State Penitentiary, was later transferred to a prison farm. From there, on May 27, 1956, Roberts had escaped.

At about 4:30 a.m. Tanner read a road sign: "Trenton, 65 miles." He nudged the accelerator gently. Suddenly, without warning, the hood of the car flew up in front of the windshield. Tanner jammed on the brakes and brought the car to a quick stop.

The man in the back seat sat upright. "What happened?" he asked.

Tanner was getting out. "The hood came unlatched," he replied. "It's a good thing there's no traffic tonight."

As Sam walked to the front of the car, Sally felt something press against her shoulder. She turned and saw, terrified, that it was a pistol in the hitchhiker's hand.

Sam slammed the hood down, got back into the car. As he reached for the ignition key, Roberts hit him on the side of the head with the pistol. Sam felt a searing pain, and blood started running down his neck. "Do exactly as I say or I'll kill you both," Roberts snarled, his pistol at Tanner's head. "Drive on down the highway."

At the intersection of a small country road Roberts ordered Sam to turn. Then, after a couple of hundred yards, he said, "Stop. Both of you get out."

Sally was crying as she and her husband stood in the road with their hands up. Roberts again struck Sam with the pistol, knocking him to the ground. Blood streamed from another head wound. The escaped lifer kicked Tanner in the side, saying, "Get up and open the trunk." Sam dragged himself to his feet and did as he was told.

"Now get in." Roberts slammed the lid.

"Please," Sally pleaded. "Just leave us here and take the car."

Now the pistol was pointed at the girl. "Get in front."

Roberts drove a short distance back toward the highway and stopped. Sally screamed as he slid over and pulled at her maternity blouse. Now she became hysterical and pleaded with him to release her husband. Roberts ordered her out of the car.

"Okay, you want to be with your husband, so get in with him," he said, opening the trunk. The lid slammed shut. Soon the car began to move. Sam and Sally could scarcely breathe in their cramped positions. After what seemed an eternity the car stopped again. The trunk lid opened, and Roberts told them to get out. After tying their hands and gagging them with strips torn from clothing he found in the car, he pushed them back into the trunk. With gags cutting at their mouths, the young couple struggled for every breath.

Five more times during the night Roberts stopped the car. Twice he pistol-whipped Sam; twice he pointed the gun at him and snapped the trigger. Each time the gun failed to fire. The last stop Roberts made was for gas, after warning the Tanners that he would kill them and the filling-station attendant if they made a sound. As Roberts drove on again, Sam managed to free his hands and untie Sally. He tried to force the lock on the trunk, but it wouldn't move. Finally, he pried open one corner of the trunk lid with a tire tool. They breathed deeply of the fresh air.

It was daylight now, and they began to hear the sounds of traffic. "We must be in Trenton. There are cars all around us," Sam whispered. He pried frantically at the trunk lid.

"Maybe if we drop some things out of the trunk we'll attract attention," said Sally.

They dropped the strips of cloth they had been bound with; they dropped small hand tools—everything that would go through the opening. Their efforts went unnoticed. In desperation, Sam forced his blood-drenched hand through the opening and began to wave. It was then that the man saw Sam's hand and alerted me.

I started my motorcycle, snapped on the radio transmitter and swerved into the westbound lane. After weaving my way around cars for about a block I spotted the Chevrolet. The sight of a bloody hand waving from its trunk caused my pulse to quicken as I reached for the microphone in front of me. "521 to headquarters—emergency."

The dispatcher answered almost immediately. "All cars stand by. Come in, 521, with the emergency."

I gave my location, direction of travel and a description of the car I was following. As he called other units to assist me and gave their locations, I realized that there were no other units in the vicinity. I was on my own. I turned on my red lights and stepped on the siren. Traffic slowed, came to a stop. The Chevrolet was stopped by other cars. I was off the motorcycle and moving toward the left rear of the Chevrolet almost before the driver had it stopped. There were screams from within the trunk of the car: "Kill him, kill him." The cries were frightened, hysterical.

Through the left rear window I saw the driver of the Chevrolet grab a pistol on the seat and turn as I leveled my revolver.

"Don't do it, fellow. One quick move and I'll shoot," I warned.

He hesitated. Self-preservation told me to pull the trigger and play it safe. The abhorrence of taking a human life—any human life—told me to wait. I could see the hatred in his eyes as he slowly made his decision. Finally, deliberately, he laid the pistol on the seat and raised his hands. With a deep feeling of relief I ordered the driver to step out. I handcuffed his hands behind him. The key to the trunk was in his pocket. Now other officers were arriving to assist me. I took the key and unlocked the trunk.

Bloody, dirty, soaked with perspiration and weakened from their ordeal, the Tanners were immediately sent to a hospital. Roberts was taken to police headquarters. Later, he pleaded guilty to a charge of first-degree robbery and was sentenced to twenty-two years in the New Jersey State Penitentiary—after which he will be returned to Kansas to finish his sentence there.

Sam and Sally Tanner had a fine baby son. But perhaps their harrowing experience with a hitchhiker will be a warning to others who are tempted to offer a ride to a stranger at the side of the road.

In a Los Angeles taxicab I spotted a neatly wrapped little box in the corner of the seat. Handing it to the driver, I said, "Looks like one of your passengers forgot something."

With a nonchalant "Thanks," he opened the glove compartment and tossed in the package, which looked as though it had come from a jewelry shop. I noticed several packages in the compartment. Then he explained: "These boxes are for a little game of psychology I play with my customers. I've found that four out of five men will return the package. But I guess women are just too curious or covetous. About four out of five can't resist."

"What's in the box?" I asked.

"Just a note," he answered. "It says, 'Crime Does Not Pay.' "

— *James Hodgson*

John Deering, a truck driver of Anderson, Indiana, was stranded along the road with a burned-out fuse. Two men drove alongside and relieved him of $5—but supplied him with a fuse before they fled. *—AP*

The Great Portuguese Bank-Note Swindle

By Frederic Sondern, Jr.

IN APPROPRIATELY austere offices at 26 Great Winchester Street, the venerable London firm of Waterlow & Sons, Ltd., in the 1920's, conducted its impressive and often delicate business, the manufacture of bank notes for governments all over the world.

There, on December 4, 1924, Karel Marang van Ysselveere, respected merchant banker of The Hague, presented his credentials as special emissary of the Portuguese government. He was received at once by Sir William Waterlow himself, to whom the suave, distinguished-looking Dutchman explained that the Bank of Portugal needed two hundred thousand 500-escudo (25-dollar) notes at once. Their issue must remain secret for political reasons; hence the negotiations had been entrusted by the Bank's governor to Marang, rather than to the usual diplomatic channels.

Sir William nodded his understanding. He would of course need authorization from the Bank's governor, and the customary contract. Naturally, agreed the courteous Hollander; the papers would be dispatched from Lisbon without delay. Thus began one of the most fantastic frauds in the history of international finance.

During the next weeks a series of imposing "Most Confidential" documents arrived at Waterlow & Sons. A letter under the seal and over the signature of the governor of the Bank of Portugal, Camacho Rodrigues, authorized the printing of the bank notes. It explained—for Sir William's eyes alone—that Mr. Marang was empowered to receive the currency and take it to Lisbon. There it would pass into the hands of a syndicate of bankers commissioned by the Portuguese government to use it to rehabilitate the finances of its colony of Angola in Africa.

Since the money was to be spent only in Angola, it could be printed from the same plates and with the same serial numbers Waterlow's had used for the last issue of 500-escudo notes, which was circulating in Portugal. To avoid confusion of the two issues the governor of the colony would later have the new notes overprinted with the word ANGOLA.

Whatever suspicion of irregularity might have existed in Sir William's mind vanished when contracts arrived signed by the high commissioner of Angola and other prominent people. Waterlow's presses produced five million dollars' worth of 500-escudo notes, which were duly delivered in several batches to Marang. He transported them to Lisbon under the customs immunity of his diplomatic status—he had a Liberian diplomatic passport. Sir William did not know that every letter and contract now carefully locked in his safe was a forgery, that the notes would never be surcharged or circulate in Angola. It was not until a year and $10,000,000 more escudo notes later that he would learn the magnitude of the deception to which he was an unsuspecting party.

On December 5, 1925, the Portuguese Criminal Investigation Division raided the Oporto branch of the Bank of Angola and Metropole—a new and extremely prosperous institution—in response to complaints that it was illegally manipulating foreign exchange. But when the investigating magistrate and his auditors went through the bank's vaults, they found something far more startling than unlawfully acquired dollars and pounds. Its strongboxes were crammed with thousands of 500-escudo notes. The bills were wrapped in Bank of Portugal packages, but they were not arranged consecutively by serial number, in the Bank's usual manner.

The Bank of Portugal's top technical expert was hastily summoned. Positively, he said, the notes were authentic. But the magistrate sent the seized currency to the Oporto branch of the Bank of Portugal with orders to check the serial numbers against those of all its 500-escudo notes. By evening, four pairs of notes with identical numbers had been found.

By December 7 all Portugal was in a panic. As the public brought thousands of 500-escudo notes to the offices of the Bank of Portugal for redemption, more and more pairs of identical notes turned up. When the extent of the catastrophe became clear, the normally solid escudo dropped gradually on the international exchanges. The Lisbon Cabinet was in almost continuous emergency session.

The facts that emerged from investigation became increasingly fantastic. Someone had not only fooled Waterlow's into printing three hundred million escudos for him, but had founded the Bank of Angola and Metropole with this worthless money. He had bought heavily into the largest industrial concerns of Portugal, acquired large blocks of real estate and pyramided these assets into a financial empire. He had also, through the Bank of Angola and Metropole, bought up a considerable portion of the privately held stock of the Bank of Portugal itself. And if the criminal had been able to continue his fabulous swindle for another month or two, he would have controlled the national Bank, have been in a position to get rid of the evidence against him and would probably never have been brought to book.

Arthur Virgílio Alves Reis was born in 1896 in Lisbon, son of a minor customs official. He became fascinated at an early age by the story of Cecil Rhodes, the great builder of South Africa, and dreamed of establishing a similar empire in the Portuguese colonies. The dream stayed with Reis as he grew older. On graduating from the Lisbon *Politécnica*, the young man wanted the post of a colonial government engineer. Competition was keen, but Alves Reis cleared this obstacle in characteristic fashion. An expert draftsman, he forged a diploma from the University of London. With this—since British-trained engineers were in great demand—he got his job. In 1916 he arrived in the territory of Angola as a railway inspector. Within two years he became manager of the state railways, and shortly afterward inspector of public works—the highest technical official in the colony—at the age of twenty-five.

Angola lies on the Atlantic coast between the Congo and the territory of South West Africa. It is rich in rubber, cotton and minerals, including gold and diamonds. Reis explored the territory and became enthusiastic. Exploitation of its mineral resources, rail links to the north and south, the harnessing of its big rivers, could make Angola one of the most prosperous sections of the continent. He resigned his post, set up the firm of Alves Reis,

Ltd., in Lisbon, obtained exclusive rights to prospect the Angola mineral belt and began searching for capital.

But money was hard to get. Angola had a bad reputation financially, and not even Reis's extraordinary eloquence could move the British and Netherlands bankers to give him even a part of the £6,000,000 he wanted. He was desperate—when opportunity beckoned unexpectedly from a different direction.

Reis had a reputation for skill in negotiating difficult financial problems. The Royal Trans-African Railway Company of Angola was in trouble with its foreign bondholders and asked him to take charge until the tangle was straightened out. In the company's treasury was over $100,000 in gold, earmarked for the payment of debts. Reis had himself made chairman of the company and used his authority to divert the funds to Alves Reis, Ltd., for prospecting ventures in Angola. A few months later the would-be empire builder was in jail awaiting trial for fraud.

It was July 1924, and the finances of many European countries were tottering. In jail Reis read about the German government's printing of countless billions of marks to bolster its sagging treasury. If he could only devise some method of getting Portuguese bank notes printed for his own use, thought Reis, he could still put over his colonial projects.

He had his friends bring him every available scrap of information about the Bank of Portugal's currency operation—and reached two conclusions: that during the past few years the Bank had issued far more bank notes than the limit set by law, a situation that could be embarrassing to both the Bank and the government; and that the Bank had no system for keeping exact track of how many bank notes of a particular denomination were in circulation at a given time. Something else also struck Reis. While the Bank's printing plant manufactured most of the currency, some of its 500- and 1000-escudo notes were made by Waterlow & Sons of London. Portugal had long been troubled by counterfeiters, and Waterlow's plates, inks and techniques were forgery-proof. In Reis's nimble brain, the Great Plan began to take shape. In August, he was found guilty of defrauding the bondholders of the railway, but three months later a superior court reversed the decision.

As confederates in his scheme Reis had selected three eminently qualified friends. Karel Marang van Ysselveere, a prosperous merchant and financier in The Hague, was to be front man; Senhor José Bandeira, brother of the Portuguese minister to The Hague, would be his assistant. Adolph Hennies, a German with a shady reputation for irregular currency transactions in South America, was Reis's personal adviser.

Marang and Bandeira, Reis decided, were to know only a small part of the whole scheme. "When a man is acting in good faith," Reis writes in his *Confessions*, which he published later, "the person with whom he is dealing, especially an honorable man like Sir William Waterlow, will respond to that good faith." Both Marang and Bandeira were to believe—and did for a long time—that while the transaction was irregular, Reis was acting with the full approval of the government of Angola to save the colony from ruin.

José Bandeira persuaded his brother, the minister, to write a letter officially introducing Marang as a diplomatic emissary of Portugal—the credentials which so impressed Sir William. As soon as Marang returned to Lisbon after his interview at Waterlow's, Reis went to

work to forge a number of remarkable documents. In the
first one the Bank of Portugal authorized the government
of Angola to issue a specified number of bank notes. The
second contained Reis's authorization by the government
of Angola to effectuate the issue. In the third, Reis appointed Marang as his representative. Some little time
later Reis forged Governor Rodrigues' letter to Sir William Waterlow authorizing the printing of the notes.
Marang, unsuspecting, took these masterpieces to London.
And Sir William, as Reis had so rightly calculated, did
"respond to that good faith."

Reis had concluded that five million dollars' worth of
500-escudo notes was all that could safely be put into circulation for the time being. But, in order to operate with
even that amount of cash without arousing suspicion, he
must have a bank. In July 1925 his Bank of Angola and
Metropole opened its doors in Lisbon and Oporto.

Alves Reis proved to be an able and imaginative
banker. His bank quickly acquired a reputation for handling loans—small ones in particular—with a dispatch
and friendliness quite different from the methods of other
Portuguese banks. Reis and Hennies had hit on the
scheme of exchanging the Waterlow bank notes for their
debtors' collateral. Within a few months they had solidly
invested $2,500,000 of their spurious currency—and in-
creasing numbers of their clients now became depositors
of the pleasant institution. Within six months the bank
was prospering.

But by June 1925 the increase in the circulation of the
500-escudo note had been noticed. There were rumors of
counterfeiting. The Bank of Portugal reacted as Reis had
always thought it would. It announced officially that all
reports of the inflation of Portuguese currency by coun-

terfeiting or other means were ridiculous. Reis concluded
correctly that the Bank had no inkling of his operation
and that the public would accept the pronouncement of
the Bank's venerated head without question. He promptly
put the rest of the Waterlow printing into sound investments. And he ordered another ten million dollars' worth
of notes from London through Marang.

At the same time Reis had been quietly buying up stock
in the Bank of Portugal. Within another two months he
would have a controlling interest in the Bank and would
probably be its governor. He would then be able to erase
all evidence of his fraud. Sure of success, in October 1925
Reis sailed for Angola. With the same high commissioner
whose name he had forged he discussed a number of
interesting projects. His bank was ready to finance the
construction of a railway to bring the produce of the rich
Bembe copper mines to the port of Luanda. A similar
development subsequently completed by others proved of
inestimable value to the Allies in World War II. Reis
also proposed to underwrite the transportation of a thousand Portuguese families as colonists to the fertile table-
lands of Angola. The high commissioner listened, fascinated, as his former inspector of public works outlined his
plans for the region.

But events in Lisbon had moved quickly. Governor
Rodrigues and his directors had learned of mysterious
efforts being made to buy the Bank of Portugal's stock.
They began an investigation. A number of leads pointed
toward Senhor Alves Reis. Then came the raid on the
bank's Oporto branch and the investigating magistrate's
discovery of the duplicate notes.

Reis arrived in Lisbon from Angola the next day and
was arrested. But the forger wasn't through. In prison, he
managed to fabricate an impressive mass of documents

indicating that Governor Rodrigues and some of the directors of the Bank of Portugal had been the real conspirators and that he, Reis, was the victim of a political plot. The material was so convincing that it split Portugal into two partisan camps for months and delayed Reis's trial for five years. But in May 1930 he was tried, found guilty on his own confession and sentenced to twenty years.

Alves Reis's weird dream of empire was over. Having served his prison term, he dropped out of sight for a number of years. Then he turned up again—once more on a swindling charge. Convicted in a Lisbon court of fraud to the tune of 60,000 escudos for coffee which he sold but failed to deliver, he was sentenced on March 5, 1955, to four more years in jail. This time all signs of his opulent past, all dreams of glory were gone.

Aging and impoverished, Alves Reis lay in bed with heart trouble throughout his trial. Six months after sentencing he died, in September 1955. Two sons who had lived with him revealed that they had been unable to find work because of their father's bad name; the family had survived only by donations of food from friends.

Thus miserably and ingloriously came to a close the career of the man who perpetrated the astounding Portuguese bank-note swindle.

Counterfeit fifty-dollar Federal Reserve notes seized in Milan, Italy, bore the words, "redeemable in awful currency of the United States Treasury."   —*New York Times*

Secret Service agents in St. Louis learned from a man they'd just caught why he produced counterfeit ten-dollar bills. "Good engraving just intrigues me," he explained.   —*Paul Steiner*

Love and the Lie Detector

By David Redstone

IN 1921 THERE was a series of baffling thefts in a girls'
dormitory at the University of California. Money,
jewelry, clothing and other articles were reported missing.
School authorities preferred to handle the matter without
police assistance, and the girls themselves were assigned to
patrol duty. But amateur sleuthing failed and Margaret
Taylor, one of the students, made a formal complaint to
the police.

William Wiltberger, a police officer assigned to duty at
the college, took charge of the investigation. He toured
the secondhand stores and pawnshops in an effort to find
the loot, but the thief had been too clever to dispose of it
in this obvious manner. He then began to question the
ninety girls who lived in the dormitory. He got nowhere.
All the girls were from good families, and none seemed to
have any reason to steal.

Wiltberger then proposed something altogether new.
He had caught the spirit of modern investigation from
Police Chief August Vollmer, who was making Berkeley,
California, famous as the cradle of scientific crime detec-

tion in America. He knew that twenty-three-year-old John A. Larson, a fellow policeman in Berkeley, had been experimenting with a lie-detecting device that measured a person's respiration, blood pressure and other physical reactions as he replied to questions. Now he persuaded Larson to set up the apparatus at the college laboratory.

Larson was no ordinary officer of the law. He was a graduate of Boston University and had a Ph.D. from the University of California. He had become interested in criminology while writing a thesis on heredity and finger-prints, which was in line with his studies in biology, physiology and psychiatry. Chief Vollmer had induced him to join the Berkeley Police Department, where he could do special research in police science. That work, however, didn't exempt Larson from pounding a four-to-midnight beat as a regular patrolman. Before proceeding with the lie tests, young Larson asked the girls to vote their consent. This they unanimously did.

An actual police investigation differs in many ways from those in fiction. In crime fiction the least likely suspect often roams at large through some two hundred pages before the detective gets around to him. In real life, when a person finds a body, witnesses a crime or makes a complaint to the police, that person is the first to be examined, so as to eliminate—or incriminate—the least likely suspect. Detectives like to solve mysteries in the shortest possible time, preferably on page one, so they can go home and soak their feet.

The least likely suspect here was Margaret Taylor, since she was the one who made the complaint. Larson had her take the test first. He did not begin with direct questions such as: "What did you do with Miss So-and-So's hand-bag?" Subjects mustn't be frightened at the start, for that would influence the graph readings. The girls should be

put at ease so that pulse, heartbeat and respiration would be normal when he began their tests.

So, for a while, Larson made casual conversation. Charming conversation it was, too. He and Margaret talked about books, parents, music. He found her intelligent and witty, as well as lovely. She was curious about his work, and soon he found himself talking of his many interests. She told him he was wonderful to be doing so much and to be so ambitious. He almost said she was wonderful too, but caught himself in time. It occurred to him that some criminals and congenital liars have been known to be thoroughly delightful people. Not that this girl . . .

Then he smiled and said, "Now shall we get down to business?" He adjusted the lie detector and began to read from a list of innocuous questions, later interpolating some like the following:

"Do your parents give you enough money to buy all the things you need at school?"

"Do you enjoy reading crime stories?"

"Do you ever envy your classmates the pretty things they have?"

"Tell me quickly, after each word as you hear it, what you associate with that word or idea: Desk. Tree. Crime. Locket. Rocker. Locker. Purse." She answered easily, without hesitation, and Larson noted the effect on the graph. Key words such as *crime*, *locker*, *purse* had caused no change from the normal in her pulse or breathing. He thanked her gravely and dismissed her.

Several days were spent in making the tests. After they were over, Wiltberger dropped in. "Any results?" he asked.

"Some."

"Any lies?"

"A few."

"Well, all girls fib a little," Wiltberger remarked. "I suppose you'll have to repeat some of the tests before you make up your mind."

"My mind's made up. But a retest of Margaret Taylor won't do any harm," Larson said. "Will you ask her to come in?"

Wiltberger did so, and left them alone. "There's a special question that I want you to be sure to answer truthfully," said Larson. "It's here on the list. Go ahead, please."

She read it. Her face flushed. Larson watched the blood-pressure indicator. His own face grew warm, because this question was not one he had asked the other subjects. Her answer was a quick "No!" The recording needle jumped with the response. He pointed to the peak on the graph, which showed that she had given an untruthful answer. Confronted with this evidence, she broke down and confessed to the truth. And then she asked *him* the same question. It was: "Do you love *me?*"

His answer—"I do"—he repeated a year later, at the altar. Which is why he looks back with warm memories to his first lie-detector case.

It was an important case for other reasons. It proved that such a test could be used successfully in a criminal investigation. Larson, by means of the instrument, found the culprit—another of the ninety girls. She confessed when shown that the detector pointed to her guilt. Most of the stolen things, which she had hidden cleverly, were restored to their owners.

Later Dr. Larson solved a number of important criminal cases that might still be mysteries but for the scientific lie detector, and he taught hundreds of police officers how to use the apparatus. His name came to rank with the top scientists in his field.

Who was proudest to see it there? Margaret Larson, née Taylor.

J. Edgar Hoover tells this story of one of his G-men: In February the G-man received an unsigned valentine. He painstakingly processed the card for fingerprints. Then for the next few weeks he obtained, without their knowledge, the fingerprints of all the girls he suspected. He finally found the matching prints and the lady confessed.   —*Leonard Lyons*

A Minneapolis suburb has been buzzing with the news that a housewife was seen holding hands with the mailman on her front porch. True, the lady in question calmly admits. It was the best way she could think of to convince her dog that postmen aren't burglars.   —*"Almanac" in Minneapolis Tribune*

"They Swore My Life Away"

By Clifford Shephard, as told to W. W. Ward

I STOOD on a curb downtown, waiting for the traffic light to change. It was a little after 5 p.m. on April 18, 1935, and I had just knocked off work for the day. I had run into Betty, my landlady, doing her marketing in town, and we were on our way home to supper. It had been a good day and I didn't have a care in the world. In fact, being a six-foot 200-pounder, the only thing I had on my mind at the moment was food. That was the last untroubled thought I was going to have for the next fifteen years. In a matter of seconds my life changed to just plain hell on earth.

As Betty and I crossed the intersection and headed for my car, a little beak-nosed man ran up beside me and peered into my face. Suddenly he shouted, "That's him! I'd know him anywhere."

People stopped and stared at us and I could feel my face getting red. "Cut it out," I said to him. "You've made a mistake."

"That's the same woman, too," the little guy went on excitedly. "She was with him."

"Come on," I said to Betty. But as I started forward somebody grabbed me by the arm.

I looked into the unfriendly eyes of a husky, blue-jowled man and caught the flash of a badge. With him was a tall, sandy-haired, thin-lipped guy with freckles.

"Look," I told Blue-Jowls quietly, "I don't know who you're after, but . . ."

"Save it," he said. "Come along."

With the thin little man beside us, they led us to a police car and shoved us in. We drove to the county prosecutor's office. I could see that Betty was plenty scared and I tried to reassure her. We hadn't committed any crime. These guys had made a mistake and I expected to clear it up fast. At the prosecutor's office the little thin-faced man told his story.

"They're the Saturday Forgers," he asserted loudly. "They was in my place of business three months ago. I cashed a check for 'em for $35. It wasn't any good. I know 'em. I never forget a face."

The blue-jowled cop sat down on a corner of the desk. "This man," he said, indicating the little guy, "runs a liquor store downtown. We were driving around when he came running out and stopped us. Said he'd seen a couple who had given him a bum check a while back. He swears these two are the pair."

This was the first I knew of the reason for bringing us in. It was, of course, preposterous. I said so. "I never had a check bounce in my life," I told the man at the desk. "There's some mistake."

He asked me my name, age and occupation. I said I was forty-nine and told him I was in business for myself.

One of the detectives chuckled. "You ain't foolin'," he said.

I explained that I'd had good sales and promotion jobs until I decided to go in for myself, handling a liquid run-stopper for women's hosiery. The prosecutor cut me off to ask some questions of Betty. She told him she ran a boardinghouse and that I was one of her regular boarders.

"How long's he been with you?"

"Four months."

"That's about the length of time this bum-check couple's been working," the sandy-haired man said. "Description fits 'em to a T."

"They hooked a lot of us merchants," the liquor-store man said. "I can get you plenty of witnesses."

"Call them in," said the man behind the desk. Then he went back to his papers. They fingerprinted us, then led us out into a hall, and one of the detectives pointed to a wooden bench. We sat down.

"Cliff," Betty said, "what can we do?"

I grinned at her. "Why," I said, "when the other merchants show up they'll tell 'em they made a mistake and they'll let us go."

"What if they don't?"

"Look," I said, "this is America. They don't throw innocent people in jail."

A door opened down the hall and the detective beckoned. Back in the prosecutor's office there were eight or nine men who stared hard at us as we walked in. "That's him," I heard a man say.

"That's the woman, too," said another. The little liquor dealer glared triumphantly at me.

Blue-Jowls took my arm. "Let's go," he said.

At the door I stopped and looked back over my shoulder at that little group of men. Fellow citizens—small-town merchants—the kind of people you buy your bread and aspirin and underwear from and talk with about the weather while you wait for change. These men were sending us to jail! They wouldn't cheat a customer for anything in the world, but they took our freedom from us as if it had been a nickel lying on the sidewalk.

I caught a glimpse of Betty's pale, frightened face before they took her away. Then a door closed between us and I was led down steel steps to the jail. The smell of stale cigarette smoke and disinfectant mingled with the body odor of men. At the last cell on the left we stopped. A jailer opened the door and the detective pushed me in. I sank down on the cot, overcome by a sense of utter helplessness. A short while ago I had been walking along the street among friendly people. Now I was behind bars.

I spent that whole night listening for footsteps that didn't come. I watched the gray dawn filter through the window bars and their vague shadows move slowly down the opposite wall. That day passed, then another. The only footsteps I heard were those of the jailer bringing food. On the third day they brought us before a judge to arraign us for forgery. As the clerk droned on, listing the witnesses against us, I felt again the chill of complete helplessness and fear.

"We didn't do it," I mumbled once, but nobody heard. It was all I could think of to say. Later, in my cell, the words came strong and bitter and clear, but there was no one to hear but a peevish old man who was now my cellmate. I spent the next five months in that cell. It wasn't until October that we were given a trial. In the big courtroom, before rows of curious, unfriendly eyes, we faced again the storekeepers who were our accusers. One by one they took the witness stand to identify us. They told how we'd acted, where we'd stood in their stores. Their voices carried the ring of truth and, God help them, the jury believed what they said.

The lawyer assigned by the court to defend us was young and inexperienced, just out of law school. Fifteen witnesses testified in my favor, swore to my integrity. They weren't believed. A repairman said I was in his garage having my car's headlights fixed on the day and at the hour some of the forged checks were being cashed. He wasn't believed.

We were each sentenced to nine months—the length of time it takes to bring a human being into the world—and it took only nine seconds for an impassive judge to blast me into a living hell. But at least the torture of uncertainty was gone. There was a day I could look forward to. Each night when I was locked in my cell at the county workhouse I made a mark on the wall. When the summer days began to shorten I began to let myself think of the things which come with freedom—walking up to a door and opening it, if I liked, ordering steaks and chops and hot biscuits and mashed potatoes with gravy.

When the day came, my hands shook so that I broke the laces on one shoe. A few of the boys called out, "So long, Cliff," and I waved. Betty, just released, was waiting in the outer office. I started toward her, but stopped at the look on her face. Then I saw the two detectives. One of them stepped forward and I felt the bite of cold steel on my wrist. Once again we were under arrest. The officers led us to a car and drove us to the county jail.

It was like dreaming a nightmare over again. There was another group of indignant local merchants, another batch of forged checks. Sure, a druggist said. I remember them. That's the woman, they said. A slick team. We never forget a face. All I could do was sit and stare, a lump of bitterness closing my throat.

We were indicted again. Our trial was a heartbreaking

repetition of the previous one. Betty got nine months in the women's detention home. I was sentenced to a year and a half in the county penitentiary. My spirit was just about broken. When they told me to eat, I ate. When they told me to turn out my light and go to sleep, I slept. Twice I roused myself from this lethargy to apply for a pardon. Both times it was turned down. The eighteen months dragged out into an eternity, an empty, desolate void. When I was released I had lost thirty-five pounds, my hair was streaked with gray and my shoulders had a permanent slump. As I walked away from the prison gates my pace was that of a tired old man. I tried to get a job as a salesman, but my prison record was against me. I washed dishes in a diner. I mowed lawns. I cleaned stables for a riding academy. Then the police got me again.

For the third time I faced the hard stares of storekeepers from a nearby town. This time I lashed back. I denounced the merchants as weak-minded old men with failing memories. But they could have railroaded me right back into jail if it hadn't been for one thing—*at the time those merchants swore they had seen me in their shops, I was already in jail!* They let me go.

Now I got my first break. On that grand jury was a banker who listened carefully to the storekeepers and suspected that the first two indictments were wrong. Through him I got in touch with the Burns Detective Agency, which acted for the American Bankers' Association in running down forgers.

Digging into their records for a man answering my description, they discovered one Edward Sullivan. Known as the Phantom Forger, he was over six feet tall and weighed two hundred pounds. The agency's handwriting experts found that the signatures on the checks that I had allegedly written were the same as those forged by the

Phantom, even to the names used. Armed with this evidence, I applied for a full pardon. In my own mind there wasn't the slightest doubt that it would be granted. And yet they turned me down cold. Under state law I couldn't apply again for two years.

I got a job peddling rugs from door to door. But still my freedom meant nothing with a prison record hanging over my head. Then one day the Burns Agency got in touch with me. Sullivan and his wife had been picked up and taken to Milwaukee, Wisconsin, to answer charges for previous forgeries. I set out for Milwaukee and on arrival went directly to the district attorney's office. There Detective Arthur Gunderman listened to my story—and believed it. On February 10, 1939, nearly four years after that grim day of my first arrest, I sat in the warden's office at the Wisconsin State Prison, where Sullivan was serving an eleven-year term. When he finally was brought into the room I saw that, while he was big and had my heavy shoulders and broad face, there the resemblance stopped. Sullivan shook hands and sat down and I poured out the whole story. I'd brought along photostatic copies of the checks I'd been convicted of signing and when I laid them before Sullivan he smiled.

"You got a bum deal," he said. Then he wrote out a full confession for each of the forgeries for which I had spent almost three years in jail. Warden John Burke and Detective Gunderman signed as witnesses.

As soon as I got back to my home state I again made application to the Board of Pardons. This time, with Sullivan's confession, I knew there wasn't a possibility that they could turn me down. *And yet they did* at their April 1940 term. There was no explanation. Just a big red "Rejected" stamped across the form. I walked out with that piece of paper in my hand and stood on the sidewalk with the tears blurring the bright spring sunshine.

That afternoon I got a job as a handyman in a bar and grill. One of the customers at the tavern was a newspaper reporter, and for four years he worked with me writing appeals every two years based on the evidence I had collected. Thirty local clergymen signed a petition asking that I be pardoned. Yet each application was turned down.

My reporter friend got my story before the governor, who ordered the case investigated. Under a recent revision of the state constitution, the old Board of Pardons had been replaced. The new three-man board reviewed my case thoroughly, then presented its findings to the governor with a unanimous recommendation that I be granted a full pardon. It was signed on June 14, fifteen years after those self-deluded merchants had stood before the court and sworn my freedom away.

I've been asked many times how I felt when handed my pardon. If I had to pick one out of the jumble of thoughts, I suppose I'd make it gratitude that I was no longer a criminal in the eyes of the law. I know that a guy can get awfully bitter holding a grudge, so I'm not looking back. There are a lot of years left ahead for me. I want them to be good.

J. Haskell Betherum was arrested in Oklahoma City when he asked two policemen why they were driving without lights. His six-dollar fine was paid with pennies donated by sympathetic citizens in response to a newspaper's invitation for contributions from "anyone who has ever sassed a policeman, wanted to sass a policeman, or who had been sassed by a policeman." Among the contributors was the judge who fined Betherum.

—Pathfinder

A Housewife Who
Confounded Two Countries

By Murray Teigh Bloom

WHEN the old Cunarder *Scythia* steamed out of Boston Harbor on November 9, 1889, among the passengers was a tall, pleasant-looking woman traveling with her two young daughters. Mrs. Leonora E. Piper was a simple New England woman with little formal education, wife of a store clerk in Boston. Yet in a brief three months she was destined to provide the world with one of the most profound mysteries of modern psychical research.

During the rough voyage on the *Scythia* Mrs. Piper more than once regretted her acceptance of an invitation to come to England so that some of her incredible phenomena could be studied closely by scientific experts. She knew that it would be a repetition of the past four years: open suspicion, minute observations for trickery, private detectives trailing her every move, people afraid to talk openly in her presence and everyone regarding her as a strange, rather fearsome freak.

It had been that way since early 1885, when she first came to the attention of Professor William James, the

great Harvard psychologist. After the birth of her first child she had visited a clairvoyant in Boston, renowned for his medical diagnoses. Mrs. Piper was then in frequent pain and as she listened to him she found herself going off into a trance. In later trances her friends found that she could accurately answer questions about friends who had died. James heard about her from members of his family who had attended a séance. He laughingly explained how unscrupulous mediums made it a point to do research in advance on all their clients, how they employed agents to get information from tombstones, directories and interviews with servants, and how they exchanged vital biographical data on potential clients.

Professor James's explanations didn't impress his womenfolk. Annoyed, he decided to look into the matter himself, so that he could show these naïve women exactly how they were being hoodwinked. But after a few sessions with Mrs. Piper, James was sure that more than trickery was involved. His mother-in-law, for example, had for some time been looking for a lost bankbook and asked Mrs. Piper where it was. The medium described the place so exactly that the book was found instantly on the return home. Another time Mrs. Piper told James that his Aunt Kate, who was then living in New York, had died early that morning. "On reaching home an hour later," the professor noted, "I found a telegram reading as follows: 'Aunt Kate passed away a few minutes after midnight.'"

Still, it was always possible that Mrs. Piper had in some way made a special investigation of the James family. So James brought a visiting professor from Oxford to a sitting *after* Mrs. Piper was already in trance. The medium gave the correct names of the Oxford don's parents and the illness from which his father died; she stated other personal facts correctly. After a number of such sittings James wrote: "I now believe her to be in possession of a power as yet unexplained."

When the report reached the British Society for Psychical Research, there were lifted eyebrows and comments about a man of James's intelligence being taken in so easily. Obviously, what was needed here was an *experienced* investigator. Fortunately, they had the very man for the job—Dr. Richard Hodgson, a brilliant Cambridge graduate who was making a life's work of exposing "psychic" wonders.

Soon after he landed in Boston, Hodgson had a sitting with Mrs. Piper. James introduced him simply as "Mr. Smith." Mrs. Piper promptly told him his real name, the fact that his mother and four others in his family were alive, but that his father and a younger brother were dead. She spoke of a cousin Fred, who went to school with him in Australia and was great at playing leapfrog.

That all this was true only served to convince Hodgson that Mrs. Piper was cleverer than he had expected.

Hodgson hired detectives to trail Mr. and Mrs. Piper to see if they were doing surreptitious research on possible sitters, or if they were having someone do the work for them. He deliberately sought out sitters who had come from far places and had no ties in Boston or even in New England. They were brought into the room only after Mrs. Piper was in trance and would leave just before she came out of it. After two years of constant search for fraud, Hodgson was nearly ready to admit that perhaps, after all, Mrs. Piper did possess some supernormal powers. But there was to be one final test. He planned to take her to a foreign country where she had no friends, family or associates, then see what she could do. Mrs. Piper felt, as she told friends, that she had to go to England "in order to prove myself an honest woman."

From the moment she landed at Liverpool she was always under the watchful eye of some member of the British Society for Psychical Research to make sure that she couldn't get in touch with any possible assistants. When she visited Professor Oliver Lodge—later knighted for his brilliant scientific work—Mrs. Lodge engaged an entire new staff of servants, none of whom had even the vaguest knowledge of the Lodge family or their friends. Lodge locked away the family Bible and albums. Mrs. Piper even let him search her luggage for biographies or dossiers of personal data on leading English figures. He found nothing.

Once in trance, Mrs. Piper would, apparently, be taken over by a "spirit control" who called himself "Dr. Phinuit," a deceased French physician of Metz. "Phinuit's" voice came through Mrs. Piper as huskily masculine and tinged with a stagy French accent. Critics were quick to point out that the alleged French doctor, curiously, knew only as much school French as Mrs. Piper did and that he didn't recognize the names of standard French drugs. The trance itself was real enough, however. Professor James once made a small incision in Mrs. Piper's left wrist. During the trance no notice was taken of it and it didn't bleed. But the moment the medium awoke the cut bled profusely, and throughout her life Mrs. Piper retained a slight scar.

After three months of investigation the members of the British group agreed that they could no longer, alas, dismiss Mrs. Piper as a fraud. Worse, some of the members were beginning to be afraid that even mind reading wasn't the whole answer. It's one thing if a medium tells you about things that happened to you years ago. After all, those events are part of your memory and she might be reading your mind, admittedly a fabulous skill in itself. But what if she tells you about the exact movements of persons who are at this moment in a distant city? Would mind reading alone explain that?

During this first visit to England Mrs. Piper gave eighty-eight sittings and produced hundreds of detailed and afterward-verified facts about her sitters. In addition, Professor Lodge compiled a carefully checked list of forty-one incidents in which Mrs. Piper gave facts about the sitters or their families that were *unknown to them at the time of the sittings*. When she returned to Boston early in 1890, news of the incredible success of her British sittings preceded her. Although she could have asked great sums for sittings, she was content to accept only the modest fees paid by investigators.

In 1892 George Pellew, a young Boston lawyer and

author who had once attended a Piper sitting, was killed in a fall. Shortly after his death, at a sitting attended by Dr. Hodgson and a friend of Pellew's, "Phinuit" suddenly announced that George Pellew was present and wished to communicate. Then followed a series of detailed statements about Pellew, his friends and various incidents that his family verified. Eventually "George Pellew" became Mrs. Piper's control, and more than thirty of Pellew's friends and relatives had sittings in the next few years. "Pellew" recognized all the people he had known in life, and failed to recognize the hundred others who had been brought in deliberately by Hodgson to trip up the "spirit." Not only did "Pellew" recognize friends but he remembered their opinions, their occupations, their habits. Once he translated a Greek phrase, composed on the spot by a classical scholar. Mrs. Piper knew no Greek. George Pellew did. He also reported accurately what his father, in another city, was doing.

The Pellew sittings convinced many investigators that here, at last, was communication with the dead. But others, more skeptical, pointed out that while these sessions indicated that Mrs. Piper might possess almost incredible telepathic powers they didn't prove she was getting her information from spirits. After all, they pointed out, everything that emerged in the Pellew sittings was known to at least one or more persons who were alive. Wasn't it more likely that this amazing woman was able, in trance, to assemble the necessary details by telepathically picking the minds of those who had known George Pellew? And what did the center of this controversy think of it all? "I don't know what happens when I'm in trance," she used to say. "I have no theories to explain the things I'm told happen."

In 1898, after Mrs. Piper returned from a second Brit-

ish visit, a new American skeptic appeared on the scene.
With the secret coöperation of Dr. Hodgson the new sitter
held seventeen sessions with Mrs. Piper. He took unusual
precautions to make sure she wouldn't know who he was.
He would drive to her home in a closed carriage and put
on a mask just before getting out. After tiptoeing into the
room he would sit behind Mrs. Piper and never utter a
word. Mrs. Piper told the mysterious visitor his name and
his father's name, and gave him a wealth of detail about
himself and his family. For the first time in his many years
of unmasking frauds, the sitter, Professor James H. Hyslop
of Columbia University, found himself bewildered. The
savant had to admit that Mrs. Piper was producing inexplicable results. In the end he said he believed that he had
actually spoken to the spirit of his dead father.

In 1901 Mrs. Piper announced that she was going to
discontinue all sittings. She had allowed herself to be
tested for fifteen years and she was tired of it. As for her
talking with spirits of the departed: "I never heard of
anything being said by myself during a trance which
might not have been latent in my own mind or in the
minds of the sitters or in the mind of some absent person
alive somewhere else in the world. The theory of telepathy strongly appeals to me as the most plausible solution
of the problem."

Dr. Hodgson, who had come to America to unmask
Mrs. Piper as a fraud, was placed in the difficult position
of having to persuade the former suspect to continue her
sittings because he and other investigators were now convinced that she had truly been in communication with
the dead. Mrs. Piper continued her work until July 31,
1911, when the "spirit controls" announced she would
have to stop because of her poor health. By this time the

British society had established a modest trust fund for her and her two daughters so that she was no longer dependent upon having a number of sittings a week in order to make ends meet. Her husband had died in 1904. In 1924 Mrs. Piper gave a special series of sittings, but these were among her last. She had been a medium for more than forty years. The records of her sittings fill more than three thousand pages. More than $150,000 had been spent on the most prolonged investigation in the history of psychical research.

Critics are quick to point out that scientists and other intellectuals have frequently been deceived by clever mediums. "Ada B.," about whom Professor Hyslop made many scientific reports, was exposed by an amateur conjurer. Sir Arthur Conan Doyle knelt and kissed the hand of what he believed was his mother's ghost, but the ghost turned up in the Police Magistrate Court one week later as a piece of cheesecloth smeared with luminous paint. Thomas Edison was taken in by a psychic mind reader whose clever tricks were later revealed by a New York novelist. Mrs. Piper is the only famous medium against whom no charges of fraud were ever brought.

For years after her retirement Mrs. Piper lived with a daughter in a quiet section of Boston. The amazing woman who could hear unvoiced thoughts thousands of miles away, in languages she never knew, became deaf and heard little of the outside world. Her address was kept secret and her telephone was unlisted. Few in the apartment house knew that the white-haired, bright-eyed old lady who occasionally went out for a stroll with her nurse or gray-haired daughter was the simple Yankee housewife whose work had convinced leading scientists of two countries that there is indeed life after death.

The State of Tennessee
versus Uncle Joe

By T. H. Alexander

AN OLD NEGRO named Uncle Joe was on trial for chicken stealing. The evidence, while not direct, was fairly conclusive, for bloodhounds had tracked to the old man's house. Uncle Joe had no money to pay an attorney and his defense was undertaken by Smith S. House. It was House's maiden court speech in Williamson County, Tennessee; as resurrected from the dim files of the county records, it reads:

"Your Honor and gentlemen of the jury: When it becomes necessary to hale an upright, respectable citizen into court to answer to a charge of purloining the fowls of a neighbor, then things have come to a high pass in the noble county of Williamson. The prosecuting attorney has asked you to send this old man, who is now engaged in the honorable calling of caring for and rearing seventeen motherless grandchildren and one fatherless great-grandchild, to the penitentiary—for what? For being suspected of having appropriated some fowls belonging to a neighboring white man by the name of Miles—recently moved here from some place in Ohio."

The prosecutor interrupted: "If Your Honor please, I object to this attempt to arouse sectional prejudice in the minds of the jury by this reference to the former home of Mr. Miles. The fact that the defendant is attired in an old Confederate uniform is enough. This is too much."

Judge Henry H. Cook: "Objection sustained."

Mr. House: "The sole evidence upon which he hopes to convict this old body servant of a major in General Robert E. Lee's army is not evidence at all. It is not proof that any jury would accept. It is the testimony of a blood-hound which, when it reached the end of the trail it was following, jumped up into the lap of the defendant and tried to lick his face, and gave other evidence of affection.

"Now Major McEwen, whom this defendant used to serve, was a fancier of bloodhounds; when he died from the effects of a wound received at Drewry's Bluff, his bloodhounds were parceled out among the Negroes on the place and a pair were given to this defendant. Whatever puppies he raised he sold or gave to his friends, last year giving a pair of three-months-old puppies to the sheriff of this county. One of these puppies, gentlemen, is the bloodhound that trailed the defendant to his cabin door.

"The defendant has admitted that he passed within a hundred feet of Mr. Miles's poultry pens on the afternoon of the day the chickens were stolen. And why did he pass that way?

"I crave your indulgence, gentlemen. Back of Glass's thicket is an eminence known as Winstead's Hill. Across that rock-ribbed hill, shuffling on ragged rock-torn feet, came Hood's army to its death in that holocaust, that shambles that was Franklin."

Prosecuting attorney (angrily): "Your Honor, I object to counsel fighting the battle of Drewry's Bluff and Franklin as part of the case against a chicken thief."

Judge Cook: "Objection overruled. Proceed, please."

Mr. House: "Winstead's Hill is covered with beautiful cedars which every year are used to welcome a person called Santa Claus. The defendant vows that he visited Winstead's Hill on that date to select Christmas trees for Douglas Church. In returning to his home he passed Mr. Miles's poultry pens. The bloodhound, sent out to catch a thief, struck a scent which since puppyhood had meant food and shelter and kindliness. A bloodhound, even a sheriff's assistant, may be forgiven a slight inattention to duty. He followed no chicken thief's trail. He followed the scent of a master who had been kind to him, and as an arrow to its mark—that dog went back home! I thank you." The defendant was acquitted.

When two convicts who escaped from a Texas prison were caught in a couple of days through a phone call from a farmer a hundred miles distant, newsmen converged on the farmer. "How could you recognize them when you've never seen a picture of them?" they asked.

"When those two fellas walked by I was out plowin'," he replied. "Of course I waved and hollered, but they just walked on. So I knew they wasn't local folks, and then I remembered about the convicts. I figured they was the only kind of folks that'd be in too big a hurry to stop for a chat."   —*Jean Mikeska*

The FBI agent in a Western state was hot on the trail of a fugitive. When word came that he was heading for a small town, the G-man called the local sheriff. "You send me a pitcher of that guy and I'll git him good," the sheriff promised. That night the agent mailed the sheriff a dozen pictures of the wanted man— profiles, fullface, standing, sitting and in various costumes. Shortly he received an electrifying telephone call: "We got eleven of those crooks locked up already," the sheriff boasted. "And I guarantee to jug the last one before morning!"

—*Fulton Oursler*

Secrets of a Soviet Assassin

Condensed from the book The Mind of an Assassin
By Isaac Don Levine

"**I** PUT my raincoat on the table so that I could take out the *piolet* [ice axe] in the pocket. When Trotsky started to read my article, I took the axe and, closing my eyes, gave him a tremendous blow on the head. The man screamed in a way that I will never forget—*Aaaaa!* . . . very long, infinitely long. He got up like a madman, threw himself at me and bit my hand—look, you can still see the marks of his teeth. Then I pushed him, so that he fell to the floor."

With these words the most celebrated and mysterious assassin of our time—the man who calls himself Jacques Mornard—described his murder of Leon Trotsky, exiled patriarch of Bolshevism. It took place on August 20, 1940, inside the steel-shuttered walls of Trotsky's heavily guarded villa on the outskirts of Mexico City. "Mornard" was convicted and sentenced to twenty years' imprisonment in the Mexican Federal Penitentiary.

In August 1960 this man was freed. All this time he had resolutely refused to disclose his identity, motives or political ties. Despite the mask, his true identity has grad-

ually been pieced together over the years. He is Ramón
Mercader del Rio, a Spaniard, fifty years old in 1964,
Moscow-trained in the art of murder. He killed Trotsky
on the orders of the world's most fearsome secret-police
organization, the Soviet State Security, then called the
NKVD. But his stubborn refusal to admit his identity enabled the organizers of the crime to disavow any connection with it.

When he was arrested, the police found on him a three-
page statement, typewritten in French, dated and signed
at the last moment in pencil. It stated that he was the son
of "an old Belgian family," that he had been caught up
in the Trotskyite movement while studying journalism in
Paris. He had met Trotsky and become disenchanted, the
"confession" said, and finally moved to kill him when the
old Bolshevik tried to force him to go to the Soviet Union
to organize an assassination plot against Stalin.

These claims, and amplifying details the prisoner gave
after his arrest, were quickly proved absurd: the people,
schools and addresses he mentioned were nonexistent or
totally unlike his descriptions. But no logic could make
him change his story. For six months "Mornard" was
given an intensive psychological examination by Dr. José
Gomez Robleda, head of the department of medical-
biological studies at the National University of Mexico,
and Dr. Alfonso Quiroz Cuarón, professor of criminology.
At first suspicious of the doctors, the prisoner gradually
came to talk freely with them. Though he never disclosed anything he considered important, he unwittingly
revealed a great deal about himself.

The two doctors found the killer a truly extraordinary
man. He was fluent in several languages. Attractive to
women, he could be ingratiating to men, and would pass
for a gentleman anywhere. He had superior intelligence,

remarkable self-possession, a gift for acting. He displayed a marked interest in gambling, mountain climbing, small-craft sailing. His coördination, dexterity and mechanical aptitudes were unusual: given a Mauser rifle, he proceeded to dismantle it in the dark and put it back together in less than four minutes.

His responses to word-association tests showed the prisoner to be deeply indoctrinated in Stalinist views, and he betrayed his Moscow training on several occasions. At one point, for example, he made a passing reference to a man named Kamo—a figure almost unknown in the West but a hero within the NKVD, whose history is taught in Soviet schools for infiltration and sabotage. A test of "Mornard's" pronunciation showed that his "native French," although excellent, bore traces of a Spanish accent, and he showed a striking familiarity with anything Spanish. The evidence suggested a Spanish Communist background.

But it was not until September 1950 that Dr. Quiroz Cuarón was able to document the suspicions. The criminologist found his proof in police archives in Madrid: the dusty fingerprints of a man named Ramón Mercader, arrested in Barcelona in 1935 as a Communist youth organizer, tallied with those of "Mornard." So did pictures.

Don Pablo Mercader Marina, a tall, elderly man living in retirement in Barcelona, took a good look at a photograph of the Trotsky killer. "Yes," he said, "that's my son." Don Pablo did not know of his son's crime. Long removed from the family, he said, "I do not want to re-establish contact with any of them."

Since then, further revelations by ex-Communists have established additional facts in Mornard-Mercader's strange history. This is the story:

Ramón Mercader was born in Barcelona in 1913, the second child of Caridad del Rio Hernandez and Don Pablo, a conservative gentleman of good but not too prosperous family. Ramón's mother, a spirited young society matron, was a strikingly attractive woman, quick-tempered and unpredictable, who at the age of thirty-three developed a compulsion to adventure. She began to associate with bohemians and revolutionaries, and in 1925 she moved to France. Here she joined the Communist Party, had numerous love affairs with French Communist leaders, and worked as an underground courier.

Ramón, who lived part of the time with his mother, part with his father, worshiped his mother and was soon drawn into her Communist associations. When the Spanish Civil War started in 1936, he and his mother were among the first to volunteer to fight Franco. At this point a new love entered the life of Caridad Mercader: Leonid Eitingon, a general in the NKVD who, under the name of General Kotov, was organizing Loyalist commando and sabotage units in Spain. One of his students was Ramón Mercader. What neither Ramón nor Caridad may have known at this time was that Eitingon was also a leading officer of a special NKVD division in charge of liquidating Soviet political enemies on foreign soil. Their number-one target was Leon Trotsky.

Lev Davidovich Bronstein, known to the world as Leon Trotsky, had designed and engineered with Lenin the Bolshevik Revolution of November 1917. Stalin was at that time a semi-obscure henchman of Lenin's, but after Lenin's death he maneuvered to isolate Trotsky politically, and in 1929 he expelled him from the Soviet Union. Since then Trotsky had lived the life of a hunted man, pursued by Stalin's killers from one place to another. One by one his retinue was picked off: his secretary was killed in Spain; his son died suddenly in Paris, and Trotskyites believed he had been poisoned. Finally, in 1937, Trotsky sought refuge in Mexico.

Caridad and Ramón were now in Moscow with Eitingon, and Ramón was receiving highly specialized training in the arts of terror. Plans for the great assassination were already being laid. What kind of man was needed to deal with Trotsky in Mexico? Spanish-speaking Ramón Mercader must have seemed an obvious choice.

In the Byzantine way of the Soviet secret police, it was decided that Mercader should ingratiate himself with the Trotsky household by seducing one of its female couriers, Sylvia Ageloff, a young American social worker and loyal member of the U.S. Trotskyite group. The NKVD arranged for Ramón to meet Sylvia "by chance" in Paris in the summer of 1938. Young, personable, well supplied with money, he must have looked like the answer to a young woman's prayer. He soon became her constant companion.

Ramón followed Sylvia to New York on a false passport issued in the name of "Frank Jacson." (The original from which this passport was drawn had been taken from a Canadian who was killed in Spain with the International Brigade. Embarrassingly, Soviet technical documentation experts had misspelled the name: it should have been "Jackson.") Sylvia and he took a temporary apartment in Greenwich Village. Then "Jacson" announced that he had been offered a job in Mexico City, and in January 1940 Sylvia followed him there. Eitingon was in Mexico to supervise the assassination, and with him was Caridad Mercader.

Ramón's role at this point, Caridad had assured a friend, was solely that of a spy—to find out the nature of the security system at Trotsky's villa at Coyoacán, a Mexico City suburb. Through Sylvia he gained entrée. During visits there, although he did not at first meet Trotsky, Ramón roamed through the house, snapping pictures with a concealed camera but relying on his photographic memory for most of the details. His material was sent to Moscow and placed in a special dossier of the NKVD. (Vladimir Petrov, the Soviet intelligence officer who defected in Australia in April 1954, has reported that he saw this dossier in 1948. It contained "complete documentation of Trotsky's life right up to his last days.")

In the early morning hours of May 24, 1940, the Soviet spy command in Mexico tried an audacious frontal assault on the Trotsky dwelling. A group of twenty men, dressed in Mexican police and army uniforms, drove up to the residence, stormed through the gate and delivered murderous submachine-gun fire into the bedrooms where the Trotskys and their eleven-year-old grandson were sleeping.

Amazingly, Trotsky, his wife and grandchild survived the attack—by throwing themselves under their beds. After a month's investigation, the Mexican police cracked the case, and some two dozen persons were arrested and later tried. Ramón Mercader, however, remained above suspicion.

Only four days after the armed attack, Mercader offered to drive Mrs. Trotsky to Vera Cruz with some mutual friends. It was on this occasion that Ramón first met his future victim. He entered the villa's courtyard and chatted briefly and courteously with Trotsky. He gave Trotsky's grandson a small glider as a present. Only a man of iron nerve could have carried on with such an assignment so soon after an attempted assassination which he had helped to stage.

Moscow now decided on a single-handed assassination attempt, and Ramón was to play the lead. Caridad arranged with the NKVD for maximum safeguards and a chance for her son to escape alive. Mercader—or "Jacson," as he was known to most of the Trotskyites— stepped up the pace of his infiltration program. During the last three weeks in July he paid the Trotskys five visits, never neglecting such friendly little gestures as bringing candy for Mrs. Trotsky. On August 17 Ramón visited the master with the outline of an article he was writing. Trotsky had agreed to check it over. The two men spent eleven minutes alone in Trotsky's study. Trotsky remarked to his wife afterward that the young man's behavior had seemed strange. That visit was the "dress rehearsal."

On August 20 Sylvia and Ramón ran into one of the Trotsky bodyguards downtown. The "Jacsons" said they were returning to the United States the next day, but would say good-bye to Trotsky first. Ramón excused himself and departed on some urgent business. Sylvia went back to their hotel and awaited a message from him. He never returned.

At 5:20 that afternoon Ramón Mercader showed up at the Trotsky villa with his completed article to show Trotsky. He was carrying a khaki raincoat. Sewn into it was a long dagger, and in one pocket he carried the ice axe, its stock cut down for easy concealment. In the back pocket of his trousers he carried a .45-caliber automatic. He hoped to accomplish his murderous mission with a single crushing blow of the ice axe, which would make little noise and thus enable him to get away quietly and

unmolested. If any mishap should occur, he had the automatic to shoot his way out.

The guards recognized him and opened the double
electric doors of the fortress villa without hesitation. One
guard led him to Trotsky, who was feeding his pet rabbits
in the courtyard. Mrs. Trotsky saw him, noticed his raincoat and commented that it was somewhat incongruous
on such a sunny day. "Yes, but you know it won't last
long—it might rain," Ramón said, holding the bulky
coat close to his body.

Trotsky obviously did not want to tear himself away
from the rabbits, but finally he took off his working
gloves and walked into the house. Ramón followed him to

the study, where Trotsky closed the door and sat down at his work table. A few inches from his hand was a loaded .25-caliber automatic. Ramón stood at his left side, blocking off the switch to the house alarm system.

Trotsky took the article and started to read. At that exact moment Ramón seized the ice axe and, closing his eyes, smashed it down on his victim's skull, penetrating almost three inches into the brain.

With a fearful cry, Trotsky threw himself at the killer and grappled with him. Mrs. Trotsky rushed to the study to find her husband stumbling dazedly from the room. "See what they have done to me!" he said, and slumped to the floor.

Trotsky's bodyguards swarmed into the room now. Ramón stood gasping, face knotted, pistol dangling in his hand. The bodyguards began to hammer away at him. Mrs. Trotsky addressed a curiously detached question to her still conscious husband. "What about that one?" she asked, gesturing toward the assassin. "They will kill him."

"No . . . impermissible to kill," Trotsky said slowly. "He must be forced to talk." Rushed to the hospital, Trotsky soon lapsed into unconsciousness. He was operated on, but he died twenty-six hours later.

A block away Caridad was sitting in a chauffeur-driven car, a bizarre parody of the anxious mother waiting for her son to come home from work. General Eitingon was waiting in another car nearby. When the police alarm sounded and an ambulance came through the streets, they realized that Ramón had not got away. Caridad drove immediately to the airport and, with a forged passport, made her way to Cuba. Eitingon drove all night to Acapulco, where he boarded a Soviet freighter waiting in the harbor.

Some weeks later Caridad rejoined Eitingon in Moscow. There Lavrenti Beria, head of the NKVD, himself presented her to Stalin. She received the Order of Lenin—Communism's highest decoration—and her son was cited as a Hero of the Soviet Union. To a friend in Moscow she proudly spoke of these honors.

Caridad spent the war years in the Soviet Union, receiving assurances from her lover Eitingon and his Kremlin superiors that an operation to rescue her son would be launched. Stalin proved reluctant to redeem the pledge, but eventually allowed her to try to organize an escape. She arrived in Mexico City in March 1945, but was unable to achieve her objective—or even to see her son, so ironclad was the regime imposed on her by the NKVD to ensure the secrecy of the identity of the Trotsky assassin.

Now seventy-two and white-haired, Caridad lives in Paris amid disillusionment. The years in the Soviet Union served to cure her of some of her Communism. "You are right," she said in Moscow to an intimate Spanish comrade of independent views. "We have been deceived. This is not paradise. It is hell."

Sylvia Ageloff, when she learned that her lover had killed Trotsky, went into a nervous collapse from which it took years to recover. (Ramón wept when he was told of this in prison, but later he lost all interest in her.) Trotsky's widow died in Paris in January 1962. Eitingon is dead, a victim—with his master, Beria—of the 1953 purges after Stalin's death.

Mercader became Mexico's model prisoner. He ran the penitentiary radio-repair shop, a small but profitable business. He was quite comfortable, having taken advantage of the lenient Mexican prison regulations to ensure special food, books and other comforts—including the regular visits of a girl named Roquelia Mendoza, a Mexico City nightclub performer. (Prisoners are allowed to have conjugal visits from wives or common-law wives.)

Double-chinned and corpulent, Ramón Mercader now looked like a relaxed bourgeois businessman. Through underground channels he kept in touch with the Communist network outside. Released from prison in May 1960, he emplaned for Czechoslovakia, and disappeared behind the Iron Curtain without a trace.

Once when I was a boy I ran away from school and late at night concluded to climb into the window of my father's office and sleep on a lounge, because I had a delicacy about going home and getting thrashed. As I lay there and my eyes grew accustomed to the darkness, I fancied I could see a long, dusky, shapeless thing stretched upon the floor.

A cold shiver went through me; I was afraid the thing would creep over and seize me in the dark. It seemed to me that the lagging moonlight would never, never get to it. I turned to the wall and counted twenty, to pass the feverish time away. I looked—the pale square of light was almost touching it.

With desperate will I turned again and counted a hundred and faced about, all in a tremble. A white hand lay in the moonlight! Such an awful sinking at the heart—such a gasp for breath. I counted again and looked—a naked arm was exposed. I put my hands over my eyes and counted until I could stand it no longer, and then—the pallid face of a man was there, with the corners of the mouth drawn down and the eyes fixed and glassy in death! I stared at the corpse till the light crept down to the bare breast—inch by inch—and disclosed a ghastly stab!

When I reached home they whipped me, but I enjoyed it. That man had been stabbed that afternoon near the office, and they carried him in to doctor him, but he only lived an hour. I have slept in the same room with him often, since then—in my dreams.   —*Mark Twain*

B. JOHNSON

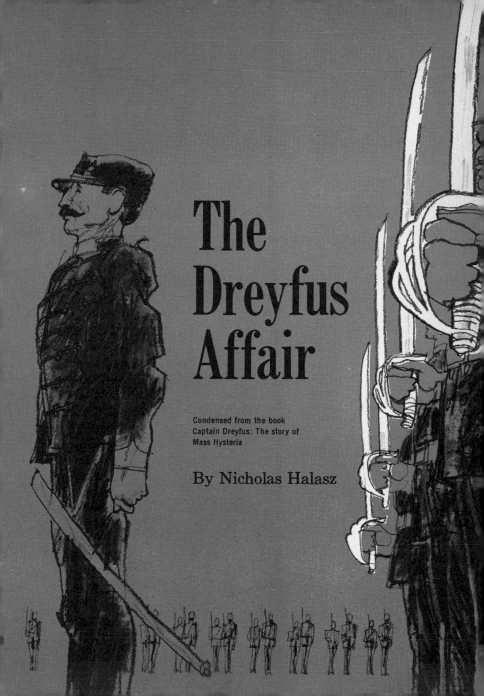

The Dreyfus Affair

Condensed from the book
Captain Dreyfus: The story of
Mass Hysteria

By Nicholas Halasz

The Dreyfus Affair

Condensed from the book Captain Dreyfus:
The Story of a Mass Hysteria

By Nicholas Halasz

The Dreyfus Affair, in which an innocent man stood branded before the world as a traitor; is perhaps the most celebrated miscarriage of justice in modern times. For twelve tortured years the question of Captain Dreyfus' guilt or innocence kept all France in a turmoil and caused the world to doubt the sanity of that obsessed nation.

Dramatic, terrible, relentlessly absorbing, the case disclosed forgers and liars in the highest places; it set family against family and poisoned a whole people with hysteria and unreason. But before the end it also brought forth heroes and patriots who risked everything to restore the ideal of rule by law and absolve the conscience of France.

In Captain Dreyfus, *Nicholas Halasz recaptured the gripping fascination of a time when a man, a nation and the very concept of justice itself were on trial.*

On July 20, 1894, a visitor was announced to Colonel Max von Schwartzkoppen, military attaché of the German Embassy in Paris. The caller was a slightly built gentleman with drawn features, deep-seated black eyes and a large mustache. He was in his early forties and wore the red ribbon of the Legion of Honor. He was unmistakably a French officer in mufti.

The visitor explained that he had come to volunteer his services as a spy. Financial difficulties aggravated by his wife's illness forced him to this expedient. He had excellent connections, he said, in the French Ministry of War. To prove it he reached into his pocket and offered to hand over a secret document. At this point the astonished Prussian terminated the interview. He refused to look at the document, and the pale, deeply disturbed Frenchman left the Embassy.

Colonel Schwartzkoppen rejected the services of the Frenchman for practical rather than moral reasons. Who can trust a man, however desperate, who comes unknown from the streets to peddle such goods? Who is to say he is not an *agent provocateur* sent by the French? However, the colonel was a soldier and did not have to make decisions on his own. He reported the unusual visit to Berlin. The reply came back swiftly: "Negotiate."

The colonel had no way of locating the French officer, but he did not have long to wait. Two days later the desperate figure in mufti called again. This time he gave his name and showed credentials: Major Count Ferdinand Walsin-Esterhazy, commander of a battalion of the French Army stationed at Rouen. He asked to be put on the payroll at a salary of 2000 francs ($400) a month. Schwartzkoppen refused this request, but agreed to pay cash on delivery for documents according to their worth. Three weeks later Esterhazy delivered general orders for the French artillery in the event of mobilization. Its value appeared unquestionable. Schwartzkoppen handed over 1000 francs.

On September 1 Esterhazy delivered several fresh

documents. He had also meant to deliver with them, written out in his own hand, a *bordereau* or itemized list of the kind careful clerks prepare to make sure that all items of a shipment may be checked by the recipient. That *bordereau* was to become world-famous, for when Esterhazy later sent it on through the mail it was intercepted and fell into the hands of French counterespionage. Its discovery set off a scandal that rocked France to its foundations and for twelve long years divided the country into factions of unparalleled bitterness. It was the beginning of the historic Dreyfus Case.

Long before Esterhazy began his traffic with Schwartzkoppen, France had been plagued by espionage leaks. As far as three years back the Second Bureau, as the General Staff's department of intelligence was called, had been aware that the German Embassy had access to secret information. New military maps of regions along the German and Italian frontiers had been mysteriously disappearing, and no one could discover how. Intelligence officers worked mightily to unearth any possible avenue into the General Staff. It was a period of grave tensions between France and Germany, and mail to the German Embassy was regularly intercepted. The military attaché's mail in particular was carefully scrutinized. This surveillance had disclosed that Schwartzkoppen was working very closely with his counterpart, the Italian military attaché, both signing their communications to each other with the same alias, "Alexandrine." One note signed in this way had especially alerted the Bureau:

Enclosed are twelve detail maps of Nice that the scoundrel D——— left with me for you. I told him you had no intention of taking up relations with him again. He said there was a misunderstanding, and that he will do his best to satisfy you.

An examination of the handwriting proved that the "Alexandrine" who wrote this note was Schwartzkoppen. But who was "the scoundrel D———" who had supplied him the maps? The Second Bureau sought in vain to learn his identity. The problem was still agitating them when Count Esterhazy's *bordereau* was intercepted from Schwartzkoppen's mail. The *bordereau* was written on both sides of a sheet of cream-colored graph paper. It read:

> I am sending you some interesting information.
> 1. A note on the hydraulic brake of the 120 mm. gun.
> 2. A note on the new plan for the supporting troops.
> 3. A note on the modification of artillery formations.
> 4. A note concerning Madagascar.
> 5. The provisional Firing Manual for Field Artillery.
>
> This last document is extraordinarily difficult to procure and I have it at my disposal only for a few days. If, therefore, you will take notes of whatever is of interest to you and hold it at my disposal, I shall take it back. I am off to the maneuvers.

When this document was delivered to Colonel Jean-Conrad Sandherr, chief of the Second Bureau's counter-espionage, he was appalled. For it was apparent that the author of the *bordereau* must be on—or closely connected with someone on—the General Staff. How else could he get secret information about such different activities of the Army? Here, Sandherr decided, was the ghost that had been haunting them, "the scoundrel D———" of Schwartzkoppen's note. No suspicion of Major Esterhazy crossed his mind, although Esterhazy's squalid financial practices were by no means unknown to his fellow officers. Although he was born in Paris, Count Esterhazy came from the high aristocracy of Hungary. He had served with distinction in both the Austrian and Papal armies before joining that of France. As a French officer, he fought the Prussians in 1870 and was decorated for valor. But he was a nearly unmitigated scoundrel. He married into the French aristocracy, soon squandered his wife's substantial dowry and for the rest of his life was never to be out of financial difficulties. He turned up now as director of a dubious finance corporation, now as shareholder in a fashionable house of prostitution.

But Colonel Sandherr was to look elsewhere for the culprit. Since the author of the *bordereau* had written "I am off to the maneuvers," he decided to consult the chief of military transportation, Colonel Pierre-Elie Fabre. Fabre scrutinized the *bordereau* and concluded that its author must be an artilleryman with contacts in other branches of the service. "A probationer!" It seemed a dazzlingly brilliant solution.

Breathlessly, they got out the file of probationers—the young officers who were not yet attached to any one bureau of the General Staff but were shifted on temporary assignment from one office to another. They went down the D's and came to a halt at the name Dreyfus. In their immense relief they found no words. Each read the other's thought: "It was the Jew!"

Many acquaintances of Alfred Dreyfus, the only Jew on the General Staff, regarded him as a very caricature of the Army caste. He was cold, unbending, brilliant, utterly devoted to his profession to the exclusion of all else. His reserve was impenetrable, his zeal for study boundless, his appetite for work insatiable.

Alfred was born in Alsace in 1859, the son of a prosperous textile manufacturer. He early decided to become an Army officer and at the age of nineteen entered the Ecole Polytechnique, that famous institution which had launched so many young men on military careers. He earned a reputation there as a daring horseman and a good fencer, but he was not popular with his classmates. They were for the most part sons of the old nobility or civil servants, had gone to the same Jesuit preparatory school and formed a closely knit group—obvious candidates for preferment in the Army and promotion to the General Staff. They thought Dreyfus a bore, and the fact that he had an independent income of $5000 a year did not make him better liked. In the Army, where he was assigned to the artillery, he devoted himself to his work with single-minded ambition. At the age of thirty he was a captain in the Central School of Explosives at Bourges. He then applied for admission to the Ecole de Guerre, open only to officers who were considered suitable material for the General Staff.

Meanwhile he had become engaged to Lucie Hadamard, a serious-minded girl from a wealthy and distinguished family of French Jews. On the day of his marriage he was notified he had been accepted at the Ecole de Guerre. After the honeymoon Alfred and Lucie settled down to a life of military scholarship, taking up residence in a fashionable district of Paris. During the next three years two children were born to them, a boy and a girl. The family was a happy one.

In the Ecole de Guerre, Dreyfus was not of the inner clique. He had to compete on unequal terms with the pick of the Army, the brightest officers of his generation, most of them buttressed by the good will from on high which goes with family connections and the old school tie. Dreyfus had nothing to buttress him but his mind and his formidable capacity for grueling work. He finished the course ninth in a class of eighty-one. In 1893 he was appointed to the General Staff as a probationer. It was a time of rising anti-Semitism in France, and to some

staff officers the presence of a Jew in this inner sanctum
came as a shock. A last-minute effort was made to fend
off Dreyfus. Colonel Sandherr entered a formal protest,
describing the appointment as a security risk. But such
a description would have struck too many people as out-
rageous, for the fitness reports on Captain Dreyfus
throughout his military career testified to his abilities
and his high standards of professional conduct. There
was nothing the anti-Semites could do to block his appointment. He had been on the General Staff a year
when Esterhazy wrote the meticulous and treasonous
bordereau.

Dreyfus' file was now brought out and samples of
his handwriting placed side by side with the *bordereau.*
Sandherr and Fabre pored over the exhibit, comparing
the two handwritings. Not being men who needed much
convincing, they noted a similarity. Sandherr informed
his immediate superior and, after a further and equally
inconclusive check of the handwriting, the news of Dreyfus' suspected guilt was passed on, through channels, to
General Auguste Mercier, the Minister of War. Mercier
at once closeted himself for a long talk with the Premier,
Charles Dupuy. Both these men were aware they were
handling dynamite. The fate of the government was involved. To announce that a spy had been caught inevitably would reveal that the General Staff had been lax
in allowing spying to be done. They must make sure of
the criminal before letting the political opposition learn
of the crime. Premier Dupuy and General Mercier agreed
that all must be kept secret until the case was airtight.

The handwriting expert of the Banque de France, who
had been called in, said the *bordereau* could have been
written by a person other than the writer of the samples
submitted to him for comparison. But Alphonse Bertil-

lon, famed criminologist of the Paris police, considered it "manifest that the identical person wrote both the samples and the incriminating *bordereau*." This opinion was accepted as proof of Dreyfus' guilt, and War Minister Mercier moved swiftly into action. The awkward fact that the writer of the *bordereau* had said he was "off to the maneuvers," whereas no probationers had attended the maneuvers that year, was somehow explained away. And the fact that the *bordereau* was full of obvious Germanisms, whereas Dreyfus wrote a flawless French, was ignored. Assuming that investigation would almost certainly disclose further evidence, Mercier ordered Dreyfus' arrest.

The arrest, which for political expedience was to be made in secret, was arranged by the Marquis du Paty de Clam, a major on the General Staff. Dreyfus was directed to appear at an inspection of General Staff probationers at the office of the Chief of Staff. The time: October 15, 9 a.m.; civilian attire. Dreyfus arrived punctually. He was astonished to discover only Major du Paty present and three men in civilian attire who obviously were not staff officers. The three stood about feigning indifference, and the bemonocled marquis did not introduce them. They were police officers. The marquis asked Dreyfus if he would write a letter for him while awaiting the arrival of the inspecting officer. He had injured his finger, he explained, and could not hold a pen.

Dreyfus sat down at a desk and du Paty began to dictate. He dictated an ordinary letter, but loaded it with phrases from the *bordereau*, meanwhile watching Dreyfus' reaction intently. Dreyfus remained unmoved and du Paty became annoyed. "Watch out," he warned, scowling. "This is very serious."

It seemed to du Paty that the blackguard had no

nerves. Phrase after phrase from the *bordereau* peppered him, yet his writing remained calm and businesslike. Du Paty gave up in midstream.

"I arrest you in the name of the law!" he shouted. "You are accused of high treason."

As the plainclothesmen moved to stand over Dreyfus, he jumped to his feet and cried out in terrible anger, "Show me proof of the infamy you pretend I committed."

"The proofs are overwhelming," du Paty replied curtly. He took out a pistol and put it on the table before Dreyfus. Then he stared silently. But Dreyfus had no intention of killing himself; when this became apparent, he was removed to an isolated cell in the Cherche-Midi prison.

Du Paty and an aide then hastened to Dreyfus' home to take Lucie Dreyfus by surprise. Mme. Dreyfus sensed disaster instantly. Du Paty was courteous but grave. "I am afraid I bring bad news," he said.

Lucie paled. "Is he dead?"

Du Paty shook his head.

"Has he fallen from his horse?"

Again du Paty shook his head. "It is much worse," he said at last. "He is in jail."

The small, slender woman straightened. "Where is he?" she demanded. "I want to be taken to him immediately."

But du Paty warned her that if she wanted to help her husband she must not try to find him; she must keep everything secret and tell no one. He appealed to her on patriotic grounds. A slip of the tongue, he said, and war might break out. Lucie apparently believed him. She did not inform even Dreyfus' brothers of the arrest. This was a mistake, as it turned out. For, at this juncture, when the Army had not yet staked its honor on conviction, energetic intervention might have rallied public opinion and freed her husband. Du Paty produced a search warrant and he and his aide ransacked every drawer, closet, bookshelf, and examined every slip of paper. They took away the household ledger and the love letters Alfred and Lucie had written during their engagement. But they turned up no incriminating documents, nor did they find any cream-colored graph paper such as the *bordereau* had been written on—which was what they were looking for.

While Captain Dreyfus raged in his cell, General Mercier pushed the investigation to develop further evidence. For a moment hope flared. Paris' network of stool pigeons produced a report that Dreyfus frequented suspicious cafés and was a gambler. But it turned out to be another Dreyfus, the owner of a police record. Police Chief Louis Lépine himself checked inch by inch over Dreyfus' entire life and found not a suspicion of perfidy. The Marquis du Paty, considered the General Staff's handwriting "expert," spent hours in Dreyfus' cell, making Dreyfus write the text of the *bordereau* in various postures. Dreyfus wrote sitting, standing, leaning against a wall, crouched over the floor—in every possible posture. Du Paty was convinced he must in the end discover the position which would make Dreyfus' handwriting identical with that on the *bordereau*. But this game proved futile.

A week went by, and du Paty succeeded in getting nothing out of Dreyfus except the truth, which he refused to believe. The police investigation was equally fruitless. There remained only the highly assailable evidence of the similar-dissimilar handwriting on the *bordereau*. It seemed Dreyfus must be released with the verdict of "not proven." Then the dreaded leak to the public occurred, which made this course impossible. It was Major Henry who pulled the plug.

Major Hubert Henry, who did the Second Bureau's dirty work, was the only officer on the General Staff to have risen from the ranks. Of peasant stock, uneducated and unversed in any foreign language, he was snubbed socially even by the Bureau's junior officers. Thus Major Henry was ready-made to be taken in when the aristocratic Count Esterhazy, for his own purposes, had set out to cultivate him as a friend. The count spoke seven languages. He knew German affairs thoroughly and had considerable background on Austrian and Italian affairs as well. For an international illiterate like Henry, the count's help in translations and in background information was invaluable. The two had become close. If Major Henry recognized his friend Esterhazy's handwriting on the *bordereau*, he gave no indication of it. Instead, perhaps on his own, perhaps prodded by Esterhazy (who had everything to gain if the issue against Dreyfus were forced), Henry now communicated the fact of Dreyfus' arrest to the press.

On October 29 the following item appeared in the popular anti-Semitic newspaper *La Libre Parole:*

Is it a fact that on orders from the military a very important arrest has been made? The prisoner is accused of high treason. If this news is true, why the silence? An answer is urgently requested.

General Mercier felt impelled to issue a guarded communique, admitting that an Army officer had been arrested on suspicion of "giving to foreigners some documents which, though of slight importance, were nevertheless confidential." But all the newspapers were now on to a big story, and within forty-eight hours Alfred Dreyfus was headlined as the traitor. Soon most of the Paris press echoed *La Libre Parole's* accusation that the

Minister of War's office was "a cesspool, worse than the Augean stables." The furor was so great that the Cabinet held an emergency meeting. It was decided that the government could not survive a quashing of the case. Dreyfus must be tried.

With her husband's name made public, Lucie Dreyfus sent a telegram to Alsace to her brother-in-law Mathieu, who had been closest to Alfred. He hastened to Paris and implored Major du Paty to let him visit his brother's cell. He gave his word of honor that, should his brother confess that he had committed treason, then he, Mathieu, would hand his own brother a revolver and demand that he kill himself then and there. Du Paty rejected his plea.

On December 4 the investigator for the court, Bexon D'Ormeschville, drew up his case. It rested mainly on the *bordereau*. No handwriting expert today would have the least difficulty in deciding that Dreyfus could not have written this. And even then, when their science was far more rudimentary, the five handwriting experts who were to testify held contradictory opinions. So this aspect of the case was a bucket of eels. Hence D'Ormeschville would have to rely on argument, painting Dreyfus as a supercriminal who was so crafty that he had left no evidence, and who had even taken the precaution to disguise his hand when indulging in criminal penmanship. The chances are he was not very happy about his case.

He was even unhappier about another document that had just come into his hands. When the Italian military attaché, Lieutenant Colonel A. Panizzardi, learned of Dreyfus' arrest he was understandably concerned lest he somehow become involved in the case. On November 2 he sent a cable in code to Rome: "If Captain D. had no relations with you, a denial would be welcome to avoid press comment." The Italian code had been broken and the message was decoded. Major du Paty made a "free translation" of it for the Second Bureau's files: "D. arrested. Precautions taken. Emissary warned." The prosecutor knew his French penal code. Article 101 reads: "All documents that might serve to convict the defendant must be shown to him." How long could du Paty's "free translation" stand up under the scrutiny of a defense lawyer who could lawfully demand to see the original? The prosecutor felt that such evidence, if presented in court, would inevitably blow up in his face.

But the pressure was on. The press was already inflating the case to monstrous proportions. "Dreyfus," wrote *La Croix*, "is an agent of international Jewry, which has decided to ruin the French people and acquire the territory of France." All unsolved treasons of the recent past were charged to the Jewish captain, and *Le Temps* and *Le Matin* joined in unearthing a love interest. Dreyfus had a sweetheart in Nice, they announced, an Italian beauty of noble birth who had seduced him into committing treason. *La Libre Parole*, *La Cocarde* and *La Patrie* all demanded that he be put to death. It was obvious what would follow a failure to convict Dreyfus: Mercier would be out, probably the government too. Possibly the entire General Staff would be replaced.

In this crisis a proposition was put forward by Colonel Sandherr. This was simply to confront the court with the Second Bureau's file on the case and classify it "secret," thus preventing the defense from examining it and tearing it to pieces. General Mercier hesitated for a long time. That Dreyfus was actually guilty he never doubted, nor did any other officer on the staff except possibly Major Henry. But a War Minister cannot ignore the law without incurring grave risks. To set aside Article 101 in the present temper of affairs would be regarded as an act of patriotism. How would it be regarded at some later date when the present temper changed? If some political opponent then brought it to light, it would be irreparably damaging. He told Sandherr that he must have time to think about it. Three days passed without word from him.

Then on December 15 *La Libre Parole* announced triumphantly: "Dreyfus is committed for trial by court-martial. Mercier with the brutal bluntness of his patriotism has prevailed over his enemies who conspired in the dark." The die was cast. The ideal of government by law and not by men was committed to its ordeal.

In searching for a lawyer to defend Alfred, the Dreyfus family settled on Edgar Demange. Demange, of high repute in criminal law, was a man of fifty-three and a devout Catholic. He would not be attracted either by the withering publicity or by a fee, however large. Nor was there any nonsense in Demange about giving the benefit of the doubt to the defendant. "Should I find the least reason to doubt his innocence," he told the Dreyfus family, "I will refuse to defend him. In effect, I shall be his first judge."

Demange studied the family's evidence on Dreyfus' career and then called for the government's evidence under Article 101. He was thunderstruck. Was this all: the *bordereau*, a dispute among handwriting experts, a prosecutor's petit-point of suppositions and theories? It was all. The decision to use the Second Bureau's secret file had not yet been taken. The lawyer went to see Dreyfus in his cell. "I am convinced of your innocence," he said, "I will defend you."

The decision to go to trial taken, Dreyfus was permitted to write his wife, "My judges are loyal and honest soldiers like myself," he wrote. "They will recognize the error that has been committed. I have nothing to fear."

Trial began December 19, 1894, in an eighteenth-century palace on the Rue Cherche-Midi. The court-room was large and gloomy, illuminated by yellow gas-light. Its tiny windows were cut into thick stone walls. The press had intimated that the court-martial would be held behind closed doors. As a result, few of the public attended. Colonel Emilion Maurel, the presiding judge, ordered the accused escorted in. Captain Dreyfus entered rigidly. The bespectacled man, a small mustache under his sharp nose, his skin drawn and shining, wore the full-dress uniform of an officer of the General Staff. He glanced around stiffly and felt reassured. Seven Army officers were to serve as judges; he was among his own. But he answered the first formal questions about his name, address and rank in a voice that, while firm and carefully emotionless, yet had an artificial intonation. This had always happened when he was fighting for self-control. He had long known it made a bad impression. But that only made it more difficult to eliminate.

Proceedings began with an argument over whether the trial should be public. The prosecution wanted the trial held *in camera*. Demange, for the defense, naturally wanted the public present. A stormy debate ensued, in which he could hardly get a word finished. In the end the trial was declared secret. It was a defeat, and Demange knew it. Dreyfus, too, sensed the significance of the ruling. The public prosecutor's ominous argument still rang in the suddenly hushed room: "There are other interests involved in this case than those of the defense or of the prosecution." Dreyfus' two brothers, Mathieu and Jacques, left grudgingly and anxiously. Only witnesses and experts, the chief of police and the official Ministry of War observer, Major Marie-Georges Picquart, were permitted to remain.

The early nervousness left Dreyfus when he began his testimony. He went over the various items listed in the *bordereau* in a matter-of-fact, almost discursive tone. He explained why it was impossible for him to have been in possession of information about the 120-mm. gun and its supporting troops, or on the Madagascar expedition, and why he could not have written,"I'm off to the maneuvers." His memory never failed him, and he did not hesitate over his answers. His testimony occupied the court's first session. When it was over it was obvious that Captain Dreyfus had made a very good impression. Official observer Picquart reported to War Minister Mercier that it seemed quite likely that the court would acquit. This report made for a busy night in the War Ministry. The lights in high places burned late.

Together General Mercier and Colonel Sandherr sifted through the Second Bureau's record and put together a long memorandum. It consisted of the files of previously unsolved espionage cases, with commentary by General Mercier deftly linking Dreyfus to each. It included du Paty's "free translation" of the Italian telegram and mentioned that Dreyfus had served at Bourges, where an explosives formula had been stolen (although the theft occurred before his tour of duty there). It was in effect a kind of criminal biography which interpreted Dreyfus' studious and unrelenting zeal as a German-inspired desire to learn all about the French Army. They sealed it in a large envelope, placed this in a still larger envelope, then sealed that too, and gave it to du Paty to deliver to the court. It was to be given to the judges as they retired to deliberate their verdict.

On the second day of the trial Major Henry asked to appear as a witness. Had he had any advance warning that Dreyfus was a spy? "Yes," he answered in a thun-

derous voice. An "unimpeachable source" had warned
Major Henry as early as the previous March that there
was a traitor in the Ministry of War. Then suddenly the
witness pointed straight at the accused. "And there is
the traitor!" he roared.

Dreyfus jumped indignantly to his feet. So did his
counsel. They demanded under Article 101 that Henry
name the person who gave the warning. Henry refused.
And the presiding judge intervened. "You do not have to
name the person," he told Henry. "It will suffice if you
affirm on your honor that this person told you the traitor
was Dreyfus." Major Henry lifted his hand to the crucifix
and in a voice that shook the courtroom cried: "I swear."

On the fourth day of the trial, December 22, the pre-
sentation of evidence concluded. The verdict would now
be deliberated. As the judges rose and prepared to retire,
Major du Paty sauntered over and unobtrusively slipped
the presiding judge the envelope from General Mercier.
Colonel Maurel opened it and found a note from the
War Minister requesting him to read the contents of the
enclosed envelope to the judges during their deliberation.
It was an impressively bulky espionage file, and whatever the commentary which accompanied it lacked in
logic it made up for in authority. It was signed by General Mercier. It would not have taken a very clever lawyer to make hash of it, but no lawyer was present—only
General Mercier's subordinates.

After an hour they called court into session again to
hear the final pleas. Demange spoke for three hours. He
concentrated on the *bordereau*. After all, it was the only
evidence the Republic had produced. The prosecutor's
speech was brief. He suggested that the judges take a
magnifying glass and examine the *bordereau* themselves.
Then Dreyfus rose. "I am innocent," he said simply.

Dreyfus was now led from the courtroom. After another brief period of retirement the judges returned and Colonel Maurel read the verdict. It was unanimous. Captain Alfred Dreyfus was found guilty of treason and condemned to dishonorable discharge from the Army, to deportation and exile for life in a fortified place. In the courtroom Demange wept aloud.

On January 5, 1895, Alfred Dreyfus was publicly drummed out of the French Army. The proceedings, formal as an execution, were held on the parade ground of the Ecole Militaire. The great crowds that came to watch had to be held at bay by a heavy military cordon. They were in a lynching mood, and "Death to the Jew!" was heard from all sides. Each regiment of the Paris garrison had sent a unit. A trumpet sounded, commands were barked, and a giant sergeant of the Republican Guard led out four soldiers with drawn swords. In their midst walked Captain Dreyfus.

The vast crowd was silent as the little group ground to a halt before General Darras, who sat awaiting them on horseback. The general drew his sword. In a voice that sounded tiny in that huge, silent space he cried: "Alfred Dreyfus, you are unworthy of carrying arms. We herewith degrade you in the name of the people of France."

Dreyfus stirred. He had been standing at attention. Now he lifted up his head. "Soldiers!" he shouted. "An innocent is dishonored. Long live France!" His voice, too, sounded tiny, but it carried to the crowd outside. The crowd roared back angrily, "Death to the Jew!"

The giant sergeant rushed at Dreyfus. He tore the epaulets from the captain's shoulders and then tore the red stripes, marking him as a General Staff officer, from his trousers. Finally he took the captain's sword and broke it in two. He threw the pieces on the ground. With the epaulets and the red stripes it made a little pile of refuse, all that remained of Dreyfus' once high place in the world. Dreyfus was then marched past the soldiers ranked column after column in lines of parade dress. He walked with the unbending precision of a staff officer on inspection. The effect was ghastly. His uniform seemed suddenly naked. At regular intervals he threw up his arms and with a face that was nearly maniacal in its effort to conceal its suffering cried: "I am innocent. Long live France!"

Six weeks later Dreyfus was en route to Devil's Island, the notorious French penal colony off the coast of South America. He need not have gone there. For General Mercier, who still yearned for proof that the court-martial verdict was just, sent du Paty to his cell with a proposition: There were many ways in which his life in exile could be made supportable. The place chosen need not be a blistering rock in a desolate sea. It could be a garden spot. His family might be permitted to join him. There could be other privileges. Dreyfus had only to confess. He need not admit deliberate treason. It would suffice if he pleaded a moment of mental aberration, perhaps only criminal carelessness. Dreyfus replied to this offer instantly, in a letter to General Mercier. The only privilege he wanted was that the search for the traitor be continued and pressed to a successful conclusion.

As he was being transported to the ship, the crowd at La Rochelle station rushed the convict train and tried to mob him. Dreyfus thoroughly sympathized with their feeling. He was a soldier to the core, and the people's trust in their Army was sacred to him. "I was transported as the vile scoundrel whom I represent deserves to be," he wrote Lucie at the time, "As long as I represent such a miserable creature, I cannot but approve."

Dreyfus made the long voyage to Devil's Island in chains, and his incarceration there was arranged with fantastic caution. He was placed in a stone hut which was surrounded by a high stone wall. The windows and door were barred and from a small anteroom of the hut a guard, who was relieved every two hours, kept a constant watch on his movements. Five men were detailed to this duty. He was never allowed to sit facing the sea. It was feared he might signal to someone in that blinding glitter. His request that work be assigned him was turned down; and Lucie's request to join him in exile—a favor the law accorded to wives of deportees— was likewise rejected. No letter containing any allusion to his case was allowed to reach him. When he was taken for a walk on the shadeless strip of rock adjoining his hut, no one was allowed to talk to him. His guards were not permitted to answer his questions.

Dreyfus maintained his rigid bearing and his military composure. But violent neuralgias began to rack his head. When storms stirred up the sea and the waves thundered against the rock, he took advantage of the sound to give vent to shrieks of despair. He waited for storms because he did not want anyone to hear him. No one heard. He and his case were entombed in silence.

This existence continued for eighteen months. Then the precautions concerning Dreyfus were suddenly doubled. All letters and packages from the outside world were stopped. Where there had been one man watching him day and night, there were now two, with orders to report Dreyfus' every gesture and change of expression. A second stone wall was erected around the first one, and for the two months until it was completed he was confined to his cot each night in double irons.

These measures were taken because Mathieu Dreyfus had made a move. The silence that had fallen over his brother's case was its worst enemy, he knew. He had resorted to a hoax to break it. Through a friend he succeeded in getting published in England a fabricated report that Dreyfus had escaped from Devil's Island. As Mathieu had expected, the item was widely reprinted and the entire Paris press took it up. It caused the Minister of Colonies immense agitation while he awaited the official report from Devil's Island; and his frenzied fears were communicated to Alfred's jailers. Mathieu's hoax accomplished nothing except publicity. But other developments, already under way in the War Ministry, were to keep the Dreyfus case very much alive.

In March 1896, some fifteen months after the case had been closed, an interesting *petit bleu*, or special-delivery postcard, came into the posession of the Second Bureau. It had been written by a woman friend of Schwartzkoppen and given to him to mail. Schwartzkoppen had never succeeded in mailing it, for it was somehow stolen from him or possibly even removed from the letterbox. The message on the *petit bleu* was innocuous, but it was intimate in tone—and it was addressed to Major Count Ferdinand Walsin-Esterhazy!

It was brought to the desk of Georges Picquart, now a lieutenant colonel and head of the Second Bureau. When Picquart first glanced at the *petit bleu* his reaction was immediate. "What, another spy?" he asked. "What is Esterhazy doing getting *petits bleus* via the German Embassy?" In view of the count's unsavory record, Picquart decided to keep an eye on him. Three months later Count Esterhazy made a mistake. Perhaps Major Henry had failed to warn him that he was being watched, perhaps it was simple brazenness. At any rate he chose this moment to make a written application for General Staff duty. The application came to Picquart's desk and it struck him that there was something familiar about the handwriting.

In his new post Picquart had recently had occasion to examine the highly secret Dreyfus file. He now went directly to the safe, got out the *bordereau* from the Dreyfus envelope and compared its writing to Esterhazy's. Immediately he summoned the criminologist Bertillon. To Bertillon's credit he did not quibble. He studied the *bordereau* again and then examined Esterhazy's application. "This is the man who wrote the *bordereau*," he said.

Picquart had once taught Dreyfus at the Ecole de Guerre. He did not like him and, unlike the other instructors, was not even impressed by his intelligence. But he was now to jeopardize his career to see justice done. His lonely crusade was to win him bitter enmities on the General Staff, cause his eventual imprisonment and all but ruin his life.

His conversation with General Charles Gonse was testified to subsequently in court. "You should have kept the two cases separated," General Gonse said, when Picquart approached him. "The Dreyfus case is closed."

When Picquart insisted that it should be reopened, General Gonse lost patience. "What do you care for this Jew anyhow?" he asked.

"He is innocent," Picquart replied quietly. He could not understand why that should not be reason enough.

But the general understood. "For me," he said, "truth is what the Minister of War and the Chief of the General Staff tell me is true." Then he added, "If you keep silent, no one need find out anything."

Picquart forgot the difference in rank. He forgot the power of a general of the Army. "General," he cried, "what you say is abominable. I do not know yet what I am going to do. But I will not carry this secret to my grave."

The general did not freeze. He did not bark. But not long afterward he ordered Picquart to investigate the intelligence service on the eastern border. When that task was done, he ordered him directly to the Italian frontier to inspect the intelligence service there. From the Italian frontier Picquart was sent urgently to Algiers, and from Algiers to Tunisia—each time with letters of praise for work well done. At first Picquart suspected nothing. But after nearly three months a friend wrote to complain that, whenever he inquired, the Second Bureau replied that Picquart was expected back momentarily. How long was a moment? the friend asked. And Picquart realized that he had been practically exiled. In his absence Major Henry took over his place and ran things with his huge fist. Picquart's mail, addressed to the bureau, came to Henry's desk for forwarding. Henry began steaming it open. A file on Picquart was started. Into it went whatever compromising material could be found, and if nothing could be found it was invented.

But there was a simpler way of disposing of the troublesome Picquart. Henry suggested that Gonse dispatch him to the Tripoli border where skirmishes were taking place. A bullet in the right place would, he felt, successfully stop any reopening of the Dreyfus case. General Gonse sent the order. Picquart, however, had already insured that the truth should survive. On a brief leave in Paris he had left with his lawyer, Louis Leblois, a letter to the President of the Republic. The letter, to be delivered in the event of Picquart's death, described how Picquart had discovered the real author of the *bordereau*. It concluded:

1. Walsin-Esterhazy is a German agent.
2. Acts charged to Dreyfus were committed by Esterhazy.
3. The Dreyfus case was treated with unheard-of lightness, with a preconceived conviction of Dreyfus' guilt, and in disregard of the law.

When Picquart told him the story in confidence, Leblois was profoundly disturbed. He finally obtained permission to impart the secret to reliable friends if he could do so without divulging Picquart's name. The lawyer felt this could be managed. He contacted Auguste Scheurer-Kestner, vice-president of the Senate, an old and trusted friend of the Dreyfus family. Senator Scheurer could do nothing until the mysterious officer Leblois represented was willing to come forward with proof. He hinted privately, however, that there was evidence of Dreyfus' innocence. When his views became known he was savagely reviled by the press and ostracized in the Senate. His interest in the case was to bring him only abuse. But it was the beginning of a Dreyfusard or "revisionist" movement in high places.

Count Esterhazy was becoming increasingly uneasy. He knew that several people now suspected him of having written the *bordereau*. And when France's largest newspaper, *Le Matin*, published a facsimile of that famous document, having somehow obtained a photograph of it, he was thoroughly alarmed. In his panic he rushed to the German Embassy and told Schwartzkoppen that their connection had been discovered and would soon be made public by a leading senator. He suggested that Schwartzkoppen go to Mme. Dreyfus and assure her that her husband had actually committed treason. Schwartzkoppen refused, and Esterhazy then said he had reached the end. He would kill himself then and there in Schwartzkoppen's office. The prospect failed to alarm the military attaché, and Esterhazy became enraged. He threatened to make public Schwartzkoppen's relations with a lady whom he named. Schwartzkoppen rang for an attendant and ordered that Esterhazy be shown out forcibly.

When he reported Esterhazy's melodramatics and growing recklessness to Berlin, it was decided that Schwartzkoppen had better get out before the brewing scandal boiled over. He was promptly recalled to Germany. On leaving Paris, he did the most that a spy can do for his own self-respect. He could not name one of his own agents. But in bidding the President a formal farewell, Schwartzkoppen assured him on his honor as an officer that he had had no dealings with Dreyfus.

Meanwhile Henry, aware of the mounting suspicion of Esterhazy, consulted du Paty, who assured Esterhazy on behalf of the General Staff that there was nothing to fear, that matters were well in hand. He was not exaggerating. In order to protect the count (who was quite capable of blackmailing him if he did not), Major Henry was busily forging fresh evidence to reinforce the case against Dreyfus. Capitalizing on Colonel Sandherr's recent death, Henry let the news leak out that he had discovered yet another secret file in Sandherr's office safe. It contained documents, he declared—shoals of them—certifying Dreyfus' guilt. There were no less than seven letters in Dreyfus' own hand to the German emperor. On one of them the Kaiser had scribbled a marginal comment to the German ambassador, saying in effect that "the scoundrel" was getting more and more demanding but was to be kept satisfied.

Some three years after his brother had been convicted, Mathieu Dreyfus learned the identity of the real traitor. It came about by chance. Mathieu had brought out a pamphlet on the Dreyfus case, to be sold in the streets of Paris. On its cover was a reproduction of the *bordereau* as it had appeared in the newspaper *Le Matin*. In a moment of idle curiosity, a stockbroker named Castro bought one of the pamphlets. He had had business dealings with Count Esterhazy, which had netted him only acrimonious correspondence. Castro now recognized the handwriting and went to Mathieu with the letters Esterhazy had written him. Mathieu embraced him in gratitude; and on November 15, 1897, he formally charged Esterhazy with having written the *bordereau*.

Since under French law anyone with knowledge of a crime can bring a charge, an investigation could not be avoided. The General Staff wanted the charge dismissed at once on the technicality that the only evidence was the *bordereau* and this was inadmissible because the Dreyfus case was closed. But they were at the mercy of an adventurer's whims. Esterhazy insisted that he could not allow his reputation to remain under a cloud. He demanded a complete vindication. So the "investigation" dragged on. Now that he was under fire, the newspapers lauded Count Esterhazy to the sky. Only the revisionist papers, a tiny segment of the press, attacked him. *Le Figaro*, a small highbrow publication, brought up from the *bordereau* that telling bit, "I am off to the maneuvers," and was now able to prove that Dreyfus had not attended the maneuvers that year and that Esterhazy had.

Le Figaro also published, side by side, reproductions of the *bordereau* and of Esterhazy's handwriting so that its readers might judge for themselves. The mass-circulation papers retorted with two voices: one group said that the handwritings were not identical; the remainder said they had been "reliably" informed that Dreyfus had imitated Esterhazy's handwriting. Esterhazy spent most of his time in newspaper offices, handing out juicy bits about "the international Jewish syndicate" and its plots to destroy the Army and thus France. At the same time, he painted his own portrait in glowing colors. He was, it seemed, a superbly courageous man of indomitable will, fanatically jealous of his honor. His every word was enshrined in print for posterity and debated avidly. Paris was at his feet.

When he was finally brought into court on Mathieu's charges, the official announcement emphasized that Esterhazy was not being tried. His innocence had already been established. The trial, it was declared, was being held only in justice to Esterhazy. The accusation rather than the accused would be tried. On the stand Esterhazy

made a calm and reserved witness. His one outburst occurred when he once cried out fervently, "All I have
said is as true as that I am innocent." It is perhaps the
one truthful statement he made.

When Mathieu's turn came, Esterhazy's attorney criticized him sharply for circulating a reproduction of the
bordereau. "You may defend your brother before the
court but no where else," the lawyer told him.

"I shall defend my brother everywhere," replied
Mathieu. And the throng in the courtroom hissed its
hate so loudly that it had to be called to order.

The bulk of the testimony was taken behind closed
doors. At the end the public prosecutor formally dropped
the charge against Esterhazy. Nevertheless, Esterhazy's
attorney spoke for five hours. The court deliberated for
three minutes, and then it voted unanimously for acquittal. A pandemonium of joy broke out. It was as if
France had won a great victory on the battlefield. Officers, newspapermen, women and men, old and young,
rushed up to Esterhazy to embrace him with tears in
their eyes. Long into the night triumphant processions
marched through the streets of Paris chanting, "Long
live Esterhazy! Long live the Army!"

One victim of the trial was Colonel Picquart, who had
been summoned from Africa to testify. At the court he
stood alone, isolated by the enmity of his fellow officers—
a proud figure, handsome and poised. Only Senator
Scheurer-Kestner talked to him, and Mathieu and Lucie
Dreyfus, and Demange, who had been retained to represent Mathieu. Despite heavy pressure he resolutely gave
his testimony about the *petit bleu* which linked Esterhazy
with the German Embassy. But it was heard secretly behind closed doors; the opposition described the *petit bleu*
as a forgery, and his sacrifice availed nothing. After the

trial Picquart was arrested, charged with having di-
vulged secret information, and held in the fortress of
Mont-Valérien for weeks.

And on Devil's Island, five thousand miles away, Dreyfus' guard was increased to thirteen men and a warden.
A tower was built to watch over the sea. A large gun was
mounted on its top. Dreyfus had no idea why. All mail
privileges had been denied him for months, and the
guards never spoke to him.

The acquittal of Esterhazy and the arrest of Picquart
made black headlines around the world. France is no
more, Europe mourned from Lisbon to Moscow. The
country that had led Western civilization in her ideas of
justice and freedom had fled from her senses. In her
madness she had created a morally upside-down world
in which, as one writer put it, "the fraudulent glorified
fraud, and the impostors erected a monument to im-
posture."

"Courageous men defying tyrants are never wanting
in history," wrote Georges Clemenceau, the Tiger, "but
it requires true heroism to defy the tyranny of public
opinion." The monster in France was now public opinion, inflamed and fed on lies by the ultranationalist press.
Few within or outside the government dared defy it.
True, there had always been Dreyfus adherents—about
one percent of the population by contemporary estimate
—and they were found in all walks of life. Early Dreyfusards included the writer Anatole France, the scholarly
director of the Pasteur Institute, Pierre Emile Duclaux,
the Senator and former Minister of Justice, Ludovic
Traitieux. Led by the aged Senator Scheurer-Kestner,
this little band of stalwarts gave voice to the dissent. And
slowly, one by one, other honest and courageous men
began to line up with them. But Picquart's arrest came

as a terrible blow, for the battle to see justice done now appeared lost.

Then came January 13, 1898—and the leaden atmosphere of despondency was dispelled as if by the elemental force of a hurricane. On that date the newspaper to which Clemenceau contributed, *L'Aurore*, published Emile Zola's *J'Accuse!*, a title which was to become a byword, forever associated with Zola by the whole world. It was a challenge to France and to every Frenchman to hold by cherished ideals and stand up and be counted. Zola was then at the peak of his world fame. His novels were best sellers in almost all civilized languages. He had been writing about the Dreyfus case in the columns of *Le Figaro*. But he came to realize that only a stark witness to faith—an invitation to martyrdom—could break the spell that had descended on the nation. He did not consult anyone but wrote for a night, a day and another night until he had finished his appeal to sanity. In publishing it he threw into the scales all he had attained in a lifetime of creative achievement.

J'Accuse! was a document of formidable power. With magic insight it pierced the smoke screen of fraud, confusion and contradictions, and showed with precision and clarity how the General Staff, having committed a fateful blunder, had attempted to cover it up and had sunk into a morass of fraud and forgery. At the close of his long plea, Zola made several specific accusations, the last being:

> I accuse the first court-martial [of Dreyfus] of having violated all human rights in condemning a prisoner on testimony kept secret from him, and I accuse the second court-martial [of Esterhazy] of having covered up this illegality by order, committing in turn the judicial crime of acquitting a guilty man with full knowledge of his guilt.

Zola knew that he could be prosecuted for making these accusations.

> The action I take here is designed to hasten the explosion of truth and justice. Let them dare to carry me to court, and let there be an inquest in the full light of day!
> I am waiting.

The repercussions were immediate. *L'Aurore*, a paper of insignificant circulation, sold three hundred thousand copies of the *J'Accuse!* number. Thirty thousand letters and telegrams poured in from all parts of the world, testifying to the relief felt everywhere at Zola's stand and to mounting revulsion over the French dim-out of reason. In France itself, the internal tensions broke into violence. In Paris huge protest meetings were held, ending in bloody clashes. In other French cities angry crowds plundered Jewish stores, publicly burned copies of *J'Accuse!* and hanged Zola in effigy. The uproar, which sometimes had to be quelled by the military, was to continue for weeks. The Cabinet was at a loss. It could not let Zola's accusations go unchallenged, for both public and press were demanding harsh punishment for him. Yet prosecuting him for libel would mean reopening the Dreyfus case because the defendant had the legal right to attempt to prove the truth of his statements. A face-saving formula was finally devised. Zola would be charged with criminal libel only for the passage of *J'Accuse!* in which he stated that a court-martial "acting on orders" dared acquit Esterhazy. This would give him the right to produce evidence against Esterhazy but not in favor of Dreyfus.

On February 7, 1898, the trial of Zola opened. It lasted for fifteen days and was followed with anxious interest throughout the world. It intensified feelings that were already high, and Army troops were held in constant readiness to control the mobs that surrounded the building. The judge made every effort to prevent the witnesses from wandering out of the narrow area embraced by the indictment. "The question is out of order" became the signature of the trial. For, on Zola's instructions, his attorney ignored Zola's defense and simply tried to reopen the Dreyfus case before the civilian court.

In his own plea Zola assured the jury that not he, and not Dreyfus, were on trial, but France. The question was whether France was still true to her character as the guardian of justice and humanity. He ended his speech with these words: "Dreyfus is innocent. I vouch for it with my life and honor. By all I have gained, by the name I have made, and my contribution to French literature, I swear to it. May all of this perish if he is not. Dreyfus is innocent."

The room was breathless. For an instant it seemed as if the Dreyfus case must be heard in public at last. But Zola was no match for the prestige of the General Staff. It was impossible to believe that these men, the cream of the Army, the backbone of national defense, could be forgers, liars and crooks. And the General Staff drew the issue clearly. It would resign *en bloc* if the jury acquitted Zola.

It took the jury only thirty-five minutes to bring in the verdict. By an eight-to-four vote, Zola was pronounced guilty. He was given the maximum penalty, one year in prison and a fine of 3000 francs. The news caused riotous joy throughout France, and political parties vied with one another in claiming the lion's share in the triumph. Abroad, the dismay was almost universal. English and Continental newspapers called the sentence savage and barbaric, and felt that France's moral decay augured ill for the Western world. The unanimous hostility abroad only strengthened the prevailing opinion in France, however, for the French public resented it and were quick to dismiss any appeal, advice or opinion coming from outside.

But the Dreyfus case would not die. The excitement Zola had touched off in France continued to rage at fever pitch. The battle over Dreyfus' innocence or guilt was carried on in hundreds of pamphlets. It seemed that almost everybody wished to make a public declaration of his stand. The scientists lined up almost to a man on the revisionist side, professors of the humanities and writers were divided. The revisionist youth set up headquarters in a bookshop in the Latin Quarter and took their work with great seriousness. Jules Renard's diary tells of a young man whose family desired him to marry a certain girl. He requested her parents to let him have her photograph and also to inform him of her views on the Dreyfus Affair. A French expedition to the arctic wintered on an iceberg and was feared lost. When they were found in the spring their first question to their rescuers was, "What about Dreyfus. Is he free?"

Godefroy Cavaignac, the new War Minister who now came into office, felt the government had mishandled the Dreyfus case and was convinced he knew what to do about it. Cavaignac firmly believed in Dreyfus' guilt, in the existence of the Jewish syndicate and, innocent that he was, in the integrity of the General Staff and its documents. He wanted to end the debate once and for all by simply bringing all the secret documents into the open and thus prove Dreyfus' guilt beyond question. From the now vastly swollen Dreyfus file (Henry had added sheaves of irrelevant documents to make examination difficult) Cavaignac selected the best evidence he could

find. It included a letter from the Italian military attaché, Panizzardi, which mentioned Dreyfus by name.
Shortly afterward, when he spoke in the Chamber, he
announced he would read from "three documents chosen
out of a thousand pieces of correspondence exchanged for
six years between people active in espionage." He felt
this evidence answered the question about Dreyfus' guilt
"definitively, conclusively and forever." The deputies
agreed, hailed Cavaignac as a soldier-statesman and voted to display his speech publicly throughout the country.

That honestly indignant speech became the turning
point in the Dreyfus case. For when Picquart read it he
at once recognized the documents cited. As a result of
his forthright testimony in the Zola trial, Picquart had
been retired from the Army for "grave shortcomings in
service." He knew the step he was taking might lead him
to prison again, or worse. Yet he now wrote the Prime
Minister:

> Up to the present I did not feel free to give an account of
> the secret documents on the strength of which Dreyfus' guilt
> was allegedly established. The Minister of War quoted three
> of these documents in the Chamber. I consider it my duty to
> let you know that two of the documents quoted do not refer to
> Dreyfus, and the third has all the characteristics of a forgery.

A careful examination of the documents, which Prime
Minister Henri Brisson now ordered, revealed that the
Panizzardi letter was indeed a forgery. It consisted of
two letters, glued expertly together. When Minister of
War Cavaignac was informed, he summoned Colonel
Henry and confronted him with the forged document.
How did he explain it? After an hour of denials Henry
conceded that he had rearranged a few sentences but
denied that he had fabricated the text. He stubbornly
stuck to his denial, then conceded one step. "My supe-

riors were disturbed. I wanted to calm them. I said to myself: 'Let us add a sentence that can pass as proof in the situation in which we are.' I acted alone and in the interest of my country."

But after further savage prodding Henry finally admitted he had manufactured the whole letter except for the signature. Cavaignac at once informed the press and ordered Henry's arrest. Shortly afterward—on August 31, 1898—Colonel Henry was found dead in his cell. He had used a razor to cut his throat.

The effect of these events on the Army was shattering. General Raoul de Boisdeffre, chief of the General Staff, resigned at once, as did General Georges de Pellieux, who was indignant at having been deceived into misleading the jury in the Zola trial.

Esterhazy, when the news of Henry's suicide reached him, fled without luggage to London. The time had come to confess for a good price and take revenge on his accomplices for deserting him. His side of the story, vividly written, was soon appearing serially in both London and Paris. The late Colonel Sandherr, he insisted, had briefed him to become an agent of the Germans, to sell them inconsequential data and garbled versions of secret documents. His mission had been to gain access to German secrets, he said.

A retrial of Dreyfus now became inevitable. Overnight everybody seemed to have turned revisionist. The government deliberated night and day. The antirevision bloc was still powerful, but Premier Brisson was determined on a new trial. He dispatched a friend to Mathieu Dreyfus, advising him to petition for one. Demange, whose large practice had crumbled away because of his defense of Dreyfus, at once complied. The Army tried every possible maneuver to block the move, including the re-arrest of Picquart; but the revisionist fold was growing constantly now, even within the government. Some six months after the petition for retrial was presented the Senate enacted a special law enabling the High Court of Appeal to review the case. The court studied it for three months, then voided Dreyfus' original sentence and ordered him to stand a new trial before a court-martial at Rennes.

Rennes was a sleepy town in devoutly Catholic Brittany. The trial was held in the high-school hall, the only place large enough to hold the crowds. When Captain Dreyfus was brought in, avid eyes were turned on him to see at last the man behind the legend. For years now every person present had known Dreyfus' name as well as his own, yet hardly anybody had ever seen him.

Dreyfus had been brought back to France on the cruiser *Sfax*. The news that he was to be retried, that the outside world had remembered his existence, had come as such a shock that he had feared he would not survive it. Only thirty-nine years of age, he was now and old man, gray-haired, frail. The eyes behind the glasses were so pale they seemed a ghostly blue. His skin, like faultily tanned hide, yellowed and browned, appeared glued to the protruding bones of his face. Even in his brand-new uniform he looked like a bag of bones. A writer reported that the audience gaped at him and felt almost spent by the force of the experience. Through an accident of time and place this man had been for years a symbol in a clash of ideas so violent that its fury nearly drove France to fratricide. But to have responded with emotion to the role foisted upon him would have struck him as indecorous and unmilitary. Clemenceau complained that "Dreyfus never understood the Dreyfus case." And a younger Dreyfusard, Léon Blum, wrote: "If he had not been Dreyfus, he would not even have been a Dreyfusard."

Dreyfus defined his point of view later: "I was only an artillery officer prevented by a tragic error from following my career. Dreyfus, the figurehead of justice, was not I. He was created by you." Certainly a courtroom appeal to the feelings of others would have violated his own deepest feeling. He would not even reveal his physical misery. His weakened condition and loss of self-control became apparent only when his eyes would suddenly stream tears. Otherwise his bearing remained militarily stiff, reserved, colorless. The defense was not well conducted, and a grave error was made in permitting the exclusion of the public after Dreyfus' testimony was taken. Demange was now an old man and had lost much of his force. His co-attorney, Fernand Labori, who had defended Zola, was shot in the streets of Rennes by a rabid anti-Dreyfusard. The wound was not serious, but until it healed the ineffectual Demange was left to conduct the case alone.

General Mercier dominated the trial. He was a poised and impressive figure, and his testimony abounded with hints that what he told was but part of the truth, that the whole truth was still too dangerous to France to tell. Mercier described the days when Dreyfus had been put under arrest. The German emperor, through his ambassador, had threatened war, he said. Those had been days and nights of anxiety. He, Mercier, had kept the chief of the General Staff on the alert to issue the order for mobilization at a moment's notice. In such a situation legal scruples were not so compelling as in less critical times, and of course you couldn't aggravate things by divulging proofs. In summing up, Mercier thrust home the final dagger. "My convictions have not changed since

1894. They have only been strengthened by a more
thorough study of the files and by the attempts I have
seen to prove that guilt is innocence."

The judges, a cross section of officers from the provincial garrison, were perhaps fair. But in a military court,
if it comes to the question whether it is a captain or a
general who is lying, the general gets the better of it.
After thirty-three sessions and a parade of 115 witnesses,
the court, by a vote of five to two, again found Dreyfus
guilty of high treason and sentenced him to ten years in
prison.

It could not stand. The world responded to the verdict
with a tempest of indignation. From Russia to America
people were shaken by the event. It was incomprehensible
to them. French embassies and consulates around the
globe were besieged by protest demonstrations. Mass
meetings were held to urge the boycott of everything
French, including the World Exhibition in Paris, scheduled for the coming year. Everywhere was echoed the
comment, "Not Dreyfus but France stands condemned."

The Premier of France, anticipating just such a reaction at home as well as abroad, had made no secret of the
fact that he would not allow a conviction to remain in
effect. Now he promptly issued Dreyfus a full pardon. On
September 19, 1899, after he had spent almost five years
in prison, Dreyfus was released. In order to recuperate
safe from mob annoyances, he moved with his family to
Switzerland. Clemenceau opposed the whole idea of pardon since it was an acknowledgment of inability to get
justice from a French court. The Dreyfusards had been
fighting not only for Dreyfus but for law in French courts.
Picquart, who had spent nearly a year in prison because
of his efforts to free Dreyfus, bitterly resented the fact
that a pardon was accepted without consulting him. He

felt that in accepting it Dreyfus had acknowledged guilt. Thus Picquart was left alone to face the hatred and contempt of that Army which he still loved. The pardon freed Dreyfus, but it did not vindicate Picquart for championing him.

Mathieu Dreyfus had not objected when his brother accepted a pardon. But he would not rest content until the Dreyfus name had been completely exonerated. He kept digging away at every aspect of the case until finally, he found an approach which was rewarding. One of the judges who voted for acquittal in the Rennes trial had since retired. Mathieu cultivated his acquaintance and eventually learned the details of how the Rennes trial was conducted. Above all, he secured the vital intelligence that General Mercier had used the same trick on the second court-martial that he had used on the first: secret forged documents which the defendant was given no opportunity to inspect. Armed with this new evidence, Mathieu presented a request for revision, and in March 1904, this was sent to the High Court of Appeal. That court, determined to leave no doubt or ambiguity unresolved, ordered a new hearing.

The hearing was long and exhaustive—a parade of witnesses and documents from the past: from the Rennes court-martial of five years before, from the Zola trial before that, from the Esterhazy trial and from the first trial of Dreyfus in 1894. When it was over the High Court, on July 12, 1906, set aside the sentence of the Rennes court-martial and declared its verdict of "Guilty" erroneous. The court announced that there existed no incriminating evidence of any kind against Dreyfus and that a retrial was unnecessary since there had never been any facts to try. At last, after twelve long years, the case was closed.

The government without delay undertook the rehabilitation not only of Dreyfus but of Picquart as well. "To liberate the conscience of France," both chambers voted to re-integrate the two officers into the Army. Dreyfus was promoted to *chef d'escadron* and awarded the Legion of Honor as "an appropriate reparation for a soldier who had endured a martyrdom without parallel." Picquart was recommended for the rank he would normally have achieved by now—brigadier general. General Picquart went on to become Minister of War in 1908, in Clemenceau's Cabinet. Dreyfus retired from the Army after a year, but was summoned back in 1914 and fought in two of the bloodiest battles of World War I—Chemin des Dames and Verdun. The other principal of the case, Major Esterhazy, survived to an obscure old age in the slums of London under the name of Count Jean de Voilemont.

Perhaps the high point in the drama of restitution—in righting the terrible wrong done Captain Dreyfus—came in 1906, immediately after his vindication. It was a ceremony at the Ecole Militaire grounds, the same spot where, twelve years earlier, Dreyfus had endured such frightful degradation. It was not public; only a few friends were invited. Dreyfus arrived at half past one and quietly chatted with a group of officers. A trumpet sounded a call. Two *escadrons de cuirassiers* formed a rectangle. A captain went to escort Dreyfus, who was in full dress. They stepped briskly along the line of *cuirassiers* and drew up before Brigadier General Gillain. The general drew his sword. Four calls sounded from the trumpet.

"In the name of the President of the Republic and on the basis of the power conferred on me, Commander Dreyfus, I make you a Knight of the Legion of Honor," the general announced, and touched his sword three times to Dreyfus' shoulders. He pinned the cross on Dreyfus' black dolman and kissed him on both cheeks.

The last trumpet calls rang out. Dreyfus stood to attention as the troops marched off to the sound of fanfares. Suddenly a boy ran up to embrace him. It was his son Pierre. Only then did Dreyfus burst into tears.

Seated in an open carriage flanked by Mathieu and his son, Dreyfus rode out of the yard. There was a surprise. A crowd estimated at two hundred thousand had gathered spontaneously in the streets. Hats were raised to Dreyfus. "Long live Dreyfus! Long live justice!" He waved greetings and thanks, a smile on his pale face.

A recent theft-prevention device may drive auto thieves crazy from frustration. When the unit is installed, any tampering with the ignition wires locks the brakes. If the brakes are released, the fuel supply is cut off. If the fuel system is adjusted, the brakes lock again and the ignition system is grounded. In one test, an experienced mechanic was unable to get the car started in 30 minutes.
— *Fleet Owner, quoted in Engineering Digest*

A Jewel Thief in Cologne couldn't believe his eyes. A window display disappeared without a trace when he reached through the broken pane for the booty. An electronic trip wire causes the endangered jewels to slide into a safety box.

— *Neue Illustrierte, Germany*

The answer to thefts of books from libraries may lie in an electronic device invented by Emmanuel Mitchell Trikilis, an engineer. A sliver of magnetized metal is hidden somewhere in a book's spine or binding, and the librarian who checks the book out simply demagnetizes the metal insert by passing the book through a coil carrying an electric current. If a thief bolts for the exit instead of the check-out desk, the magnetized metal inside his book is detected by an instrument that trips a device hidden in the door; the turnstile is automatically locked, and the librarian is alerted by a buzzing noise. A sign over the door explains all with a succinct message: "If turnstile is locked, please report to loan desk".
— *Time*

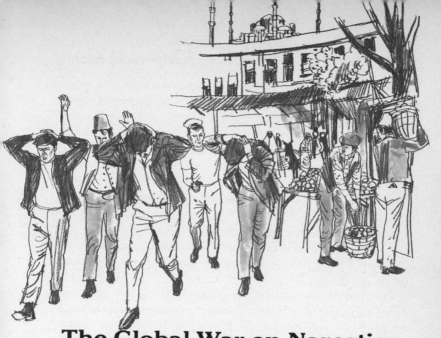

The Global War on Narcotics

By Frederic Sondern, Jr.

IT WAS late afternoon in the ancient city of Istanbul. As street vendors, beggars, people of every race and dress jostled along the Rue Cabristan, no one paid much attention to a group of workmen digging a ditch outside a little café. Suddenly, at a window above the café a shade jerked up. Immediately the ditchdiggers dropped their tools, rushed into the café and up its stairs, pistols in hand. In a few moments four cursing men emerged from the building, prodded forward by an American seaman. Before a crowd could gather, police cars had whisked them off.

Within the hour Harry J. Anslinger, then commissioner of the U.S. Treasury Department's Bureau of Narcotics, received a cable from the American seaman—U.S. Narcotics Agent George White: "Able today to buy quantity pure heroin from biggest ring of dealers here and arrest same. Brilliant support from Turkish police who have seized refining plant and 900 ounces of narcotics, source large shipments to the United States."

Agent White's triumph in a city on the other side of the globe was not an unusual project for the Narcotics Bureau. A tightly knit organization of some three hundred officers, the Bureau deals with one of today's most intricate law-enforcement problems.

With the end of World War II, habit-forming narcotics began to flow again to Europe and the United States from dope racketeers in the Far East, the Middle East and South America. In the United States the drug traffic climbed rapidly back toward prewar levels. By 1949 more than 10 percent of the inmates of U.S. federal prisons were men and women convicted under the narcotics laws. Drug trafficking and addiction were contributing more and more to crime of all kinds—from gang warfare and murder to prostitution and larceny by addicts in need of money to satisfy their expensive craving.

Some months before the raid in the Rue Cabristan, field offices of the Bureau of Narcotics reported to Washington that heroin, most vicious of the opium derivatives, was getting into the illicit market from a new source. Examination showed it to be of Turkish manufacture. Narcotics-squad detectives of New York's police department ferreted out a Greek sailor and two friends who seemed to be doing most of the peddling. They were shadowed to their cache—a suitcase in the parcel room of a bus terminal. After arrest, the sailor told of a big heroin ring in Istanbul which sold to seamen.

Commissioner Anslinger decided to push right into the enemy's camp. A few years ago that would have been difficult. Owing to the work of the United Nations, however, new weapons have been put into the hands of the men who fight the illicit drug traffic. Anslinger telephoned the chief of the narcotics section of the Turkish police, then sent for Supervising Agent George White of the San Francisco field office. A few days later, in Istanbul, the Turkish police welcomed their American colleague. They briefed him on persons in the Turkish underworld who might be involved, on their habits and headquarters, warning that undercover men had a way of being found in the Bosporus with their throats cut.

Disguised as an American merchant sailor, White began frequenting waterfront bars. He dropped hints that he had money to spend, had connections in New York and was open to business if the profits were right. The scouts of the dope syndicate reacted almost at once. For more than a week he was put through a grueling inquisition. Questioned and cross-questioned by Turks who seemed to know a great deal about our underworld, he was aware that one slip would mean a quick bullet or a knife in the back. White's answers, based on an encyclopedic knowledge of our criminal elements, passed muster. He was finally taken to the Rue Cabristan café, where he met the four men he had come five thousand miles to catch. They agreed to let him have six thousand dollars' worth of heroin the next day.

The gangsters arrived at the appointed hour. White was to signal the ditch-digging police outside by raising the window shade when the deal was consummated. After endless delays and arguments the precious carton containing the drugs was produced. White said that he wanted to examine it in better light. And then—the shade stuck. White fought with it, too violently. The others reached for their guns, but the agent managed to draw first. At that moment the disturbed shade flew up with a bang, and the police pounded up the stairs. Other raiding squads converged on headquarters and plants of the gang in and near the city. It was a clean sweep, the biggest catch in Turkey in recent years.

Almost as soon as a gang in one of the drug capitals is knocked off, however, another takes its place. With heroin selling in New York or Paris for $300 to $600 an ounce, the returns for drug racketeers are high. A single shipment which U.S. customs inspectors found in the tail assembly of an airplane at La Guardia Airport would have been worth over a million dollars in the underworld retail trade.

When Charles Lucania (Lucky Luciano), former New York racketeer, was deported to Italy in 1946 after serving ten years in prison, he had big plans. In Rome he allied himself with the cream of Italian black-marketeers and arranged for a flow of drugs from the eastern Mediterranean. Then he obtained an Italian passport and permission to visit Cuba. In Havana the suave Signor Lucania began to establish contact with correspondents in Miami, New York and Chicago.

Actually the Narcotics Bureau knew his plans before he left Italy. They let him carry them out—up to a point—to see what contacts he would make. Then the commissioner suggested to Cuban authorities that Lucania be deported. Just as Lucky saw his dream of another empire coming true, Havana detectives appeared at his door one morning and asked him to pack; his plane was leaving shortly.

This swift and silent international coöperation often results in underworld catastrophes. The steward known as "Louis" was nervous as the S.S. *Santa Luisa* from South American ports steamed into Charleston harbor not long ago. He was carrying a big load this trip. The customs men made their usual careful search, apparently found no contraband, and cleared the ship. Louis was relieved. The next day he decided that the coast was clear. His runner, a newsboy, had come aboard and the two sauntered to the cleverly concealed cache in the forepeak. No one was around except a steam fitter, who seemed absorbed in his work. Quickly Louis opened the cache; the boy slipped several small bags into his clothing and shuffled off. The steward had just closed the compartment when he felt a hand on his shoulder. It was the steam fitter, but he had a badge. The newsboy found agents waiting for him at the foot of the gangplank.

Louis' cache had been under guard from the moment customs searchers had found it—not many minutes after they had come aboard. A message from narcotics men in a Latin-American country, who had been watching a big new syndicate that was building up a coastal trade, told Washington that the ship was "hot." They had not been able to identify the runner, however, and the Bureau wanted him. So, from the time the ship landed, narcotics and customs agents dressed as electricians, steam fitters and longshoremen took turns staying in sight of the cache until their quarry sprung the trap.

A nemesis to many a narcotics trafficker has been the International List of Narcotics Violators, which is kept up to date by the Bureau of Narcotics from reports sent in by other nations. Besides names and descriptions of all known illicit drug traders, the International List describes every unusual smuggling trick tried in recent years. There are some classics. An Egyptian syndicate discovered a new method of concealing narcotics in the camel trains which they dispatched across the Sahara Desert to Casablanca and Tangier. Metal capsules containing morphine and heroin, fed to a camel, would lodge in one of the storage compartments of his peculiar digestive system. Each animal could carry tens of thousands of dollars' worth of drugs. At the end of the journey the camels were killed, the capsules recovered. It was expensive transport, but the returns justified the investment.

Egyptian customs inspectors missed this trick until the price of camels went up sharply. Then an Egyptian officer investigating the phenomenon had a bright idea: he examined the camels by fluoroscope. The syndicate had to look for a new transportation scheme.

It takes time, infinite patience and ingenuity to build up an ironclad case against the shrewd operators catalogued in the International List. Take Joseph "Pip the Blind" Gagliano, for a long time No. 121 in the book. Several facts were known about him. His New York headquarters were modest—in the back room of a bar on East 107th Street. His runners smuggled in opium from Mexico, brought it to his secret New York factory to be converted into heroin. From there, dealers and peddlers fanned out across the country, did a huge business. Pip never handled dope himself and would discuss a deal only in his back room with no witnesses present.

A Bureau agent whom we'll call Jackson, after months of building himself up as a prosperous racketeer from the West Coast, finally succeeded in developing an acquaintance with the gangster. But to obtain a conviction he had to get Pip the Blind to hand over narcotics and accept payment—or order a man to do so—before witnesses.

Jackson drove up to the gang's headquarters one morning and honked his horn. One of the boss's musclemen responded to the summons. "I've got to see Pip," said Jackson. "Big deal. But I've banged up my leg. Can't walk on it." He exhibited a foot swathed in bandages;

crutches leaned against the seat. "Pip don't never talk to nobody on the street," the gunman replied. "But since it's you, I'll see what he says." The agent held his breath. Behind his seat, in a reconstructed baggage compartment, crouched another agent with his eyes at a peep slot from which he could see and hear anyone who came to the side of the car. Across the street, in an innocent-looking truck, were more agents and a camera.

Pip the Blind walked toward the car with his chief henchman. What he said in the next few minutes and the orders he gave his assistant sealed his doom. The next day Jackson and his helpers repeated the process with his two principal lieutenants. Police traps snapped shut from New York to the Mexican border. Pip the Blind later hanged himself in his cell.

Narcotics Bureau agents thus concluded another case—with quiet satisfaction. For, as the commissioner's executive officer said to me: "When you break a narcotics case, you not only nab some of the nastiest specimens in existence but you save a lot of people from a lot of misery. An ounce of cocaine sold in New York may account for a hop-headed holdup man who kills a peaceful citizen in Dallas or a doped-up driver who rams a school bus in Ohio."

A man walked into a Yonkers pharmacy and handed the druggist a doctor's prescription for a narcotic. The druggist took one look, asked the customer to return in the afternoon, then phoned the doctor. It turned out that the man had visited the doctor's office the day before. When his request for narcotics was refused, he stole a pad of prescription blanks and, after studying a book on the subject, forged the prescription. What had aroused the druggist's suspicions? "That prescription," said the druggist, "was too legible to have been written by a doctor." — *Theodore Irwin*

Bond of Reunion

By Carl Carmer

Tʜɪs sᴛᴏʀʏ was told me by my wife, one of the six young people who made the vow that night on the shore at Pascagoula. The other four surviving members of the group all corroborate the details of this extraordinary experience.

The four girls had been childhood neighbors and close friends. Two of them would graduate from college in New Orleans in the spring and after that there would be no more sun-drenched vacations at the rambling seaside home of Jane's mother. The two boys were Bud and Jimmie, Jane's brothers; they had grown up in Pascagoula, Mississippi, helping their widowed mother with her pecan orchards.

It was a starlit night at the end of summer. As the drift-wood fire lighted the weathered pillars of the house behind them and the line of shore ahead where dark ripples winked on white sand, the six young companions—who had parted in many previous Septembers with the knowledge that in the following June they would be together again beside Mississippi's Gulf waters—vowed that they would come back again to Pascagoula.

"The vow won't mean anything," said Jimmie, the youngest of the party, "unless each one of us leaves in this spot something that he likes."

"What do you like most of all?" said Bud.

"Why, the *Sparrow*," said Jimmie. They all looked toward the black outline of his catboat as she rocked at her mooring just offshore.

"The *Sparrow* is just like one of us," Elizabeth said thoughtfully. "We've sailed her over every drop of water for miles and miles around here. She's taken us swimming ever since we were little. We all love her as much—well, almost as much—as Jimmie does."

"Then why not let it be the boat that we leave here?" said Jimmie. "If we do that, each one of us will be leaving in Pascagoula the one thing that he loves most, and she'll make sure we'll be back—all of us—when the time comes."

The five who still live say that their vow was all but forgotten in the six years that followed. They were so scattered that a reunion had become impracticable. Elizabeth became my wife and came to live with me in New York. Of the other three girls, one was a social worker in Virginia, one was a housewife in Baton Rouge and Jane was teaching in a New Orleans school.

Then a letter brought each one of them a great sorrow. "Jimmie has been murdered," wrote his mother. "He took a load of pecans to New Orleans and left the truck there for repairs. On his way to the railroad station he was hit over the head and robbed by someone who must have seen him get the money for the pecans. He died, still unconscious, in Charity Hospital."

On reading this letter the girls were so overcome with

grief that the postscript made little impression on their
minds at the time, though they all remembered it later:
"The *Sparrow* has gone. On the day Jimmie died she
slipped her moorings and drifted away. Bud has looked
everywhere. He told the Coast Guard, and they searched
every inch of shore line but found no trace of her."

The end of this story occurred three years later. Elizabeth went to New Orleans for a minor operation. While
she was recovering, the social worker came home from
Virginia on her vacation and the Baton Rouge housewife
came downriver to visit Jane. Thus they were together
again, for the first time since the night of their vow nine
years before. A sunny Saturday found them motoring to
Pascagoula.

"It won't be the same without Jimmie," said Elizabeth.
"I don't know whether I can stand it."

When they reached the house, Jane's mother stood in
the doorway. Elizabeth jumped from the car and ran toward her, expecting the usual affectionate embrace. She
stopped, puzzled and hurt at seeing no gesture of welcome. The older woman was deathly pale, her arms hung
limp, and she shook with emotion.

"The *Sparrow* has come back!" she said. "She drifted in
only a few minutes ago, all covered with mud. She's down
there now, on the shore."

They looked—and saw the top of a little mast bobbing
up and down. Suddenly Bud, who had quietly come from
the house, was beside them, an older Bud whose eyes
seemed to burn with grief as he spoke: "Jimmie said that
when the time came, the *Sparrow* would see that we would
all be together again, and now she's done it. He's down
there—"

"*Don't say it!*" said Jane sharply—and they were all
silent in the shock of their inescapable surmise.

The Trial That Rocked the Nation

By John T. Scopes

A BUZZ ran through the crowd as I took my place in the packed courtroom in the little town of Dayton, Tennessee, on that sweltering July day in 1925. Seated near me at the defense table was my chief counsel, the famous criminal lawyer Clarence Darrow. Opposite us, languidly waving a palm-leaf fan, sat the prosecution's star, William Jennings Bryan, the silver-tongued orator, three times the Democratic nominee for President and leader of the fundamentalist movement which had brought about my trial.

A few weeks before, I had been an unknown high-school teacher in a little mountain town. Now I was involved in a trial reported the world over. Seated in the courtroom, ready to testify in my behalf, were a dozen distinguished professors and scientists, led by Professor Kirtley Mather of Harvard. More than a hundred reporters were on hand, and even radio announcers, who for the first time in history were to broadcast a jury trial.

"Don't worry, son, we'll show them a few tricks," Darrow whispered, throwing a reassuring arm around my shoulder as the judge ascended the bench.

The case had erupted around my head not long after I arrived in Dayton to teach science and coach football at the high school. For a number of years a clash had been building up between the fundamentalists and the modernists. The fundamentalists interpreted the Old Testament literally. The modernists, on the other hand, accepted the theory of the nineteenth-century English biologist Charles Darwin—that all animal life, including monkeys and men, had evolved from a common ancestor.

Fundamentalism was strong in Tennessee, and the state legislature had recently passed a law prohibiting the teaching of "any theory that denies the story of creation as taught in the Bible." The new law was aimed squarely at Darwin's theory of evolution. An engineer, George Rappelyea, used to sit around Robinson's drugstore and argue with the local people against the law. During one such argument, Rappelyea said that nobody could teach biology without teaching evolution. Since I had been teaching biology, I was sent for.

"Rappelyea is right," I told them.

"Then you have been violating the law," druggist Robinson said.

"So has every other teacher," I replied. "Evolution is

explained in Hunter's *Civic Biology*, and that, of course, is our textbook."

Rappelyea thereupon made a suggestion. "Let's take this thing to court," he said, "and test the legality of it."

When I was indicted on May 7, no one, least of all I, anticipated that my case would snowball into one of the most famous trials in U.S. history. The American Civil Liberties Union announced it would take my case to the U.S. Supreme Court if necessary to "establish that a teacher may tell the truth without being sent to jail." Then Bryan volunteered to assist the state in prosecuting me. Immediately the renowned lawyer Clarence Darrow offered his services to defend me. Ironically, I did not know Darrow before my trial, but I had met Bryan when he addressed my college graduating class. I admired him, although I did not agree with his views.

By the time the trial began on July 10, our town of 1500 had taken on a circus atmosphere. The buildings along the main street were festooned with banners. The streets near the three-story red-brick courthouse sprouted with rickety stands selling hot dogs, religious books and watermelons. Evangelists set up tents to exhort the passersby. People from the surrounding hills, mostly fundamentalists, arrived to cheer Bryan against the "infidel outsiders." Among them was John W. Butler, the genial state legislator who had drawn up the anti-evolution law. Butler was a forty-nine-year-old farmer who, before his election, had never been out of the county he was born in.

The presiding judge was John T. Raulston, a florid-faced man who announced: "I'm jist a reg'lar mountaineer jedge." At the prosecution table with the aging and paunchy Bryan sat his son, also a lawyer, and Tennessee's brilliant young attorney-general, Tom Stewart. Besides the shrewd sixty-eight-year-old Darrow, my coun-

sel consisted of the handsome and magnetic trial lawyer
Dudley Field Malone, forty-three, and Arthur Garfield
Hays, quiet, scholarly and steeped in the law. In a trial
in which religion played a key role, Darrow was an agnostic, Malone a Catholic and Hays a Jew. My father had
come from Kentucky to be with me for the trial.

Judge Raulston called for a local minister to open the
session with prayer, and the trial began with the selection
of a jury. Of the twelve jurors, three said they had never
read any book except the Bible. One admitted he couldn't
read. My father growled, "That's one hell of a jury!"

After the preliminary sparring over legalities, Darrow
began his opening statement: "My friend the attorney-
general says that John Scopes knows what he is here for. I
know what he is here for, too. He is here because ignorance and bigotry are rampant, and it is a mighty strong
combination."

Bryan sat nibbling on his palm fan as Darrow walked
slowly around the baking courtroom. "Today it is the
public-school teachers," Darrow continued, "and tomorrow the private. Next, the magazines, the books, the
newspapers. After a while, it is the setting of man against
man and creed against creed until we are marching backward to the glorious age of the sixteenth century, when
bigots lighted fagots to burn the men who dared to bring
any intelligence and enlightenment and culture to the
human mind."

"That damned infidel," a woman whispered loudly as
he finished his address.

The following day the prosecution began calling witnesses against me. Two of my pupils testified, grinning
shyly at me, that I had taught them evolution, but added
that they had not been contaminated by the experience.
Howard Morgan, a bright lad of fourteen, testified that I

had taught that man was a mammal like cows, horses, dogs and cats.

"He didn't say a cat was the same as a man?" Darrow asked.

"No, sir," the youngster said. "He said man had reasoning power."

"There is some doubt about that," Darrow snorted.

After testimony was completed, Bryan rose to address the jury. The issue was simple, he declared. "The Christian believes that man came from above. The evolutionist believes he must have come from below." The spectators chuckled and Bryan warmed to his work. In one hand he brandished a biology text as he denounced the scientists who had come to Dayton to testify for the defense.

"The Bible," he thundered in his sonorous organ tones, "is not going to be driven out of this court by experts who come hundreds of miles to testify that they can reconcile evolution, with its ancestors in the jungle, with man made by God in His image and put here for His purpose as part of a divine plan."

As he finished, jaw outthrust, eyes flashing, the audience burst into applause and shouts of "Amen." Yet something was lacking. Gone was the fierce fervor of the days when Bryan had swept the Democratic convention like a prairie fire. The crowd seemed to feel that their champion had not scorched the infidels with the hot breath of his oratory as he should have.

Dudley Field Malone popped up to reply. "Mr. Bryan is not the only one who has the right to speak for the Bible," he observed. "There are other people in this country who have given up their whole lives to God and religion. Mr. Bryan, with passionate spirit and enthusiasm, has given most of his life to politics." Bryan sipped water as Malone's voice grew in volume. He appealed for intel-

lectual freedom, and accused Bryan of calling for a duel
to the death between science and religion. "There is never
a duel with the truth," he roared. "The truth always
wins—and we are not afraid of it. The truth does not
need Mr. Bryan. The truth is eternal, immortal and
needs no human agency to support it!" When Malone
finished there was a momentary hush. Then the courtroom broke into a storm of applause that surpassed that
for Bryan. I found myself pounding Malone on the back
of his damp jacket. But although Malone had won the oratorical nod over Bryan, Judge Raulston ruled against
permitting the scientists to testify for the defense.

When court recessed, we found Dayton's streets swarm-
ing with strangers. Pitchmen hawked their wares on every
corner. One store announced: "Darwin Is Right—Inside."
(This was J. R. Darwin's Everything to Wear Store.) One
entrepreneur rented a store window to display an ape.
Spectators paid ten cents each to gaze at the simian and
ponder whether they might be related. "The poor brute
cowered in a corner with his hands over his eyes," West-
brook Pegler noted, "afraid it might be true." H. L.
Mencken wrote his sulfurous dispatches sitting in his
shorts with a fan blowing on him, and there was talk of
riding him out of town on a rail for referring to the local
citizenry as yokels. Twenty-two telegraphers were sending out 165,000 words a day on the trial.

Because of the heat and a fear that the old courthouse
floor might collapse under the weight of the throng, the
trial was resumed outside under the maples. More than
two thousand spectators sat on wooden benches or squatted on the grass, perched on the tops of parked cars or
gawked from the courthouse windows.

Then came the climax of the trial. Because of the wording of the anti-evolution law, the prosecution was forced

to take the position that the Bible must be interpreted literally. Now Darrow sprang his trump card by calling Bryan as a witness for the defense. Judge Raulston looked startled. "We are calling him as an expert on the Bible," Darrow said. "His reputation as an authority on Scripture is recognized throughout the world."

Bryan was suspicious of the wily Darrow, yet he could not refuse the challenge. For years he had lectured and written on the Bible. He had campaigned against Darwinism in Tennessee even before passage of the anti-evolution law. Resolutely he strode to the stand, carrying his palm fan like a sword to repel his enemies.

Under Darrow's quiet questioning he acknowledged believing the Bible literally, and the crowd punctuated his defiant replies with fervent "Amens."

Darrow read from Genesis: "And the morning and the evening were the first day." (This was a slight misreading—the words "evening" and "morning" were switched—but it appears this way in the trial transcript.) Then he asked Bryan if he believed that the sun was created on the fourth day. Bryan said that he did.

"How could there have been a morning and evening without any sun?" Darrow inquired. Bryan mopped his bald dome in silence. There were snickers from the crowd, even among the faithful. Darrow tugged on his lavender galluses and twirled his spectacles as he pursued the questioning. He asked if Bryan believed literally in the story of Eve. Bryan answered in the affirmative.

"And you believe that God punished the serpent by condemning snakes forever after to crawl upon their bellies?"

"I believe that."

"Well, have you any idea how the snake went before that time?"

The crowd laughed, and Bryan turned livid. His voice rose and the fan in his hand shook in anger.

"Your Honor," he said, "I will answer all Mr. Darrow's questions at once. I want the world to know that this man who does not believe in God is using a Tennessee court to cast slurs on Him. . . ."

"I object to that statement," Darrow shouted. "I am examining you on your fool ideas that no intelligent Christian on earth believes."

Judge Raulston gaveled the hubbub to a halt and adjourned court until next day. Bryan stood forlornly alone. My heart went out to the old warrior as spectators pushed by him to shake Darrow's hand.

The jury got the case at noon the following day. The jurymen retired to a corner of the courthouse lawn and whispered for just nine minutes. The verdict was guilty. Judge Raulston fined me $100 and costs.

Dudley Field Malone called my conviction a "victorious defeat." A few Southern papers, loyal to their faded champion, hailed it as a victory for Bryan. But Bryan, sad and exhausted, died in Dayton two days after the trial.

I was offered my teaching job back but I declined. Some of the professors who testified in my behalf arranged a scholarship at the University of Chicago so I could pursue the study of science. Later I became a geologist for an oil company in South America and Louisiana.

Not long ago I went back to Dayton for the first time since my trial thirty-five years before. The little town looked much the same to me. But now there is a William Jennings Bryan University overlooking the valley.

There were other changes, too. Evolution is taught in Tennessee, though the law under which I was convicted is still on the books. The oratorical storm which Clarence

Darrow and Dudley Field Malone blew up in the little courtroom in Dayton swept like a fresh wind through the schools and legislative halls of the country, bringing in its wake a new climate of intellectual and academic freedom that has grown with the passing years.

A lawyer of the old school in San Antonio, Texas, had a way with a jury. His voice would make the courthouse windows rattle, his flailing arms stirred up a breeze like an electric fan. One day, defending a damage suit, he put on a long, loud and impressive show. When he finally sat down, exhausted, his opponent rose to reply.

This lawyer loosened his collar, waved his arms, pounded with his fist and jumped up and down in front of the jury a full two minutes—never uttering a word. Then he buttoned his collar, smoothed his hair and said quietly: "Gentlemen of the jury, now that I have fully and completely answered the arguments of my learned opponent, I would like to discuss with you the facts in this case."   —*Clifford W. Potter*

While Dr. Hawkins was rector of Woodchester [England], gravediggers had brought up to the surface indubitable fragments of Roman mosaic; and Dr. Hawkins became convinced that there, waiting to be discovered, lay a Roman pavement. As he was anxious to bring it to light, his problem was how to do so in the face of local opposition to disturbing the bones of the dead whose descendants still lived in the parish.

What he did was very bold and very simple. He imported from a distance workmen vowed to secrecy, whom he paid well and hid in the rectory attic (supplied with food and drink) during the day. When at night he brought them forth to their nefarious job of circumventing pious prejudices, he himself played ghost and, standing on the churchyard wall in a sheet, frightened intruders away. And that is how the mosaic of Orpheus and the Beasts (a sample portion of which is now in the British Museum) came to be unearthed. —*Laurence Housman*

The Amazing Mr. Means

By J. Edgar Hoover with Courtney Ryley Cooper

EVEN the prison term at the end of his life did not divorce Gaston B. Means, one of the most amazing figures in recent criminal history, from his fraudulent activities. He kept sending me offers to solve the mysteries confronting the Federal Bureau of Investigation—if he could only get out for a while. We regarded him as the greatest faker of all time. Accusations against him, proved and unproved, ran all the way from murder and will forgery to the supreme fraud by which he obtained $104,000 on his promise to restore the Lindbergh baby.

Means was the son of a reputable lawyer of Concord, North Carolina. He attended the University of North Carolina but left it in 1900 without a degree. He became a small-town superintendent of schools under the less stringent requirements of those days, and then a traveling salesman. About 1915 he talked himself into a job with a New York detective agency; his qualifications were largely self-manufactured. Once assigned to a case, he would do little work other than mental gymnastics. His report would create so many clues, direct so much suspicion into divergent channels, that either his story had to be accepted or a crew of detectives assigned to untangle it. His stories were regarded as examples of efficient investigation. His fame spread.

On the eve of World War I, Means was asked to further Germany's cause in the United States. His career for the next three years was filled with plots and counterplots, sensational charges, lost documents and skulking spies. He discovered "mysteries" that he was hired to solve at a salary of $100 a day. Just when he had really warmed to the task, America went to war and Means became a private detective again.

Soon, however, another big opportunity loomed. The widow of a wealthy lumberman had fallen into the clutches of a European swindler. Her family appealed to the detective agency for which Means worked. Means circumvented the villain and assisted the widow with her business affairs. Then, in an old tin box the widow had given him he found a crumpled paper. He summoned the family.

"I've found a new will—which bequeaths practically the whole estate to my client!"

"Is it genuine?" they asked.

"That," said the amazing Mr. Means, "will have to be investigated."

He got together a staff which consisted of his brother, his brother's wife, his brother's father-in-law and his own father-in-law. They investigated and investigated—for two years. Meanwhile, Means gained more and more of a hold on the widow's finances. At last, with practically every cent gone, the widow went out shooting rabbits with him one day. Friends with them heard him calling frantically, crying that she had shot herself. They brought her body back. A jury in his hometown acquitted him in fifteen hours.

There remained the will, in which Means had a substantial interest. It was declared a forgery. A trial of the case went steadily against him. Any other man might have withdrawn as best he could. Not Means. He was determined to prove his high character. So he decided to perform a service for the government. He told high-ranking Army officers a weird story about the existence of a trunk crammed with documents obtained from the German spy organization. He would get that trunk. All he asked in return was recognition of his great feat, addressed to the trial judge. An intelligence officer was detailed to go south with Means.

After many mysterious comings and goings, Means produced a trunk and suggested that it be sent north intact. Then, with the baggage check, he rushed back to Washington to get that letter of recommendation. He insisted that he had delivered the documents and that the Army should pay its debt. In the midst of the argument, the trunk arrived—but the documents were gone. Means stormed and strode about. He knew exactly who had done this despicable thing. He would find the scoundrels and recover the papers—that is, he would if only he could get that letter to the judge. But the Army investigated and found that the weight of the trunk when sent was the same as when received. So Means washed his hands of the whole affair.

The forgery case dragged on, but Means did not again enter the jurisdiction of the court. Then came an election, and the head of the detective agency for which the fictioneer had worked was made director of the Federal Bureau of Investigation. A gasp ran through the organization when, in October 1921, we learned that one of our co-workers was to be Gaston B. Means.

Presently word went through the underworld that a man in the Department of Justice could "fix things." Envoys from the bootleg rings sought him out. If they questioned his authority, Means would suggest a conference at his house. He would arrive, all in a dither, greet his visitor and then inquire of his secretary: "Any calls?"

"Yes. Senator Blank called, and the Attorney-General, and the Secretary of State. And the White House."

By the time Means had "answered" his calls, the underworld visitor would be convinced that he really ran the nation.

"You see," he would explain, "I'm a great friend of the President. I know everybody in the Cabinet. And I'm on close terms with the National Committee. Now, the Committee is a little short of funds, so if you'll just pay me so much a barrel, I'll see that you get all the whiskey you want."

After paying amounts running into thousands of dollars, the whiskey man would wait and wait, while the great Mr. Means was "called" here and there about the country on his official duties, with no time to spend on opening liquor warehouses. Naturally, his "clients" hesitated to make a complaint, but rumors of his activities permeated Washington. Finally, the Attorney-General stepped in and ended Means's mad career as an agent.

The Teapot Dome scandal had just broken and Means immediately turned his dishonor to his own ends. His name flashed across the front pages. He was telling, before a senatorial committee, the "inside story of a crooked Administration." He "confessed" to handling tremendous bribes for high Administration officials. The country was being sold out, said Gaston Means, and he knew the name and address of every despoiler. The committee asked for documents. He promised to produce them the next day.

But he came empty-handed, and, when asked for the papers, he said that the sergeants at arms had them. The officers denied it. Means appeared nonplussed. "Strange," he said. "Two sergeants at arms of the Senate appeared at my house last night with this order and took the documents away with them."

The committee head examined the paper bearing his purported signature. "That's a forgery," he announced. Means leaped from his chair. "Forgery! I've been tricked by my enemies. I'll run them down—if it's the last thing I do."

But Means never got around to it. There were so many other things to do—among them, trying to keep out of the penitentiary. With others, he went on trial for conspiracy to violate the Volstead Act. He gave a weird defense, claiming to be a tool of "higher interests," but he was sentenced to two years in Atlanta.

We thought we had put Means away where he would cease to bother. Means had a different idea. He began writing me letters, promising, in return for favors, to "solve" a tremendous conspiracy in diamond and whiskey smuggling and a dozen other plots. Then he became dangerously ill, and begged to get out so that he could die in the bosom of his family.

While he suffered this approaching death, a woman interested in prison welfare visited Atlanta. Means forgot his illness. Would this woman care to hear the inside facts about the President's death? Thus came into being that horrible hoax, *The Strange Death of President Harding*, which the honest woman who had been victimized repudiated shortly after publication.

Means also repudiated it, somewhat gleefully. He had collected his royalties and now had found a new set of victims, a group of men in New York interested in alleged subversive Soviet activities. Means, just out of prison, knew all there was to know on that subject. Did they realize that two most dangerous Russian secret agents were in America with $2,000,000 to spend on destruction? If these gentlemen cared to have him make an investigation lasting about six weeks—at $100 a day—he was sure he could bring these two fiends to justice and, furthermore, capture twenty-four trunks and eleven suitcases full of secret orders, plans and diaries. The investigation dragged out for three years. Time after time Means almost got those trunks and suitcases. Once a sponsor paid $25,000 to get the documents from imaginary foes who had held Means prisoner in a mountain cabin. Means got the papers, but, in returning them to New York, the inevitable happened. The dreaded secret agents stole them back again!

The wilder the story became, the more his sponsors trusted him, one of them spending his entire life's savings. Finally, Means burst in upon his employers with the news that one of the Russians had murdered the other and that all the documents had been burned. Means told his story with such attention to detail that warrants were actually sworn out against a nonexistent killer for a murder that happened only in the imagination of Gaston B. Means. The great sleuth followed the slayer; several times he almost had him. Then suddenly his interest lagged. Colonel Lindbergh's baby had been kidnaped.

Immediately he sought several rich men and told them of a strange coincidence. A former Atlanta convict had approached him in a speakeasy and asked him to take part in the kidnaping. He had refused, but he knew the whereabouts of the baby. Perhaps he could establish contact. While the rich men pondered, Mrs. Evalyn Walsh McLean sent for Means and, without knowing of his claims, told him that since he was a crook and knew the underworld, he should be of assistance in finding the baby. Means set forth at once to "contact the kidnaper." Back he came, announcing that the baby stealers wanted $100,000.

Then began a fabulous chase. Following his usual pattern, he worked with a confederate who telephoned Mrs. McLean from time to time, telling of his difficulties. Finally, Means promised to deliver the baby at a Southern resort. Mrs. McLean went there. Means appeared with a confederate who posed as "King of the Kidnapers," and who, after mysterious talk and actions, told her how and when the baby would be restored. But nothing happened. The telephone calls began again. By this time everyone was designated by code. Means was No. 27, the King, No. 19; Mrs. McLean, No. 11; the baby was The Book.

Now, it seemed, hijackers were after the baby. Then the King complained that Means had placed two gunmen on his trail. Means said that the King was trying to double-cross him. Finally Means made a demand for $35,000 in addition to the $100,000 he had received plus $4000 expense money. Failing to raise it, Mrs. McLean thought the matter over and demanded that Means return all the money. Hurt, but bowing to the inevitable, Means agreed. He would get it at once. He hurried away—and did not come back. After a time a friend of the McLean family went to Means and demanded the money. Means displayed the greatest surprise: "Didn't Mrs. McLean get it? She must have it. Her messenger met me at the bridge outside Alexandria as I was returning to Washington. He said, 'I am No. 11.' So what was I to do? I gave him the money." Only Gaston Means knew where that $104,000 is hidden, and the secret has died with him. Perhaps the money is concealed with many other thousands he collected in his life of fraud. Or it may be, as some said, that he spent it all and there is no treasure cache to be found anywhere—Means's final triumph of deception.

He got fifteen years for the Lindbergh hoax, and from prison continued his fabulous lies, all with the purpose of creating sympathy. When one wild story failed, he could always try another. Nor was he shamed by being called a liar. During Means's trial for the Lindbergh hoax he testified in his own defense, and after he had finished his fantastic tale he sat down beside me. "Well, Hoover," he asked, "what did you think of that?"

"Gaston," I answered, "it was a pack of lies."

"Well," he said seriously, "you've got to admit it made a whale of a good story!"

Gaston Means's many attempts to shorten his prison term for the Lindbergh hoax were unsuccessful. He would have been eligible for parole in 1943, but he became ill and died—of complications following a gallbladder operation—on December 12, 1938.

Indiana's Governor Matthew E. Welsh informed an audience that, despite problems, strides are being made in certain areas, including education. He was informed by the Department of Correction of a reformatory prisoner who, while serving a term for armed robbery, was taught to read and write in the institution's education program. "Now he's serving a term for forgery," concluded the governor. "And I say this is progress."

—*Roger Allen*

A Killer Is Loose

By Joseph P. Blank

As THE residents of Jerseyville, a town of 7500 people in southwestern Illinois, started about their daily affairs on the mild, sunny Friday morning of October 9, 1959, alarming news wildfired among them: a cold-blooded killer was hiding somewhere in their area.

The twenty-one-year-old killer, James Gordon Palmer, was a Jerseyville man. Police Chief Herman Blackorby described him as "a nice-looking, nice-talking boy who didn't mind killing you." In a ramble through Missouri, Illinois and Tennessee he had robbed and murdered a bait-shop owner, a young waitress and a filling-station attendant. He had fired bullets into the backs of their heads—in the case of two of them, while they lay face down on the floor—until they stopped moving.

On the night of October 8, sheriff's deputies had spotted Palmer as he drove up to his Jerseyville apartment. He raced them to the outskirts of town, jumped from his car and escaped into a cornfield. An hour later he shot and wounded a railroad brakeman shining a lantern near a ditch where he lay hidden.

Now more than a hundred police, state troopers and sheriff's deputies had converged on Jerseyville. They put bloodhounds around the spot where Palmer had fled, but the dogs couldn't pick up a scent. They patrolled all roads and searched hundreds of buildings. Each school bus carried an armed policeman. A helicopter and four small planes kept crisscrossing nearby farmlands. Radio broadcasters warned listeners to lock their doors. Police feared that Palmer might massacre an isolated farm family to steal a car. As the hours passed, the people of Jerseyville grew increasingly jumpy. By afternoon sporting-goods stores had sold out their supplies of guns and ammunition. Several farm families drove into town to stay at the hotel. One woman, hearing a noise in the basement, riddled her kitchen floor with buckshot.

In the squat brick building that housed the two office rooms of Gorman Brothers' Construction Company on Franklin Street, business continued as usual. But that evening Louis Gorman found his wife and two children frightened. Gorman, a quiet and gentle man, fifty-two and graying, tried to reassure them. "Palmer is probably well on his way to Mexico by now," he said.

Nevertheless, he slept restlessly. He arose before five, dressed and drove down to Sandy's Café, where he drank coffee and talked with two men from a posse that had searched for Palmer through the night. Then, shortly after seven, Gorman drove to the office. Two truck drivers, Charles Kroeschel and his son-in-law, Robert Cordes, arrived at the same time.

When Gorman put his key into the lock he found it unlocked. He made a mental note to remind his men to check the doors before leaving at night. Entering the building, Gorman went to the washroom. He saw that the glass pane in the rear door had been broken and covered with cardboard, but he assumed that one of his men had broken the window on the previous day. Meanwhile, Charlie Kroeschel walked around the counter in the outer office, stepped into the inner office—and was confronted by a man pointing a .22-caliber semi-automatic rifle. Kroeschel's mouth fell open. He backed away, repeating incredulously, "Louie, he's here. That guy is *here*."

Palmer, tall, lean, blond, with a boyish face, said, "Do as I tell you and you won't get killed. Sit down on the floor of the inside office and don't move." Kroeschel and Cordes obeyed.

Gorman, in the washroom, heard Kroeschel's astonished words. Quickly he opened the washroom window, but he couldn't push out the screen. Palmer banged on the door and said, "Are you coming out or will I have to shoot you through the door?" Gorman came out.

"Sit down with your buddies," Palmer directed, then asked the trio if the owner of the business was among them. Gorman answered. The killer nodded toward him and said, "Open the safe, brother."

"I can't," Gorman said. "It's a tricky combination lock and our office manager, Ernie Pohlman, is the only one who knows how to open it."

"Brother, you're lying," Palmer said evenly. "I've got a notion to kill you right now." He moved his rifle.

"I'm not lying. Ernie will open the safe when he comes in." Gorman later admitted he was scared. He had no way of knowing at what point a twisted whim might prompt the killer to start shooting.

At that moment truck driver Edward Fitzgibbons drove his pickup to the back of the building. Palmer crouched behind the service counter. Fitzgibbons, noticing the broken pane in the rear door, ambled into the office saying, "Hey, it looks like somebody broke in here."

Palmer rose from behind the counter, his gun leveled. "And I'm still here," he announced. "You just sit down on the floor there with your buddies." Fitzgibbons did so.

The next captive was William Kuehnel, a railroad engineer for the local freight line, who dropped in to tell Gorman that a car of cement had arrived. The engineer was followed by Herschel Andrews, a construction-equipment operator, and then truck driver Darrell Smith.

Ernie Pohlman was a little late that morning. Reluctant to leave his wife and three children in the house six miles out in the country, he had stayed to show his wife how to fire his shotgun. His first sensation when confronted by Palmer was relief: at least he knew his family was safe.

When Pohlman identified himself, Palmer said, "Just the man. Open the safe, Ernie."

Pohlman knelt before the safe, which for a long time had been difficult to open. He twirled the knob. He failed on the first try. He failed again. In a warning tone Palmer said, "Ernie!" Again Pohlman muffed the combination. Palmer said, "Ernie, I'll give you one more minute. If you don't open that safe, you're a dead man."

"Take your time, Ernie," Gorman urged. "A minute's a long time."

Pohlman's face was white and wet with sweat. He carefully turned the dial again, heard the tumblers click and slumped with relief. He dumped the contents of the money box on the floor. Palmer nodded to Bill Kuehnel and said, "Now, sir, I want you to get the bills from the wallets and put all the money into that paper bag."

When Kuehnel had completed his task, Gorman said to Palmer, "You've got all we can give you. Why don't you take off?"

Palmer ignored the suggestion and stared at the men for a minute. "Brother," he said to Gorman, "write out a

sign saying 'Closed till 1 p.m.' and put it on the window
of the front door." Palmer seemed to have a plan in mind.

Gorman penciled the words on a rectangle of cardboard. As he taped the sign to the door window he saw a
man step onto the porch of the house across the street. He
kept rubbing the sign, hoping to attract the man's attention. But Palmer grew aware of his excess motions and
said, "Brother, you're having a hard time with that sign.
Get away from there." Each time Palmer gave an order,
he moved the rifle decisively.

Palmer then addressed the group: "Do any of you have
a knife?" Nobody answered. To Kuehnel, he said, "Take
a piece of glass, sir, and cut that telephone wire." Palmer
seemed to enjoy using the word "sir" in giving orders.

After Kuehnel had cut the cord Palmer asked, "Is there
any rope around here?" Again nobody answered, al-

though Gorman and his employes knew there was rope in the shed behind the building.

To Gorman, Palmer repeated, "Is there any rope?"

"On top of that elevator outside." Gorman pointed to the elevated sand-and-gravel bin and cement chute about forty feet away. A wood ladder rose from the ground to the top of the bin where two lengths of rope dangled.

Palmer spoke to Kuehnel. "You, sir, get up that ladder and bring down a rope." As Kuehnel started out, Palmer said, "Wait! It might not look right unless it was the owner." He nodded at Gorman. "Better if you did it, brother."

He ordered the seven other men to lie on their bellies, face to the floor and hands behind their backs. "Not a false move out of any of you," he warned, "or your boss'll get it." He posted himself at the door and told Gorman to climb the ladder and get the rope. "And if you try anything funny, there are going to be a lot of dead men in here."

Gorman climbed the ladder. As he began fooling with the rope, he stood close to the top edge of the sand bin. He wanted terribly to be free of Palmer. "I could roll into the sand bin and Palmer could never hit me," he thought. "Then I'd yell for help. Maybe when the men heard me they could make a break for it. But, no, Palmer would start shooting." Gorman gathered up the rope and climbed down.

In the office, Palmer told Gorman to tie the men's hands behind their backs as they lay face down on the floor. First in line was Kuehnel. As the railroad man felt the rope go around his wrists he resigned himself to death. "I figured this was my time," he later recalled. "I knew he was going to shoot us."

Palmer tested the knot and said, "Brother, you tie a

loose knot. If I find another knot like that, I'm going to
shoot the man through the head."

Gorman retied the knot. Then he bound Fitzgibbons'
wrists. "As the seven of us lay there," Fitzgibbons said
later, "I swear I felt the floor vibrate from our heart-
beats." Gorman was feeling sick at the thought that he
was tying up the men so that Palmer could shoot them
while helpless. This was the killer's pattern, he knew.

After Gorman had tied the wrists of the next man,
Darrell Smith, Palmer said, "Three down and four to go.
When they're all tied up I'll have to shoot them through
the head." On the floor the silent men lay tense as boards,
listening to the blood pound in their ears, waiting for the
shots.

"I was never more scared in my life," Gorman later recalled, "but I knew I had to do something. If I lunged at
Palmer I'd probably get a bullet in the head. If I simply
obeyed him, I'd still get the bullet in the head and so
would the seven other men."

Palmer sat alertly on his haunches, his rifle muzzle following Gorman's every move. Gorman, about seven feet
away, knew that if he tied up the fourth man he'd be a
step farther away from the killer. He had to contrive a
means of getting closer.

During his seventy-five minutes of captivity Gorman
had noticed that whenever Palmer rose from his haunches
he invariably pointed his rifle at the ceiling before bringing it to bear on his victims. If attacked, would Palmer
stick to this habit, giving his assailant an added fraction of
a second—or would he fire from his haunched position?

Gorman said, "Their legs are too jammed together for
me to step between them."

"Then step on their legs, brother. They won't be hurting for long."

"I'll be able to do a better job if I can work from around their heads," Gorman said. This would put him a little closer to Palmer.

"You have my permission," Palmer said.

Then Gorman had a sudden idea, felt his guts twist in fear, and acted. He stepped between the second and third man and, without haste, pretended to stumble. He tottered, then, in a seeming effort to regain his balance, stepped over the second man, moving closer to Palmer. To make the action seem innocent he stepped *backward*, giving the killer a clear shot at his back. Again Gorman took a step backward, over the remaining man between him and Palmer.

The killer hesitated a moment, then—following habit—rose from his haunches, pointing the rifle toward the ceiling. In the split moment it took Palmer to bring the rifle down, Gorman was next to him and felt the gun barrel on his shoulder. He swung his left fist at the trigger guard, scraping the skin off his knuckles as he knocked the gun from Palmer's hands. Then, with all his power, he shot his right fist at Palmer's jaw. The killer went down, and Gorman fell on him. Palmer groped for the gun six inches away. Gorman jammed a knee on his wrist and hit him again, yelling, "Come on, boys!"

Galvanized into action, the four free men dived at Palmer. As they subdued him, contractor Ralph Russell came in the door. Hearing the scuffling and exclamations, he peered over the counter and said, "What's going on, a crap game this time of the morning?"

One of the men looked up and grunted, "Palmer!" Charlie Kroeschel ran to the nearest telephone. In three minutes the sheriff's car skidded to a halt in front of the office. Deputies handcuffed Palmer, now meek and whimpering a little, and hauled him away. It was all over.

Gorman and the seven men stood staring at one another. The thought of what might have happened was coursing through each of them like an electric shock. Gorman looked at his bloody hand. Then, in a dazed but businesslike tone he said, "Okay, boys, we've got concrete to haul."

That broke the spell. Almost in chorus, the four truck drivers demanded, "Who the hell is going to haul it?"

Gorman felt a flush of relief, and grinned. "This morning," he said, "I guess nobody is."

For his brave action Louis Gorman received the Silver Medal of the Carnegie Hero Fund Commission. Palmer is serving a 180-year prison term and will not be out—unless paroled—until 2020, when he will be eighty-two.

Some years ago a group of Army intelligence officers walked into the office of Ellis Parker, widely known detective of Mount Holly, New Jersey. A sergeant at Camp Dix had disappeared three months before; they had just discovered his body in a clump of bushes. He had been murdered; but time and weather had obliterated all clues. Parker established the fact that the victim must have been slain by one of 175 men in his own company.

The next step was to question each as to his actions on the day of the sergeant's disappearance. Only ten were able to give a detailed account. Parker ignored those who had no alibis, but he interviewed again the ten men who knew all their movements on that day three months before. This time nine became involved in contradictions. The tenth was still sure of his actions—the day of the murder, the day before, the day after. So Parker knew he had his murderer. Nobody could normally remember that much about his actions on three consecutive days three months before. (Try it—what were *your* movements three months ago today?)

Parker then found enough material evidence to force a confession. The sergeant, it seemed, had been a small-scale loan shark. To wipe out a debt, the prisoner had wiped out the sergeant.

—Fletcher Pratt

One Alaska Night

Condensed from the book Alaska Holiday
By Barrett Willoughby

A ROOT tripped me and threw me flat on the forest
trail. I lay for a moment, face on my arms, too
tired to stir. I had been foolhardy to start out alone on a
ten-mile hike across an unfamiliar Alaska peninsula.

For some time I had been breasting through the brush,
which met thinly above my trail, but had failed to take
this as a warning that something was wrong. Now, nose
to the ground, I became aware of a rank, musky odor and
of something queerly crawling that touched my cheek.
It was a tuft of coarse brown hair, dangling from a twig.

One startled glance and I knew it had been raked from
an Alaskan brown bear—the largest carnivorous animal
that walks the world today. Earlier in the afternoon I had
seen an enormous track in a patch of damp clay beside
my path. The imprint, from heel to claws, was twice the
length of my boot. The truth came with a shock—I had
been following a bear trail, not a path traveled by man.

I'm not a hunter. I'm not even a brave woman. Early
that morning I had left town in a boat with some fishermen and had reached the vicinity of a fox ranch, where

a schoolmate of mine, Lonnie, was spending the summer with her father, who owned the place. This part of Alaska was strange to me; but the fishermen pointed out a trail crossing the peninsula to the ranch. I persuaded them to put me ashore so that I might walk over while they fished. They were to call for me in the evening on their way home.

Now I was lost on a bear trail. Panic came upon me. I had an almost uncontrollable impulse to dash madly through the trees regardless of direction. But I got hold of myself, decided on a course and went forward.

I was nearly exhausted when I burst through the timber and saw a log cabin in the middle of a small, wild meadow. There was something sinister about that cabin. The boarded windows on each side of the closed door stared back at me like eye sockets in a brown and weathered skull. I turned to go back, but after one glance into that black forest I changed my mind.

At the edge of the dooryard I came upon a stump on whose broad top was a crosshatch of axe marks. I moved on to the cabin and paused before the closed door. There was a rawhide latch-thong hanging outside. I gave it a pull, and the creaking door swung in of itself, revealing an interior so dark I could distinguish no detail. The room gave off the faint rancid odor that clings to a place in which raw furs have been dried. I bumped against a crude table and my outflung hand encountered a candle. I struck a match and turned to inspect my shelter.

In one corner was a rusty stove, in another a stout pole frame laced with strips of cured bearskin to make a bunk. There was a chair and a steel bear trap with a broken jaw. Nothing to alarm even the most timorous woman.

As I raked ashes from the stove, I searched my memory for all I knew of this region. The first thing that came to mind was the story of five prospectors who, a few years before, had vanished without a trace. Rumor said they had met with foul play at the hands of a crazy trapper, "Cub Bear" Butler. I glanced uneasily over my shoulder, wishing I hadn't thought about that. Axe in hand, I went out to the chopping block to cut firewood. A large blood-gold moon, just topping the hemlocks, threw long tree shadows across the meadow. Each blow of my axe rang out unnaturally loud. My sense of isolation deepened.

I chopped an armload and was reaching for the last stick when my groping fingers touched something which made me recoil violently. I struck a match—and stood transfixed with horror. It was a fleshless skeleton hand, severed at the wrist. Then I saw another, and another—ten

altogether. There wasn't a bone of any other kind. I tried
to scream, but could make no sound. I tried to run,
but my legs turned to water. Somehow I got back inside
the cabin and shoved the door shut. The fastening was
a sturdy wooden bar. I pulled the latch-thong inside.
The door was strong and no one could enter. I was
hollow with dread and my hands trembled so I could
scarcely build the fire. My mind kept swirling about
Cub Bear Butler, the crazy trapper, and the five prospectors who had vanished. Had I stumbled onto Butler's
cabin? Could those skeleton hands belong to the five
prospectors?

I didn't intend to go to sleep, but gradually fatigue
began to triumph over nerves.

I don't know what awakened me; but suddenly I
found myself sitting bolt upright, heart pounding, ears
straining, eyes wide open. Some sound had penetrated
my sleep. I was about to light the candle when it came
again: *Thump!* . . . *Thump-thump-thump!* Someone knocking to get in!

The stillness tightened around me. I put from me the
thought of a dead man with no hands and tried to convince myself that the knocking had been born of my over-
wrought nerves when—*Thump!* . . . *Thump-thump-thump!*
The sound seemed as if the visitor were knocking not
with firm knuckles but with the fleshy stub of an arm.
Leaden with fright, I managed to reach the door and
press my ear against it.

"What do you want?"

Silence.

I lifted the bar, flung open the door and looked out.
Nothing; neither movement nor sound. Puzzled as well as
frightened, I went back inside.

No sooner had I dropped the bar in place than it came

again—*Thump! . . . Thump-thump-thump!* I jerked open the door. I ran around the cabin, scrutinizing every inch of the meadow, bright with moonlight. The nearest cover, a tall hemlock, was fifty feet away. Nothing human could have traversed that distance so quickly. Only one thing knocks and remains invisible to mortal eyes!

I kindled a roaring blaze just outside the door and sat on the threshold to watch the clearing. After a while I began to nod.

I woke with a start, thinking I heard someone calling my name. The morning sun flooded the clearing. Then I saw a slim, blonde young woman in breeches and a windbreaker running across the meadow toward me. It was Lonnie, my friend of the fox ranch, and behind her strode her father, a lean sourdough Alaskan. I could have rushed upon them and fallen to embrace their knees, but pride kept me from betraying myself to the quizzical eyes of her father, already on the alert for some sign of feminine asininity.

"Dad had a fit when you failed to show up last night," said Lonnie, "and sent ranch hands to search the woods as soon as daylight came."

"A woman," declared Dad, "should never go into the woods alone. Women have no bump of location. They're always getting lost. You can thank your lucky star you stumbled onto Butler's cabin."

"It's not only women who get lost," I retorted. "How about those five prospectors who disappeared in these woods a few years ago?"

"Oh, those chaps! It's likely they were drowned off the Cape."

"No they weren't," I said quietly. "They were killed— murdered—right here at Butler's cabin."

"What are you staring at now, Sis?" Dad broke in on my concentration.

"Those marks on the door."

He laughed. "You must have been pretty excited when you got here last night—knocking that hard."

As we were walking away I glanced back at the cabin in which I had spent the most terrifying night of my life—and at the marks on the door. I knew that my two small fists had never made them. For I had never knocked on the door of that grim, deserted cabin in the clearing.

The *Mary Celeste* sailed from New York to Genoa in November 1872. The master was a man with a splendid reputation both as a mariner and a gentleman, and his family was with him. The ship made a good passage at first; early in December two vessels recorded in their logs that they had sighted her three hundred miles off Gibraltar. Then, on December 5, the captain of a British brigantine that fell in with her noted that her course was queer and sent a boarding party over to see if she needed help.

On deck all was silent. Not a living thing was in sight—nor a dead one. The visitors called out but got no response. Every soul aboard had simply disappeared. The ship was in perfect condition. The cargo was well stored and in good order. There was plenty of food and water aboard. The cash box was intact. In the forecastle were the seamen's chests and clothing, dry and undisturbed. Some underclothes had been hung out to dry; in the mate's cabin was a piece of paper with an unfinished sum on it. A child's dress was still in the sewing machine, and there were four half-eaten breakfasts on the table.

The *Mary Celeste*'s lifeboat hung on its davits. There was no sign of violence, nor of any sort of trouble. The ship's papers and chronometer were the only articles of importance that were gone. The ship's log contained not a hint of tragedy. There was not a clue that might lead to the solution of the riddle of where those two-score people had gone, and to this day there has never been a word which threw sensible light on the extraordinary mystery.   — *The Log of Bob Bartlett*

Life and Death
of a Twisted Genius

By Lester Velie

O NE JANUARY day in 1955, newspapers the world over used their blackest type to proclaim a murder that was a sensation on three continents. It was the flamboyant death of a flamboyant man, forty-six-year-old Serge Rubinstein.

In Tokyo, in London, in Toronto, Paris, Zurich and New York, men had reason to remember Rubinstein. From Japan he had smuggled out close to a million dollars' worth of closely guarded yen to explode a currency crisis. In England he had seized a great mining corporation without investing a shilling, then filched its assets from under the noses of Great Britain's shrewdest money men. In New York he had amassed $5,000,000 in less than eight years, despite Securities Exchange Commission charges of fraud and lawsuits by outraged investors.

Had you told Rubinstein that this made him a historic cheat on the scale of a Charles Ponzi or a John Law of Mississippi Bubble fame, he would have parted his sensuous lips in a roar of happy laughter. To himself Rubinstein was one of the great financial geniuses of his time.

But he lived by his own rules. This didn't apply just to making millions. He lived the love life of a shah. On the day he died he had lunch with one lady friend, dinner with another, and at 2 a.m. was calling for further female companionship. He'd fly off for weekends in Miami Beach or Montreal, taking not just one girl but three.

A stocky man, with piercing green-gray eyes and a shrill voice, Rubinstein lived like a grand duke. Winters he spent in his six-story Fifth Avenue mansion in New York, summers in a home in Beverly Hills. He gave three grand balls yearly and would invariably tog himself out as Napoleon—with cowlick plastered over his high forehead in striking resemblance. Another pose he liked was that of a Russian noble, and during winter he would affect an ankle-length, mink-lined and mink-collared greatcoat, old-Moscow style.

Rubinstein's murder posed a mystery which the police couldn't solve. In his richly carpeted bedroom, with its marble-manteled fireplace and satin-canopied bed, a police inspector thumbed in amazement through the slain man's address books. They contained two thousand names. Great bankers were in them, and call girls; respected lawyers, and blackmailers; judges, playboys, headwaiters, press agents and mistresses. Somewhere in those two thousand names, probably, was the name of the murderer. "Where do you start with this man?" agonized the police inspector. . . .

Serge Rubinstein was born in St. Petersburg (Leningrad) in 1908. His father had made a fortune as a banker under the czars, and the Rubinsteins lived in opulence. Then in 1918, with the rise of the Bolsheviks, they fled from Russia, wandering through Europe and settling eventually in Paris. At eighteen Serge was resolved to remake the fortune his father once had. But first he knew he must train his mind. He could already speak Russian, English, French, Swedish and German, but he didn't have the Latin that would open his way to a European university education. Rubinstein went to London, locked himself in a boardinghouse room with a Latin dictionary, Caesar's *Commentaries* and other texts. In three months he had taught himself the Latin he needed to enter Cambridge. The brain that could turn this trick easily sopped up—in three years—all the economics the professors could teach. So dazzling a student was he that John Maynard Keynes, England's top money authority, told him: "You'll be one of the world's great financial figures."

At twenty-one, laden with scholastic honors, Rubinstein got a job with the Banque Franco-Asiatique in Paris, as a clerk. Within a few months he was its managing director. His first move was to staff the bank with White Russian refugees whom he felt he could trust. The boy banker then discovered a chain of restaurants in whose till were francs worth about $450,000. Control could be bought for $60,000. Rubinstein helped himself to $60,000 of his depositors' money, moved in on the restaurant chain and used its assets to gamble in the international money market. He manipulated the French franc into such a tailspin that the government ordered him deported. He took a nice profit with him.

Back in England, Rubinstein launched the moves which made him a multimillionaire in his twenties. Here is how he did it: Rubinstein received a proposition from an accused English swindler who controlled the board of a mining firm, the Chosen Corporation, with properties in Korea. The accused faced jail because of illegal deals in the shares of his own company. Would Rubinstein buy a block of 173,000 shares at a price that might help the accused promoter beat the swindle rap? Rubin-

stein was glad to, since it cost him no money. For the
173,000 shares he gave Chosen a "deposit"—a bookkeeping entry—in his Banque Franco-Asiatique in Paris.
The bank didn't have the money, of course, but this didn't
matter. When the English swindler went to jail and
Rubinstein became the new managing director of Chosen,
he never troubled to claim his company's "deposit."

Rubinstein set himself up in regal style in a suite in the
posh Savoy Hotel. He invited London society, members of
Parliament and bigwigs from "The City" (London's Wall
Street) to lavish parties. They came to see this Russian-
born financial prodigy with the Cambridge accent and
the Parisian charm—and gave him the respectability he
needed to press his schemes further. Rubinstein then
brought over his cohorts from Paris and introduced them
to Chosen stockholders as an "important French syndicate" which wanted to invest in Chosen. The board of
directors obligingly sold Rubinstein and his pals another
150,000 shares, on a part-payment plan which Rubinstein
turned into a no-payment plan. So the control of the
Chosen Corporation and its six million dollars' worth of
Korean mining properties fell into Rubinstein's hands.

Rubinstein now headed for Japan, taking for companionship a Hungarian charmer who called herself the
Countess Natasha. There, in short order, he sold the
mines, formed a half-dozen dummy corporations and
transferred to them the proceeds of the sale—some
$3,500,000 in yen. But a problem arose. Japanese currency
couldn't leave the country in 1937. And while the Japanese government allowed Rubinstein to take out about
two thirds of the yen in British sterling, more than a million dollars' worth remained blocked. How to get it out?

About the waist Japanese women wear an obi—seven
yards of material which comes wrapped around a card-

board tube. A Rubinstein agent posing as a silk merchant bought a huge batch of obis. Then he stuffed close to $1,000,000 in 100-yen notes inside their cardboard cylinders—and sailed them safely past the noses of Japanese customs men. When Rubinstein unloaded his yen in San Francisco, St. Louis, Chicago and New York, the Japanese currency took a tumble from which it didn't recover for years. Of this coup the British stockholders of Chosen knew nothing. They learned about it only after the British government smelled a swindle and started probing. When the investigators could find no Chosen assets, the stockholders hired an American lawyer, Harry Zucker, who after four years of sleuthing traced the stolen funds to New York. (Rubinstein, describing himself as a Portuguese citizen, Sergio Manuel Rubinstein de Rovello, had arrived in America with them in 1938.)

The stockholders entered suit, and Rubinstein hired a small army of lawyers. He fought so stout a delaying action that, in 1946, the British stockholders were glad to settle for about half the assets their company once held in Korea. This left Rubinstein with close to $2,000,000. Using this loot, Rubinstein proceeded to clean up another five million in America. He would gain control of a company, loot it or juggle its stock and walk away with a profit. Three million came from deals in an oil-company stock, for which the government tried to send him to jail on charges of mail fraud and stock manipulation. Rubinstein hired the best legal brains, and was cleared.

It seemed that Rubinstein could live happily forever by flouting the rules other men live by. By taking persistent delight in outraging people and then calling the world as witness, however, he brought on himself a chain of disasters. Although of Jewish descent, he once rose before a distinguished group of war refugees to declare: "The

world belongs to leaders like Hitler. Someday I'll be one
of the greats in it." In 1941 he boasted that he had
crashed the United States with a phony passport. This invited the interest of the Immigration Service, which
launched its first effort to deport him. Soon after, he
bragged of how he had outwitted his draft board. Thinking of himself as a Napoleon, he didn't feel that he should
go into the Army as a private. To dodge the draft, he tried
bribery; also he bought an aircraft factory and swore he
was an executive vital to war production. Altogether, he
spent half a million dollars in his attempts at evasion and
on his subsequent trial. This time the angry attention of
the whole country was turned on him, and in 1947 he was
convicted and sentenced to serve two years in prison. Like
a theme in a symphony, this pattern of incitement and
self-exposure repeated itself until the end of his life.

So, despite his millions, Rubinstein by 1954 was a tar-
nished golden boy. An army of government officials was
working full time to deport him, and federal agents kept
him under constant surveillance. His draft-dodging conviction had made him *persona non grata* in many places. He
had to work his deals from the shadows. When men heard
he was in a venture, they rushed for the exit—or for their
lawyers. The end came abruptly, on the morning of
January 27, 1955, when Rubinstein was found strangled
in his New York bedroom. His mouth was taped, his
hands and feet bound with curtain cord. His bedroom
was in wild disorder.

Whoever the killer was, he ended the career of a man
who at death was on his way toward achieving a fantastic
and sinister dream. Screened behind dummy companies
in Panama and Cuba, he was making an extraordinary
deal with a respected Wall Street firm. Had he lived, he
might well have broken his way into this firm and thereby

have gained control of two important banking subsidiaries. With these in his grasp, he could have had power over the issuance of millions of dollars of new securities—and with it, opportunities for corporation-looting and stock-rigging on a vast scale. He would have become a wolf such as Wall Street has never seen.

Other historic swindlers cheated little people; Rubinstein cheated the shrewdest money men of his time. Other cheats wound up in prison; Rubinstein, charged with every business crime in the book, was never convicted of one. He had the genius and vigor to have earned his millions honestly. But by defrauding others he defrauded himself of the chance to become one of the giant financial figures of our time. And in the end, the great cheat was himself cheated of the one thing he would have given all his millions to save—his own life.

The Capture
of Adolf Eichmann

By Bela W. von Block

THE TALL, gaunt man with protruding ears and a receding hairline got off the bus and started to walk along the murky Buenos Aires street. Outwardly he was relaxed, just another working man after a hard day. Inwardly he was tense, watchful—as he had been, day and night, for fifteen years.

He saw nothing to cause him alarm. In the middle of the block a tramp squatted on a discarded crate. Fifty feet beyond, two housewives stood gossiping. Farther along, two day laborers were lighting cigarettes. A dark, nondescript sedan turned into the street. The jug-eared man saw it coming and edged instinctively toward the buildings on his left. The sedan drew closer, braked to a sudden halt. The doors were flung open, and four men leaped out. He tried to run, but it was useless. He was surrounded.

"Guten Abend, Herr Obersturmbannführer!"

He heard the snarled words and opened his mouth to scream, but something struck him a crushing blow on the head. He slumped, and strong hands thrust his unconscious body into the waiting car. The four men piled into the sedan; the driver blinked his headlights twice, then drove away.

The great manhunt was over. Adolf Eichmann—the man who had often boasted that he was the "World's No. 1 Jew-Killer"—had been taken prisoner by the people he hated most, the people who had tracked him relentlessly for a decade and a half.

During World War II, SS *Obersturmbannführer* Adolf Eichmann had ruled as chief of that department of the Nazi Reich Main Security Office charged with providing the "final solution" to what the Nazis called the "Jewish problem." Eichmann was responsible for the death camps, the gas chambers, the crematories, and ordered the mass deportations and mass executions. Because of him at least six million men, women and children were put to death. "When I am finished with my work, there will be no more Jews in Europe!" he promised SS Chief Heinrich Himmler in 1942.

In May 1945, American troops nabbed Eichmann, but they didn't know it. He was wearing the torn and stained uniform stripped from a dead Luftwaffe corporal; he carried the dead soldier's identification papers. To the U.S. troops he was just another Kraut to be herded into a POW cage. In time, Eichmann escaped from the prisoner-of-war stockade—and vanished.

After V-E Day Eichmann's name was near the top of the "Most Wanted War Criminal" lists of the Allies and the occupied countries. A gigantic search for him was launched by Great Britain, France, the United States and most other nations that had fought against or suffered under the Nazis. But in time most relaxed their efforts. Before long, much of the world forgot about Adolf Eichmann. Some people, however, remembered. As early

as June 1945, Jewish refugees—particularly those who
had gone to Palestine—took steps to ensure that the
search for Eichmann would continue. Scores of secret
agents, some of them members of the Israeli intelligence
service, combed both hemispheres. Eventually all of
their activities were coördinated in Tel Aviv by a central
office.

There were a few leads. Eichmann had grown up in
Linz, Austria, and his wife and children lived there. One
agent was sent to Linz to buy a small shop located near
the house occupied by Eichmann's wife. He was to keep
constant watch. Even after Frau Eichmann moved from
Linz, the agent remained—on the slim chance that Eichmann might return to his hometown.

At various times Eichmann was reported to be in West
Germany, Syria, Egypt, Turkey, Spain. Each time his
trail was followed; each time the agents drew a blank.
Once, in 1957, Eichmann was spotted in Buenos Aires,
but the operative who saw him bungled the job of following him. More than twenty additional agents were rushed
to Buenos Aires. They combed the city for three months
but were unable to pick up his trail again.

Then, in 1958, the West German government established in Ludwigsburg the "Central Office for the Prosecution of National Socialist [Nazi] Crimes." Headed by
Dr. Erwin Schüle, senior law officer, and eight other West
German judges, this office was set up to gather evidence
and prepare cases against all former Nazis charged with
war crimes who had not yet been tried. The West German
government notified Israeli authorities that the "Central
Office" would exchange information on Nazi war
criminals.

In 1959 a picked squad of crack Israeli intelligence operatives was sent to West Germany. Several of them were originally Hungarian Jews. (This is not surprising, for it was in Hungary that Eichmann committed some of his most heinous atrocities; he sent an estimated 450,000 Hungarian Jews to gas chambers and crematories.) One of these Hungarian agents used the cover-name "Sandor Fekete"; his parents, brothers and sisters had been murdered, and he had sworn to avenge their deaths and bring Adolf Eichmann to justice. He had already spent years as a member of a group working on the Eichmann case.

While in West Germany the Israelis picked up a reliable tip that Eichmann was still in Buenos Aires. They decided on a full-scale follow-up. Sandor Fekete and another former Hungarian Jew whose cover-name was "Lajos Molnar," plus four other men and a girl, were dispatched to Argentina. They traveled separately, as tourists and businessmen. Molnar, a man of fifty-five, would be especially useful, because he had met Eichmann several times in Budapest in 1944. Neither Fekete nor Molnar "looked" Jewish. Their orders were to pose as unreconstructed Hungarian Nazis who had fled ahead of the Russian armies, and to gain entrée into the large colonies of self-exiled Nazis, many of them war criminals, who had sought asylum in Argentina during the regime of dictator Juan Perón.

In Buenos Aires, Fekete and Molnar soon made contact with the Nazi elements and gradually became accepted by various groups. But although the German expatriates talked freely about their own exploits during the war, there was never even the most casual mention of Adolf Eichmann.

Months passed. Then, in January 1960, at a drinking party, Molnar heard a single sentence that gave the first definite clue: "Poor Eichmann—making parts for automobiles when he was once one of the most powerful men in the Reich."

At once the agents narrowed their search to automobile factories, watching workers enter and leave. One day a tall, lean man with a gaunt face and protruding ears was spotted leaving the Mercedes-Benz plant in Buenos Aires. He was followed onto a bus which took him to another section of the city. The agent did not dare shadow him any farther. It was enough. His trail could be picked up again the next day. Headquarters in Israel was notified by coded cable. Fekete and the others were informed that "reinforcements"—nearly twenty agents and commandos—would be dispatched to Buenos Aires.

Much remained to be done. Eichmann's identity had to be proved beyond any possibility of doubt. The suspected man was followed to his house, where discreet inquiry revealed that he lived under the name of "Ricardo Clement." Photographs of Frau Eichmann taken while she was in Austria were shown to people living in Eichmann's neighborhood. "*Sí*, we know her. Those are pictures of Señora Clement." A large bribe—and a promise of an even larger one to come—brought final confirmation from a man who had been a highly placed police official during the Perón regime. "Clement is Eichmann," he revealed.

In Israel, a furious debate now ensued among top-level government, intelligence and military officials. Some felt that Eichmann should be assassinated for his crimes without further ado. The majority, however, felt that he should be brought to Israel for a fair trial. They realized, nevertheless, that Eichmann's capture and transfer to Israel could not be accomplished legally, for the Argen-

tine and Israeli governments had no agreement for the
extradition of wanted war criminals living in Argentina.
Eichmann would have to be kidnaped and smuggled out.

"How can we do it?" was the next question. The Ar-
gentines themselves unwittingly provided the answer. To
attract tourists to the annual Independence Day celebrations in May, the Argentine government announced it
would waive most customs and immigration formalities
for all aircraft landing in the country during the festival.
Eichmann was to be kidnaped and held in hiding until an
Israeli commercial aircraft arrived in Buenos Aires. He
would then be taken aboard the plane and flown to
Israel. Sent to Buenos Aires to command the operation
required for Eichmann's capture was a tough, battle-
hardened commando officer.

Ricardo Clement—Adolf Eichmann had allowed himself to become a creature of habit. He always took the
same bus, getting off at the same corner. He always went
home alone.

Sandor Fekete and three of the best Israeli commandos
were chosen to form the actual striking force. Some members of the group would act as lookouts and guards. Others
would drive spare automobiles in case the kidnap car became disabled—or to block traffic in the event of pursuit.
Still others would prepare the hideout, a farm several
miles outside Buenos Aires, where Eichmann would be
held until it was time to get him aboard the plane for
Israel. The operation was set for Wednesday, May 11,
1960. The aircraft would not arrive from Israel until several days later, but the commandos decided it was necessary to strike without further delay. The Israelis were in
luck. May 11 proved to be a dull, dirty, drizzly day.
There would be fewer people in the streets.

In late afternoon the rain stopped. Everything was ready. At last it was quitting time at the Mercedes-Benz plant. The workers poured out through the gate. Ricardo Clement–Adolf Eichmann was among them. He queued up for his bus, climbed aboard. An Israeli agent, dressed in nondescript work clothes, got on behind him. Another agent—a pretty, olive-skinned girl who looked like a wife waiting for her husband at the gate—went to the nearest public telephone. "He's on the way," she said, then hung up.

Two automobiles trailed the bus, keeping well behind the vehicle but never losing it. The timing was perfect. As Clement got off his bus, the sedan turned into the street and stopped. The commandos got out and surrounded their quarry. A blackjack came down on Eichmann's skull. When Eichmann regained consciousness, he was in the farmhouse, surrounded by more than a dozen Israeli agents.

Adolf Eichmann had changed somewhat in physical appearance, but he was still the same coward he had always been. "Don't kill me—please don't kill me!" he pleaded.

The Israelis had no intention of killing him—but they didn't tell him. At that moment, Sandor Fekete had an inspiration. "You have one chance to save your life," he said. "Sign a letter stating that you are going with us of your own free will, and we'll take you to Israel to stand trial for war crimes. . . ."

Eichmann wrote the letter. In the days that followed he offered to write other letters, to give information about other fugitive war criminals. He offered to betray former comrades and friends—he offered anything and everything. Every word that he said was taken down on a tape recorder and also by a stenographer.

On May 19 an El Al Airlines' Britannia turbojet airliner was cleared to land at Buenos Aires. The plane was listed as being on a charter flight. The Argentine Independence Day celebrations were just getting under way. Then, toward midnight of the next day, the plane took off again—with a full load of fuel and a manifest that showed it was carrying nineteen crew members. No one at the airport counted the people who boarded the plane or checked to see who they were.

On May 23, 1960, Adolf Eichmann was arraigned before a court in Tel Aviv–Jaffa, Israel. He was charged under an Israeli law that provides for the trial and punishment of Nazi war criminals and their collaborators. The charge against him was that he caused and ordered the extermination of six million Jewish men, women and children. The trial began on June 20, 1961, and lasted six months. The verdict, on December 15, was guilty. Eichmann's appeal in March 1962 was unsuccessful.

Adolf Eichmann based his defense on the principle of *"Befehl ist Befehl"*—the German military axiom that "Orders are orders." He contended that he did nothing but carry out the orders of his superiors—and that he thus could not be held responsible for anything he did. This was also the defense offered by Hans Frank, Wilhelm Frick, Colonel General Alfred Jodl, Gestapo Chief Ernst Kaltenbrunner, Field Marshal General Wilhelm Keitel, Alfred Rosenberg, Fritz Sauckel, Arthur Seyss-Inquart, Julius Streicher and Nazi Foreign Minister Joachim von Ribbentrop at the 1946 international war-crimes trials at Nuremberg.

This defense did them no good. They were found guilty of war crimes and hanged. Adolf Eichmann met the same fate at Ramle Prison near Tel Aviv–Jaffa on May 31, 1962.

The Abraham Lincoln Murder Mystery

Condensed from the book The Web of Conspiracy

By Theodore Roscoe

*This is a story of murder—a day-by-day account of the
tragedy of 1865 and its aftermath. The conspiracy that ended
in the death of Abraham Lincoln left behind
it a trail of unanswered questions. It is
now clear that some of the questions will
never be answered, but this book probes
deeply into all the circumstances
surrounding that baffling and tragic crime.
It lays old ghosts to rest, raises
new ones and provides suspense
on every page.*

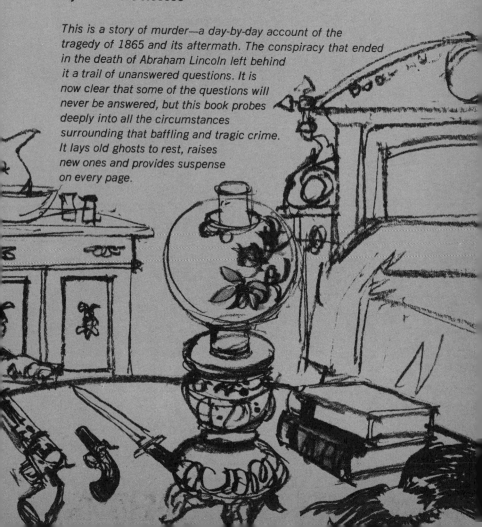

SHORTLY before noon on Good Friday, April 14, 1865,
John Wilkes Booth strolled into Ford's Theater in the
nation's capital to pick up his mail. As he approached,
theater manager Harry Ford called attention to the
jaunty twenty-six-year-old stage star. "Here," he said,
"comes the handsomest man in Washington."

In the manager's office Ford handed Booth some inci-
dental correspondence. As the renowned actor was turning to go, a stage carpenter asked Ford, "What about
tonight? Do you want the State Box ready?"

Harry Ford nodded. Yes, they'd received word that
the Presidential party was coming. Booth looked up.
"Lincoln here? To see *Our American Cousin?*"

"That's right," Ford said cheerfully. Maybe with this
attraction the stale old comedy would do more business.
Dropping an indifferent comment, Booth went out front
to read his mail on the entry steps. No witness later recalled anything remarkable in his demeanor. Here was a
truly marvelous actor! For in a trice Booth's plan to as-
sassinate the President of the United States had crystal-
lized. Within ten hours he would be able to carry it to
completion.

Mail finished, Booth purposefully reentered the theater,
mounted to the mezzanine and slipped down a side passage to President Lincoln's empty box. There he sat
watching a rehearsal of the evening's play. In the third
act Mrs. Mountchessington (the comic dowager) bawls
out Asa Trenchard (the rube) and sweeps off stage.
Trenchard, alone, flares: "Don't know the manners of
good society, eh? Well, I know enough to turn you inside
out—you sockdologizing old mantrap!" The line, recited
with gestures, could be counted on to bring down the
house.

Booth instantly came alert. The audience would be

guffawing, the stage almost empty. This was the time!
You sockdologizing old mantrap!

Booth left the theater, walking fast, and from this
point on his movements were hectic—uptown, downtown,
crosstown. He was noticed by scores of people. He made,
in fact, a great show of himself, waving to friends, tipping
his hat to ladies, calling to passersby, one of whom later
recalled: "He was faultlessly dressed, wearing elegant
riding boots and spurs." He went from the theater to a
livery stable and engaged a lively mare; next he went to
a boardinghouse near Ford's Theater in which he had
been meeting a strangely ill-assorted group of men for
several months. Then, after consuming a bottle of brandy
in a saloon, Booth was known to have disappeared at
about six o'clock.

As far as can be guessed, he circuited back to the now
deserted theater and made his way to the door of Lincoln's box. Working swiftly with a knife, he whittled a
small peephole in the upper panel, a little below eye
level. Then he scooped up the shavings and left.

Back at the National Hotel, where he lived, he had
dinner. In his room he picked up a wig, a false beard, a
dagger, a pair of revolvers and a single-shot brass derringer that fired a ball the size of a small marble. He left
the National about 8 p.m. In passing he asked the desk
clerk if he was going to Ford's that evening. No? Booth
told him he ought to go. "There'll be some fine acting
there tonight!"

Again Booth disappeared for an hour or so. Evidence
indicates that he had a final conference with henchmen
who were involved with him in the complex plot that
was to unfold before the night was over. About 9:30 p.m.
he turned up at the stage door in "Baptist Alley" behind

Ford's Theater, then walked down 10th Street, past the President's waiting carriage, to another saloon. Presently, flushed by successive drinks, he turned to go. Someone at the bar flung a taunt: "You'll never be the actor your father was!" Booth wheeled around, nettled. Then he smiled abruptly, and, walking out, he called back: "When I leave the stage, I'll be the most famous man in America."

No one knows precisely when Booth determined to murder Lincoln. But without question the assassination was not—as has been alleged—the unpremeditated act of a lunatic who had suddenly gone berserk. The evidence available concerning Booth's years prior to the fatal encounter in Ford's Theater very plainly contradicts any such assumption.

The ninth of ten children born to Junius Brutus Booth, a half-insane drunkard generally considered the greatest actor of his time, John Booth went on the stage at seventeen. In 1858, two years later, he played *Hamlet* in Richmond, Virginia, and, though critics rebuked him for "leaping about like a circus acrobat," he became an overnight sensation. Women thronged after him on the street, screamed when he walked on stage, pawed him for his autograph.

He remained in the South until February 1861. Then, with war threatening, he accepted theatrical bookings in the North. For Booth was not born a "deep Southerner." He was a Marylander with neither an emotional nor a monetary investment in slavery.

Nevertheless, when cannon fire exploded at Sumter, Booth told a theater audience in Albany, New York, that the attack characterized the "most heroic deed of modern times." A mob threatened the theater, and he was

ordered to leave the city. Despite his sympathies, he did
not rush south to join the Rebel army. While thousands
of Confederate patriots died for the Stars and Bars, John
Wilkes Booth remained on the stage, dying as Hamlet,
Macbeth and Othello to the tune of $500 a week. But
he soon became involved in a more dangerous offstage
role. By 1863 he had taken the step of joining the Rebel
underground.

The Confederate secret service was highly organized,
with spy rings in every major city of the Union. Booth's
profession made a perfect disguise. He moved across
state and front lines at will; backstage he met messengers
and secret agents. Documentary evidence shows him in
communication with Rebel intelligence even in Canada.
So much for the legend that it was an irresponsible maniac
who assassinated Lincoln. John Wilkes Booth was a secret
agent, working with numerous accomplices in an intri-
cately organized conspiracy.

Late in December 1864, Booth visited a certain Mrs.
Mary Eugenia Surratt's boardinghouse at 541 H Street,
in Washington, four blocks from Ford's Theater—as he
would again on the afternoon of the assassination. In addition to two known Confederate agents, a number of
shadowy personages—a Major Somebody, a vague Mr.
Downing, callers unknown to the permanent lodgers,
most of whom were innocent "fronts"—had been enter-
tained in Mrs. Surratt's parlor. Soon after Booth called
at the H Street house, a grubby transient applied for a
room there, giving his name as George A. Atzerodt.
Presently another stranger arrived—an enormous, hulking young fellow who said he was a Baptist preacher, the
Reverend Lewis Paine. Not long after that, a shiftless ex-
drugstore clerk, David Herold, called. These were the
chief conspirators.

By February 1865, John Wilkes Booth was a frequent visitor at 541 H Street. By March, landlady Surratt must have known that Atzerodt, Paine, Herold, Booth and her own son John, a Rebel partisan, were engaged in underground activity. Yet to the day of her execution she would resolutely continue to deny any complicity in Lincoln's murder.

The assassination of the President was not the plotters' goal during the early stages of the conspiracy. In a sense, their initial plan was perhaps even more dramatic: to kidnap Lincoln and carry him south. The strategic objective seemed valid enough. The capture of the President would deal a staggering morale blow to the North and inspirit the desperate South. Too, there was the possibility that Lincoln could be used as hostage for a massive prisoner exchange.

Unfortunately for the conspirators, Booth's abduction plans, though months in the making, were masterpieces of folly. Booth first proposed to trap Lincoln in his box at Ford's Theater. On a given signal a hand would turn off the main gas valve, plunging the theater into darkness. The abductors would dash into the box, manacle the President, lower him to the stage (a good ten feet) and rush him out through the wings to a waiting carriage which would spirit him off to Richmond. The alternate plan was to ambush Lincoln on the winding woodsy road that led to a military hospital three miles outside Washington, which the President frequently visited. It was the custom of the newspapers to announce the intended visits beforehand.

Booth prepared for the first attempt—at Ford's—on January 18. Code signs, passwords and secret orders went out to his band of conspirators. At Piscataway, at Pope's

Creek, at Allen's Fresh, at Mathias Point, Virginia, the Rebel underground was alerted. A vehicle with appropriate side curtains was at the stage door. But the attempt was a stunning flop. The night was stormy, and the President stayed at home.

The second attempt came just two months later, on the road to the hospital. The whole band from the H Street boardinghouse, charged up with brandy, was on hand, mounted, in a stand of timber well beyond the city limits. Booth issued final orders. Surratt would grab the coachman. Paine and Booth were chosen to handle President Lincoln himself.

A polished carriage flashes into view on schedule. The horses rear. The coachman lashes out with his whip. Booth roars a curse in frustration. The man in the carriage is not Lincoln. At that hour, it later develops, he is elsewhere, reviewing a regiment of Union battle veterans—the 140th Indiana—which has unexpectedly arrived in town that day to present him with a captured Rebel flag.

A third kidnap attempt failed when Lincoln again canceled a scheduled theater appearance at the last moment. Thwarted, the chief abductor must have had bitter reflections. All that mobilizing, all that rushing and girding to spring a trap on nothing but air! He could imagine the resentment among the underground partisans he had alerted. How could he face their derision and the ignominious failure of the master stroke which, he had calculated, would make the name of John Wilkes Booth a household word?

At some point while brooding upon these repeated failures, Booth decided to abandon the kidnap scheme in favor of more violent action. The exact date remains a mystery. But a significant body of evidence shows that he

cherished homicidal intentions well before April 14. Lee
had surrendered to Grant at Appomattox on April 9.
Booth must have realized then that kidnaping would not
actually help the Southern cause. It would have to be
nothing less than murder.

By Good Friday of 1865 Booth's resolve was firm. The
information that the President would be in his box at
Ford's Theater on that night merely fixed the time and
place for the strike. And the central drama was to have
its equally murderous subplot. On that night Booth
designated George Atzerodt to attempt the life of Vice
President Andrew Johnson. Paine and Herold were to
kill Secretary of State William H. Seward. At one devastating stroke the Union's most eminent leaders would be
wiped out.

John Wilkes Booth made no effort to conceal himself
as he entered the passageway leading to the President's
box. A number of people noticed him. The entrance to
the cubicle was not guarded. In spite of the kidnap attempts and the fact that the capital seethed with Rebel
agents and zealots, the guard's chair outside the door
stood empty. Lincoln had in his White House desk an
envelope containing eighty letters threatening his life. An
uncaught sniper had fired a bullet through his hat. A
group of Virginia gentlemen was raising a fund to be offered as a reward for his assassination. Yet there were no
guards of any kind outside the door, no civil or military
police.

According to a White House guard, Lincoln personally
had asked Secretary of War Edwin M. Stanton for a
bodyguard that night, after he had been threatened by
a group of hoodlums in the street during the afternoon.
Lincoln asked for one of Stanton's aides, a husky major

named Eckert, but Stanton said he had important work for Eckert that night and could not spare him. Yet at 10 p.m. the major was home shaving. He had been home since suppertime.

A Washington policeman, John F. Parker, was supposed to have been in the chair guarding the door. He had been assigned to the duty. Where was he at the crucial hour? Days afterward newspapermen would be asking that question. Parker would be investigated. Metropolitan police records would show that Parker had one of the worst records on the force—a mass of demerits and reprimands for insubordination, unbecoming conduct, drunkenness while on duty, one black mark after another. But, strangest of all, this dissolute good-for-nothing had been assigned to White House duty at the special request of Mrs. Lincoln herself. To this day nobody knows why. When her sponsorship came to light, the whole affair was at once hustled under a veil of censorship. Incredibly, this wretch was soon thereafter returned to duty with the White House guard—the man who was not in the chair in Ford's Theater when Booth appeared.

Stepping softly past the empty chair, Booth peered through the peephole he had cut earlier in the day. The President sat in an upholstered rocker with an overcoat over his shoulders. Changing position, squinting, Booth could make out Mrs. Lincoln at the President's side. A young lady, Clara Harris, a guest of the Lincolns, sat forward in an armchair, and on a divan against the inside wall of the box was her escort, a dapper young Army major named Rathbone. Booth drew his derringer and waited for his cue line. The voices were faint but distinct. Presently it came: . . . *you sockdologizing old mantrap!*

Amid the roars of laughter that rose from the audience

Booth turned the doorknob—one quick, quiet turn—and stepped swiftly forward. There was a flash, a muffled explosion. Lincoln's chin dropped to his chest, and he sat very still, as though fallen asleep.

Major Rathbone looked around, startled. He saw a shadow behind the President's chair. A little cloud of smoke drifted over the President's head. As Rathbone sprang, Booth's steel blade flashed and Rathbone took a savage gash to the bone of his arm.

Rearing back, Rathbone lunged again and clung. Booth wrestled him to the ledge of the box, flung him off and got a leg over the rail. As Rathbone made another grab, Booth rolled himself over the ledge and let go to drop to the stage. In dropping he hooked one of his elegant steel spurs in the flag which draped the box, and as he landed in a blur of red, white and blue he felt a sickening *snap* above his left ankle.

Brandishing his dagger, Booth charged into the wings. An actress was there, awaiting her cue. He struck her aside and was gone like a shadow down the dim passage toward the stage door. The orchestra leader was in the passage. Booth cut at him twice, through his coat and into his neck, and flung him aside.

From a front seat of the orchestra a Washington attorney named Stewart had glimpsed the scuffle in the President's box. Booth's leap to the stage had brought the lawyer up and over the footlights and across the stage in pursuit. But just as Stewart reached the stage door it was slammed shut. By someone in the darkness there? A stage hand? Stewart grappled with the door handle. On the delay of a few seconds hinged a nightmare of history.

In the alley the man who had been holding Booth's horse waited, expecting a tip. "Here comes Mr. Booth out of the door," he later testified. "I had hold of the bridle and Mr. Booth struck me on the breast with the butt of a knife he had in his hand and knocked me down. Then he kicked me."

Stewart burst from the stage door, shouting, "Stop! Stop!" and grabbed for the bridle just as Booth drove a spur into the mare's flank. His grab missed. The little horse shot down the alley into the night. It was shortly after 10:30 p.m. The most important phase of the triple plot had been successfully carried out.

All day Good Friday, David Herold, Booth's most intelligent and dependable underling, dashed around town on errands. To George Atzerodt's lodgings, to hide weapons and gear. To the National Hotel, looking for Booth. Then to Naylor's Livery Stable, where he rented a roan mare. As the conspirator swung into the saddle, the stableman reminded him that the horse must be returned at nine that night. But Herold did not return at nine. At ten minutes after ten, guiding Lewis Paine, who was too stupid to remember the simplest directions, he crossed deserted Lafayette Square in front of the residence of Secretary Seward and reined up. He watched Paine enter Seward's house. Quickly he dismounted and tied Paine's horse to a tree. Then he sprang back into the saddle and took off.

At almost the same moment the despicable Atzerodt, too frightened to carry out the assassination of Vice President Johnson, was fleeing from bar to bar, hoping to drown his fears and drink his difficulties away.

The Secretary of State, William Henry Seward, lived in a mansion with his wife, his two sons, Frederick and Augustus, and his daughter, Fanny. He had recently been in a carriage accident in which his jaw had been broken, his right arm fractured, ligaments torn in his foot, his body mottled with bruises. For some time there was fear that he might not recover.

On the evening of April 14, in his third-floor bedroom, Seward lay propped in bed, his right arm in a sling, his chin fixed in a rigid tilt by a leather-and-steel brace. Beneath his white hair, his patrician features wore the chalky pallor of suffering. The side of his face was puffed, the sockets of his eyes discolored. Sergeant George Robinson, a veteran, presided as male nurse. Fanny sat by the bed, waiting for the relaxed breathing that would mean her father was asleep.

As the Secretary dozed in a haze of pain, a sudden disturbance broke the quiet of the house. In dressing gown and slippers, Frederick Seward hurried to see what was happening. As he recalled the episode: ". . . A tall, well-dressed man presented himself and, informing the servant that he brought a message from the doctor, was allowed to the door of [Seward's] room. . . . [I] refused him admission. . . . Suddenly he sprang up and, having drawn a revolver, pulled the trigger." The Colt misfired.

The visitor was Lewis Paine. Enraged by the Colt's failure, Paine charged. Before Frederick Seward could fend off the blow, the giant assassin brought the weapon smashing down. He struck again and again—terrific blows that broke the pistol. Paine hurled the gun at his victim's head, stepped back and drew a bowie knife. Ribbons of blood streaming down his face, Frederick Seward slumped over, unconscious.

Paine now threw himself at Secretary Seward's door. The barrier burst inward, and the killer leaped at the figure in the bed. Seward barely had time to see the knife. Recoiling, rolling, he gasped as the blade slashed the side of his face from cheekbone to jaw.

Uttering a choked cry, Seward tried to escape from

the bed. Paine was on him, kneeing him, clutching him by the hair in an effort to jerk his head back and expose his throat. Twice and again the killer slashed. Two stunning blows struck Seward's broken jaw. Each time the blade flashed sparks, and the knife was jarred in Paine's grip. Through the heat of animal rage, Paine saw that his victim wore some kind of surgical collar. Infuriated, he hacked at the neck brace. Crimson spattered Seward's shoulders. Paine slashed again and again. Somehow Seward managed to slide to the floor.

Hands grabbed Paine's arm, yanking him back. Somewhere behind him a girl was screaming. Whirling from the bed, Paine found himself fighting two men. They struggled across the floor. Paine slammed one man against a table, gashed him with the knife, spun around and cut at the other man. Rampaging, he kicked the furniture aside and charged into the hall.

Behind him he left a scene as bloody as any in the annals of crime: Frederick Seward lying unconscious in a crimson welter; Augustus Seward, staggering with hands to head, half scalped; George Robinson, maimed, chest and shoulders stabbed; Fanny Seward fainting, hysterical; and Mrs. Seward, shaking with terror, groping into the wrecked room to her husband. On the bloodstained carpet, the Secretary of State lay prostrate (though he was to recover), his broken arm grotesquely bent, his head askew, his broken jaw unhinged.

With blood-smeared coat and crimson hands, Paine hurled himself down the staircase, bellowing: "I'm mad! I'm mad!" A man came out of a lower room and started up the stairs; Paine flung himself upon him, drove his knife to the hilt into the man's chest. The body crumpled. Paine bounded down to the street door.

In an instant, he realized Herold had deserted him.

From an upper window a woman was screaming, "Murder! Murder!" Paine untied his horse and mounted. Then, with the cry of "Murder!" alarming the night, he calmly walked the animal up the street. He could not have contrived a more deceptive retreat.

Augustus Seward reached the door brandishing a revolver, but he was too dazed to shoot. Blood streamed from his scalp into his eyes. Now shadows were running under the street lamps, boots pounding on the cobbles. Still Paine held his horse to a walk. He was heading in the wrong direction. Although Herold had explained the escape route to him six times that evening, he could not remember it. He reined up for an instant to mop his mouth and cheek.

William Bell, one of Seward's servants, ran into the street. He pointed at Paine and wailed: "Murder!" Paine walked the animal forward. "Murder!" Bell shrieked. The little Negro cried the alarm over and over again. Stubbornly he followed Paine's horse, keeping about twelve paces behind. Paine glanced contemptuously at his lone pursuer. Then, with a snort, he kicked his mount into a trot. Little William Bell gave up.

Now three conspirators were racing through Washington's dark, muddy streets—Booth, Paine and weak-chinned David Herold. Behind them, but not far, raced wildly inaccurate rumors: Vice President Johnson had been slain, General Grant shot; Lee's surrender had been a ruse to disarm the North; the capital was under Rebel attack. Runners sprinted through the residential districts, and alarmed citizens armed themselves with shotguns, pistols and knives.

Lincoln, mortally wounded, had been carried to a residence across the street from Ford's Theater. In the back parlor of the house, next to the room where the President lay dying, Secretary of War Stanton assumed supreme command of the nation. Making a desk of the top hat on his knee, he scribbled a nonstop torrent of orders, mandates and directives to the Army, the Navy, the State Department. He mobilized the eight thousand troops in the District to man the forts. Shouting, snapping, beckoning, he called out the military police, city constabulary, Federal detectives and all available guards to protect the public buildings and patrol the streets. He commanded the seizure of Ford's Theater, the arrest of everyone in the cast of *Our American Cousin*. When Mrs. Lincoln became hysterical he ordered her away from her husband's bedside.

And, meanwhile, what of Vice President Andrew Johnson? By one account, after a brief conversation Stanton "dismissed" him. In any case, Johnson played no significant part in the events of this evening.

For more than ten hours Stanton was Supreme Police Superintendent, High Judge and National Dictator all in one. A one-man junta, he was, in effect, acting President of the United States. To this day some of his dictatorial moves remain inexplicable. To block the escape of the assassins from the capital he dispatched police to the rail terminals. He ordered naval forces to blockade the Potomac. He flashed alarms to Army forces to barricade the six turnpikes that ran east, northeast, north, northwest, west and due south out of Washington. That left two others—escape routes which horsemen could reach by crossing the Anacostia River via the long wooden span called Navy Yard Bridge. Both of these roads led into lower Maryland, a region "pro-Secesh" to the core and the gateway of the Confederate underground to Richmond. Inexplicably, though Stanton closed off every other exit, he left these crucial routes wide open throughout the entire night of the assassination.

As a wartime measure the gate across Navy Yard Bridge was supposed to be closed at 9 p.m. About 10:45 on the night of the fourteenth, Sergeant Silas T. Cobb, in command of the bridge guard, heard fast hoofbeats coming down the dark reach of 11th Street. A bay mare raced up. The rider reared the horse and brought her to a standstill as one of the sentries grasped a bridle rein.

"Who are you, sir?" Cobb asked.

"My name is Booth."

"Where are you going?"

"I'm going home."

Cobb later stated that he thought the horseman some rich man's son who had been "pleasuring" in the capital. He sauntered around the animal, scrutinizing rider and mount. Then he stood back and nodded. "All right, you can pass." Booth urged the nervous mare onto the bridge and crossed at a hurried gallop. The War Department never investigated or censured the sergeant's conduct. His superiors accepted his "decision" as an unfortunate but excusable error. Cobb had no reason to suppose that this late-going horseman had just murdered the President of the United States.

The records of history contain many holes. John Wilkes Booth rode through one of them that night. Was it there through "error in judgment"—meaning military blunder? Or was it there through design? Allowing Booth to pass was not Cobb's sole contribution to history that night. A few minutes after Booth fled, a second horseman (David Herold) galloped up. The sergeant demanded identification. Herold said sullenly, "My name is Thomas."

"What are you doing out so late?" Cobb asked.

"I been seeing a woman," Herold exclaimed. "I gotta

get home!" The rider seemed harmless enough. So Cobb nodded to the sentries. They swung the gate open.

A few minutes later a third rider galloped up. This was the liveryman from whom Herold had earlier rented his big roan horse, to be returned to the stable at nine o'clock. In fleeing from Seward's house Herold had ridden past the establishment, and the foreman, John Fletcher, on the lookout for the overdue horse, had spotted him. Leaping on his own horse, Fletcher pursued Herold to the bridge. "I've got to get across," he insisted, after telling Sergeant Cobb about the stolen horse. But Cobb now made his third mistake of the night. "The bridge is closed," he said, and he turned Fletcher back.

Irate, Fletcher galloped to Washington police headquarters to report the theft. The superintendent at once connected the southbound horsemen with the shootings and applied to Army headquarters for horses to send a posse in pursuit. Horses for a detail of city police? Army headquarters replied that there were no mounts available. They told the police, in effect, to sit tight at headquarters and let the military handle the chase. And then they themselves did nothing about the clue until next day, long after the assassins had escaped.

Why? Was it the result of red-tape tangles and bureaucratic confusion? Or was there sinister method behind Edwin M. Stanton's inexplicable behavior? The answers remain unknown.

Somewhere across the Anacostia, Herold overtook Booth, and the two pounded southward together. By midnight Booth was in agony. In his leap from Lincoln's box he had snapped the tibia in his left leg, and now every jolt of the stirrup grated on the fracture. The pain was making him sick at his stomach. He thirsted for brandy.

At Surrattsville, ten miles south of Washington, was a tavern in which the conspirators had secreted a bundle of guns and gear for one of their previous kidnap attempts. Here they stopped, rapped on the door and raised innkeeper John M. Lloyd, a habitual drunkard. Blearily Lloyd fetched the hidden weapons while Booth drained a bottle of whiskey. (Lloyd would later swear that he had no idea what the guns were to be used for.) Then, quickly, the two fugitives rode on toward Port Tobacco, where a boat waited for their flight across the Potomac.

As his injured foot swelled in his boot and the leather tightened like an iron vise, Booth's nerve collapsed. He had to find a doctor, he told Herold. The nearest was a Dr. Samuel Mudd in Bryantown. Booth had visited him casually the previous winter, but was not entirely sure of the man's political sentiments. Nevertheless, they decided to risk the ten-mile detour from their well-planned escape route. It was a fatal decision. About 4 a.m. Herold led Booth up to the roadside gate at Mudd's farm and hammered on the door. Presently a voice called, "Who's there?" Herold answered that a man had been hurt by a fall from a horse. He was in great pain. Could the doctor fix him up?

The doctor aided Herold in lifting Booth from the saddle, and between them they carried him up the stairway to a bedroom. Booth, whom Herold identified as "Mr. Tyson," kept his face turned aside, a shawl pulled up to his eyes. Or so Dr. Mudd would testify later in trying to explain to skeptical authorities why he and his wife failed to recognize the injured fugitive. Mudd cut Booth's boot open and contrived a makeshift splint. When he had finished applying it, the doctor covered Booth with a quilt and went out in the breaking day to do his farm chores. At noontime Mudd examined the leg again, and

Booth kept his face turned away. That in itself should have troubled any inquiring physician, but Mudd (according to his statement) asked no questions. Instead, he went to the barn and made Booth a crude pair of crutches—a couple of sawed-off lengths of wood with crossbars screwed on top. Late that afternoon the riders departed.

Dr. Samuel Mudd was going to pay dearly for setting Booth's leg. The government would contend that he was a prime accomplice of the Booth gang. Mudd may have been guilty; he must have recognized Booth. And it appears that he told the fugitives of a Colonel Samuel Cox, who had a boat in which they could cross the Potomac. Had Booth and Herold followed Mudd's directions and found Cox without undue delay, they might have escaped. But after nightfall, somewhere near a tiny church in the wildwood, they lost their way. The track they took ended in a marsh through which the fugitives proceeded at snail's pace. Riding bruised Booth's leg at every jog. When he walked, his crutches sank in muck. Again and again he went sprawling. They didn't get to the Cox place until after midnight Saturday, and by then it was too late to risk crossing the Potomac. Federal soldiers were all about, thicker than fiddlers in hell. So for six days, while thousands of soldiers and police hunted, Colonel Cox concealed and provisioned the fugitives in a swamp two miles from the Cox house.

During this period Booth recorded some of his thoughts in a diary which stands as a masterpiece of self-pity and self-glorification. Seeing himself as a heroic figure unappreciated by a people "too degenerate" to comprehend his superior mission, he whined: "If the world knew my heart, that one blow would have made me great, though I did not desire greatness. . . . After being hunted like a dog through swamps and woods, wet, cold and starving, with every man's hand against me, I am here in despair. And why? . . . I have never hated nor wronged anyone. . . . I have too great a soul to die like a criminal." Soon enough, the man with the "great soul" would be pleading for a chance to escape from an encircling cordon of Federal soldiery.

On the night of the assassination the superintendent of the Washington police, Major A. C. Richards, had been in the audience and recognized Booth at once. After unsuccessfully trying to locate the guard assigned to Lincoln's box, Richards, a tough, capable officer, hurried to police headquarters. Within minutes he had briefed the duty force, summoned his reserves and dispatched detectives to Ford's Theater. By two o'clock in the morning of Saturday, April 15, after interrogating dozens of witnesses, he had linked three names: *John Wilkes Booth, David E. Herold, John H. Surratt.* He also had secured a vital address—541 H Street. Richards immediately ordered detective John Clarvoe to raid this boardinghouse and arrest Booth and Surratt. Clarvoe and ten men scouted up to the H Street house about 2:15 a.m. Lodger Louis Wiechmann answered the bell, and the detectives moved swiftly through the house. When they had reassembled in the lower hall, Wiechmann scolded them.

"Gentlemen, what do you mean by searching this house so early in the morning!"

Clarvoe stared. "Do you mean to tell us you don't know what happened last night?" The boarder blankly shook his head.

Clarvoe held out a piece of black cravat. "Do you see the blood on that?" Wiechmann stared at the ugly stain.

"That's Lincoln's blood!" Clarvoe said grimly. "John

Wilkes Booth has murdered the President." When Mrs. Surratt came out of her bedroom, Wiechmann blurted the news to her. The widow raised both hands in a startled gesture. "My God, Mr. Wiechmann! You don't tell me so!"

Clarvoe would recall that her shocked expression seemed genuine. Under questioning she readily admitted knowing Booth, and she told Clarvoe she'd seen the actor "at two o'clock yesterday [Good Friday] afternoon." But Mrs. Surratt insisted that she had not seen her son John for two weeks. Clarvoe was stalled. His orders had been to arrest Booth and John Surratt. They weren't in the house. Wiechmann volunteered to report at police headquarters at 8 a.m. to assist the officers, and "with this assurance the detectives left."

No character involved in the Lincoln murder case remains harder to analyze than Louis J. Wiechmann. We know he informed the authorities of Booth's abduction plot. Yet he seems to have told only part of the story. A halfway informer, did he play both ends against the middle? He would be so accused.

Time was running out now for Mary Surratt. On Monday night, April 17, General Christopher C. Augur, commander of the Army forces in charge of the capital, ordered the arrest of everyone in her boardinghouse. Augur's men waited in the parlor while the ladies dressed. Other soldiers stood outside in shadow, screened from view. Then, about 11:20 p.m., footsteps sounded on the pavement. A pedestrian with a pickaxe over his shoulder paused before 541 and rang the doorbell. In reply to the detectives' inquiries, the caller said Mrs. Surratt had sent for him that morning, to dig a gutter. As the police were questioning him, Mrs. Surratt entered the room. Asked if she knew the husky workman, the widow threw up her hands. "Before God," she said agitatedly, "I have not seen that man before!"

Cornered, the intruder faced a battery of revolvers. Told to identify himself, he mumbled a sullen reply and extended a signed Oath of Allegiance. The certificate bore the name "Lewis Paine." Paine stuck defiantly to his "ditchdigger" story until, at Augur's headquarters, the police brought in William Bell. Seward's houseboy recognized him immediately. Paine, locked in double shackles, was cast into "solitary" on board the Navy monitor *Saugus*, in the Potomac, and the War Department announced that they had captured Seward's assailant.

This Easter Monday, April 17, 1865, had been a red-letter day for the man hunters! True, Lincoln's assassin and his companion were still at large. But the catch thus far was impressive: Mrs. Mary E. Surratt; Lewis Paine; two of Booth's minor henchmen, Michael O'Laughlin and Samuel B. Arnold; and a lackey of Booth's, Edward Spangler. Within two days still another of the central conspirators was captured. Sodden drunk, George Atzerodt was apprehended at his cousin's farmhouse on the evening of April 19. He was thrust into the foul hold of the *Saugus* with the other male captives.

None of these prisoners had been indicted. They had merely been accused and thrown into prison to await trial. But even the case-hardened jailers aboard the monitor were appalled at the torture to which they were submitted. On April 23 Stanton issued an order which directed that ". . . the prisoners on board the ironclad shall have a canvas bag put over the head and tied around the neck." The hoods fitted like certain types of modern gas masks. Eyeless, they had only slits for nose and mouth. Cotton pads pressed tightly over the wearer's eyes and ears. Caught in this headlock, the prisoners were stifled, blinded, deafened. The prison surgeon protested to Stanton, urging that the hoods be loosened lest the prisoners suffocate. His appeal drew a blank. Driven beyond endurance, Paine, the physical giant of the group, went raving mad. He tried to commit suicide by dashing his brains out against the iron bulkhead of his cell. The other prisoners waited, apprehensively.

By Easter Monday the search had developed into a nationwide witch hunt. People who knew nothing whatsoever about the assassination were arrested in droves. Charges ranged from "accessory" to "suspicious conduct." Regional military units forwarded suspects to Washington. Soon, with city police and backwoods sheriffs entering the field, the harvest of suspects swamped the jails. Booth's relatives felt the impact of the hysteria immediately. Asia Booth Clarke, John's sister, five months pregnant, almost suffered a nervous breakdown when the police avalanche descended upon her home. Her husband was summarily dragged off in handcuffs to the Old Capitol Prison in Washington. He was guiltless.

The shadow fell with more stunning violence upon Junius Brutus Booth, Jr., John's brother. He was playing in Cincinnati on the night of the murder. When the news reached the city, an infuriated mob stormed his hotel. Junius Brutus fled by a side exit and managed to travel east incognito, until he was arrested in Philadelphia on April 26. He must have been dumb with anger when they locked him into an Old Capitol cell. He had supported the North during the war. Another brother, Joseph Booth, was astonished when he was arrested at a steamer landing in New York. Just arrived from San Francisco, he could hardly have had a hand in the assassination. Released after a few hours' grilling, he never forgot the experience. For years he refused to refer to John Wilkes Booth as his brother. The members of Booth's family were symbols. When Stanton could not lay hands on anything of substance, he was all for jailing the symbolic.

Another symptom of the frenzy that gripped the country the first days after the assassination was that Booth himself was reported in a dozen Northern cities at once. Persons in Washington sighted him on Pennsylvania Avenue. New Yorkers glimpsed him skulking down Broadway. Furtive "Booths" went through Niagara Falls, Boston, Chicago. Police closed in on one John Wilkes Booth (the wrong one) at Tamaqua, Pennsylvania. Still another innocent bearer of the name was chased across Detroit and hunted in Montreal. It was all wasted effort, but it was almost inevitable that sooner or later some of Booth's pursuers would begin to pick up the genuine scent.

The all-out manhunt for Booth commenced on Monday, April 17, 1865, and soon the mounting tide of soldiery galloping into lower Maryland—ten thousand of them, according to some accounts—had cast a formidable dragnet across Prince Georges and Charles counties. The soldiery had little difficulty in uncovering Booth's track. In places like Allen's Fresh and Port Tobacco, half the villagers seemed acquainted with John Surratt, David Herold, George Atzerodt. In Surrattsville, tavernkeeper Lloyd should have quaked in his boots when the cavalry swooped down on him. Instead, this boozy pawn responded so abundantly to interrogation that he wormed himself out from under the shadow of the noose and into the favor of Federal authorities as a prime government witness. Lloyd swore that Mrs. Surratt had visited him on the evening of the assassination and told him that some weapons secreted in his tavern "would be called for that

night"—testimony later used to hang Mrs. Surratt. And
he admitted that John Wilkes Booth had stopped at his
establishment in the course of his escape from Washington. The assassin's line of flight was pinpointed.

The next important suspect to fall into the dragnet was
Dr. Samuel Mudd. Acting on an anonymous tip, the
same cavalry lieutenant who had apprehended Lloyd
rode his squadron to the doctor's farmhouse and interrogated him. Uncommunicative at first, Mudd admitted
only that two riders had come to his place at about daybreak on the fifteenth, and that he had set a broken leg
one had sustained in a fall from his horse. He insisted that
the men were complete strangers. The lieutenant persisted. Finally Mudd "acknowledged . . . it was Booth
whose leg he set, and [whom he] helped through the
swamp." Mudd was arrested forthwith.

The dragnet was tightening. On April 20 War Secretary Stanton issued a stern proclamation: "All persons
harboring or secreting [Booth and Herold], or aiding
their concealment or escape, will be treated as accomplices in the murder of the President, and subjected to
trial before a military commission, and the punishment of
death." This decree must have sent a shiver through the
counties of lower Maryland. Booth was in hiding there—
somewhere—and the local grapevine's party line doubt-
less muted down to a whisper.

But information continued to seep out. Provost Marshall James R. O'Beirne, who kept a record book of his
party's activities, made a most significant entry on April
21: "Sam'l Cox's servant states that Cox had been cooking provisions lately and carrying them to persons in the
swamp. . . ." Here was big game! O'Beirne's detectives,
however, were slow in tracking it. By the time Federal
troops got to the swamp behind Cox's home, Booth and

Herold had crossed the Potomac to Virginia. This was
sometime Friday or Saturday night, a week after the murder. There Herold located a Mrs. Quesenbury of the Confederate underground, and the pair were passed furtively
from hand to hand until they reached the backwoods
cabin of a freedman named Lucas. Lucas later testified:
"One of the men said, 'We want to stay here tonight.' I
said, 'You cannot do it; I am a colored man and have no
right to take care of white people. I have only one room
in the house and my wife is sick.' The one with the
crutches took out a bowie knife, saying, 'Old man, how
do you like that?' My wife and I went out on the step and
stayed there all night. In the morning they took my horses
and went."

Sometime on Monday the fugitives met three ex-
Confederate soldiers. Testing their sentiments and finding
them sympathetic, Booth and Herold identified themselves and asked for help. One of the veterans, Captain
Willie S. Jett, eighteen years old, volunteered to guide
them to the Richard Garrett farm three miles south of
Port Royal, Virginia, seventy-eight miles out of Washington. There he introduced Booth as his friend "John
William Boyd, a Confederate soldier wounded in the
battles around Richmond." He asked Garrett to take
care of Booth until Wednesday morning, when he would
call for him. From this point on, nothing written or testified in respect to the doings at Garrett's farm can be
taken at face value. Nobody knows exactly what Booth
said to the Garretts or to Jett. Nor can the reports of the
Federal officers who now were scouting from Port Royal
to Bowling Green be accepted as wholly truthful.

But about suppertime on Tuesday, Jett gallops up to
the Garrett gate and calls out to Booth that Federal blue-

coats are crossing the Rappahannock on the ferry to Port Royal. Booth is visibly alarmed. A bit later a drum roll of hoofs echoes through the gloaming. The pounding grows louder. Then, with guidons flying, sabers jangling, a Yankee cavalry troop batters past the Garrett gate—on the trail of Captain Jett, as it turns out. On the veranda young William Garrett exclaims, "They must be going to Bowling Green!"

Booth and Herold are going somewhere, too. To the family's surprise, the pair are seen racing for the pine woods beyond the tobacco farm—Booth making grotesque speed on his crutches and Herold sprinting for dear life. They plunge into the thickets, disappear for a little and leave behind them a troubled, suspicious family.

Staying at the Garrett home at the time was farmer Garrett's sister-in-law, Miss L. K. B. Holloway, a schoolteacher and loyal Southerner. As she later told it, her nephew, William Garrett, decided to investigate their guests' odd behavior. From neighbors he learned that the bluecoats were hunting a cripple and his companion. When young Garrett returned he told Booth, who had reappeared, "You must leave first thing in the morning. I don't want you to bring any trouble upon my father."

And now occurred perhaps the strangest episode of that strange day. When the hour came to retire (Miss Holloway related), Booth refused to sleep upstairs. Anywhere would do rather than that. So young William Garrett conducted Booth and Herold to the tobacco barn. After they entered he padlocked the door behind them and gave the key to Miss Holloway. He told her that she must not let anyone have it, "as it was his opinion that they intended to steal horses and escape."

Here, surely, is a fantastic business. That Booth, his life at stake, a much-publicized $100,000 reward on his head, would consent to being locked in a barn! Booth and his accomplice were heavily armed. Had they feared a trap, they could have shouted dire threats at the Garretts or shot the hasp off the door—or quietly pried their way out. But apparently they made no protest.

About midnight a second strange thing happened: a Yankee cavalry troop, commanded by Lieutenant E. P. Doherty, raced into Bowling Green and surrounded the hotel where Captain Willie Jett was in bed asleep, partly undressed. Somebody—was it young Garrett, or one of the dozens of farmers and villagers who could have seen him in company with the wanted men?—had tipped the Federals off. The Yankee troop's action report never explained the tip. It merely said, "We took Jett downstairs and informed him our business, telling him that if he did not forthwith inform us where the men were, he would suffer. . . ." Young Jett had seen enough suffering. And a lad hauled from bed and rushed downstairs with a revolver at his neck may well do some talking. The net was about to close on John Wilkes Booth.

Miss Holloway wakens bolt upright in her bed in the Garrett farmhouse. (Or that, at least, is how she later told it.) There are sounds outside—a thrashing in the underbrush—boots trampling on the porch—metallic jingle of scabbards and spurs—a sudden, savage pounding on the kitchen door. Doherty's men have arrived.

"Open up in there!"

Miss Holloway hears a window raised, Garrett's voice calling down: "Who's there?" Miss Holloway scurries to the window. Damn Yankees! A whole passel of them—overrunning the barnyard, trampling the flower garden, pawing through the lilacs. The ugly gleam of carbines and buckles and spurs is everywhere.

"Unlock this door, or we'll smash it in." Miss Holloway starts for the hall. She sees farmer Garrett, a rumpled figure in a nightshirt, half tumbling down the stairs.

"Wait! Wait!" Garrett calls out. The door latch rattles in his frantic hand. He recoils as the door lurches inward. Two soldiers stomp into the kitchen. Muddy boots and yellow gauntlets and U.S. insignia!

"We want those two men," the officer says harshly.

Farmer Garrett blurts, "They've gone!"

The officer catches the old man by the throat left-handed, pins him against the doorjamb and holds the revolver to his temple. "Come up here and get this Rebel, boys!" he calls over his shoulder. "Maybe a little neck-stretching will loosen his tongue!"

The farmer is hustled down the porch steps and across the yard to a chopping block. A coil of hemp appears. One of the soldiers hastily fashions a sliding bowline. The shivering figure on the block emits a despairing moan. Surrounded by this lynch party, he stands on his pedestal like a speaker who has forgotten his lines. He sees on the porch his wife and terrified daughters. Miss Holloway cries out aghast as the free end of the rope is tossed over the tree limb. Fortunately for Garrett, one of his sons has the good sense to intervene. "Gentlemen," William Garrett offers, "I will take you to the place."

In sixty seconds a cordon of soldiers is thrown around the fateful tobacco barn. The key is obtained and the padlock removed. Lieutenant Doherty barks a savage command. "Come out of that! Can you hear?"

No answer.

"Look," someone shouts, "we'll have a little bonfire and burn the bastards out. Fetch some brush."

Behind the barn door there is a rustle of activity. A mutter of oaths. Cautiously, men stack an armload of brush against the barn wall. They add some old lumber.

The lieutenant calls, "Last chance, you two! We'll give you five minutes."

A pause while the night waits in silence. Then Miss Holloway hears Booth's voice, high-pitched: "Who are you? What do you want with us?"

"You've got five minutes!" Five minutes. On the porch the shawled women stand like Biblical figures. Miss Holloway feels slow tears crawl down her cheek. Propped upright on the block by threatening pistols, farmer Garrett in his nightshirt poses like an absurd monument.

"Time's up!" the lieutenant calls.

From the trap comes a pleading whine. "Give me a chance for my life, can't you, Captain? I am but a cripple—a one-legged man. Withdraw your troopers a hundred yards from the door, and I'll come out. All I want is a fighting chance."

Now the soldiers hear Herold's voice for the first time, in a blurred dialogue within the dark barn. Then a savage outburst. "You're a goddam coward. Go, go! I won't have you stay!"

A rattle is heard at the door, and a voice saying, "Let me out! I want to surrender!" Sidling up to the entry, Lieutenant Doherty orders the man who wants to surrender to thrust both hands out. The door inches open a little way. Out comes one hand. With a savage yank Doherty brings his captive lunging from the barn. Instantly the door is slammed. Herold is caught by the soldiers in a flying tackle. Doherty, lacking handcuffs, hauls the captive across the yard to rope him to a tree. The soldiers whoop joyfully around this $25,000 prize.

Now Booth, alone in the barn, begins to rant hysterically. He challenges the Yankees to combat, promising to fell them one after another. Baffled by all this claptrap, the soldiers fire the heap of brush. In a sudden gust of

combustion, the barn's interior is revealed in hot light. Through the openwork planking, all can glimpse the shadowy figure within. To and fro on his crutch the man hops like an injured raven in a cage. Everywhere he turns his escape is blocked. Suddenly a shot cracks out and he pitches headlong to the floor. Lugged from the burning barn, Booth begins to die in the best opera-house tradition. Revived with a splash of water, he whispers, "Tell Mother . . . I die for my country."

While the saddle-weary, sleepless regulars, their thoughts on breakfast and reward money, wait with ill-concealed boredom, Booth takes his time about dying. Finally, about daybreak, he expires.

Who shot him? All orders had been to bring him back alive. As a prisoner, Booth might have answered some interesting questions. For instance: Where is John Surratt? Who backed you in Richmond? How many people helped you in Washington? And a good deal more. But now he was dead. No one knows with absolute certainty who fired the shot that dispatched Lincoln's killer—but the informed consensus is that the trapped cripple committed suicide.

Lieutenant Doherty and his men must have been eager to get back to Washington with their prize. All were due for a share of the reward money. Doherty jerked a blanket from a horse at the gate and dashed to the porch. "We'll sew up the body in this," he told a subordinate. The corpse was treated to vehicular travel, though not out of respect. With four prisoners on his hands, Doherty was short of mounts; otherwise the cadaver could have gone packsaddle. The war had stripped the countryside of vehicles, but Ned Freeman, a local Negro who had an old ambulance, agreed to make the haul to the Potomac at Belle Plain, whence the body would travel by boat. Roped to a board, it was chucked into Freeman's ancient cart. From the porch Miss Holloway watched the ghastly parade form up in the road. The last glimpse she had of the celebrated visitor: the soles of his feet—one boot, one shoe—as the wobbly ambulance started Booth on his last trip to Washington.

By dawn of April 27 the news was abroad in the capital. The body of John Wilkes Booth was on board the monitor *Montauk*. Workers abandoned their breakfasts and dashed for the horse cars. Gentlemen ordered their carriages. Congressmen requisitioned coaches. The populace of Washington swarmed to the Navy Yard. A canvas awning was stretched over the deck to shield the corpse and discourage the inquisitive public eye. Under this airless tent, a rapid inquest was held in midmorning. No official on board had been personally acquainted with Booth. And now a peculiar difficulty arose: the body bore little or no resemblance to the known photographic portraits of John Wilkes Booth. This contorted corpse with matted hair, wild eyes and snarling teeth— could it really have belonged to the matinee idol, once the Apollo of the footlights and the glass of fashion?

Since the identity of the body seemed doubtful, one may believe responsible officials would have called many witnesses—close friends of Booth, members of his family. At the time, Junius Brutus Booth was no farther away than the Old Capitol Prison. He was not summoned to identify the body! With the utmost secrecy, Booth's body was spirited off the *Montauk* that same day, placed in a gun box and hastily buried in a shallow hole in the corner of an ammunition vault at the Washington Arsenal. But this body was not going to rest.

On May 9, 1865, the trial of Booth's accomplices opened before an extemporized Military Commission which convened in a makeshift courtroom at Washington's Arsenal Penitentiary. It was held that, since the President was killed "while actually in command of the Army, as Commander-in-Chief," the assassination was a military crime. The prisoners must have known they were doomed.

On June 30, all eight defendants were found guilty of participation in the assassination conspiracy. Dr. Samuel Mudd, Samuel B. Arnold and Michael O'Laughlin were sentenced to life imprisonment. Edward Spangler was sentenced to six years. Lewis Paine, David Herold, George Atzerodt and Mary Surratt were sentenced to death by hanging.

But nobody believed that Mrs. Surratt would be hanged. Long afterward, the story leaked out that the sentence passed against her was contrived through deception. At first the military judges had stood four to five against the capital penalty, but apparently at Stanton's instigation (and certainly with his approval) Judge Advocate General Joseph Holt arranged a compromise. If the tribunal would vote a unanimous death sentence for Mrs. Surratt, a petition for mercy would then be forwarded to President Johnson. Five of the generals signed the petition recommending that Mrs. Surratt's sentence be commuted to life imprisonment. Holt promised to present the appeal to Johnson. According to Johnson, he never saw it. On the morning of July 6, he signed the four death warrants. *The execution was set for the following day!*

And there was another suspicious peculiarity about the management of this trial. Yankee troopers had retrieved Booth's diary from the dying man's pocket and delivered it to Stanton in Washington. "I examined it with great care," Stanton recalled, "and read over all the entries in it." But in spite of its manifest importance, the book was not presented as evidence, nor even mentioned during the trial. Did it list conspiracy leaders? Mention accomplices? Nobody knows. For after it was given to Stanton the little book disappeared. In 1867 it was "rediscovered" in a forgotten War Department file. And now eighteen pages of it were missing, cut from the section leading up to the night of Lincoln's murder.

On the morning of July 7, the scaffold stands ready in the Arsenal Penitentiary yard. Sweat streams down the faces of the spectators, the troops, the newsmen waiting in the stifling sun. A door opens in the prison wall. Mrs. Surratt comes out, fainting, supported by two priests.

Next comes Atzerodt, shambling in chains. Then Herold, tottering, weeping. Finally, Paine, chin up, shoulders squared, the personification of Spartan defiance. The nooses are lowered and adjusted. Death caps are drawn over the four condemned heads. The victims are positioned over the traps.

The New York *World* observed: "The traps fell with a slam, the four bodies dropped like a single thing."

It would be neat, but inaccurate, to conclude that with the execution justice had been meted finally to all those who had conspired in the murder of Abraham Lincoln. Yet one—at least one—evaded retribution entirely. This was John Surratt.

That Secretary of War Stanton deliberately permitted Surratt to escape there is not the slightest doubt. He was informed that Surratt had fled to Canada, but not a single military agent was put on the trail. Four months after the assassination, Surratt was recognized in England. The American consul immediately informed Washington and received the reply that "upon consultation with the Secretary of War, it is thought advisable that no action be taken." Recognized later by a friend in Italy, Surratt confided that the conspirators "acted under orders of men not yet known." Again Washington was informed and, in a note to Stanton, Seward suggested sending a special agent to expedite the fugitive's arrest. Stanton made no reply. Prodding letters went unanswered. Finally, in December 1866, Navy Secretary Welles, at Seward's behest, dispatched a corvette to apprehend Surratt in Egypt. Surratt was tried twice. The first jury deadlocked. The second trial was dismissed because the statute of limitations had run out. One can only conclude that his apprehension and trial were deliberately delayed. No man can say why.

At his family's request, the body of John Wilkes Booth was disinterred from its makeshift grave in February 1869, to be removed to a cemetery in Baltimore. By Presidential order, no monument was to be erected over the remains. But when the coffin was opened at a Baltimore funeral parlor, another controversy arose over the identification of the corpse. Those who had been dissatisfied with the hasty necropsy aboard the *Montauk* were quick to point out that a dental examination performed here conflicted with the records of the Washington dentist who had treated Booth. Minor discrepancies in the accounts of those who were present at this inquest were sifted, discussed, debated. The questions thus raised have been argued for nearly a century.

Qualified historians believe that the Booth family's acceptance of the remains decided this issue once and for all. But what of the larger issue—how to account for the myriad instances of official malfeasance which indisputably overshadow the entire case?

Before he died in 1926, Robert Todd Lincoln burned a collection of his father's private papers. A friend visiting him at the time remonstrated, and the President's son replied, according to the visitor, that "the papers *contained documentary evidence of the treason of a member of Lincoln's cabinet*, and he thought it best for all that such evidence be destroyed."

And so the identity of the man at the center of the web will probably never be known. But whoever he and his confidants were, to the extent that they withdrew the President's protection, exposed him as a target for the suspected enemy and facilitated the escape of known conspirators, they were *particeps criminis*—master accomplices to one of the greatest crimes in American history.

Slaughter by Airplane

By Terrence F. Flahiff

S AFE IN our comfortable hotel room in Quebec City's
Château Frontenac, my wife and I stared at each
other in mounting alarm. The radio was just then announcing: "Canadian Pacific Airlines Flight 108 from
Quebec City to Baie Comeau is overdue. It is feared that
the aircraft may have crashed in the vicinity of Ste. Anne
de Beaupré."

The color left Françoise's face. Only a short time before,
we had been on Flight 108, traveling from Montreal to
Quebec. I had been ticketed to continue on to Baie Comeau, a river town 270 miles to the northeast, but had let
Françoise persuade me to get off and spend the weekend
with her in Quebec. Meanwhile, of the nineteen passengers who took off for Baie Comeau, more than half were
friends or acquaintances of ours.

What could have happened? The day of the flight—
Friday, September 9, 1949—was bright and sunny. The
plane had been behaving beautifully. We touched down
at Quebec that morning about ten, and eight passengers
disembarked. Among the seven who took our places

aboard the plane was Rita Morel Guay, a plump, twenty-eight-year-old Quebec housewife and mother. Mme. Guay, we learned later, was happy in the thought that after many stormy months of estrangement she and her jewelry-salesman husband had just become reconciled. She was flying to Baie Comeau to pick up two suitcases of jewelry which he had stored at a warehouse on a previous trip. Three days earlier, at the Canadian Pacific Airlines' office in the Château Frontenac, her husband had bought her a round-trip ticket on Flight 108, plus a ten-thousand-dollar life-insurance policy. Then he had taken her for a gay evening of dinner and theater.

At 10:45 a.m. on Friday, a few minutes after its takeoff for Baie Comeau, Flight 108 was clearing the northern tip of Ile d'Orléans. Suddenly, several people three thousand feet below on the sun deck of the cruise steamer *St. Lawrence* saw a puff of smoke dart from the left side of the plane. The stricken aircraft veered sharply away from the river, passed above two railway hands who were tamping ballast on the Canadian National Railways roadbed at the riverside, and disappeared inland. The two workmen ran to a trackside telephone, near the prominent "Mile 40" marker, meaning forty miles distant from Quebec. It would later make a good starting point for search planes.

Toward 4 p.m., anxious to find out what might have happened to my friends aboard 108, I visited the airline office on the main floor of the Château Frontenac. Relatives and airline officials crowded around the ticket counter, waiting for news. Each hour lessened their hope. There was subdued sobbing, from men and women alike. Perhaps the most pitiful sight was a slim, rather dapper young French-Canadian father who approached the Canadian Pacific desk, holding his pretty four-year-old daughter by the hand. His wife, Mme. J. Albert Guay,

had been on Flight 108, he told the hard-pressed clerk. Was it true that the plane was missing?

The clerk nodded sadly. The husband put his face in his hands and collapsed in a chair. The small girl was weeping her heart out, pressing her face into her father's sleeve. She was the only child in the lobby, and the spectacle of her grief was so heartrending that the hotel management offered father and daughter a room and airline officials summoned a priest to comfort them.

Sometime after 4 p.m., a search plane reported sighting the flash of metal in a small clearing just below the crest of a 2600-foot peak named Cap Tourmente. A party of six police and airline officials, whom I joined in case I could help out with identification, drove the twenty-four miles to St. Joachim. There we crowded onto a small, gasoline-driven railroad maintenance car for the run to the "Mile 40" marker. This marker, with an approximate direction reported by the search plane, provided our first bearing. It was dark on the densely forested mountainside, and we hadn't climbed four hundred yards when one man dropped out because of a heart condition. Shortly afterward, two others had to drop out from exhaustion. The woods were too thick for us to see anything fifty feet away. But, almost magically, a full September moon appeared at about eleven o'clock, and somebody yelled, "Hold it!"

There was the plane—Flight 108. Silver, ghostly, beautiful. The DC-3's back was broken. The soft whiteness of the full moon played like a great floodlight on the aluminum fuselage. The tail assembly, driven straight into the ground and rising thirty feet in the air, looked like a silver cross. We stood, listening. There was nothing to hear. Then, as we moved forward, I stumbled over a fallen tree and fell face down on something soft. Instantly a confusion of memories and impressions came to mind. From a country boyhood the smell of scorched spun sugar candy came back to me. Then I recalled, during the war, standing alongside artillery guns. The spent explosive from the shell casings had the same heavy, sweetish odor that I was smelling now. I had fallen next to the body of a boy, my face in the dew-moistened fur collar of his jacket. Trapped in the wet fur, as though to serve a purpose, was the sweet, burnt-sugary smell of high explosive.

We got back to Quebec, dead tired, at 2 a.m. Later that day the lobby of the Château Frontenac bristled with federal, provincial and local police. An airline official introduced me to two alert and powerful-looking gentlemen, Jean Bélanger and Jules Perrault, top investigators for Canadian Pacific. As a former Crown prosecuting attorney I felt that I could recognize a good detective. These two, I sensed immediately, ranked with the best When I told them of the smell I had noticed on the mountainside, they heard me out in detail. Perrault, his eyebrows raised inquiringly, had the look of a man who was filing away for future reference a special card.

Investigation of the wreck established that nothing mechanical had been wrong with the plane. The engines had run until impact. Fuel still remained in the tanks. There had been no fire. The controls were in order. Nothing in the plane's operating equipment—batteries, fire extinguishers, circuits—had caused an explosion. Experts found that some sort of blast had gone off just behind the pilot, in the left forward (No. 1) baggage compartment. This was a fact of great interest to the Canadian Pacific investigators. The No. 1 compartment was empty when the plane arrived from Montreal; everything that was in it when the plane crashed had been put aboard at Quebec. The investigators, in checking the airline copy of Flight 108's cargo manifest, could account at the crash scene for everything loaded at Quebec except one twenty-eight-pound parcel marked "Fragile" and addressed to Adrien Plouffe in Baie Comeau.

Now came the key findings. First, the baggage agent at Quebec airport vaguely remembered that the parcel had been delivered by a short, stout woman dressed in black who arrived and left in the same cab. Second, Bélanger's men found that no Adrien Plouffe lived in Baie Comeau.

On Wednesday morning, September 14, the coroner's inquest announced its verdict: "Death by accident—caused by explosion of unknown origin, although not from an integral part of the aircraft." That night at the Château Frontenac, Perrault caught my eye from across the lobby and sauntered casually toward the airline counter where we could talk privately. "That smell you noticed," he said—"it's turning into another, a stronger smell now." He told me why.

Bélanger's team had located the cabdriver who had brought the woman in black to the Quebec airport. He said he would recognize her. Meanwhile, Perrault, in

checking the backgrounds of Flight 108's passengers, had
stopped at the name of Rita Morel Guay. Because he
knew nothing of her he checked with the local police.
Their records showed an arrest the previous June of an
Albert Guay for threatening a waitress named Marie-
Ange Robitaille with a revolver. Guay, it turned out, had
been intimate with the shapely brunette nineteen-year-
old. When Mme. Guay learned that her husband was
keeping a Quebec apartment for the girl, she left him and
moved with their child into the home of her mother. Soon
afterward, when Marie-Ange also left Guay and returned
to her parents, Guay had gone to the restaurant where she
worked and threatened her with the gun. As for the
"woman in black," Marie-Ange told the police, the description could fit only Guay's great friend Mme. Mar-
guerite Pitre, who lived on Monseigneur Gauvreau Street.

On Thursday the cabdriver was posted discreetly outside Mme. Pitre's house, but she happened to remain in-
doors. Both she and Guay were now being watched, but
cautiously. As far as these two or the public knew, official
interest was over, and the plane crash would soon retreat
from the news as a deplorable but inexplicable mystery.
Then, fortunately or unfortunately, the frustrated cabdriver talked to a reporter from *Le Canada*, of Montreal.
The newspaper broke a sensational story that night under
the banner headline: "Who Is the Woman in Black?"

Guay somehow did not learn of this story during the
weekend. On Sunday, in fact, he managed a date with
Marie-Ange and told her that "after a decent interval"
they would be married. Guay learned only on Monday of
the police hunt for "Madame le corbeau"—the Crow, the
woman in black. He rushed to Mme. Pitre's house with a
bottle of sleeping pills, plus a line of persuasive talk such
as few other salesmen anywhere in the world would think

of attempting. The police knew that she was directly responsible for the destruction of Flight 108, Guay told her. He urged her to commit suicide to escape punishment. While she was about it, she should leave a note explaining that Guay had been her intended victim, that she thought it was he, not Mme. Guay, who was taking the plane.

Before taking a moderate overdose of pills, Mme. Pitre told a friend about Guay's advice. The friend passed the news indirectly to Bélanger and Perrault. Discharged from the hospital a few days later, Mme. Pitre was questioned in her home by the police. She readily admitted having taken the parcel to the airport—but only as a favor to Guay, who had told her it contained a statue.

The news that the hunt for the woman in black had ended, and that Mme. Pitre was talking to the police, was broadcast on Friday the twenty-third, just two weeks after the awful crash. Guay heard it over his mother-in-law's radio and pounded the table. "*La maudite salope* [damned slut]!" he shouted in rage, and stormed out the door.

A warrant had already been issued for Guay's arrest. Now police picked him up. Chafing in Quebec Men's Jail through the long weekend, Guay talked at some length to a sympathetic cellmate—who had been provided by the authorities for just this purpose. Among other things, Guay said that a watchmaker named Généreux Ruest, a brother of Mme. Pitre, had fashioned a timing mechanism for the parcel in which the police were now taking such an interest. Guay, Ruest and Mme. Pitre had met during World War II, he explained; they worked together in a Quebec munitions factory. Later, Ruest had repaired watches and jewelry for him. Questioned in his cluttered repair shop on Monday, shifty-eyed Ruest admitted having made a timing mechanism at Guay's request. He insisted, however, that all he knew was what Guay had told him—he wanted to "blow out stumps on his place in the country." Guay had no place in the country.

Private and public investigators, working hand in hand, had done a superb job. Now Captain J. A. Matté, chief of detectives of Quebec provincial police, enlisted the aid of Dr. Lucien Gravel, a professor of chemistry at Laval University. Gravel designed and constructed a detonating mechanism from familiar materials such as could have been used in Guay's fateful parcel. When this device was demonstrated in court and other evidence was presented by the Crown, Guay was ordered to stand trial for "having killed and assassinated Rita Morel [Guay], your wife."

Curiously enough, it fell to the lot of my wife's father—Albert Sévigny, chief justice of the Superior Court, Province of Quebec—to preside over Guay's trial. It began February 24, 1950, in the grim stone Palais de Justice on the terrace high above the St. Lawrence River, where Guay had watched the doomed plane disappear into the northeast five months earlier. The Crown's preparation of its case had not been easy. It was not enough that scientific investigators and police experts were certain that Guay was guilty, nor to prove, as Dr. Gravel had done at the preliminary hearing, that the plane *could* have been dynamited. The prosecution had to prove that the plane actually *had* been dynamited.

For four months Dr. Gravel and experts of Quebec Province's Medico-Legal Laboratories in Montreal sifted the wreckage until traces of burnt dynamite and fragments of a dry-cell battery which was not part of the plane's equipment were found. Canadian Pacific hired chemists to make more than two thousand tests of fragments of damaged clothing and suitcases from the airplane; then similar clothing was purchased and packed in similar suitcases and blown up by gasoline, TNT and other explosives. Only dynamite, it was shown, produced the identical chemical and physical effects that were found in the debris at the scene of the crash.

As a witness I testified merely to the unexceptional character of the flight from Montreal to Quebec, and to the evident fitness of the crew. The scientific evidence against Guay was overwhelming.

At the thirteen-day trial's end, Chief Justice Sévigny spent three hours scrupulously instructing the French-speaking jurymen, warning them clearly that if they had any reasonable doubt of the defendant's guilt they were to find him innocent. The jury took just seventeen minutes, probably the shortest time ever recorded in a Canadian murder trial, to return to the courtroom with the dread verdict: "*Coupable!*"

The chief justice ordered Guay to stand while sentence to be hanged was pronounced. "Your crime," he said, "is a crime of infamy. For what you did, there is no name!"

From his death cell Guay managed to strike twice again. Now it was not a forbidden lust and a dead wife's ten-thousand-dollar life insurance policy that he was after. He sought revenge. At the outset of his difficulties with the law Guay had warned Mme. Pitre and her brother, "Remember, if you talk to the police, you will have me to deal with." So, as he awaited execution, he wrote a minutely detailed forty-page document which helped to seal the doom of his two partners in crime. Both were duly convicted.

Today, as we see newspaper stories of other ghastly "murders by airplane," Françoise and I remember the words that Guay heard in guilty silence the day my father-in-law pronounced his doom. "*Rien n'échappe à la justice de Dieu!*" the judge thundered to the jury, to Guay and to the world. "*Nothing escapes the justice of God!*"

The Archer-Shee Case

By Alexander Woollcott

Alexander Woollcott, who died in 1943, was a drama critic, radio personality and essayist who became a kind of American legend—enshrined in the Kaufman-Hart play The Man Who Came to Dinner. *He was known for his biting wit, but also for the warmth, humanity and love of liberty which come through in this story of a court case which aroused all England over the rights of one small boy.*

F ROM time to time, since the turn of the century, there has issued from a publishing house in London and Edinburgh a series of volumes called *Notable British Trials*. Now, as an avid subscriber to the series, I have long been both exasperated and puzzled by the fact that it contained no transcript of that trial which, more and more in recent years, has taken definite shape in my own mind as one of the most notable and certainly the most British of them all.

Nowhere in England or America is there available in any library a record of the Archer-Shee case. But within recent months, by a series of curious chances, a complete private record of the entire case has come into my possession, and it is my present plan to put it into print for the use of anyone who needs it as a light or craves it as a tonic. For the Archer-Shee case is a short, sharp, illuminating chapter in the long history of human liberty, and a study of it might, it seems to me, stiffen the purpose of all those who in our own day are freshly resolved that that liberty shall not perish from the earth.

In the fall of 1908, Mr. Martin Archer-Shee, a bank manager in Liverpool, received word, through the commandant of the Royal Naval College at Osborne, that the Lords Commissioners of the Admiralty had decided to dismiss his thirteen-year-old son George, who had been proudly entered as a cadet only a few months before.

It seems that a five-shilling postal order had been stolen from the locker of one of the boys, and after a sifting of evidence the authorities felt unable to escape the conclusion that young Archer-Shee was the culprit. This devastating news brought the family hurrying to Osborne. Was it true? No, Father. Then why did the authorities accuse him? The bewildered boy had no idea. The offish captain could only refer the father to the Admiralty; and the Lords of the Admiralty—by not answering letters, evading direct questions and all the familiar technique of bureaucratic delay—retired behind the tradition that the Navy must be the sole judge of material suitable for the making of a British officer.

Thus the elder Archer-Shee found himself faced with a maddening, cruel opponent—the massive, complacent inertia of a government department which is not used to being questioned and does not like to be bothered. He was challenging a bureaucracy to battle.

At a dozen points in the ensuing struggle a less resolute fighter might have been willing to give up, and one of

smaller means would have had to. But I think the father
knew in his heart that his son was innocent. Probably he
was strengthened by his memory of how bitterly his little
boy had wept on the day they took him away from Osborne. While there was a breath left in his body and a
pound in his bank account, he could not let the youngster
go out into the world with that stain on his name.

The first great step was the retaining of Sir Edward
Carson, then at the zenith of his incomparable reputation
as an advocate. It was only after he had heard the boy's
own story (and raked him with such a bracketing fire of
questions as he was famous for directing against a witness)
that he agreed to take the case at all. From that interview
he rose, saying in effect, "This boy did not steal that
postal order. Now, let's get at the facts."

This took a bit of doing. It was the nub of the difficulty
that the small embryo officer had, by becoming a cadet,
lost the rights of an ordinary citizen without yet reaching
that status which would have entitled him to a court-
martial. But Carson was determined to get the case into
court. Resisting him in this was Sir Rufus Isaacs, later to
become, as Lord Reading, Chief Justice of England, but
then Solicitor-General, and compelled by professional
tradition to defend the Admiralty's action at every step.

Carson finally had recourse to an antique and long-
neglected device known as the Petition of Right. If a subject approach the throne with a Petition of Right and the
King consent to write across it "Let right be done," His
Majesty can, in that instance and on that issue, be sued
like any commoner.

Instead of welcoming such a course as the quickest way
of settling the controversy, the Admiralty, perhaps from
sheer force of habit, resorted to legal technicalities as a
means of delay. Indeed, it was only the human impatience

of the justices, to whom a demurrer was carried on appeal, that finally cut through the red tape. They would eventually have to decide whether or not a Petition of Right was the suitable remedy, but in the meantime, they asked, why not let them have the facts?

So at long last, on a hot day in July 1910—nearly two years after the postal order was stolen and too late for any hope of finding out who really had stolen it—the case came before a jury. By this time it was being treated by the press as a *cause célèbre*, and all the Empire was following it with bated breath. Carson was on his feet in open court speaking for the Suppliant:

> A boy thirteen years old has been labeled and ticketed for all his future life as a thief and a forger. Gentlemen, I protest against the injustice to a child, without communication with his parents, without his case ever being put, or an opportunity of its ever being put forward by those on his behalf. That little boy from the day that he was first charged, up to this moment, whether in the ordeal of being called in before his Commander and his Captain, or whether under the softer influences of the persuasion of his own loving parents, has never faltered in the statement that he is innocent.

These reverberant words had overtones which all Englishmen could hear. Now the case was being followed with painful attention by plain men and women slowly come to the realization that here was no minor rumpus over the punctilio of the service, indeed no mere matter of a five-shilling theft and a youngster's reputation, but a microcosm in which was summed up all the long history of British liberty. Here in the small visible compass of one boy's fate was the entire issue of the inviolable sovereignty of the individual.

The Archer-Shees had as their advantageous starting

point the inherent improbability of the boy's guilt. There seemed no good reason why he *should* steal five shillings when he was in ample funds. But if, out of sheer deviltry, he *had* stolen his classmate's postal order, it seemed odd that instead of cashing it furtively he would openly get permission to go to the post office, which was out of bounds, and loiter about for some time in an effort to get a schoolmate to go with him. This inherent improbability, so visible from this distance, had quite escaped the attention of the college authorities.

When young Terence Back dolefully reported that the postal order which had arrived that morning was missing from his locker, the Chief Petty Officer at once telephoned the post office to find out if it had been cashed. It had. Oh!

There followed a rush of officialdom to the post office and much questioning of the chief clerk, Miss Anna Clara Tucker. Now, Miss Tucker, had there been any cadets at the post office that day? Yes, two—one to buy a 15*s*. 6*d*. postal order, the other to buy two totaling 14*s*. 9*d*. And was it one of them who had cashed the stolen order? Yes, it was. Would the postmistress be able to pick him out? No. They all looked so alike in their uniforms. But this she *did* remember—the stolen order was cashed by the boy who had bought the postal order for fifteen and six. And which one was that? Well, her records could answer that question. It was Cadet Archer-Shee. (He had needed that order, by the way, to send for a model engine on which his heart was set, and to purchase it he had that morning drawn sixteen shillings from his funds on deposit with the Chief Petty Officer.)

On her testimony the authorities acted. But so muddle-headed was this investigation that the very first précis of that testimony filed with the Admiralty was careful to omit the crucial fact that at the college next morning,

when six or seven of the cadets were herded past her for
inspection, the postmistress had been unable to pick out
Archer-Shee. This failure became patently crucial when,
two years later on that sweltering July day, Carson, with
artfully deceptive gentleness, took over Miss Tucker for
cross-examination.

The cashing of the stolen order and the issuing of the
order for fifteen and six had taken place at the same time?
Well, one transaction after the other. She was in sole
charge of the office at the time? Yes. There were the
telephone to answer, telegrams to take down as they
came over the wire? Yes, and the mail to sort. These
matters often took her away from the window? Yes. So
if one cadet should go away from the window and another step into his place during any one of the interrup-
tions, she might not notice the exchange? That was true.
And, since they all looked alike to her, one cadet in this

very instance *could* have taken the place of another without her realizing, when she returned to the window, that she had not been dealing throughout with the same boy? Possibly. So that now she couldn't say it was Archer-Shee who had cashed the stolen order? She had never said that exactly. Nor could she even be sure, now that she came to think of it, that the stolen order had, in fact, been cashed by the same cadet who bought the order for fifteen and six? Not absolutely sure. That, in effect, was her testimony.

Well, there it was—a gap in her story wide enough to drive a coach through. As soon as he saw it, Sir Rufus knew the jig was up. Wherefore, when court opened on the fourth day, the Solicitor-General announced:

> As a result of the evidence that has been given, I say now, on behalf of the Admiralty, that I accept the statement of George Archer-Shee that he did not write the name on the postal order, and did not cash it, and consequently that he is innocent of the charge.

Then, while the jury swarmed out of the box to shake hands with Carson and with the boy's father, the exhausted advocate turned to congratulate the boy himself, only to find that he wasn't even in court. When, blushing and grinning from ear to ear, he later went to Carson's room in the Law Courts to thank him, the great advocate ventured to ask how in his hour of triumph the boy had happened to be missing. Well, sir, it seems he went to the theater the night before and so had overslept. Overslept! For weeks Carson himself had hardly been able to get any sleep. Overslept! Good God! Hadn't he even been anxious? Oh, no, sir. He had known all along that once the case got into court the truth would come out.

Carson mopped his brow. Then he laughed. Perhaps that *was* the best way to take such things.

Thanks to the House of Commons, neither the public nor the Admiralty was allowed to forget the Archer-Shee case. Several members promptly gave notice that England would expect some specific assurance that the lesson had been learned, that never again would a boy be thus cavalierly dismissed from Osborne without a chance for adequate defense. In this instance, of course, it was too late for anything but apology and indemnification. But month followed month with no word of apology, and, as for indemnification, no offer to pay more than a fraction of what the boy's father had already spent in his defense.

So in March of the following year the attack was renewed. The quaint but familiar device of moving that the salary of the First Lord of the Admiralty be reduced by £100 started the ball rolling. All those who moved to the attack spoke as if nothing in the world could matter more than the question of justice to one small, unimportant boy. The unhappy First Lord was firmly jockeyed into the position where he went on record, at long reluctant last, as expressing in this case his unqualified regrets. He even consented to pay to the boy's father whatever sum a committee of three (including Carson himself) should deem proper. This ended in a payment of £7120, and with that payment the case may be said to have come to an end.

The case—but not the story. That has an epilogue. The characters? Most of them are gone. The boy himself? Well, when it came to him, the author of the epilogue dipped his pen in irony. If you will remember that the boy was thirteen when they threw him out of Osborne, you will realize that when the Great War began he was old enough to die for King and country. And did he?

Of course. As a soldier, mind you. August 1914 found him in America, working in the Wall Street firm of Fisk & Robinson. Somehow he managed to get back to England, join up with the South Staffordshire Regiment, win a commission as second lieutenant and get over to France in time to be killed—at Ypres—in the first October of the war.

So that is the story of Archer-Shee, whose years in the land, all told, were nineteen. To me, his has always been a deeply moving story, and more and more, as the years have gone by, a significant one. For this can be said about the Archer-Shee case: that it could not happen in any totalitarian state. It is so peculiarly English, this story of a whole people getting worked up about a little matter of principle; above all, the story of the foremost men of the land taking up the cudgels—against the state, mind you—because a mere youngster had been unfairly treated.

The defendant was charged with slaying a beautiful girl. Though her body had never been found, the prosecution had woven a tight net of circumstantial evidence. Meanwhile, the defense lawyer kept harping on the theory of reasonable doubt; and, in his address to the jury, he began talking about the dead girl. Then he exclaimed dramatically as he pointed toward the courtroom door: "There she is now!"

Every member of the jury turned to look. "What more proof of doubt that this girl was murdered," the lawyer demanded, "than that every one of you turned to see if she had walked into this room?"

Nevertheless the jury returned a verdict of guilty.

"But you all looked," protested the defense lawyer. "Everyone in the courtroom did!"

"Everyone," said the foreman, "but your client."

—*Grant Cooper*

Mr. Hard-to-Catch

By Irwin Ross

THE ESCAPE of convict Robert L. Balgar was one of the simplest on record. Balgar was in a Chicago office building, in the custody of a guard, when he asked permission to go to the washroom. The guard consented, and the prisoner was not caught again for twenty-two years. The hunt for Balgar became the longest active chase that FBI old-timers can remember—a classic instance of how the FBI's far-flung apparatus, running down hundreds of leads, following a shadowy trail back and forth across a continent, finally trips up its man.

By trade, Robert Balgar was a lawyer; by profession and innate talent, a master swindler. In 1920, he was a handsome, slightly built man, past his first youth, who wore pince-nez glasses, groomed himself meticulously and always bore a stiff air of probity. His run-in with the law resulted from a $500,000 stock swindle. Convicted of using the mails to defraud, during the early 1920's he began a seven-year prison term at Leavenworth. In September of that year he was brought to Chicago under guard to testify in a civil suit. The relationship between guard and prisoner on this junket was congenial. Except for leg irons at night, the prisoner was free of physical restraint.

In Chicago they were met at the train by Balgar's sweetheart, Rosie Niktin, and his brother Charles. They visited Balgar's divorced wife and went to the movies. There they lost each other in the crowded theater, but after the show the prisoner dutifully sought out his guard. Balgar made his court appearance, and the following morning before leaving for Leavenworth he and the guard dropped by Charles Balgar's law office, where Robert tried to phone a sister in order to procure $5000. He couldn't reach her and suggested that his brother write a note asking for the money. Charles sat down at the typewriter, and at this point Robert asked permission to visit the men's room. The guard did not accompany his prisoner because he was intrigued by what the brother was writing. He couldn't understand what Balgar wanted with $5000. Five minutes passed, and Balgar did not return. The guard looked for him in the washroom, in adjoining offices, then questioned the elevator operators. He phoned friends of the convicted man to ask whether they had seen Robert. Not until the end of the afternoon did he conclude with reluctance that his prisoner had escaped.

At the outset there was nothing to indicate that Balgar would prove an elusive fugitive. His trial and dramatic escape made him a figure of considerable notoriety; he was not the average anonymous citizen. The FBI immediately began a careful manhunt. They kept Rosie Niktin, Charles Balgar and other members of the fugitive's family under close surveillance. They interviewed every

person Balgar saw in Chicago in the two days before his
flight. They interviewed friends and relatives in New
York, West Virginia, Massachusetts. The FBI operates on
the principle that if you talk to enough people someone
will ultimately make a slip, someone else will pay off an
ancient grudge.

But for a long time they could learn nothing of Robert
Balgar's whereabouts. He was that exasperating type of
criminal who associates with decent folk and never with
fast women or underworld characters—a delicacy of
taste which cut off potential sources of information. It
was fifteen months before the FBI got its first distant
glimpse of him. A Chicago businessman reported that he
had recently been approached by Balgar in the Continental Hotel in Paris. The fugitive said he was living in
Berlin and Paris, making a good deal of money setting up
corporations along American lines. It would be a great
embarrassment if he were picked up, but no danger: he
had discovered that his offense was not extraditable. The
FBI had no alternative but to alert immigration and customs officials at all U.S. ports.

Later the FBI learned that Balgar had fled to Canada
after leaving Chicago. In Montreal he was arrested for
some offense and promptly freed himself with a thousand-
dollar bribe. With a U.S. passport under a false name he
sailed for Europe. He was now married to Rosie Niktin.
The next tip did not come until several years later. It sent
a New York agent to the office of a small corporation in
downtown Manhattan. Officials there identified Balgar
from his picture as a man named A. B. Danton, who had
recently called to arrange for the incorporation of a British company in Delaware. He had mentioned that he was
stopping at the Roosevelt Hotel. Investigating, the FBI
man learned that Balgar had checked out within an hour

after his departure from the downtown office. He had given a San Francisco address when registering at the hotel, but by the time agents in San Francisco reached it, Danton-Balgar had skipped altogether—with his wife and $70,000 in other people's money. For a time he had lived in style at the Mark Hopkins Hotel, having founded and become president of a loan company whose stockholders unwittingly provided the wherewithal.

Three years after that (seven after his escape) Balgar was reported again in Paris, under the name of Roger Dilton, but he still could not be extradited. Another nine years passed. Then one summer the Los Angeles police arrested seventeen-year-old Joseph Clinton on the charge of stealing ninety-seven dollars' worth of stamps from a dental supply company. Clinton said he'd sold the stamps at half price to a mild-mannered, portly chap named Albert B. Danton. Faced by the police, Danton blandly denied the accusation, said he did not even know the youngster. But they booked him on suspicion of receiving stolen property, then released him on $500 bail. His fingerprints were mailed to the FBI in Washington, where they were quickly identified as Robert Balgar's. A teletype order went immediately to the Los Angeles FBI to pick him up. Agents raced to his home, but Balgar had again left town. This time he had absconded with a mere $1500—collection money, belonging to his clients.

Balgar had by now achieved an excellent disguise. Formerly a thin man with sharply etched features, he had become heavy, with sagging face, thick jowls and large bags under the eyes. Add a receding hairline and a thin mustache, and his present picture bore little resemblance to the man who had gone to jail in the 1920's. He had come to Los Angeles in the 1930's and started a legitimate bill-collection agency. But on the side Balgar had dabbled in stolen stamps and in conning middle-aged ladies out of their savings. He and his wife led a secluded social life.

A good many details of his latest flight were available. Balgar left town on the day after his arrest—in his 1935 Chevrolet sedan. He was accompanied by his wife and their young son. Soon word came from Illinois that the car, identified by serial and motor numbers, had been transferred to an M. Lassenger, who had a Chicago street address. Lassenger was the name of Rosie Balgar's sister. The Chicago office immediately put the Lassenger residence under surveillance. They queried all 360 elementary schools in Chicago, on the chance that the Balgars' son might be enrolled. Finally the Lassengers were approached directly. They were cordial, even agreed to let their house be searched. But there was no trace of the Balgars.

Meanwhile, all state motor-vehicle bureaus were requested to watch for Balgar's car. Also, thinking that Balgar might stay in the bill-collection business, the FBI obtained copies of his past advertisements in classified columns—he prided himself on being able to compose a catchy ad—and asked newspapers in large cities to report if any individual placed an ad with similar wording. On top of this, all known friends, relatives and business associates of Balgar—more than two hundred in all—were searched out and reinterviewed. In March of the next year—it was now seventeen years after his escape—the FBI was notified that Balgar's Chevrolet sedan had been registered under the name of Mildred Lassenger, who gave a Newark, New Jersey, address. But the address was that of a nonresidential YWCA hall; nobody there had ever heard of Mildred Lassenger.

Nearly five more years passed without another useful clue. Then, almost twenty-two years after Balgar's escape, the FBI again circularized all state motor-vehicle bureaus for new data on his Chevrolet. Florida wrote that the car had once been registered in that state by Mildred Lassenger, who gave an address in Miami Beach. But the superintendent of the apartment house at that address did not remember the Lassengers, nor could he identify photographs of Mr. or Mrs. Balgar. The lead looked like another dead end. The agents obtained a list of tenants during the season for which the car had been registered and painstakingly tracked each one down. One of them, Milton Campbell, readily identified the Balgars' photographs as Mr. and Mrs. Ronald Smith. Moreover, the "Smiths" had returned to Florida one winter, and Campbell directed the agents to the apartment house where they had lived that second season. Each tenant there was visited. One man remembered Ronald Smith and had recently seen him in New York, coming out of an office building on 42nd Street. This information was phoned to New York and two FBI men immediately visited the 42nd Street building. They found Ronald Smith's name listed in the lobby; he was running a collection business.

A mature, gray-haired man greeted the agents. They asked him about a mythical individual they said they were investigating. Smith amiably explained that he did not know the man. Then the agents produced Balgar's old "Wanted" circular from the 1930's. "This is really what we're here for," one said. "It rather looks like you, Mr. Smith."

"It does," he said softly. "It's been a long time, gentlemen."

Why the Choir Was Late

By George H. Edeal

IT HAPPENED on the evening of March 1, 1950, in Beatrice, Nebraska. In the afternoon the Reverend Walter Klempel had gone to the West Side Baptist Church to get things ready for choir practice. He lit the furnace— most of the singers were in the habit of arriving around 7:15, and it was chilly in the church—and went home to dinner. But at 7:10, when it was time for him to go back to the church with his wife and daughter, Marilyn Ruth, it turned out that Marilyn Ruth's dress was soiled, so Mrs. Klempel ironed another. Thus they were still at home when it happened.

Ladona Vandegrift, a high-school sophomore, was having trouble with a geometry problem. She knew practice began promptly and always came early. But she stayed to finish the problem.

Royena Estes was ready, but the car would not start. So she and her sister, Sadie, called Ladona Vandegrift and asked her to pick them up. But Ladona was the girl with the geometry problem, and the Estes sisters therefore had to wait.

Mrs. Leonard Schuster would ordinarily have arrived at 7:20 with her small daughter, Susan. But on this particular evening she had to go to her mother's house to help her get ready for a missionary meeting.

Herbert Kipf, lathe operator, would have been ahead of time but had put off an important letter. "I can't think why," he said. He lingered over it and was late.

It was a cold evening. Stenographer Joyce Black, feeling "just plain lazy," stayed in her warm house until the last possible moment. She was almost ready to leave when it happened.

Because his wife was away, machinist Harvey Ahl was taking care of his two boys. He was going to take them to practice with him, but somehow he got wound up talking. When he looked at his watch, he saw he was already late.

Marilyn Paul, the pianist, had planned to arrive half an hour early. However, she fell asleep after dinner, and when her mother awakened her at 7:15 she had time only to tidy up and start out.

Mrs. F. E. Paul, choir director and mother of the pianist, was late simply because her daughter was. She had tried unsuccessfully to awaken the girl earlier.

High-school girls Lucille Jones and Dorothy Wood were neighbors and customarily went to practice together. Lucille was listening to a 7-to-7:30 radio program and broke her habit of promptness because she wanted to hear the end. Dorothy waited for her.

At 7:25, with a roar heard in most of Beatrice, the West Side Baptist Church blew up. The walls fell, the heavy wooden roof crashed straight down like the weight in a deadfall. But, because of such matters as a soiled dress, a catnap, an unfinished letter, a geometry problem and a stalled car, all the members of the choir were late—something which had never occurred before.

Firemen thought the explosion had been caused by natural gas, which may have leaked into the church from a broken pipe outside and been ignited by the fire in the furnace. The Beatrice choir members had no particular theory about the fire's cause, but each of them began to reflect on the heretofore inconsequential details of his life, wondering at exactly what point it is that one can say, "This is an act of God."

One December afternoon I was walking along Michigan Boulevard, Chicago, when suddenly street and people vanished from my vision. Before me, as on a motion-picture screen, unrolled a strip of grass with an iron fence; three young trees in spring green stood at one side; in the far distance factory smokestacks trailed sooty plumes across the sky. Near the trees stood a small circle of men and women in black, and on the road by the grass was a limousine, from which alighted two men and a woman in black. The woman was I. Gently the men urged me forward until I was among the others, looking down at a two-foot hole cut in the grass, in which someone was placing a small box with infinite tenderness. What was I doing there? I recognized the faces of my husband's family, tear-stained and sad. Only he was missing. Then I knew what was in the box.

The reality of Michigan Boulevard slid back across the vision. My good sense urged me to dismiss the whole thing as a crazy vapor, conceived of loneliness for my husband.

The next February I received word from China that my husband had died and that they were sending his ashes to Chicago. On May 30, I went with my brothers-in-law, in a limousine, to Rosehill Cemetery, which I had never seen. The men got out and waited for me. For a second I could not raise my eyes. At last I looked: there was the spring grass, there the three young trees and the iron fence and the smokestacks in the distance. And there was the little square hole just big enough to take the box with my husband's ashes.

On that December day I had seen over the bridge of time to this day which marked the end of a phase of my life.

—Irene Kuhn

The Letter the Birds Wrote

By John William Rogers

This true story was told to the writer by Mrs. William Bacon of Dallas, Texas—a native of Greenville and the daughter of Daniel Upthegrove. The story is so remarkable it deserves to be preserved among the colorful and unexpected dramas that occasionally happen in courts of law.

DANIEL UPTHEGROVE was a distinguished lawyer in the pioneer days of Texas. In the early 1870's, when he was a young man just making his reputation, there lived not far from Greenville two prominent families who were neighbors and great friends. In one there was a boy named Tom and in the other a girl named Julia. Tom and Julia became sweethearts, and it was understood that the families would give this match their blessing.

One of the customs of the time was for the young people to have gay weekend parties at a ranch home. All the young men, of course, came armed, but to avoid any possible complications guns were taken and locked up in the bunkhouse, to be returned when the party broke up.

Tom and Julia were at one of these ranch-house parties when one of the guests was a visitor from the East, a handsome, vivacious girl who seemed to take Tom's fancy the moment he saw her. He was so attentive that by Sunday afternoon Julia was in a frenzy of jealousy and the two had a violent quarrel. Angered, Tom refused to cease his attentions to the visiting Helen, and that night the party was alarmed by the discovery that Julia had altogether disappeared. A search for her was begun and the next morning they found her. She was lying some miles from the ranch house beneath an oak tree in the Sabine River bottom. She had been shot and beside her lay a gun—Tom's gun.

The members of the house party knew of the lovers' quarrel, and immediately angry, menacing suspicion fell on Tom as the murderer. He protested his innocence and a complete lack of knowledge as to how his gun got there.

The two families which had been such close friends were now bitter enemies. Tom's father came to young Daniel Upthegrove to get him to defend the boy, and, after talking to Tom, Upthegrove was convinced of the boy's innocence and took the case. But the ugly fact that Tom's pistol was lying beside the dead girl could not be explained. Neighborhood resentment against Tom reached such an emotional pitch that it was clear he could not have a fair trial.

In such an atmosphere Upthegrove succeeded in having the case delayed. He remained convinced of Tom's innocence, but he could not discover one detail to cancel out the strong circumstantial evidence that pointed to Tom as the murderer. At last, feeling that only Providence could show the way, he prayed for guidance.

One of Daniel Upthegrove's least impressive friends was an old Indian who had lost a toe and was known by the Indian name of Four Toes. Four Toes liked the bottle, but drunk or sober he liked the young lawyer, and when he was in town he had a way of dropping in for a friendly call. One day Upthegrove noticed that Four Toes carried in his hand a piece of weather-stained paper which he handled with obvious respect.

"What is that paper?" asked the lawyer, curious.

"Letter the birds wrote," answered the Indian.

"You're drunk. Birds don't write letters."

"Me no drunk—this letter birds wrote. I found it in crow's nest."

"Let me see it."

Upthegrove looked at it and his eyes widened. There was a little tear out of the center, but on it he could make out clearly:

Dear Tom:
    You know my great love for you and I thought you loved me, but it is plain after last night that the first hussy who comes along and swishes her skirts can lead you by the nose. I see now there is no future for us—and this is the quickest way out for me.
                                                        Julia

The note was in Julia's handwriting. When the news of it spread, the people who had found Julia's body recalled that on her breast had been one mystifying thing. Caught under a gold pin on her breast was a scrap of paper.

Four Toes seemed convinced that his letter had been

written by the birds in whose nest he had found it. But what Daniel Upthegrove made clear to a jury was that, before Julia's body had been found, a curious crow had seen the letter she had pinned to her breast fluttering in the breeze and, after the manner of crows, had swooped down and torn it loose to carry it to the nest he was building. And so the letter the birds had written saved a man's life in a court of law.

One night, when the river steamer *Pennsylvania* lay in St. Louis, Samuel Clemens (Mark Twain), employed as steersman, slept at his sister's house and had this dream: He saw his young brother Henry lying in a metallic burial case in the sitting room; on his breast was a bouquet of white flowers with a single crimson bloom in the center. When he awoke, the dream was so vivid he believed it real. He dressed, intending to look at his dead brother, but went out first on the street and had walked to the middle of the block before it flashed on him it was only a dream. He told his sister the dream, then put it out of his mind.

The *Pennsylvania*, with both Samuel and Henry on board, made a safe trip to New Orleans; there Samuel was transferred to the *A. T. Lacey*, which left two days behind the *Pennsylvania*. Just below Memphis, the *Pennsylvania* blew up. Samuel Clemens found his brother at Memphis in an improvised hospital, with about thirty others desperately injured. His case was hopeless, and he died on the sixth night after the accident.

Samuel saw the dead boy taken to the "dead room." Then, worn out with the long strain and grief, he slept. Many hours later he went to where Henry lay. The coffins provided for the other dead were of unpainted wood; but the youth and striking face of Henry Clemens had aroused such interest that the ladies of Memphis had bought for him a metallic case. Samuel Clemens saw his brother exactly as he had seen him in his dream, lacking only the bouquet of white flowers with its crimson center—a detail made complete while he stood there. At that moment an elderly lady came in with a large white bouquet, and in the center was a single red rose. —*Albert Bigelow Paine*

Tillie Scrubbed On

By William F. McDermott and Karl Detzer

WHEN pretty, dark-eyed Terry Colangelo went to work as a cub reporter on the Chicago *Daily Times* in 1943, one of City Editor Karin Walsh's instructions to her was: "Read every word in the *Times*, every day." Terry did—and on the afternoon of October 10, 1944, she found Chicago's story of the year in three lines of small type among the classified advertisements. Circling the terse announcement with black crayon, she placed it on Walsh's desk: "$5000 reward for killers of Officer Lundy on December 9, 1932. Call Gro. 1758, 12–7 P.M."

"Might be a story behind it," she suggested.

Walsh agreed, and called reporter Jim McGuire, who had once been a detective and who had dug out some difficult crime stories for the *Times*. "Find what this is all about," Walsh directed.

McGuire went to work. "The ad was placed by a woman named Tillie Majczek," he reported shortly. "Her son, Joe, was convicted of killing this copper eleven years ago. He's serving ninety-nine years in Joliet prison."

"Find out where the woman got the five grand,"

Walsh said. "Maybe there's a feature story in it." There
was. In a few weeks it had all Chicago talking.

When reporter McGuire went to see Tillie that October
afternoon he found her in the kitchen of her drab little
house in the smoky, raucous district back of the Chicago
stockyards. "I'm from the *Times*," McGuire said. "I came
about your ad." Before him stood a short woman, spare
and muscular; streaks of white were beginning to make
chalk marks on her black hair. Age accentuated her high
Slavic cheekbones, and her shoulders were stooped,
obviously from hard work.

"Sit," she bade McGuire, and then sat down across
the kitchen table from him, speaking slowly as she
searched for the English words.

"Joe good boy," she said. "Joe don't kill nobody."

Did she have any proof? McGuire asked. No, she said,
only the same proof which the jury had refused to believe
in the trial. That was why she had advertised—to find
out who murdered Patrolman Lundy and thus prove that
her Joe could not have been guilty. She was ready to pay
$5000 for the truth. "How did you raise the money?"
McGuire asked.

"I scrub floors," Tillie answered. "In office building
downtown, at night. For eleven years. Ever since my boy
Joe is gone."

Tillie's husband worked in the stockyards, she said.
He was often laid off, and she knew she could not depend
on his pay envelope to purchase the truth that would set
Joe free. So she took the only kind of job she could get.
She worked eight hours a night, six nights a week, on her
hands and knees, scrubbing floors in a Loop office building. Eleven years she had scrubbed—3500 weary nights.
Acres of marble floor, oceans of soapy water, years of
backache and heartache. Yet her courage had never

wavered. It took a lot of scrubbing for Tillie to make enough to save $5000, but now she had the money.

"Has anybody answered the ad?" McGuire asked. Tillie shook her head. She said she had tried before, with $3500, and no one had answered that ad, either. Justice, she was discovering, could be an expensive luxury.

Back in his office, McGuire told Walsh what he had learned. It would make a nice feature for the paper, Walsh agreed. But the story wasn't complete. "Any chance the kid really wasn't guilty?" he asked.

McGuire said: "That's what I'm wondering. The old lady is sure he's innocent."

"Better check up on that angle too," Walsh decided. "If the kid's had a raw deal, let's set him free."

For ten and a half months McGuire and another *Times* reporter, Jack McPhaul, dug up hidden evidence, scoured the town and the nation for witnesses to this long-forgotten crime. They had to overcome the slick maneuverings of shabby politicians who did not want the case revived. Meanwhile, Tillie scrubbed on. Every week she put her savings in the bank. And while she scrubbed, McGuire and McPhaul dug for facts and the *Times* printed them.

The sordid story began on an afternoon in December 1932. The foreign quarter back of the yards was a rash of speakeasies. One of them, on South Ashland Avenue, was run by a frowzy, middle-aged blonde named Vera. At 2:45 p.m. on December 9, Patrolman William D. Lundy, just off duty, stepped into the illicit barroom and ordered a drink. Vera served him. There was one other customer in the dingy back room. Lundy and the customer talked about Vera's foolish habit of keeping several thousand dollars concealed in her icebox. The whole neighborhood

knew the money was there. Some day . . . At that moment
two tall men stepped into the room with guns in their
hands. They were startled to find a policeman there.
Lundy had his overcoat on, and his pistol was hard to
get at. As he reached for it the men shot him and fled,
leaving him dying.

This was the year before the opening of the Chicago
World's Fair, and Mayor Anton Cermak, distressed at
his city's shabby reputation, ordered a cleanup. There
was hue and cry back of the yards that afternoon.
Detectives swarmed through the streets, questioned informers, hunted down known gunmen, belabored all
witnesses. On that day Tillie Majczek's son, Joe, a
machinist's helper, was at his home, a mile from Vera's
speakeasy. He had not gone to work because his wife,
Helen, was about to have a baby. First he did the housework for her; then some coal which he had ordered arrived at 2:30, and at 2:45 he was still shoveling it into his
cellar. Three neighbors testified to this at the trial.

But Joe and his wife had made one mistake. They knew
nothing about the murder and the frantic police search,
so when an old acquaintance knocked on their door that
night and said he was "in trouble," they let him spend the
night in their home. What's more, they told neighbors
that the man had been there—and some neighbor told
the police. Joe did not answer the description of either of
the gunmen; he was too small, too slight. Two men who
had seen the fleeing murderers said positively that he was
not one of them. Vera also stated that Joe was not involved; but later, after a private talk with the police, she
changed her story and said Joe was one of the killers. She
alone identified him in court. The judge who heard the
case was not satisfied; he called each of the witnesses back
and questioned them. McGuire found out that after Joe's

conviction the judge had told his family he was convinced
that a grave injustice had been done. He had worried
about it and had planned to try to right the wrong, but
died before he had an opportunity to reopen the case. So
Chicago forgot Joe.

Joe's wife used to take their baby to see him in prison,
and Tillie would go along. Tillie tried to cheer Joe up;
she told him that as soon as she had earned enough money
everything would come out all right. Joe was working
hard at his prison tasks and was learning bookkeeping and
shorthand. One day, after five years, Joe's wife came to
see him alone. "Joe," she said, "I know you are innocent,
but you'll never get out of here. And our child needs a
father in the home. A man has asked me to marry him
and I'm going to get a divorce."

That didn't seem right to Tillie. Joe had so much to
worry about without Helen making life so much harder
for him. But Tillie didn't say anything. She just kept on
scrubbing.

The *Times* reporters pored over the court records. They
checked the characters of all the witnesses. They found
public documents which they believed the police and the
State's Attorney's office were trying to conceal. They
traced the members of the jury which had convicted Joe
and from four of them got sworn statements that they
would not have convicted him if the newly uncovered evidence had been presented at the trial. Joe's old neighbors,
still resentful that their honest testimony had been brushed
aside by a trial prosecutor avid for a conviction, were
anxious to tell again the truth as they knew it. The *Times*
arranged a lie-detector test for Joe. "The man is telling
the truth," was the report. Then the *Times* engaged a
lawyer, who marshaled all the facts dug out so arduously

by the reporters. These facts were so convincing that the state pardon board made a top-to-bottom investigation, then recommended that Joe be immediately released.

On August 15, 1945, Joe Majczek walked out of the Joliet prison gate. Tillie, waiting in the shadow of the tall stone wall, threw her arms around her son. She didn't weep. Joe was free, wasn't he? Jim McGuire took Tillie and Joe to Chicago in a car. There was a little family party that evening in the Majczek kitchen. Tillie had prepared the things Joe liked best. He sat at the head of the table and she stood beside him, piling his plate high. Everything was all right now—her boy was free again.

The *Times* refused Tillie's offer of the $5000, and she kept it for Joe. He might need it some day, she said. Just then Joe didn't need it: after his release he got a fine job as secretary to a manufacturer and began making a new life for himself. That was enough for Tillie, who had no idea that her long years of indomitable faith and drudgery were an epic of silent, shining courage.

Supreme Court Justice Arthur Goldberg has made an interesting suggestion—that defendants acquitted in criminal trials be reimbursed by the government. Such a radical departure from custom isn't anything the nation should leap into, but it might well bear examination, and on a wider scale than Goldberg has suggested.

Today we live under such a multiplicity of laws and regulations that any of us could find himself accused of violating one of them. If you are a businessman, you are vulnerable also to a vast number of quasi-judicial regulating agencies. Hearings before such agencies may be costly as well as time-consuming. Financially vulnerable organizations may "win" their cases but be put out of business by the cost. Since our vast machinery of government does embody such hazards to its citizens, new aids to justice along the line Justice Goldberg suggests may be needed to make legal defenses meaningful. —*Minneapolis Star*

The Curse of Amen-Ra

By Edgar Wallace

*"The Curse of Amen-Ra" is a small gem by one of the twentieth
century's most popular and prolific masters of mystery, who died
in 1932. Modern experts in Egyptian archaeology do not confirm
all its statements in their own writings, but twelve men connected with the opening of Tutankhamen's tomb in 1922 did die
within seven years after the event. "The Curse" is such a classic
that the editors are happy to include it among the stories in this
volume. Howard Carter, described as the only man among the
discoverers who remained alive, survived until 1939.*

A PORTLY DRAGOMAN watched the little group of helmeted Europeans who were directing the excavations of Tutankhamen's tomb. He turned to his employer, the special correspondent of a London newspaper, and said: "They will find gold and death." The startled newspaper man asked why.

"Because," said the dragoman, "the old gods live. This man"—he waved his hand contemptuously toward the tomb—"was an unbeliever. He found the old gods too late; and he offended the god of all gods, Amen-Ra."

Somebody told Lord Carnarvon this story. He did not laugh at it. He was a very sane, unemotional man. In all seriousness, he immediately said: "I recognize that possibility." And this is the curious fact, that every mummy which is supposed by popular tradition to be "unlucky" is the mummy of one who has defied the great gods.

Tutankhamen was buried with elaborate ceremonial, but they made no image of Ra in yellow for the bow of the boat which carried his swathed body; nor did they paint on suitable plaques the figures of the gods Tem, Shu, Tefnut, Seb, Mut, Osiris, Isis, Suti and Nephthys and anoint them with cedar oil. And the Spell of Peace did not go into the closed cavern where they laid the body of the young king. Only a great unrest. For though Tutankhamen was hastily recalling the exiled divinities, and had changed his very name to propitiate them, the Old Ones who sit on the Parapets of Hell were not with him, and their wrath dwelt in the pitch-dark chamber where they laid the embalmed shell of the unbeliever.

Some day we shall discover that thought has substance and that love and hate are as material as the rays of the sun; then we shall know that the stories we dismiss as myths and the frantic imaginings of half-demented priests are terribly well founded in sober fact. Hate may not lie like a cloud over the Valley of the Kings, nor stand, an invisible and vengeful shape, to bar intrusion into the mysteries of the dead; but hate is there, a tangible and everlasting factor.

Very clearheaded scientists viewed the excavations with uneasiness. Such men do not believe in ghosts; but they do not preclude the possibilities of psychic phenomena. There are hoodoo men and women—who doubts this? There are ordinary people who carry with them an aura of disaster or fortune. The x which produces such phenomena is a mystery as yet unsolved. In Tutankhamen's tomb was the supreme x, which was death.

With Lord Carnarvon were Howard Carter and his secretary, Dick Bethell; M. Benedite, the French archaeologist in charge of the Department of Antiquities at Cairo; and M. Pasanova. Of those men only one remains alive. When the tomb was opened, two other notables entered. One was Colonel Mervyn Herbert, Carnarvon's half brother; the other was H. G. Evelyn-White. When Herbert entered the cavern he shivered and stopped, reluctant to go on. "I wish to God Carnarvon hadn't found this tomb. Something dreadful is going to happen to our family." Before the year was out he was dead.

When the door was forced Carnarvon walked into the tomb with a smile and a jest. "I wish he hadn't laughed— he will be dead in six weeks," said Arthur Weigall, the writer. Something stung Lord Carnarvon on the cheek. He was a dead man before the wonders of the tomb were fully revealed.

Evelyn-White, Egyptologist and scholar, became a changed man after the tomb was opened. It was as though he were haunted by some unseen and dreadful presence. Within a year he had committed suicide. "There was a curse upon me," he wrote in the letter he left behind him. The Egyptian authorities brought Sir Archibald Douglas Reed, a great radiologist, to X-ray the mummy. Within a year he was a dead man. Professor Laffleur of McGill University was the first American scientist to examine the chamber of death. He did not leave Luxor alive.

Young men, old men, men in the prime of life, men for whose lives any insurance office would have exacted the minimum premium, died, mysteriously, tragically. Only Howard Carter remains. Almost every workman who entered the tomb has passed into the shadows.

Seven French authors and journalists visited the tomb; six were dead within two years. When they unveiled Tutankhamen they found a mark upon his face—the mark left on Lord Carnarvon's face was in exactly the same position. On the day the tomb was opened, a cobra, which was the sacred snake of Egypt, went into Howard Carter's house and destroyed his favorite pet, a canary that the explorer took with him wherever he went; the cobra is the rarest snake in Egypt. Woolf Jocl visited the tomb, and was dead within a year. Jay Gould was taken ill in the tomb and died. To every man without exception who has visited the tomb, misfortune has come.

The most skeptical admit that there is something more than coincidence in the fatalities which have followed association even with minor articles from the tomb. Pieces which have been placed in the Cairo Museum have been "working." Attendants whose duty it is to look after these exhibits have sickened and died for no known reason.

The famous Dr. Mardus was convinced that the opening of Tutankhamen's tomb would bring death. "The Egyptians for seven thousand years possessed the secret of surrounding their mummies with some dynamic force of which we have only the faintest idea," he said.

The Killer,
the Mother and the Boy

By Ernest Havemann

SHORTLY after nine o'clock the night of February 29, 1956, a woman in the little town of Paoli, Pennsylvania, heard six shots. She ran to her window and saw a black De Soto pull away. Lying dead in the street was Patrolman Gerald H. Mitchell, who had been shot when he stopped the car for a routine traffic violation. Within minutes an alarm was out for the killer. A dramatic manhunt, which before its finish would bring terror and a strange kind of heroism to a housewife and her eleven-year-old son, was under way.

The De Soto roared down Route 30 and turned left into Route 202. Two patrol cars, attracted by the reckless driving, took chase. With throttles wide open, hitting up to 110 miles an hour on the straight stretches, this strange caravan bore down on the quiet town of Gladwyne, where most of the residents were by that time on their way to bed.

One of the patrol cars radioed ahead and asked the township police to set up a roadblock. There were two patrol cars parked abreast on Route 23. Their headlights shone brightly to warn the approaching fugitive. As the De Soto approached the roadblock, the driver, blinded by the headlights of the patrol cars, did not see the concrete sides of the bridge. He swung his car around the patrol cars, then tried to swing back. The right side of the De Soto slammed into the concrete with a shower of sparks and was practically sheared off. Bouncing away from this terrible crash, it skidded to a shuddering stop against the left-hand railing of the bridge.

The police got there while the twisted metal on the right side of the car was still burning hot. They played their flashlights on the wreck. What they saw made their flesh creep. The De Soto was empty. And nobody was on the bridge. It was almost as if there had never been a driver at all. Whoever had been in the car had miraculously escaped injury, and presumably had jumped off the bridge into the dense underbrush below. All night long the police searched the woods. And during that time they also found out about the wrecked De Soto. It had a Massachusetts license number and belonged to a filling-station owner near Boston. It had been stolen a few days before by a gunman who held up the station and took $100 in cash as well as the car. The gunman's name was Danny Metcalf and he had a record for minor larceny charges. He was described as young and very small. He stood about five feet three inches, weighed about 130 pounds and had dark, curly hair. The police set up a roadblock on every highway in the area and waited for a smallish young fellow with a New England accent to show up.

On the morning of March 1, the alarm clock in Mrs. Margaret Loweth's bedroom went off as usual at seven. She threw on a dressing gown and began to get breakfast. Her husband, William, a salesman for a chemical company, was off on one of the trips that kept him away from home several nights a week.

One thing that Margaret Loweth definitely did not like was to be left alone, even though her husband's business regularly required it. When he was gone, she was likely to jump a little at any unexpected noise in the house. At the hospital where she worked she was a calm and efficient nurse. In her private life, however, she was the first to admit that she was a timid woman and easily frightened. That morning the three family dogs seemed extraordinarily restive, so Mrs. Loweth chained them to the wire in the backyard, where they could run a little, and came back in. She was in a hurry to get her only son, Billy, eleven years old, off to a dance festival in which he was to appear at a nearby school.

As she was dressing, there was barking and a knock at the back door. It was probably Billy's young friend Ed, stopping by on his way to school. Mrs. Loweth, partly dressed, still barefoot and with her hair not yet combed, slipped on her bathrobe and opened the door. A most extraordinary stranger pushed his way in. He was small, muddy and in tatters. His eyes had the wild look of a hunted animal, and in his right hand he carried a heavy monkey wrench taken from the Loweth garage. He shut the door behind him.

In his own bedroom, Billy had also heard the knock and the wild barking of the dogs. He hoped whoever it was would go away quickly. He was still in his pajamas and he hurried, then, to finish getting dressed. Suddenly he heard his mother scream. It was repeated, and the sounds of a struggle came through the bedroom door. Billy listened tensely. Who was there? What was happening? He heard something fall in a clatter to the floor. His first impulse was to cry out for his mother, as any boy of eleven might. But he stifled the cry and tried to think like an adult. Standing in a closet was his .22-caliber rifle. There was a rule in the family that he could use it only when his father was present, but he felt that this was one time the rule could be broken. He took a box of cartridges but found that his hands were trembling. He managed to get one bullet into the rifle.

By this time the house was strangely quiet. No sound came from the living room. Standing at the closed door of the bedroom, Billy alternated between bravery and cowardice. Finally, he threw the door open and ran into the living room holding the rifle before him. His mother lay near the front door, her head in a pool of blood that still dripped from her scalp. Near her stood a small man with a heavy monkey wrench in his hand. There was blood on the monkey wrench. Billy pointed his rifle.

"Don't shoot!" cried the man. He backed slowly toward the far end of the room, where he could turn a corner into the den. The only thought in Billy's mind was that he might be losing his last chance. He fired the rifle. The bullet struck the man's little finger, tearing the flesh and breaking the bone. He was in pain but not badly hurt. The boy waited, paralyzed by fear. His one bullet was spent and now he was at the fugitive's mercy.

Long seconds went by. Metcalf realized that he had nothing more to fear from this small boy with the crew cut and wide, scared eyes, a baby come to the defense of his mother. He took the rifle away from Billy, almost gently. Billy dropped to the floor beside his mother, begging her to speak to him.

When Margaret Loweth recovered consciousness, the intruder was well armed. He had found the cartridges for the rifle. He had also found a .25-caliber automatic pistol her husband kept in his top drawer. He was listening to

the radio, trying to get a news program. As Mrs. Loweth's
mind gradually became clearer, the man spoke to her.
"I'm going to rest," he said. "Both of you come in here."
He motioned toward the bedroom.

As he lay on the unmade bed, the sight of the blood on
Mrs. Loweth's head seemed to bother him. Finally he
said, "Boy, get some hot water and towels. Help your
mother clean up."

Billy did as bid. The boy seemed perfectly calm. The
fact that her son was not hysterical helped Mrs. Loweth
keep level-headed too. Moments dragged on. All the
while her brain was straining for some plan, some method
of escape. Her head began to ache horribly; she felt a
little faint. She found herself praying: "Dear Lord, please
help me. . . ."

The man on the bed interrupted. "What are you
saying?"

At that moment the phone rang. The man made Billy
answer. It was a neighbor whom Meg Loweth was supposed to pick up and drive to the festival. "Aren't you
ready yet?" the neighbor asked.

Billy hesitated, looking first at the man on the bed and
then at his mother. Mrs. Loweth would not have been
surprised if he had blurted out something that would
have got them both killed. Instead he thought for a moment and said calmly, "We're almost ready."

"Well, I guess we'll walk on," the neighbor said.
"Good-bye."

The intruder was visibly agitated. "That woman's
coming over here," he said. "We've got to get out."

In vain Mrs. Loweth tried to persuade him that the
neighbor merely planned to walk on to school without
waiting for a lift. Danny Metcalf called for some clean
clothes. Billy brought shoes, trousers and a jacket belong-

ing to his father. The shoes and trousers were far too big.
"Let's have a pair of your blue jeans and your sneakers,"
the man told Billy.

At the roadblock north of Gladwyne the patrolman
who stopped a black-and-white Ford at about 8:45 a.m.
figured he was just going through the motions. A woman
in a dark coat and white hat was driving. Two young
fellows who might have been her sons sat beside her. But
the patrolman noticed that the woman had blood
trickling down her left cheek. Under her white hat could
be seen the edge of a towel. "You're bleeding," he said.

One of the "boys" spoke up. "She hurt her head.
We're taking her to the doctor."

The Boston accent registered. At the same moment the
patrolman noticed that the woman was making frantic
motions with her left hand held outside the window. "My
God!" the patrolman shouted. "It's him!"

Danny Metcalf held a pistol against Billy's temple and
said, "Drive on fast or I'll shoot!" One policeman fired a
shot at the Ford. Another policeman cried out frantically, "Hold your fire! He's got a gun to the boy's
head!"

The Ford pulled away, going north and picking up
speed. Margaret Loweth had never driven over sixty
miles an hour before. Now she saw the speedometer
needle hit ninety. "From now on you better do what I
say," the man said. Then, still holding the pistol to
Billy's head, he lapsed into silence.

Mrs. Loweth could see a string of police cars in the
rear-view mirror, but they never seemed to move any
closer. At almost every crossroad there stood another
police car. Yet none of them tried to stop her. Why
weren't they helping her? She did not know that a call
had gone out on the police radio: "Subject sighted pro-

ceeding north in car driven by woman. He has gun to head of small boy. Withdraw all roadblocks. Do not crowd him. Repeat, he has gun to head of small boy. Do not crowd him."

Meg wondered how much longer she could keep going. She knew she was weak from loss of blood, suffering from shock and on the verge of passing out. But she swore to keep going until her boy was safe. The wild ride continued for twenty miles. Mrs. Loweth knew that she was just about at the end of her rope. The attacks of nausea and blackness were coming closer together now. Her arms felt weak, unable to cope any longer with the steering wheel of the speeding car. But before she passed out she was determined to make one last try to save her son and herself.

Ahead of her, as she rounded a curve, she saw a gray sedan going much slower than she was. She could not pass because a truck was coming from the opposite direction. She was going only about fifty now. When the truck was out of the way she started around the sedan. As soon as she was abreast she turned the steering wheel slightly to the right. The two cars grated, swerved and headed into a ditch. Mrs. Loweth took her foot off the accelerator and jammed on the brake. Metcalf grabbed the wheel, but too late. The Ford rocked, pitched, nearly went on its side and then stopped, still on all four wheels.

Danny Metcalf scrambled out of the car, his arm around Billy's neck. Holding the boy in front of him as a shield, he backed into the woods. The police had arrived. "Don't move any closer," Danny Metcalf shouted, "or I'll kill the boy!" The police watched him warily. And then he stumbled in the underbrush and toppled backward. In the next few seconds everything happened. Billy Loweth broke loose and ran. Seeing Billy freed, the police began firing. Danny Metcalf lay dead from a dozen bullets.

Meg Loweth, the timid woman who had suffered a horrible beating, driven a car on a wild ride and wrecked it at the right instant, had been struggling with police officers in an attempt to get to her boy. Now, when she saw Billy safe and sound, she cried, "Thank God!" She looked at the police officers and added, "And thank you gentlemen too." Then she finally fainted.

Alfred Hitchcock, director of movie mystery thrillers, stepped into a New York hotel elevator with a friend and immediately began talking as though continuing a conversation: "So I turned on the light, and there was this girl in the middle of the floor. Her throat was slit and there was a great puddle of blood. Beside the body was a knife. I was in a spot. If I called the police, there'd be a nasty row, and if I didn't somebody would find me there. So I took out my handkerchief and carefully . . ."

At this point the elevator stopped at Hitchcock's floor and he quietly stepped off with his companion, leaving everybody in the car goggle-eyed. —*Chicago Tribune*

Ghost Dog of Sunnybank

Condensed from The Book of Sunnybank

By Albert Payson Terhune

IN TACKLING ghost stories of any kind the teller lays himself open to the charge of lying or of loose mental gear. But dog ghost stories are tenfold more vulnerable than are those of white-robed ex-humans. So I start by refusing to express any personal belief or disbelief. I shall give only objective testimony on Sunnybank's one alleged ghost.

I had a big crossbred dog, Rex, who was almost the size of a Great Dane, short-haired and fawn-colored, with a jagged scar across his foreface. Rex was a lovable chap. From puppyhood he was slavishly devoted to me. He would lie for hours at my feet, staring up into my face. If I moved he would get up quietly and follow me, lying down again close to my feet. It was the same at meals. Rex was not allowed in the dining room. So always he went out on the veranda and stood looking in at me through the French windows just behind my chair, never stirring until the meal was ended. He used also to lie in one particular spot in the hallway outside my study door while I was at work. It was his favorite and *only* resting place. You will presently see why I have dwelt so long on these details.

In March 1916, Rex was killed. Perhaps you have read of his death in my book, *Lad: A Dog*. In the summer of 1917, my lifelong friend the Reverend Appleton Grannis came back from a long sojourn in the West. He had not been at Sunnybank in years. One hot afternoon he and I were chatting at the dining-room table. As usual, I sat with my back to the long veranda window. We were leaving the room when Grannis said to me:

"I thought I knew all your dogs. But there's one I never saw till now. The big dog with the short fawn-colored coat and a scar across his nose."

"We have no short-haired dogs at Sunnybank," I told him. "And none with a scarred foreface."

"But this dog has been standing outside the window staring in at you all the time we were there," he protested. "He's gone now. Which of your dogs is he?"

"I—I don't know," I answered truthfully.

Another close friend, Henry A. Healy, used to drop in often at Sunnybank. He was keenly interested in problems of crossbreeding. Thus he had made more or less of a study of Rex. One evening in the autumn of 1918, Healy and his wife dined with us. Afterward we sat lazily in the firelight for an hour or two. As the guests were starting for home, Healy said:

"Bert, I wish there were some creature so utterly devoted to me as Rex is to you. I've been watching him as he lay at your feet. He kept looking up into your face every minute with a queer kind of adoration. He—"

"Good Lord, man!" I sputtered. "Rex has been dead more than two years."

Healy frowned worriedly for a moment. Then he said, "Yes, I know he's dead. I remember now. . . . Just the same," he said with something like defiance, "I can swear he was lying in the firelight at your feet all evening."

My collie Bruce in those days was the one dog allowed in my study. He lived four years after Rex's death. Never once in that time would he set foot on the stretch of floor just outside the study where Rex had been wont to lie. He would skirt it as though walking around something that lay there. Again and again—before guests who can attest to the truth of this—I have ordered Bruce into the study. Invariably he would make that needless detour. Why? I don't know.

How did Grannis chance to see a dog peering in through the window at me? Grannis, who never had heard of Rex.

I don't know.

Healy was a level-headed business executive, not given to indulging in fancies. What did he see lying at my feet in the firelight?

I don't know.

S. S. Van Dine was a man who couldn't be fooled. He wrote detective stories. He knew dogs.

Mr. Van Dine had a blue-ribbon terrier named Scotty. Scotty ate breakfast with Mr. Van Dine every morning. One morning he didn't show up. Mr. Van Dine went to look for him, and found a man's footprints in the yard. "That man snatched my dog," said Mr. Van Dine.

He measured the footprints to a thousandth of an inch. Took plaster casts of them. Swore he'd catch the thief if it kept him sleuthing until doomsday! Late that afternoon Mr. Van Dine heard a howling and a yowling under his tool shed. Discovered his dog wedged in there hunting a rat.

What about the mysterious footprints in the yard? Mr. Van Dine, by painstaking comparative measurements, determined that they were his *own* footprints. That's the end of this detective story.   —*Princess Alexandra Kropotkin*

The Great Armored-Car Robbery

By Frederic Sondern, Jr.

SHORTLY after noon one hot August day in 1934 a big armored car of the U.S. Trucking Company lumbered up to the Rubel Ice Company's plant in Brooklyn, New York. Inside, packed in canvas sacks, lay almost half a million dollars to be delivered to various banks. As the truck stopped, its three crewmen, peering through the peep slots, saw only the usual ice peddlers at the loading platform, a few children in the street, some people playing on a nearby tennis court. The three men started their prescribed, unvarying routine. The driver gave an order and unholstered his gun. One guard swung open the car's heavy steel door, stepped to the office to make his collection. A few moments later the second guard opened the door to get down and cover his partner's return. Then it happened!

One hand still on the open door, one on the butt of his pistol, he found himself looking into the ugly snout of a submachine gun held by one of the ice peddlers. "Reach! And don't close that door!" The voice was quiet but deadly. The driver, pistol in hand, stared unbelievingly into another machine-gun muzzle, then dropped his weapon to the floor. On the ice plant's steps, two men stuck pistols against the first guard's ribs and quickly disarmed him. Two cars had suddenly appeared and hemmed in the armored car. Armed men made a ring around the real ice peddlers, who obeyed a curt order to lie face down. Other bandits began carrying sacks of currency from the truck to the cars. In the center of this smoothly operating formation stood a stocky, dark-haired, stubble-chinned man in tattered clothes and a soiled white apron—one eye on the gangsters, one on his wrist watch. "Three minutes!" he suddenly shouted. "Everybody scram!" Car doors slammed, motors raced and the bandits melted away.

Minutes later the voice of the radio dispatcher at police headquarters lost its usual bored calm and changed to a staccato bark. All of New York's 420 police patrol cars were alerted. The three crowded East River bridges leading into lower Manhattan were blocked by emergency squads. Men in uniform and plainclothesmen covered subway stations, trolley lines and bus terminals. Within thirty minutes the huge borough of 2,500,000 people was bottled up. Or so the police thought. But, as evening came, it was clear that the bandits had escaped—by water; their cars had been found at a pier about a mile from the Rubel plant. Workmen near the pier had seen a "whole bunch of men"—who looked like a fishing party but carried canvas sacks—leave two cars and climb into two boats. The boats had vanished. And so had the bandits—with $427,950 in untraceable bills of small denominations. Not a cent of it, incidentally, was ever recovered. It was, up to that time, the biggest, quickest, most perfectly planned cash holdup in the history of crime.

Inspector John J. Sullivan—New York's hard-driving

chief of detectives—took charge of the case, assisted by Brooklyn's Inspector John Ryan. One lead after another petered out. The crew of the armored car could not find a single picture in the Rogues' Gallery to identify. "It happened so quick," they explained. "You look at the tommy gun, not the guy holding it." The cars which the bandits had used revealed nothing. There were no fingerprints on anything. The bandits had all worn cotton gloves. All over the city detectives made contact with their underworld stool pigeons—to no avail. It looked like the perfect crime.

Some hours after the robbery the holdup men met a few miles away in a hideout to divide their loot. It was an impressive gathering, by underworld standards; each man was an expert in his field. There were kidnapers Percy Geary, John and Francis Oley; experienced robber Archie Stewart; forger Stewart Wallace; crack auto thief Joseph Kress; and two ex-bootleggers, Thomas Quinn and John Hughes. Most unusual of all, however, was the stocky leader, soft-spoken and imperturbable John Manning. The underworld knew little about him. But he had a reputation for his "jobs," and though suspected by the police to be a criminal he had never been arrested. Manning had spent three months planning and perfecting his greatest coup. The idea of the robbery had come to him when he saw an armored car picking up sacks of money from a branch of the Brooklyn Trust Company. His professional eye noticed that there was a moment in the drilled procedure when the truck was exposed to attack.

Slowly and carefully collecting his gang, Manning held endless reconnoitering and planning sessions. For days he and Benny McMahon—a shrewd ex-bootlegger and his only trusted friend—trailed the armored car. They found that the car's schedule was changed every day so that it was impossible to know when it would arrive at a certain point. But they did observe that it always visited the bank and the Rubel ice plant on the same day of the week. The Rubel plant seemed the ideal spot. Since it was near water, a getaway by boat would be possible—avoiding the danger of traffic snarls and radio-directed police cars. Ex-bootleggers Quinn and Hughes agreed to supply a speedboat and a fishing dory. Kress, the auto expert, would get the cars.

Every day for three weeks before the holdup the principals rehearsed in front of the Rubel plant. Manning, wearing an ice peddler's white apron, would push a cart in front of the office where the armored car always stopped. Geary, who had made friends with some of the real ice peddlers, would lounge around the loading platform; Stewart and the Oleys, apparently fascinated by the tennis players, lay in the grass near the courts. Everyone became accustomed to them. After a while Manning would buy some ice and trundle it away. On the morning of the robbery Manning was at his post early. Two submachine guns were concealed under the burlap in his cart. The getaway cars, manned by Kress and McMahon, were parked within view. As the armored car hove in sight, Manning reached into his cart and grasped one of the guns. Geary dropped from the loading platform and took the other. The rest was clockwork.

After the holdup Manning and his men cruised around for fifteen minutes to confuse their trail, then made for the pier where their boats were tied up. While crossing the bay they had a serious accident. Transferring the currency from the canvas sacks to suitcases, McMahon caught a drawstring in the trigger of his sawed-off shotgun. The blast ripped through his legs. Unruffled, Manning ordered two of his men to take Benny to a brothel in upper Manhattan and call in a certain shady doctor. When Benny died a day later, his body was dismembered, stuffed into a trunk and deposited in the areaway of a house in the West 70's that was closed for the summer. When Manning was told, he is reported to have said, "Too bad about Benny. But they'll think it's a gang killing. It won't cause us any trouble."

The two boats were sunk off piers in Queens. The bandits proceeded to their hideout in a covered truck which met them at the piers. After sharing the currency, the gang agreed to break up and quit the rackets for a while. Manning retired for the remainder of the summer to his favorite hiding place, which he rightly considered the safest possible spot in which to escape police surveillance—a respectable nudist camp in New Jersey.

Months went by. As far as the public was concerned the case of the Great Armored-Car Robbery was stone cold. But Inspector John Ryan was determined that, no matter how long it took, the bandits would be tracked down. As his executive officer for the job he selected Frank Phillips, a shrewd young detective with an encyclopedic knowledge of the underworld and patience equal to the inspector's own. A few days after the robbery the getaway boats were found floating near the Queens waterfront. Manning had made one mistake. He had left pneumatic life-preserver cushions in the scuttled craft and they had finally raised the hulls to the surface. But when their registration numbers were traced they led to a nonexistent "John Donahue" at the address of a warehouse. The warehouse, it developed, had been the hangout of the ex-bootleggers—Quinn and Hughes. The detectives went back over Quinn's and Hughes's activities during the past months. One clue led to another, and, not two weeks after the robbery, having checked on scores of suspects, Frank Phillips laid on Inspector Ryan's desk a "score card" containing, as it later proved, the names of all the bandits. The inspector smiled one of his rare, wintry smiles of approval. "And now," he said, "we've just got to get the proof." He did not know that this was to take four more long years.

On a July evening in 1936, almost two years after the robbery, John Manning was delivered at the morgue with four pistol slugs in his body. According to the underworld grapevine, he had been lured to a fatal rendez-vous by members of his armored-car gang. They had heard that he had decided to go straight and were afraid that sometime he might talk. The police agreed it was the most unnecessary murder in their experience. Manning would never have talked—to anyone. Shortly after Manning's death Archie Stewart and Stewart Wallace held up a bank in Pine Bush, New York. It was a clumsy job, and they were both wounded and captured. They were sentenced to from thirty to sixty years. Vainly Inspector Ryan hammered at them; they would talk about anything except the armored-car robbery.

About a year later an employe of the U.S. Mint in Denver saw in a detective magazine a picture of Francis Oley, wanted for the kidnaping of wealthy John J. O'Connell, Jr., in Albany, New York. The mint employe told the police that the picture resembled a man who frequented a bar in his neighborhood.

Oley was arrested. In his apartment they found letters implicating in the kidnaping his brother John and Percy Geary. Within twenty-four hours they were arrested in New York. Francis Oley hanged himself in his cell during the trial. Geary and John Oley were sentenced to seventy-seven years in Alcatraz. Inspector Ryan tried again with these convicts, and again he learned nothing about the robbery.

One day, however, the inspector discovered that a younger brother of Archie Stewart had become a probationary patrolman on the New York police force. He watched the young man for a while, then sent him to Clinton Prison to persuade his brother to tell the story of the armored-car holdup.

Finally the older Stewart agreed to talk. For the next two months Ryan and Phillips worked—with Archie Stewart's help—to build up an airtight case. Witnesses were marshaled for corroborative evidence. Hughes had disappeared, and there was reason to believe that he had been disposed of by the gang. Quinn, Stewart Wallace and Kress were located, tried and sentenced to long terms. They were the only members of Manning's gang who had not already been clearly accounted for.

I was shown a picture of John Manning, taken as he lay in the morgue. A sardonic grin still raised the corners of his mouth. "Looks as though he smiled when he got it, doesn't he?" said an officer. He looked as though he had been saying, in his quiet way—"The dopes."

A favorite "vanishing trick" of American criminals after committing a serious crime is to get jailed in a smaller community for some minor offense—under another name, of course—until the hue and cry has pretty well died down.

A while back, a newer expedient was brought to light: a smart crook had been "hiding" on the detective force of a large city, where for several years he had been detailed to search for himself.
                                                    —*Freling Foster*

CELEBRATED SCAMP

Condensed from the book The Legendary Mizners

By Alva Johnston

He was not a man to admire, for by ordinary standards and by prefer-
ence he was an outlaw. But neither was he a man to ignore—it would
have been easier to ignore a circus parade. Wilson Mizner rode
through life at a pace that never slowed down. He was a gambler who
used his wits for coin, and he turned up wherever things were stirring.
San Francisco, Alaska, New York, Florida and Hollywood all saw him
in his heyday. Many men still bear the scars of his practical jokes.
Everywhere he went he was the liveliest man in town. His life, like
this book about him, does not contain a dull page.

Damon Runyon called Wilson Mizner the greatest man-about-town that any town ever had. He was a celebrated wit, confidence man, cardsharp, prizefight manager and playwright. He lived on familiar terms with most of the great prizefighters, beauties, showmen, gamblers, bunco steerers, fences and international crooks of his time. Conversation was Wilson Mizner's hobby, profession and neurosis. His fame as a wit has grown steadily. Although he wrote practically nothing, he is probably quoted more than any other American of this century. Scores of men have won recognition as sparkling conversationalists because they have made small private collections of Mizner sayings.

Many of Mizner's lines have passed into the language. Some, like "The first hundred years are the hardest," are passing out again after long and hard service. Among his philosophical maxims were "Be nice to people on your way up because you'll meet 'em on your way down," and "If you steal from one author, it's plagiarism; if you steal from many, it's research." H. L. Mencken, in *A New Dictionary of Quotations*, attributed to Mizner, "I respect faith, but doubt is what gets you an education," and "A good listener is not only popular everywhere, but after a while he knows something."

As a wit, Mizner belonged to two distinct schools—the scientific and the O. Henry. His scientific method consisted of bringing a calm spirit of inquiry to bear on boiling emotion. When an excited man rushed up to him exclaiming, "Coolidge is dead!" Mizner asked, "How do they know?" The O. Henry school was the school of fantastic exaggeration. Telling of a Klondike pal who had frozen to death in the act of tying his shoelaces, he said, "We had to bury him in a drum." A strutting little fellow went through bankruptcy and then strutted more than ever.

"Failure has gone to his head," said Mizner. Describing his own flight from a madman armed with a revolver, he said, "I got up enough lather to shave Kansas City."

He hated to write, but Jim Tully once badgered him into writing a short story, which appeared in *Liberty*. A little shamefaced over his effort, Mizner said, "I wanted to see something in print besides my thumbs." Shortly before he died, a publisher asked him to write the story of his life. "It would be blowing a police whistle," replied Mizner. This was a reasonable excuse. He was fundamentally a confidence man whom circumstances occasionally induced to go straight. He had a sixth sense for locating chumps with detachable bankrolls.

Mizner was born in Benicia, California, the youngest of seven children. In addition to being one of the most eccentric families America has produced, the Mizners were the oldest of the old families of Benicia, which is twenty-five miles northeast of San Francisco. They had been in the diplomatic service for three generations, and collateral branches of the family teemed with governors, judges, generals and cotillion leaders. The four older Mizner brothers were professional men and seemed on their way to eminence. The parents expected the younger boys, Addison and Wilson, two exceptionally knowing youths, to become illustrious figures in national life. The Mizner house, a cottage that had been enlarged into a kind of rambling hotel, was the headquarters of fashionable Benicia. It was normal for the family to have twelve or fourteen people at dinner. The plentiful seafood around San Francisco Bay made it comparatively inexpensive to run the place like a country club. "When the tide was out, your table was set," Wilson Mizner once said.

A large-headed, spindle-shanked boy during his Benicia

days, he had a genius for getting into trouble with school-
teachers and village authorities, but he always emerged
triumphant because of the glorified status of his family.
When he was thirteen, his privileged place in the world
was recognized by international law when his father was
appointed minister to the five Central American repub-
lics. The law of nations forbade the arrest of any member
of the family for anything except murder. For the rest of
his life Mizner had a sort of subconscious belief that
treaties had been entered into by the nations of the
world authorizing him to commit anything except capital
crimes. His only conviction—for running a gambling
house in Mineola, Long Island, in 1919—came as a terrific shock because of his lifelong assumption that he was a
man to whom the statutes didn't apply. Sentence was suspended, and Governor Al Smith pardoned him and restored his rights of citizenship.

The family returned to California after two years in
Guatemala. Mizner's enjoyment of diplomatic immunity
had given him too strong an I-do-as-I-please spirit for
school discipline. After being expelled from softer institutions, he was sent to Santa Clara College, famous for
changing young hellhounds into saints. Mizner caused a
panic at Santa Clara by tying a steak to the rope of a fire
gong after curfew. The alarm was sounded when the meat
attracted the attention of the large dogs that roamed the
campus at night to encourage students to stay in their
dormitories. He was expelled for heating a cannonball for
several hours and then bowling it from a fire shovel along
a corridor. He correctly forecast that the severest dis-
ciplinarian of the faculty would rush out and pick it up.

The elder Mizner died at about this time. For a while,
Wilson enjoyed an allowance of $150 a month from the
estate. He already had expensive tastes, and he made

both ends meet by gambling, borrowing from his mother and working at strange occupations. From time to time he visited mining camps in California, Nevada and Colorado, both as a prospector and as a gambler. He boxed professionally a few times. For a year or so the telegraph wire was his lifeline, but finally a request for $100 brought from his mother the reply, "I didn't get your telegram."

When Wilson was about eighteen years old he was hired by Dr. Silas Slocum's traveling medicine show in the Northwest. Having learned to speak Spanish fluently in Guatemala, he won the respect of Dr. Slocum as a Latin scholar. Slocum appointed Wilson professor of internal medicine and manager of the trained bear. The "doctor" had beautiful green, red and yellow maps of the internal arrangements of the male and female anatomies. Standing on a platform, pounding the maps with a rattan stick, Wilson would describe how Dr. Slocum's medicine, in a grand steeplechase through the nerves, arteries and vital organs, drove the devils of disease out of the human constitution. Dr. Slocum had instructed Mizner to describe the more embarrassing parts of the human geography in the modest obscurity of a dead language. So, on coming to one of these, Mizner would whack the area with his rattan stick and swear frightfully in Spanish.

Mizner resigned from the medical fraternity after his activities had come to the attention of his Uncle Eugene Semple, former governor of Washington Territory. Semple telegraphed to the Mizner family, and they sent Addison into the Northwest to locate Wilson and bring him home. Addison found his younger brother managing Dr. Slocum's trained bear in sparring matches with dogs. (This was invaluable in his later work with prizefighters, among them Bob Fitzsimmons and Stanley Ketchel.)

In the next chapter of his career, from 1897 to 1902,
Mizner was on the Klondike River and in Nome. The
primary authority on the Klondike chapter was Sid
Grauman, proprietor of the famous Egyptian and Chinese
theaters in Hollywood. Going to the Klondike as a boy,
Grauman sold newspapers from the States for a living—
$1.50 apiece in Dawson City and $2.00 on the creeks,
where deliveries were made by dogsled. The price was always paid in gold dust poured from a tomato can into
scales. Sometimes weeks passed before Grauman received
a shipment of newspapers. The Spanish-American War
was on and the Klondikers were crazy for news. Once,
when a dogsled shipment arrived, Mizner offered Grauman $25 for the first paper, provided no others were sold
for forty-five minutes. Grauman accepted, but regretted
the bargain. Mizner filled an empty store with miners at
fifty cents a head and read the news aloud to them.

Mizner was a debunker of the arctic literary tradition.
The noblest characteristic of the land of ice and snow, according to Robert W. Service, Jack London, Rex Beach
and other writers of the Northern Lights school, was the
undying loyalty between pal and pal. "Nothing whatever
to it," said Mizner. "I never knew the meaning of in-
gratitude until I had one of those arctic pals. I had faith in
that man. He made the first set of burglar's tools ever
turned out in Alaska. I elected him chief of police. I paid
his expenses, managed his campaign, organized a reception for him the day he took office and pinned a gold star
on his shirt, and the first man he arrested was me. At that
time there was only one typewriter in town. Somebody
had stolen it and sold it to a butcher who thought it was a
cash register. Three friends of mine were in danger of being put away for life. We needed the typewriter to draw
up the appeal, and in the emergency I borrowed it from

the butcher shop when the butcher was out. My new chief
arrested me. That is the comradeship of the North."

Saloons, gambling hells, dance halls, sporting houses
and vaudeville shows were sprouting everywhere in Daw-
son City. Wilson became a faro dealer and a professional
singer, and for a while was a cashier, or "weigher," at the
famous Monte Carlo, operated by Swiftwater Bill Gates
and Jack Smith. A weigher was a rather distinguished
creature who presided over large, shining brass scales into
which gold dust was poured to pay for drinks, dance-hall
tickets, poker chips and other items. "I weighed a million
and a half dollars' worth of gold dust and nuggets at
Swiftwater Bill's," Wilson said in a newspaper interview
in New York years later, "and never made a mistake that
wasn't in favor of the house."

Paying in raw gold was a complicated transaction. The
dust was first poured from the miner's poke into a small
brass container called a "blower." From the blower it was
poured out until the scales balanced. The excess gold in
the blower was then returned to the miner's poke. Nobody could cheat a careful and sober miner. Weighing in
the gambling hells was generally above suspicion. But
weighing at the bars in the dance halls was different.

A sourdough who was having a big night expected to be
fleeced and was seldom disappointed. When the profession was very young, weighers let their fingernails grow
long and cleaned them frequently. Some weighers kept
their fingers wet with beer and would wipe off dust and
small grains into their leather pockets. Mizner, however,
was a spiller. He had a thick piece of carpet under his
scales. In an interview in the New York *Review* in 1911, he
was quoted as saying, "Once a week I burned the carpet
and never made less than $2500 out of it." The figure
seems high. (Arctic reminiscences generally require more

than the usual discounts.) The carpet would have had to
absorb about twelve pounds of metal to have been worth
$2500 at the then prevailing rates.

A clever battler named Young Jack McKernan, who
was later known as Jack (Doc) Kearns, the manager of
Jack Dempsey, learned the art of weighing from Mizner.
Kearns, a pink-cheeked youngster, was fumbling with a
pair of scales in Nome when Mizner took pity on him.
Kearns went to Mizner's room with him. "Sit down, my
boy," said Mizner. He got out a jug of syrup and plastered the boy's hair down with it. "Handle the stuff all
you can. Keep running your fingers through your hair,"
said Mizner. The young Doc had a long mane. He ran
his hands through it conscientiously as he worked at the
scales. Between the syrup and the metal, his hair would
gradually take on the consistency of peanut brittle. After
every shampoo the Doc had a pleasing addition to his
pocket money. "Mizner was a wonder at the business,"
Kearns recalled. "He could make a pair of scales do
anything."

In 1899 Wilson turned up in Nome, where he made a
small fortune fleecing suckers at card games and badger
games; ran it into a big fortune by speculating in mining
claims; and lost it all by mixing with heavyweight gamblers at Tex Rickard's Northern Saloon and Wyatt Earp's
Dexter Bar. Broke, he was forced to work. He dealt faro;
managed hotels, actresses and prizefighters; he even did
an occasional column for the Nome *Chronicle*. One night
he would buy champagne for the house, and the next he'd
be stealing coal to keep from freezing to death. He was the
Grover Whalen of Nome when he was in clover. He
greeted the steamers and serenaded the newly arrived leading ladies. One of the most popular actresses to arrive in
Nome asserted some years later that Mizner had married

her there, but he said he couldn't remember the incident.

Mizner drifted down from Nome to San Francisco and eventually found himself in New York. His first New York headlines were the biggest. They came on February 2, 1906, three days after he had secretly married Mrs. Mary Adelaide Yerkes in her mansion at 864 Fifth Avenue. Mizner was twenty-nine years old, Mrs. Yerkes forty-eight. He was penniless; she was reputed to be worth $7,500,000. The news got three-column headlines on the front pages of some of the papers.

Mrs. Yerkes had been a widow for exactly one month when she married Mizner. Her previous husband was Charles T. Yerkes, whose name is known today mainly because of the Yerkes Observatory, which he gave to the University of Chicago. At the time of his death he was the celebrated Traction King, builder of the Chicago "El" and part of the London Tube. He was the hero of Theodore Dreiser's novels *The Titan* and *The Financier*. He served a sentence for embezzlement in 1871 and boasted of wholesale bribing of city officials in Chicago.

Mizner was highly pleased at being Yerkes' successor. In one moment of enthusiasm he exclaimed, "I own everything that runs on wheels in Chicago!" and in another he said, "I'm the only man who was ever accused of stealing a subway." It had taken Yerkes a lifetime of industry and rascality to build up this estate; Wilson had sung himself into it in a few weeks. His good looks and his wonderful line of conversation helped, but it was his singing of sad old ballads that made him irresistible to the widow.

Mizner was also proud of his neighbors. He was close enough to the Astors to run over with a plate of soup in case of illness. Thomas Fortune Ryan lived next door. Andy Carnegie was a few blocks up the Avenue. Mizner was now as close to the Fricks, Garys, Vanderbilts,

Goelets and Whitneys as he had been in the Klondike to Diamond-Tooth Gertie, the Scurvy Kid, Nellie the Pig, Two-Toothed Mike, Deep-Hole Johnson and Jerkline Sam. Yerkes had fixed the house up very much to the taste of Wilson Mizner. He had spent several million dollars building the stately four-story edifice on the south corner of Fifth Avenue and 64th Street. He had poured out additional millions on carving, painting, gilding and inlaying the interior and had stocked it with art treasures selected with considerable judgment.

Addison Mizner hurried to the Yerkes mansion on hearing the news of the marriage. He found Wilson in a bed that had once belonged to the Mad King of Bavaria; it was on a dais with two green velvet steps; gold cupids were putting an enameled Goddess of Night to sleep at the head of the bed and listening to her songs at the foot. Propped up among pillows of peach-colored satin, covered to the waist with point lace, the bridegroom was wearing a gray woolen undershirt, the sleeves of which had shrunk nearly to the elbow. He was holding a sack of Bull Durham between his teeth and rolling a brown-paper cigarette. Addison excitedly asked the reason for the marriage. "The service is good here," said Wilson.

The mansion was a marvelous playhouse for Mizner and his sporting pals. Yerkes, who belonged to the old school of miscellaneous collectors, had picked up a vast variety of antique handbells, enameled and jeweled with saints, heroes and landscapes, and Mizner could ring for his servants with any one of a hundred little instruments of exquisite workmanship. Yerkes had also been a collector of antique timepieces. He had gathered together an estimated two thousand of them, and Mizner, a perpetual adolescent, lost his mind over the clock room.

The clocks were silent when he became master of the

mansion, and one of his first directions to his servants was to wind them all up and bring in experts to deal with the recalcitrant ones. Every hour on the hour the clock room was pandemonium. A whole aviary of stuffed birds began to whistle and sing. Muscular men of cast metal stepped out of hidden doors and smote gongs with sledge hammers. A full orchestra of tiny musicians swung out on a turntable, slowly raised their bows and then frantically sawed away at violin strings. Nineteenth-century railroad clocks clanged and whistled as locomotives emerged from one tunnel with a train of passenger coaches and disappeared into another. Steamships came out screeching, paddled under bridges and cruised back into their cases. Peasants came forth and called their cows. Clocks pealed, tolled and jingled, and rendered minuets from hidden music boxes. The cream of the fun for Mizner was showing the room to friends with hangovers and seeing their nervous systems murdered when all the clocks let go at once.

Mizner said that his first serious domestic strife arose over the clock situation. He came home sober in the wee hours one morning, went to bed a little after three and was roused at four by the shrieking of a cuckoo clock in his own room. He had ordered his servants to make every clock run, and they had taken him literally. He got up, cursing, and located the clock, high up on the wall and out of reach. He went to the Yerkes arsenal on the fourth floor, returned to his room and went to bed again. When the cuckoo screamed at 5 a.m., he lit the lights and gave it both barrels of one of the Yerkes shotguns. That episode started the bride wondering whether her new consort had the true Fifth Avenue spirit.

The romance was on and off the rocks several times. The *Press* reported on June 16, 1906, that Mrs. Mizner had developed a disconcerting thrift. On one occasion,

Mizner left her after a financial argument. She waylaid him near an elevator in the Hotel Astor and pelted him with greenbacks. Describing this in after years, Mizner said, "The greatest humiliation I ever underwent was picking them up." He contradicted himself slightly in another version, saying: "I picked up $8000 before I realized I'd been insulted." In 1907, Mrs. Mizner obtained a divorce and the right to resume her former name. Shortly after this, Mizner resumed living by his wits. "Why should I work?" he said in a newspaper interview. "I've committed no crime. Work is the poorest excuse for an education. I hate work like the Lord hates St. Louis."

In 1910 Mizner was New York's most flamboyant sport. He was a glittering object, on display in all the leading Manhattan showcases, from the Haymarket to the Horse Show. A first-nighter and ringsider, he traveled about with startling exhibits like Diamond Jim Brady and Bet-a-Million Gates. He was a conspicuous figure at races, baseball games and backstage celebrations, in the company of mature birds of paradise like Lillian Russell or younger specimens like Grace Washburn of the Winter Garden, Evelyn Nesbit of the Thaw case, and a few of the breathtaking Mrs. Nat Goodwins and Mrs. Kid McCoys.

He was noted for his spectacular entrances. Hatcheck girls being almost unknown at this time, he walked into restaurants wearing a made-to-order silk hat two inches higher than the norm. He was a little over six feet three, with a gigantic head and a large, statesmanlike face; the caricatures of the time made him look like Woodrow Wilson. According to the Broadway sage Swiftie Morgan, Mizner had the highest collars in the world specially made for him, partly for the insolence of the thing and partly to conceal a frantically bobbing Adam's apple. He carried a white-handled, white-shafted cane three or four inches taller than any other known walking stick and wore an Inverness cape thrown back over his shoulders to show its white satin lining and a spacious white shirtfront. The novelist Djuna Barnes, describing him in the *Morning Telegraph*, said that his fingernails were "ovals of opalescent opulence."

Wilson Mizner's big year was 1911. He had suddenly become important and legitimate. He was a successful Broadway playwright. His play *The Deep Purple*, written in collaboration with Paul Armstrong, was a landmark in American culture—the first effective drama about modern city-bred criminals. In preparation for their second play, *The Greyhound*, Armstrong took Mizner on a transatlantic voyage. *The Greyhound* was a melodrama about ocean-going crooks—"sea serpents," "deep-sea fishermen" or "pearl divers," as they used to be called. Mizner had a scholarly grasp of this subject. He knew international low life as Henry James knew international high life. For years he had been practically a commuter from New York to London and Paris, and had made a total of thirty transatlantic round trips. Mizner was also something of a sea serpent or deep-sea fisherman himself. He said he was always able to win the confidence of strangers by warning them against strangers. He knew every twist of fraud and larceny on the high seas, but Armstrong didn't, and Armstrong insisted on the trip so that Mizner could brief him on background and atmosphere for their drama of deviltry in the steamship lanes.

Mizner usually won when he played games of chance, by land or by sea, but he never claimed to be a really great cardsharp. He was, however, a supreme artist at taking a lot of people thrown together by chance and quickly converting them into one big, happy family. His

power to produce mirth in a small or moderate-size group
of people is said to have been unequaled. On the first night
out he would have the whole ship's population of prospective suckers bellowing. His function was to deprive them
of their reason with Mizner gags; once the brain was completely abstracted it was time for the cardsharps, dice
wizards and con men to go to work. Mizner, his mission
accomplished, might then disport himself as he pleased
for the rest of the trip. If his crooked friends prospered,
they would make a suitable recognition of his contribution to the success of the voyage.

Mizner seldom joined the big card games, but he
earned considerable sums by winning ship's pools with
enlightened guesses as to the distance that would be covered by the ship in each twenty-four-hour period. Because
of the generally high caliber of ship's officers, the steamship pool is usually regarded as an unfixable form of gambling, but Mizner and two confederates drew the lucky
number three times in succession. It all started with a
ship's officer who was practically a clotheshorse for med-
als. His chest, as Mizner described it, was ablaze with
chafing dishes. Mizner couldn't believe that an honest
heart beat beneath a whole showcaseful of jewelry. Standing outside the cabin of the glittering officer, Mizner mentioned to a confederate the number he had drawn in the
pool for the next twenty-four hours, and added in a loud
voice, "You know what I would do to show my gratitude
if I won? I'd stick $1000 under the right officer's pillow."

Somehow or other, the day's run came out exactly right
for Mizner, and $1000 of his winnings turned up under
the medal collector's pillow. There were two more conversations outside the cabin and two more miraculous
strokes of luck for Mizner and his confederates. The fourth
time they approached the cabin, however, a hoarse voice

growled through the door, "Get out of here, you bastards. I'm four hundred miles off my course now!"

He was at times content with a very small advantage. In the Klondike he had trouble with the Northwest Mounted because he had five deuces in a deck, the minutest possible degree of dishonesty. His approach to any topic was a calculation of odds. Writhing with agony from appendicitis, he was told that he was to be operated on by a surgeon who had performed eighteen successful appendectomies in a row. Mizner handed a roll of bills to his pal Lew Lipton, of Broadway and Hollywood, saying, "See what odds you can get that I don't break his run."

He preferred odds of 100 to 0 in his favor and often made arrangements that ensured those odds. He was also ready to accept odds of 51 to 49 in his favor, and he would rather gamble honestly than not at all. Once a ferryboat stopped at the cry of "Man overboard!" A lifeboat was lowered and the sailors found Mizner treading water, a stopwatch in his hand. He had a bet on the length of time necessary for his rescue. He was walking across Times Square once with Honest John Kelly, the famous gambler and referee, when a streetcar knocked over a fish wagon. A lobster and a crab landed side by side on the pavement and started for the streetcar tracks. "A hundred on the lobster," said Mizner, but Kelly wouldn't bet.

Mizner won a good deal by betting on Jess Willard to beat Jack Johnson in their bout in Havana in 1915. By a simple device he had convinced himself that the fight was fixed. A few days before the bout he cabled, "What shall I do?" to Jack Johnson. Johnson and Mizner were close friends. Mizner reasoned that if the fight was on the level, Johnson would cable enthusiastically about his chances of winning, and that if it was a fake, Johnson would not reply at all. After two days without word from the black champion, Mizner bet everything he had on Willard.

He won a roll of bills at Atlantic City once, by a game that was halfway between a lucrative practical joke and a crooked gamble. He and some other sports were lounging along the boardwalk, betting on anything in which they could find an element of chance, such as which of two sunbathers would be the first to go into the water or which of two swimmers would be the first to come out of it. One of the party noticed a pair of gigantic feet sticking out of a window on the first floor of a boardwalk hotel. The owner of the feet was out of sight, apparently lying back in a chair.

Mizner and his friends began to guess how tall the man was, from the evidence of his feet. Finally, they backed their guesses with money. Most of the bettors placed the man's height at well over six feet. Mizner made the lowest estimate. With a curious disregard of the principles of human symmetry, he guessed five feet one. When the money was up, they called on the man in the hotel room. He was a dwarf, four feet six inches tall, with size eleven shoes.

Mizner had brought him from New York and planted
him there, figuring he could probably win a few bets on
the man's paradoxical physique.

On another occasion Mizner used a practical joke to
remind a young woman friend that he had given her a
warning. He had advised her not to spend a weekend with
some people with whom he had quarreled. He had insisted that she would be bored; she had insisted she
wouldn't. During her visit a present arrived for her. It was
a bulky object, fussily beribboned. She started to unwrap
it in the presence of her hostess. Finding Mizner's card in
it, however, she hurriedly introduced another topic of conversation and then carried the gift to her room. It was an
enormous pie. A rope ladder and a file were concealed
in it.

The Millionaires' Club was another of Mizner's New
York enterprises. Among its appointments was a three-
hundred-pound man with a resemblance to William
Howard Taft, who at the time had only recently left the
White House. This man was always seated in a huge armchair in the reading room, with a highball in his hand and
a newspaper before his face. As people could tell at close
range that he was not Taft, strangers were led to the door
of the room for a look but were requested not to enter.
They were told that the ex-President hung out there because it was the most exclusive club in town and the one
place where he was sure of not being disturbed. Although
chief owner of the club, Mizner posed as a casual patron
so that he could bring suckers in without embarrassment.
He had steered in a gorgeous prospect one evening when
the place was suddenly thrown into an uproar; "Taft"
had sunk a knife into a waiter for persistently bringing him
highballs with hardly any whiskey in them. During the

turmoil the sucker fled. Meeting him a few days later, Mizner said, "Can you beat it, the way they kept that story about Taft out of the papers?"

Mizner was a star witness on March 14, 1918, at a John Doe inquiry into gambling in the Court of General Sessions. According to the *Sun*, which treated the inquiry with some flippancy, it all started when a German baker who had lost $35,000 to Mizner at *chemin de fer* started to pay off in doughnuts. The *Sun* asserted that tens of thousands of doughnuts were piled up in front of Mizner's apartment, on West 43rd Street near Sixth Avenue. One of the questions put to Mizner was how long he had played *chemin de fer*. "Since infancy," he said.

On rare occasions he picked the wrong man. He once drew a simple-looking stranger into a poker game and let him win for a while. Suddenly they began raising each other wildly and the stakes became enormous. Mizner laid down four queens and reached for the pot. The stranger laid down four kings. Mizner pushed the pot back across the table. "You win, stranger," he said. "But those are not the cards I dealt you."

Men who were in Wilson's confidence tell of the wide range of devices by which he raised money. A rich young man of Seattle, on a visit to New York, complained to Mizner of a hangover and a complete inability to remember the events of the preceding night. Mizner hopped over to confer with the maître d'hôtel of a reigning lobster palace and concocted an itemized bill for nearly $2000, to be split two ways. It was collected from the Westerner, who was informed that during the period about which his mind was a blank he had thrown one of the biggest and wildest parties of the season.

In the early 1920's Addison Mizner, who had achieved

a modest practice as a landscape architect on Long Island, fell ill and moved to Palm Beach, fully expecting to die in the near future. The atmosphere of the Florida real-estate boom revived him, however, and he launched on a fabulous career as an architect. He sent for Wilson and together they promoted the gaudiest of all the subdivisions, Boca Raton—"Beaucoup Rotten," rival real-estate men called it.

Boca Raton was the Bride of the Gulf Stream, the Anteroom of Heaven, the Miznerized Venice. It had a built-in ocean to carry electrically driven gondolas, steam yachts and Cleopatra's barges to your doorstep. It had Palm Beach, a few miles north, for servants' quarters. As Addison dipped his maps and sketches in the colors of paradise, Boca Raton became a blaze of tropical splendor. The parks and gardens of the oceanfront estates were to flow rhythmically into one another. The whole coastline was to unroll like a Persian rug, causing people on passing steamers to scream with delight.

The Miami *News* compared the stampede of the wealthy into Boca Raton with the footrace of the original Okies into the Cherokee Strip when it was thrown open to homesteaders in 1893. The Mizner brothers sold eleven million dollars' worth of lots the first day their property was offered to the public. "It's a platinum sucker trap," said Wilson, describing the subdivision to Ashton Stevens.

The boom intoxication, which made Addison a dreamer, made Wilson a man of action. He became the secretary and treasurer of the Mizner Corporation—a dignified climax to a lifelong career of larceny. There was as much as $10,000,000 in down payments in the treasury at one time, but apparently very little of it stuck to Wilson's fingers. He occasionally cut up an unethical melon for himself and his friends, but so did nearly every other subdivider in Florida. A "melon party" was always held at Wilson's house in Palm Beach on the eve of a public sale of Boca Raton lots. Wilson and his friends would study the blueprints and pick out for themselves the properties that had the best talking points. It was a certainty that investors would bid extravagantly for these lovely locations and that the prices would double and treble very rapidly.

By 1925 the Florida phenomenon, which had become vaster than the Mississippi Bubble or any other real-estate mania in history, showed signs of exploding. During the summer and fall, the question constantly being asked was "When will it all end?" On January 13, 1926, *Variety* stated, under the headline "Florida Slipping," that everybody was anxious to unload.

The Mizners put on a brave front at a housewarming in February for the Cloister, the clubhouse and hotel at Boca Raton, but it was fighting after the bell. In March, in a dispatch to the *Herald Tribune* from the training camp of the New York Giants in Sarasota, W. O. McGeehan wrote that a number of the destitute realtors had been caught disguising themselves as Giant rookies so they could get free meals by signing checks at a restaurant that catered to the ballplayers. Most of the little speculators charged those who speculated on a very large scale with fraud. "The good people went in for a gamble," said Wilson Mizner, "and they are full of moral indignation because they lost."

Lawsuits were filed by the thousand. In a letter to Arthur Somers Roche, Mizner wrote: "I never open my door but a writ blows in. I spend my evenings shuffling these fearsome documents and can already cut to any complaint I desire. This proficiency may prove valuable, should the judge wish to decide by chance what case to try next."

In the same letter Wilson expressed regret about his failure to imitate the wisdom of the lame Confederate general who, on seeing disaster ahead, said, "Boys, things look tough. But remember, the eyes of Dixieland are on you. The beauty and chivalry of the South know our desperate plight and thank God for it, as only in extremities like this are heroes made. The hated Yankees are preparing to charge—let them come! Don't shoot until you see the whites of their eyes. Then, my brave fellows, fight it out hand to hand, until the case is hopeless. Then you can retreat—but, seeing I'm lame, I'll start now."

Wilson didn't start to retreat until 1927, and then he didn't stop until he reached Hollywood, where he became a restaurant man and screenwriter. Addison, who had demonstrated his faith in Boca Raton by assuming personal responsibility for the debts of the company, lived mainly on loans from wealthy friends throughout the remaining years of his life. When he died, in February 1933, his estate was found to be insolvent.

When Wilson went to Hollywood, he posed as a millionaire idler, but he was really looking for a job. The crash had wiped him out completely. His experiences had broken his spirit to the extent that he was willing to do honest work, and he got a job as a writer. Sound pictures were just coming in. Mizner scored heavily with the dialogue he wrote for *One Way Passage*, one of the most successful of the early talkies. Deciding to settle down in the picture colony, Mizner joined H. K. Somborn, one of Gloria Swanson's former husbands, in opening the Brown Derby restaurant.

While Wilson Mizner devoted much of his leisure to

the denunciation of suckers and chumps, his routine evening in Hollywood consisted of coming to the Brown Derby with a thick roll of bills and giving them away a few at a time to professional moochers. By midnight he would be reduced to getting his paper from his newsboy on credit. He offered a feeble resistance to some of the demands on his purse. Once, when a borrower asked for $50, he said, "Here's $25. Let's both make $25." When a burglar came to him for a loan, he said, "Doesn't it get dark any more?"

Most of Mizner's motion-picture work was done on the Warner Brothers lot. He was a writer who never wrote. His method of collaboration was unique. After thirty-five years of strictly nocturnal life, he was a dormouse in the daytime. At the studio he slept most of the time, in a huge red plush chair which so closely resembled an archiepiscopal throne that he was called "the Archbishop." When Mizner's literary partners needed some lines or ideas from him, they would shake him gently and start him talking. After half an hour or so, they would order him back to sleep while they sat down at their typewriters and worked up his conversation into script form.

The only time Mizner was ever known to show excitement in Hollywood was when his friend Jack Johnson arrived at the Warner lot to play a small part. To most people, Johnson was just a has-been, but Mizner threw his arms around him and kissed him on both cheeks. He introduced the former heavyweight champion with great ceremony in order to make sure that the heads of the studio realized how much they were being honored.

There were large gaps in Mizner's pose of being the hardest, coldest and most callous man in the world. He used to visit narcotic hospitals to cheer up old pals. In conversation, however, Mizner did his best to suppress

the instincts of humanity. His later comic style was largely
ridicule of all sentiment and feeling. Although at times
he could be soft in his behavior, he aimed at being as
satanic as possible in speech.

In 1910, when Mizner was close to the prizefighter
Stanley Ketchel, news was telephoned to Mizner that
Ketchel had been shot and killed that day. "Tell
'em to start counting ten over him, and he'll get up,"
said Mizner.

Mizner got all possible comedy value out of his own
last illness. In March 1933, in his fifty-eighth year, he
had a heart attack at the Warner studio. When he recovered consciousness, he was asked if he wanted to see a
priest.

"I want a priest, a rabbi and a Protestant clergyman,"
he said. "I want to hedge my bets."

His heart attack, President Roosevelt's inauguration,
the bank holiday and a California earthquake came at
almost the same time. Mizner criticized this piling up of
climaxes. "Bad melodrama," he said.

Told that death was only a few hours away, Mizner
rallied strength to send a postcard notifying a friend.
"They're going to bury me at 9 a.m.," wrote Mizner.
"Don't be a sucker and get up."

When they arranged a tent over him for the administration of oxygen, he said, "It looks like the main event."

Coming out of a coma shortly before his death, he
waved a priest away disdainfully. "Why should I talk to
you?" he said. "I've just been talking to your boss."

The priest gently reproached Mizner for levity at such
a time. He told the sick man that his death might come at
any moment. "What?" said Mizner. "No two weeks'
notice?"

Portrait of Harry

By Arthur Trevenning Harris, M.D.

A<small>T THE END</small> of the war I was practicing medicine in Laguna Beach, California. Several service camps were located nearby, and we members of Rotary worked as waiters and dishwashers at a USO club that was thronged nightly with returning veterans.

One of the most popular features of the club was the work of Kathryn Olsen, a local painter, who sketched lifelike charcoal portraits of GI's and mailed them free to their relatives. One evening I noticed that Miss Olsen's sitter was a sad-faced young Marine, who was talking to her jerkily and frowning often. I watched her face expectantly. For Kay was more than an artist; she was also a mother confessor. Many a boy had poured out his troubles in the two-hour sitting and gone away comforted. Now she was shaking her head sympathetically, nodding encouragingly. But no answering smile broke over the young man's face. For the next hour I was busy; I forgot the painter and her subject. Then Kay came rushing up to me. "Dr. Harris—please—"

She gestured toward the boy who was sitting beside the

easel, head in hands. "He insists that it—that I"—she was confused—"and the strange part of it is that I did!"

"Did what?"

"Please—come and see—talk to him!"

She introduced me. The boy was swallowing convulsively. Now and then he gave his head a sidewise jerk, as if to shake away an impossibility.

"I—I've upset him," mourned Kay. "You can see that he's a Marine, and I've put Army insignia on the portrait. I don't know why. I drew what I thought I saw!"

"That's easily explained," I said. "You were talking—just absentmindedness."

The boy pointed toward the portrait and said nervously: "That isn't me! It's my brother. Don't change it!"

The portrait was a good likeness of the boy, so I said: "Then you must be twins!"

"Were," he mumbled, and dropped his head again.

Kay whispered: "His brother was killed in action. He's been telling me . . ."

"But I didn't tell you he was Army—and an officer. That's why this"—he nodded toward the portrait—"gets me!" He laced and unlaced his big rawboned fingers. It was late now, and the crowd had thinned. I drew up a chair and sat knee to knee with the Marine. Clearly we could not turn this distraught lad out into the night. Besides, knowing how closely linked the personalities of identical twins are, I thought I might help.

"Coffee?" I asked. Kay went for it, and he began to talk.

"My folks adopted me from an orphanage," he said. "I didn't know that there were two of us until I was around twelve. Then we bumped into each other at the county fair. First off, we just stared at each other. It was like looking in a mirror; then we laughed together! But he was dressed different—city clothes—he was ritzy! I was wearing blue jeans, same as I always did on the farm."

"Did he know he had a twin somewhere?" I asked. The youth took long drinks of the hot coffee, then fumbled for a cigarette.

"No, sir, he hadn't been told either. But Harry—that was his name—said, 'Hey! Did you come from an orphanage? If so, there were two of us.' I was glad—very glad! First, we figured we'd ask his folks and mine pointblank that very day. Then Harry said, 'Let's stay together until they find us!' I said, 'Okay, let's stay together.'"

Every once in a while the boy would lift his eyes and look from Kay to me anxiously. He seemed to be begging for understanding. Perhaps he found it in our eyes, because the words came more and more easily.

"We sure had fun!" At the memory a smile crept around his mouth. "I only had the four bits Pa'd given me to spend. Harry had a whole five-dollar bill—enough to buy a shoat! He said if I didn't help him spend it he'd tear it up!" He chuckled. "He dragged me to where you throw baseballs at a clown's head sticking up—three balls for a dime. We used up almost all his money. And Harry kept saying, 'We *must* be brothers, Jud. We sure look like twins!' I never was so happy in all my life before.

"I don't mean that I was miserable with my folks on the farm. They were good to me. But I'd never had a warm feeling all through, like I had that afternoon. Anyway"—he gave a short, hard laugh—"it was lucky we had that much time together, because as soon as Harry's folks came along they snatched him away as if I was a toad. But Harry called back, 'So long, Jud! I'll be seeing you, Jud!'" For a long moment the boy was silent. When he spoke again, it was slowly, huskily.

"Maybe they wouldn't let him see me on account of we really were twin brothers. My folks told me how it hap-

pened. When they adopted me from the orphanage they tried to get him too. But Pa wasn't so well fixed, and when a city guy asked for my brother Pa lost out.

"I begged Pa to let me go see Harry in town, but he wouldn't hear of it. Said Harry's folks were high-class—about as fine as they come in Nebraska—and I had no call to be trailing him. That's the way Pa put it! Thinking how friendly Harry and I'd been, I got sort of bitter. Those days sure were miserable!"

"And did you ever see Harry again?" I asked, to end another silence. Jud gave a nod in Kay's direction. "I just told her some of it," he said dully. "I told her about the night on Guadalcanal, just after the Army got there. Machine guns and rifles and mortars—everything was popping. For a moment a flare lit up my foxhole—and Harry rolled in. 'It took a war to do it, Jud!' he said, and pounded me on the back. 'My double—Jud!' I sensed right away that his folks hadn't told him we were brothers. We buttoned our ponchos over us and lit a match—just once—to look at each other. He told me he was married and an officer. I decided I couldn't tell him about us being brothers then—twins even! . . . And I didn't tell her"—he jerked his head toward Kay—"that Harry was Army, and a captain."

His eyes strayed toward the portrait. Mine followed. There were the captain's bars, the Army insignia. When I turned back, the boy's eyes met mine. "Can you explain it, sir?" he asked. "What she drew, I mean?"

"Tell me the rest," I suggested.

"Well—Harry and I talked about what we'd done since the fair. Harry was bright—educated, too! University. When the Japs quieted down, Harry said he'd better move on. But he gave me his home address. I must look him up when . . . Well, I didn't see him again on 'Canal, because our outfit was shipped out next morning."

We were almost alone in the club now. I realized that perhaps Kay had heard the end of the story, and a glance showed that she was struggling against tears. When the boy spoke again, he kept his eyes fixed on the portrait.

"Okinawa!" Jud's voice was thin, only a whisper. "War was old stuff then. A guy didn't shake—you were too tired. And I knew what grunting breathing meant—even in the dark. Someone badly shot up. It came from behind a rock. I crawled along carefully, my knife ready, and waited for a flare. No Jap trap here. One of our guys. I told him I'd find a corpsman with a slug of morphine. The guy groaned and tried to sit up. Then he spoke. 'Jud? It is Jud—isn't it?' Yeah, it was Harry. When he coughed, there was blood. I tried to tell him it was just his shoulder, but Harry wasn't dumb. He begged me not to leave him. He wanted me to strike a match so he could see me again. The rock was good cover, so I did. He whispered about his wife—for me to be sure to see her when I got home. And then, the last words he said were, 'Gee,

Jud, I wish that we two were really brothers—twins!'"

The boy spoke on, slowly: "So—I told Harry that I'd known from the day at the fair that we were twins. I told him I'd been too scared to tell him on 'Canal—him class and an officer. I held him against my shoulder. But now he couldn't talk. His eyes were half shut and . . . then he wasn't breathing. . . . I don't know if he heard me saying over and over again, 'Harry, we *are* brothers—twins! Harry . . .'" There were tears in Jud's eyes. "We'd found each other for keeps this time—we'd be brothers for keeps. I know that, sir! And ever since Okinawa, it's been like I've been walking through fog, wondering if he heard me, wanting to know for sure."

With a shake of the head he muttered, "You can see that picture isn't me! That face—why, it's happy, like Harry was. Me—I'm always scowling. And the uniform—"

"I wish I knew how it happened," Kay said tearfully.

The doctor in me had been pondering—identical twins . . . an almost inseparable entity. At that moment I had what may have been a glimpse of the unknown.

"Just a minute," I said. "There is something Jud wants to know, and I believe the picture holds the answer. Now think, Jud—think! Why, when looking at you here, did Miss Olsen see Harry, even to his insignia?"

The youth gripped my arm. "You mean he heard me—she saw him because he's here, somehow?" I nodded.

"Look, sir—if only I could believe that . . ." He stopped. Kay was beginning to understand her "mistake." Jud turned to her, a new light in his eyes. "Send it to Harry's wife, will you, please, ma'am?" His very voice had changed. "I won't need it. From now on, wherever I go, he goes too." He chuckled, and suddenly cried out, surprised: "Say! That sounded like Harry laughing! And me—I haven't laughed since he—since Okinawa!"

Fortune in the Grave

By J. Edgar Hoover

NO ONE was watching, that summer night, when two
figures—one tall and the other small—stepped
warily between the rows of soldier graves. The big man
hugged a bulky package against his chest; he took jumpy,
nervous steps and often peered over his shoulder. The
little one, who carried digging tools, marched sedately,
looking neither to the right nor to the left. Behind the cold
white headstone of a long-dead legionnaire they picked
and shoveled the damp earth and buried the package
in a four-foot hole.

"Even if they kill me, I'll never tell where we hid this stuff," the short man muttered greedily.

"Me neither!" promised the other.

Before dawn they had scrambled over an eight-foot wire fence and vanished into the living world. In the ground they left a treasure, but in the Los Angeles field headquarters of the FBI they left a real headache. For buried behind that grave on the night of July 30, 1945, was $100,000 in loot from a holdup—one of the most impudent bank robberies ever to confront us. This is the story of how we found the men—and, in spite of their vow, the cash.

In Hollywood, California, at seven o'clock that morning, six bags of silver coins and a cardboard carton stuffed with bills, in all $111,300, had been placed on the rear seat of an Oldsmobile coupé. The money was for cashing weekly checks of Lockheed Aircraft employes at the Burbank plant. Two messengers of the Hollywood State Bank sat in front—Thurston M. Patterson at the wheel and Victor H. Lohn beside him as lookout—and between them were loaded .38-caliber revolvers. They drove through the Cahuenga Pass toward Burbank. As they neared the factory their route led off the highway. Suddenly at a back-street corner they were confronted by an MP uniform and an uplifted hand. As Patterson brought the car to a sudden stop, he was startled to see that the uplifted hand held a .45 automatic, aimed straight at him. More shocking still, this tall, incongruous MP—dowdy, unshaven, hollow-chested—was shaking all over with nervousness.

"*Get out of there!*" he cried in a shrewish voice. A second armed figure, shorter, chunkier and infinitely calmer, sprang from behind a tree and joined him in the bright sunshine of the street. Both robbers thrust guns through the car windows. Lohn and Patterson had to do as they were told.

"Get into the back seat. Put your heads down. Look at the floor. Hands behind your head." So the messengers were kidnaped into the hills. After bouncing over dirt roads for twenty minutes the car halted on the brink of a lonely canyon, and the captives were rustled down the steep sides. Neck and hands, Patterson was tied to a sapling; and Lohn, after his wrists were corded behind his back, was hurled face down in the weeds. Both were blindfolded with adhesive tape. The bandits, clambering back to the car with its box and bags of money, mouthed bloodcurdling threats, lest the bank men cry for help.

As soon as he dared, Patterson began to rub the right side of his face violently against the rough bark of the tree. Soon his cheek was bloody, but he persisted until he had scraped the adhesive from one eye. Then he called directions to his partner, who was struggling to rise:

"Stand up; come nearer! . . . You are going to move around me—behind the tree I'm tied to. I can reach the knife in your hip pocket. Careful . . ." Lohn's hands were free. He ripped off the sticky hoodwinks, cut the ropes that fastened Patterson, and they staggered up the ravine to the highway.

This outrage was a challenge to the FBI because the thieves had violated national as well as state statutes: kidnaping, impersonation of Army personnel and theft of the uniform; moreover, the bank funds were guaranteed by a federal agency. We had to break the case with all possible speed; otherwise its cynical simplicity and audacity would encourage the underworld to a new upsurge of violence. One clue we had: while Lohn's eyes were being taped, he had glimpsed a Lockheed employe badge on the shirt of the short robber. Undoubtedly the thief had worn it to make us believe he worked at the plant. Even so, it was something to start with.

At the same time that the Los Angeles police department, the sheriff's office and FBI agents were interviewing hundreds of persons, checking out suspects and following tips and leads, we were pursuing our own precise lines. For example, experience teaches that robbers often ride to the scene of a crime in a stolen car. So we carefully searched for stolen cars; in one, a jalopy with doctored licenses left in a parking lot, we found a cardboard box on which were scribbled a name and address. Agents were about to explore the address when a Mrs. Abelar, who lived there, notified the police. "Come and see what we've found at our place," she invited.

An extra garage at the rear of her home had been rented by two young men for the last few weeks. On the evening of the holdup a child's ball rolled under the doorway; the Abelar children removed the hasp from the locked door and inside the garage beheld six bags of silver money. Found in addition were an Army blouse with an MP brassard on the sleeve, a .45-automatic, a .38 belonging to the bank messengers and a sport jacket on which was pinned that Lockheed identification badge!

Of course the badge number was a fraud; the original number had been ripped out and false figures had been substituted with a black grease pencil. However, in Washington, FBI scientists took the badge into the laboratory. By daylight it revealed nothing. But under an ultraviolet lamp the empty surface of the cellophane cover suddenly produced images. The printed digits of the original badge had left unseen traces. Within an hour our Los Angeles agents were checking the plant records. Employment files proved that those old numbers once had been assigned to a tall, nervous workman called John Joseph Uckele. As his nearest friend, Uckele had named another Lockheed employe—Stanley Matysek. And Stanley, according to plant gossip, was a short, chunky fellow with a reputation for never getting excited. Almost certainly we had found the names and partial histories of the criminals.

While the pair had long since quit Lockheed, their recent movements were easily traced to the University of California in Los Angeles, where, by using forged credentials, they had been posing as summer students. Their rooms in the dormitory contained drills and files, keys to the Abelar garage, blueprints for a burglar-alarm system, a bayonet, an electric drill—and, final bizarre touch, the twelve-page manuscript of a story written by the jittery, imaginative Uckele about a hitchhiking soldier who killed an insurance salesman.

Where to look for Uckele and Matysek? In planning the search, we had to guess at their own thinking. Probably the holdup men believed they had committed a perfect crime and would soon return after a temporary absence. If so, there was no need to search afar. Fortified with photographs from Army records of the two men, we started looking around Los Angeles bars. Strange as it sounds, two of our agents stepped inside a tavern on the Sunset Strip, and there was Uckele, sitting on a high stool before a stein of beer. Just as he buried his nose in the foam, the FBI men took him, each by an elbow, and lifted him through the folding doors. Then they relieved him of his loaded .45 automatic.

That thief howled until the street resounded; he shrieked appeals to corner loafers and swore they were his relatives and friends; he was energetically pretending to be crazy. Catching him off guard, an agent asked him, "Where's Stan?" He answered, "Haven't seen him for months." Then, realizing his self-betrayal, he fell into a bleak and shaky silence. Not an hour later we surprised Stanley lurking near the same bar. In his car we confiscated a device that recalled the assassination of President McKinley—a sheet-metal contraption, wrapped with gauze, fashioned like a splint for a broken hand and arm. Within this fake was a fully loaded and cocked .45. If Matysek had been wearing it, he certainly would have started shooting.

At the FBI office the accused men blamed everything on a character they invented, a mythical "Nick." By blackmail Nick had forced them to do his evil bidding, and he had kept all the loot for himself. To shake our skepticism Uckele screamed Nick's name in the middle of the night. In court for routine arraignment, he yelled Nick's name to the judge, and then fell to the floor foaming at the mouth; it was the ancient trick of swallowing a small cake of soap.

During the months before the trial we naturally tried to coax out the secret of the money. Not if we killed them, they told us. Besides, only Nick knew. And yet from under Uckele's bed came a most betraying clue—a water-filled carton with a soggy dollar bill floating in it. The meaning of this absurd experiment was plain. The loot was buried in damp ground, and Uckele wanted to find out how soon a wet dollar would rot.

Then Matysek, from solitary confinement, began smuggling grapevine notes to his pal. Eventually these notes reached Uckele, but somehow they always came into our hands first. Thus we read the description of "Nick" which they were concocting; their plans for an insanity defense. Also they had a master plan for escape, to be followed only if they were given long sentences.

In these intercepted notes we found what we were seeking—discussions about the money, sometimes cryptically referred to as "18," again as "the paper": "If we go to a federal penitentiary the winter rains will rot the paper in no time." Another read: "One advantage about my sister is she's only seventeen, and they can't prosecute a juvenile. But how the hell can she go to—" Matysek was too cunning to name the hiding place, but from his note we had learned that we must find not only a cache in damp earth but one inaccessible to a young girl.

We began our search where the pair had lived on the campus of the university, at the foot of the Santa Monica Mountains, which divide West Los Angeles from the Lockheed plant. Through admissions of the prisoners, we found $5000 in one-dollar bills buried in a campus flower bed. Nick, they swore, took the rest. We heard that Uckele and Matysek often took walks through fashionable suburbs in the canyons; a map disclosed that fire trails, which wind among the mountain trees, were numbered. Even thrill-hardened agents felt a tingle when they put their finger on Fire Trail 18—which by an isolated and lonely route ran from near the campus to the ravine where the bank messengers had been abandoned. We felt so near the goal—but where next?

From a high point west of the college dormitory our men surveyed the footpaths as they tried to reconstruct the known events—and imagine the rest. The criminals must have driven from the ravine down Trail 18 and, after leaving the loot in the garage, abandoned the Oldsmobile about a mile away. At night they had buried the bills in damp ground. Scanning the countryside, the agents noticed how one path led to an eight-foot wire fence bordering the Sawtelle Veterans' Facility Cemetery. Their reasoning began to fit in with recent reports. A gravestone is a landmark easy to remember. And a girl would have a hard time getting over that fence! Painstakingly agents moved along the endless rows of graves, searching for some telltale trace. Presently they came to the resting place of a soldier who had died in 1922. Behind his headstone was an inexplicable hump of leaves.

Our men began to dig and soon had exhumed a gunnysack and duffel bag. When these were opened the wind fluttered stacks of greenbacks: $100,000 cash. Uckele was told of this, and the court gave him another chance to make a clean breast of it all. Instead, he made a violent attempt to escape from the U.S. Marshal in the elevator of the Federal Building. Battered from the struggle, he limped into court and finally confessed the whole desperate story. For that, his sentence was reduced from thirty-five to twenty years. But for some time afterward Matysek stood firm; when he too finally confessed, his sentence was reduced to twenty-one years.

Forty years ago this bank robbery might never have been solved. An ultraviolet ray broke the case, plus persistence and patience and—a frequent reward of hard-working officers—good luck!

My brother-in-law, a plainclothesman in the Los Angeles police department, was watching a detective story on television with us one evening. The cunning crook brilliantly outmaneuvered the pursuing sleuths for almost a half hour before, in the last half minute, he was caught and trapped into a confession. "Now, honestly, Joe," I said, "are real criminals as clever as that?"

"Not usually," he answered, "but neither are we—so it comes out about the same!"
—*Bette Atwater*

Ship of Sleepless Men

By Anthony Abbot

It ONCE happened that an American woman, thinking about a crime she did not witness, reading the testimony of murder trials she did not attend, helped to overcome the judgment of two juries and two judges and to obtain a Presidential pardon for the man she considered innocent.

The story begins on the night of July 13, 1896, aboard

the *Herbert Fuller*, a barkentine out of Boston for the Argentine. During a squall Lester Hawthorne Monck, a twenty-year-old Harvard student voyaging at sea because of delicate health, sprang up from a dream so vivid that he could not tell whether the sounds he heard were nightmare or real. Above the creaks and groans of the ship's timbers, the wash of the rain on the afterdeck overhead and the wind in the halyards, what was that other sound?

Monck opened his cabin door and peered out. The chartroom looked peaceful enough; a lighted oil lantern swayed from its hook. The doors to three other staterooms, where the captain, his wife and the second mate slept, were closed. The mysterious, frightening sound must have been part of his dream. Monck bolted his door and tried to go back to sleep. Then it came again. *There was a scream this time. It was not a nightmare!*

Monck scrambled out of bed and shouted: "Captain Nash! Is that you?"

No answer! Trembling, Monck reached for his revolver, sat on the bunk and loaded it. He lost another minute pulling on his pants and searching for his slippers. Then he unbolted his door and looked out again into the chartroom. The body of Captain Nash, head split open, lay sprawled on the floor amid a growing pool of blood. Monck stumbled across to Mrs. Nash's cabin. One horrified glance was enough. Laura Nash lay nude in her own blood, slain after a terrific struggle.

Monck turned toward the companionway that led to the unlighted afterdeck. Overhead he heard the heavy pacing of the man on watch, Bram, the first mate. Bram, looking down, saw Monck with his revolver. Seizing a piece of loose planking, he hurled it at the student. "Why?" Bram was one day to be asked in court. "Why did you throw that board at Mr. Monck?"

"Who wouldn't? He was pointing a gun." And no one could quarrel with such a reasonable answer. Monck dodged the flying board, called to the first mate and told him what he had seen. Bram finally came down, and groaned at the sight.

"This is mutiny!" he said. "The second mate must be up forward by now, taking command." He made no attempt to look into the cabin where the mate was supposed to be sleeping. Instead he said: "We better wait till it gets light. . . ." As the two men waited for dawn, Bram began to weep. "They'll murder me next," he wailed. "I've been hard on all of them, I guess. They must have drugged me so I wouldn't hear in there." Yet Bram, Monck remembered, had been pacing the deck, keeping his watch. If he could walk, why could he not hear? He stowed this question away in his mind.

At dawn, Bram and Monck cocked their revolvers and crept to the crew's quarters. There was no sign of mutiny: the sailors were fast asleep. The first to be roused was the steward, an intelligent West Indian named Spencer. He refused at first to believe their story. But he followed them to the chartroom, and when he saw the bodies of Captain and Laura Nash he nearly fainted. Then he flung open the door of the second mate's cabin—and screamed. For the second mate had also been murdered!

The three men hurried back on deck, where Bram began searching for the murderer's weapon. Suddenly he shouted: "This is what did it!" And from under some planking he lifted a long-handled axe, its blade stained crimson. Before anyone could stop him, he had pitched it overboard. "Why did you throw the axe away?" was another question Bram had to answer later in court.

"I was afraid it would be used to kill others of us," he said. And who can quarrel with that answer, either? Bram

admitted he even wanted to throw the three bodies overboard. But common sense, in the form of the steward,
intervened. Why not, asked Spencer, call a powwow of
everyone on board?

Cigars, whiskey and three corpses in the chartroom—
was there ever another conference like that one? For
everybody knew that the murderer sat smoking, drinking
with the rest of them. Bram offered his theory of the
crime: the captain and the second mate had fought over
the brown-haired, attractive Laura Nash and killed each
other and her in a hysterical shambles.

There was talk about some spots on the clothing of
Charlie Brown, a Swedish sailor who had been at the
wheel during the murder watch, and about drops of
blood on the deck. But no one came to any conclusion.
Finally it was decided to preserve the bodies for the coroner; they were sewn into canvas, lashed in a tiny skiff and
towed astern.

Monck wrote an account of all that had happened, and
every man on board signed it. It was decided to make for
the nearest port. But now that some kind of order reigned
again aboard ship, a fuller realization of the horror of
their plight settled over the crew. Of the nine men left
alive, one was a killer. But *which* one? Until that was
known, who could be safe? For six days and nights no one
slept on board the *Herbert Fuller* as she plowed through the
seas with her dismal burden astern. The men grew thin
and pale. Fear deepened in them like a disease.

One day a seaman burst out that he had seen the
wheelman, Charlie Brown, change his clothes on the
night of the murder. Why not? countered Charlie. He was
cold after the rain. Another sailor remembered that
Charlie was sailing under an alias; his real name was

Julius Leopold Westerburg. Then the question arose: Could the steersman have left the wheel long enough to kill three persons without the ship getting off course? Later, able-bodied seamen testified that he could have lashed the wheel and the ship would have kept her course. Other experts said that this might be done on some types of ship but not on a heavy-sailed barkentine like the *Herbert Fuller*. Bram, Monck and Spencer ordered the wheelman put in irons.

"You do me wrong," was all that Charlie Brown said.

"Now that we have caught the murderer, let's tear up the paper we all signed," Bram proposed. But Monck said he was not at all sure that they had the murderer.

After Brown's arrest the tension lessened for a few hours. Then some of the men who had been talking with Charlie Brown brought up new suspicions. Charlie had a tale of his own: he *had* heard the noise of the murders; through a window into the chartroom he had actually seen the axe rising and falling, though he could not see who held it. Could a man at the wheel see anything through that window? Jurymen were to board the ship and grasp the wheel, and some were to decide they could see a great deal through that window. Charlie also said that he had seen Mate Bram come from the chartroom to the afterdeck. Some of the other nerve-racked, sleepless crewmen remembered that Bram had once remarked that Laura Nash was built for the entertainment of a man much younger than the captain; all knew that Bram and Captain Nash had not liked each other.

Sunday night a group of crewmen, led by the steward, grabbed Bram and chained him to the mizzenmast. "I am innocent," was all he said. Either Bram or Charlie must have done it—so the remaining seven reasoned. But was it common sense to believe that Bram could kill the second mate, the captain and his wife—with an axe—and yet have no small spot of blood on his clothes?

After eighteen days at sea, the ship's company staggered down the gangplank. They still seemed dazed when they told their story to a Boston grand jury. Appalled, the jurymen listened to the testimony, to theories and to a great deal of gossip. It was said that Bram once had plotted mutiny with the crew of another ship. There was the motive; the man wanted to be a pirate—to attack a ship in ancient style, kill all hands, escape with a fortune and live happily ever after. And of Charlie Brown it was said that he had once been accused of homicide. The grand jurors indicted Bram. He was assigned two excellent lawyers. On New Year's Day, 1897, twelve good men and true were locked in the jury room. After twenty-six hours and more than fifty ballots, they returned a verdict of guilty. Mate Bram was sentenced to be hanged.

The next year Bram was tried again, the first judgment having been reversed for errors by the Supreme Court. Meanwhile the laws of the land had undergone a change: now a man found guilty of murder in a federal court might hope for life imprisonment if the jury felt like recommending it. The second Bram jury did. In July 1898 the first mate was condemned to life imprisonment. For fifteen years nothing more was heard of him. Then, on August 27, 1913, he was paroled.

Mary Roberts Rinehart, seeking a plot for a new mystery novel, heard from a friend the yarn of the *Herbert Fuller*. After studying transcripts of the two trials and doing some independent research, she was swept with an overwhelming conviction that injustice had been done, that Bram's name should be cleared. She wrote her novel in a fervor of protest.

In her story Mrs. Rinehart naturally added some beauteous ladies and a love affair for the young man, but it was the same weird yarn of a murderer at large on the high seas—except that her villain turned out to be not the mate but the man at the wheel. She called him "Charlie Jones," a homicidal maniac. Her book, *The After House*, was published in 1914. Shortly afterward ex-President Theodore Roosevelt, excited by the tale, questioned Mrs. Rinehart and declared that something should be done.

Just what was done Mrs. Rinehart was never told. President Wilson was one of her most admiring readers; whether he acted merely because he had read *The After House* or whether Colonel Roosevelt's letters to various authorities also helped, she never knew. She did know that in the midst of the struggle over the League of Nations in 1919, Woodrow Wilson took time out to sign a full Presidential pardon for Bram.

"Bram," stated Mrs. Rinehart in her autobiography, *My Story*, "wrote me a letter in which he said: 'Permit me to say to you, in the presence of Almighty God, that I never committed the crime for which I have unjustly suffered behind prison bars.' I never believed that he had. And by that time I was in possession of information which he did not have. The other suspect, Charlie Brown, had some years after the murders been taken with a sudden attack of homicidal mania in a hospital in Stockholm and had tried to kill his nurse with a knife."

Many years ago, the reluctance of seamen to sail on a Friday reached such proportions that the British government decided to prove the fallacy of the superstition. They laid the keel of a new vessel on Friday, launched her on Friday, named her H.M.S. *Friday* and sent her to sea on Friday. The scheme had only one drawback—neither ship nor crew was ever heard from again.
—*Our Navy*

Miracle on the Gallows

By Jerome Beatty

THE MIRACLE occurred at Columbia, Mississippi, on February 7, 1894, when Will Purvis, a twenty-one-year-old farmer, was hanged. . . .

In Marion County, in 1893, a secret band was terrorizing planters and Negroes. The men called themselves White Caps, and their latest crime was to horsewhip a Negro who had left a widow's farm to work for Jim and Will Buckley for more money than the widow could afford to pay. The Negro recognized some of his torturers, and the Buckleys announced that they would report the names to the grand jury. The White Caps threatened the Buckleys with death if they did, but Jim and Will were brave and angry men. Unarmed, they went to town and testified before the grand jury. The White Caps ambushed them on the way home. Will Buckley dropped from his horse, shot to death; Jim escaped. He said that two men had hidden behind a clump of bushes, and that the one who fired the fatal shot was Will Purvis.

Will Purvis was from an old family for whom the nearby town of Purvis was named. Three relatives and

two neighbors testified that he was at home when the
murder was committed. His shotgun hadn't been fired for
months. But the jury doubted the testimony of relatives
and friends, and the verdict was "Guilty." Purvis was
sentenced to be hanged.

On the day of the hanging three thousand men, women
and children thronged the scene at Court House Square.
The sheriff and his deputies, experienced in their duties,
had seen to it that the trapdoor and the rope were carefully tested with sandbags, and the hangman's knot expertly tied. Everything was ready. Will Purvis was led up
the steps. Deputy sheriffs tied his hands behind him, tied
his ankles together. One held the black hood ready. The
sheriff, who had arrested Will and believed firmly in his
guilt, asked grimly, "Would you like to say anything?"

In a clear, cool voice, Will declared, "I didn't do it.
There are men out there who could save me if they
would."

Near the courthouse steps was the Reverend J. G. Sibley, pastor of the Columbia Methodist Church. He had
visited Purvis in jail and converted him; until then, Will
had belonged to no church. The minister believed the
condemned man was innocent, and so did scores of others. Throughout the months while Will's futile appeals to
higher courts were being heard, the Reverend Mr. Sibley
and church members prayed for him every Wednesday
night in the little church. At first only a handful came to
the meeting, but the attendance grew until the church
was crowded. Their one hope was that God would act.
The night before the hanging the Reverend Mr. Sibley
held a prayer meeting by torchlight in the Court House
Square, where hundreds knelt. After this meeting the
Reverend Mr. Sibley went to pray again with Will. He

found the condemned man, chained to the floor but completely calm. "I have no worry," he said, "over the destiny of my soul."

The next day, as the black hood was placed over Will Purvis' head, the Reverend Mr. Sibley and those who doubted Will's guilt again prayed together aloud: "Almighty God, if it be Thy will, stay the hand of the executioner." The sheriff said, "God help you, Will Purvis," and threw the lever. The crowd cried out as the body shot down through the opened trapdoor and the rope jerked hard.

Then there were screams and shouts as they saw that Purvis lay on the ground under the gallows, the black hood still over his head, his hands and feet still bound. He was very much alive, and the hangman's noose swung high above the open trapdoor—empty. What had happened? No one can put a noose tied with a hangman's knot around a man's neck in such a way that the man's head will slip through as his body drops. If the knot slips, the noose becomes tighter. And the sheriff performed no trickery, for he believed Will Purvis was guilty. Yet Purvis had fallen free of the noose.

Later he declared, "I heard the door creak, my body plunged down and all went black. When I regained consciousness I heard somebody say, 'Well, Bill, we've got to do it all over again.'" And the two deputies dragged him like a sack of potatoes back up the steps to be hanged again. As they reached for the rope, the Reverend Mr. Sibley leaped to the scaffold and cried to the crowd, "People of Marion County, the hand of Providence has slipped the noose. Heaven has heard our prayers. What do you say, friends? Shall Will Purvis be hanged again?"

"No! No!" they shouted. The miracle had changed their minds. They began to sing, to shout, to praise the

Lord. Undoubtedly they would have rescued Will Purvis had the executioners tried to go on with their work. So the bewildered and frightened sheriff took Will Purvis back to jail. The governor, no believer in miracles, ordered an inquiry. The investigators exonerated the sheriff; the preparations for the hanging, they reported, had been thorough. They couldn't explain why it wasn't successful.

But Will Purvis had been sentenced to hang *until dead*, and the governor, believing him guilty, refused to commute the sentence. Will's attorneys pleaded that he had been hanged once and that he could not be hanged again until he was convicted in another trial. However, three appeals were rejected by the State Supreme Court and Will was sentenced to be hanged again on December 12, 1895, nearly two years after his life had been spared. Most men would have lost their minds under month after month of such torture. Will Purvis, praying constantly, was sure that the Lord would save him again.

No new evidence was discovered, but public opinion turned. The God-fearing citizens of the community were convinced that a sign from Heaven had declared Will Purvis' innocence. And now the hand of man took hold. Will was granted an extraordinary favor by officials of Marion County. He was transferred from the strong Columbia jail to the shabby little prison in his home town of Purvis, "so he could be near his friends for the last weeks of his life." Probably the officials were not surprised when, a few days before Will's sentence was to be carried out, a mob overpowered the guards at midnight and rescued him. The governor, furious, offered a reward of $750 for Will's capture and $250 for evidence that would convict his rescuers. But the rewards were never claimed, although almost everybody knew who had broken into the jail and almost everybody knew that Will was living with kinfolk in the forests and hills.

Then a new governor was elected. During his campaign he had declared that a miracle had been performed, and he had promised to commute Will's sentence. Will gave himself up, and his sentence was commuted to life imprisonment. Two years later, in response to a petition signed by thousands of citizens, including the district attorney who had prosecuted him, Will was pardoned. He was free not because any new evidence had been found but because the majority of the people of Mississippi believed that God had overruled the jury's verdict. He moved onto a back-country farm, and a few months later married the daughter of a Baptist minister. They became the parents of eleven children. Every Sunday Will and his wife went to the Reverend Mr. Sibley's church and gave thanks to God for saving his life.

And then, when Will was forty-seven, the last chapter in this amazing case was written. An old planter named Joe Beard, dying, confessed that he and another member of the White Caps had committed the Buckley murder. The news was a Mississippi sensation and for weeks those who had believed Purvis was innocent went around saying, "I told you so," to those who hadn't. The state legislature paid Purvis $5000 to atone for the state's errors.

Will Purvis died in 1943, a respected citizen of his community. Doubt if you will that his life was saved by a miracle. Call it an accident, an accident that might happen once in the history of the world. But Will Purvis has testified, "God heard our prayers. He saved my life because I was an innocent man." Will Purvis believed. And it was *his* neck.

The Unmasking of
Paul "The Waiter" Ricca

By Louis Sidran

O N JUNE 4, 1954, a fifty-five-year-old laborer named
Angelo Ciola walked, as usual, the fourteen blocks
from his factory job to his home on Chicago's South Side,
opened his door and stepped directly into one of the most
incredible crime stories in recent history.

Angelo Ciola was not accustomed to drama. A man of
almost monotonous habits, he had lived in the same
neighborhood for thirty-four years, had never missed a
day at work. He was good-natured, friendly—and not
easy to fool. He wondered, then, what was going on when
he was met at his door by an investigator for the U.S.
Immigration and Naturalization Service. The agent
wanted to know if Ciola really was Ciola. Ciola showed
him his U.S. citizenship papers. Had Ciola ever heard of
a man named Paul Ricca? He hadn't. Paul "The Waiter"
Ricca? Still no reaction. But *everybody* in Chicago had
heard of Ricca. Ciola explained that his English was not
too strong; he read only Italian papers.

The agent persisted. Had he ever heard of Felice
DeLucia? No. Then how about Paul DeLucia? No again.

Ciola protested that he was an honest man who had never had any trouble with the law. What was this all about? The agent explained that Paul Ricca, Felice DeLucia and Paul DeLucia were one and the same man. And by a fluke of fate the lives of this man and Angelo Ciola had become irrevocably entangled.

The man known as Paul Ricca is soft-spoken and has the manners of a gentleman. He looks like a chairman of the board—which he is. But the corporation he heads is the Midwest division of the infamous crime octopus called the "Syndicate." As heir to Al Capone in the Midwest, Ricca had for years been watched by the police and the FBI. But only once in his criminal career had he slipped up. In 1943 he was convicted as a ringleader in an extortion gang which had shaken down the movie industry. He served three years in prison, then returned to Chicago to live like a baron. Protected by the best legal counsel that money could buy, Ricca seemed invulnerable to prosecution for his criminal activities. But in 1945 an anonymous tipster phoned the district director of the Immigration and Naturalization Service in Chicago to assert that Paul Ricca's true name was Felice DeLucia and that he had entered the United States illegally under the name of Angelo Ciola. The tip set off a chain of investigations that culminated in a tale far stranger than fiction.

Ricca had indeed masqueraded as Angelo Ciola. More than that, he had used Ciola's identity for years, without the slightest suspicion that the real Ciola was not only alive but actually living in Chicago only a few miles from his own home!

The story begins in Naples, Italy, in 1915. A girl named Amelia DeLucia was keeping company with one Emilio Perillo. The DeLucia family was, to say the least, unsavory, and the Perillo boy was ordered by his parents to break off with Amelia. She pleaded for one last moment with Emilio. The boy never returned from this final good-bye. He was found dead on the street the next day. Felice DeLucia, Amelia's seventeen-year-old brother, confessed to the killing, received a light sentence and in two years was home free. But a young man named Vincenzo Capasso had had the bad luck to be an eyewitness to the murder. One day Felice emptied his gun in Capasso's back—and this time he decided to flee the country. However, as a draft dodger in World War I, as a former convict and now as a fugitive in the Capasso murder, he couldn't travel under his own name. He needed a false passport. The man to see was a certain travel agent.

From his files the travel agent pulled out a legitimate client's passport, that of the town clerk of Apricena, a town some ninety miles northeast of Naples. According to the documents, the clerk was practically the same age, like DeLucia had five sisters and no brothers, and was headed for the United States to look for a more prosperous future. The clerk's name was Angelo Ciola.

After having waited some four months for his papers to be cleared, the real Angelo Ciola sailed from Italy on the *Duca degli Abruzzi*, arriving in New York on August 5, 1920. Felice DeLucia, sailing from France as "Angelo Ciola from Apricena," arrived five days later. In a short while both men were settled in Chicago—Ciola in a neighborhood where he found work as a laborer; DeLucia as a waiter in the employ of "Diamond Joe" Esposito, whose restaurant was virtually a meeting hall for the men who were even then organizing the Syndicate. DeLucia's rise was meteoric. He stayed with Esposito only long enough to pick up his nickname—"The Waiter." For the

Syndicate, he managed the Dante Theater in Chicago's Little Italy section, and then the World Playhouse Corporation for Al Capone. It was as a specialist in the entertainment business that, years later, he combined with Louis "Little New York" Campagna, Frank "The Enforcer" Nitti and others to muscle Willy Bioff and George Browne out of their lucrative extortion racket, which had terrorized the movie industry. Some time after World War II he became Midwest boss of the Syndicate.

Being a man of many aliases proved complicating to DeLucia-Ciola-Ricca. In 1928 he applied for citizenship and asked the court to change his name from Angelo Ciola to Paul DeLucia, because he had been "married under that name." With no questions the court granted the change, and he had his original surname back. Still, however, the name Ricca, one of his earlier aliases, stuck to him; its sound had apparently endeared it to headline writers.

Until 1928 he carefully signed all official papers as Angelo Ciola, birthplace Apricena, birth date July 10, 1898. Even after the legal name change he cautiously continued to employ Ciola's background. The single major lapse into honesty had occurred in 1926, when he was married in a Chicago church: confronted by the cloth, he identified himself as Paul DeLucia, born in Naples on November 14, 1897. The only other name lapse of consequence came to light in connection with a bank account at the First National Bank of Chicago that he forgot to close out. The account, with $1.39 left in it when he was brought to trial in 1957, carried his real signature and listed his honest birth date. Ironically, while this midget account remained active, Ricca had $300,000 in cash secreted in the attic of his River Forest mansion.

Even with the discovery of the real Angelo Ciola, fed-

eral agents knew it would be a long time before they had
their case against Ricca nailed down. So a five-man,
twenty-four-hour guard was put on the Ciola family.
During the three years that this lasted, one thing irked
Ciola: the guards insisted on driving him to and from
work, even though he felt he needed the daily walk to
keep healthy. The guards considered driving in a car
healthier. Witnesses in any case involving Ricca had had
an alarming way of vanishing. On December 8, 1955,
Alex Louis Greenberg, a local hood and government witness against Ricca, was found murdered. In 1953 Ricca's
chauffeur mysteriously disappeared—and has never been
found.

In September 1956 the accumulated evidence of years
was turned over to the office of Robert Tieken, U.S.
Attorney for the northern district of Illinois. John H.
Bickley, Jr., an ex-Marine who, although only twenty-
seven years old, already had a reputation in the prosecution of deportation and denaturalization cases, was ordered to drop everything and concentrate on Ricca.

Suddenly came a "break" which could have given
Bickley what he most desired: an eyewitness who could
positively identify the accused. Margaret Perillo Terribile,
sister of Ricca's first victim, Emilio Perillo, was discovered living in Brooklyn. She remembered Felice DeLucia.
Shown pictures, she picked Ricca out every time as the
man who had killed her brother. She wanted revenge and
would testify. But then two "tourists" from Italy paid
Mrs. Terribile a visit. Immediately she lost all appetite
for the case. She and her husband got down on their knees
and pleaded with Bickley not to make them testify. Days
before the case came to trial, the Terribiles disappeared—
gone back to Italy, someone said.

Bickley took his case to court in April 1957, with some two hundred documents and exhibits detailing the family origins of Felice DeLucia and outlining the crime career of Paul "The Waiter" Ricca. The prosecutor could trace a host of "coincidences" linking Ricca with Felice De-Lucia, who had entered the United States illegally and was a fugitive from an *in absentia* murder conviction. But only one witness could prove to the court's satisfaction that Paul Ricca was not, as he had claimed, Angelo Ciola of Apricena. That witness was Angelo Ciola himself—and on his small frame rested the weight of the case.

On the second day of the trial, after Bickley had paraded a succession of witnesses and exhibits, each barely a pinprick in Ricca's armor, he suddenly called as his next witness "Angelo Ciola." Ricca, sitting beside his attorney, blinked in astonishment. Did Bickley mean *him?* Bickley repeated slowly, "The government calls as its next witness the *real* Angelo Ciola." And the little man entered—nervous but not frightened.

After the preliminary routine of identification Bickley asked Ricca to rise and face the witness. As the two men confronted each other, Bickley asked Ciola the questions necessary to establish an unshakable fact in a court of law. Did he know this man? No. Had he ever seen him before? No. Did this man come from Apricena? No. Was his name Angelo Ciola? Oh, no. How did the witness know? Because, as town clerk of Apricena, he had personally kept the birth and death records. There were only 6000 people in Apricena. Only one Ciola family. Only one Angelo Ciola—himself. Ricca's attorney did not cross-examine.

The trial ended the following day, with Ricca offering nothing in his own defense. His citizenship was taken away, and he was later ordered deported to his native

Naples. But first, in July 1959, he entered the federal prison at Terre Haute, Indiana, to serve a three-year sentence for income-tax evasion. At the end of his term, Italy refused to take him back—*no* country would have him—but Ricca is today appealing a scheduled deportation to his native land.

What gave quiet little Angelo Ciola the courage to testify, in spite of the obvious risk to himself and his whole family?

His reasons were as simple as his way of life. America had been good to him, he said, and if he could help his adopted country by testifying he would do it. Moreover, Ricca had besmirched the good name of Ciola. It was up to him to redeem the name—and in a sense the names of many thousands of Italian immigrants who, unlike a few notorious gangsters, live quiet, law-abiding lives in a country they have chosen for their own.

A policeman told us recently about a thug they had in the line-up. He was a beetle-browed, hard-looking chap who had been interrupted doing a job on a delicatessen. During the routine questioning, his belongings, among which was a pair of brass knuckles, were inspected.

"Be careful wid dem knuckles, Sarge," he requested a bit bashfully. "They mean something to me."

The knuckles were examined more closely and this inscription was found inside the little finger: "With truest love, from Mildred."   —*PM*

A Chicago man admitted in court that he stole seventy-five checks, worth $600, from mailboxes, but asserted he always sent $5 from every stolen check he cashed to the chaplain of the Federal Penitentiary at Terre Haute "for the betterment of prison conditions."   —*Camp News Service*

No Clues

By Karl Detzer

SHORTLY before midmorning the day of the murder—
August 4, 1955—thin rain began to fall from a lead-
colored sky on Kansas City, Missouri. In a beauty shop at
6313 Brookside Plaza, Mrs. Wilma Frances Allen, pretty
thirty-four-year-old wife of the president of a prosperous
automobile agency, was having her hair done. Between
12:25 and 12:30 she left the shop, paused in the door to tie
a scarf over her head and stepped out into the rain. Her
Chevrolet convertible stood in a nearby parking lot. Mrs.
Allen hurried toward it. She was not again seen alive.

According to everyone in the beauty shop, her mood
was gay. She was looking forward to dining out with her
husband that evening, and the visit to the hairdresser was
in honor of the occasion. As she sat under the drier she had
asked the manicurist to change the shade of her nails to go
with a beige dress she would wear. Hairdo and manicure
came to $5. She paid with a $30 check, put the change in
her blue handbag and vanished into the rain.

The Allens were a happy, highly respected couple.
They lived with two sons, aged nine and seven, in a big

ranch-type house on exclusive Vivion Road. No servants "slept in," but Mrs. Allen had employed a baby-sitter for the evening. At five o'clock her husband phoned her. Startled that she had not returned home, he spent an hour calling friends, seeking news of her. That evening he sent out his agency salesmen to hunt for the convertible. They couldn't find it. Allen, greatly disturbed, notified the police. They broadcast a "missing persons" lookout and a request for information concerning the car.

It was 2:10 a.m. when Patrolman Ronald Ehrhardt discovered the Chevrolet under a dark viaduct near the Union Station. The motor was cold, proving the car had been there several hours. Doors and trunk were locked. Detectives broke in and found bloodstains on the rear floormat and seat cushions. Then the detectives pried open the car trunk and came upon most of the clothing Mrs. Allen had been wearing. It was bloodstained and torn. All jewelry and money, the scarf and blue handbag were missing. Grimly the police shifted their search for a young woman to one for a young woman's body.

Experts discovered several latent fingerprints in the car, too blurred to be of value. There were also what appeared to be palm prints, useless at the moment because there was no classified file of palm prints against which to check them. By dawn the authorities had dug up only one slim, useful fact. The Allens kept a mileage-gasoline record, which enabled the police to estimate that the car had traveled some sixty or seventy miles after it left the beauty shop. Police drew a thirty-five-mile circle on a large map. It covered parts of several counties in two states, Missouri and Kansas. The area embraced some fifty towns, many suburbs and some sparsely settled rural regions. Somewhere in that circle, police told themselves, somewhere . . .

By eight o'clock that first morning fifty Kansas City detectives were at work on the case. As yet there was no evidence that any federal statute had been violated, but Percy Wyly, agent in charge of the local FBI office, stopped at police headquarters to offer every coöperation short of actual investigation. The law rigidly restricts the FBI from participating in local investigations unless a federal statute has been broken. Under the Lindbergh Act, if the assailant crossed the nearby state line in committing this crime, or trying to evade capture, the case would be in the jurisdiction of the FBI. But until this was proved Agent Wyly could not enter the case.

Most officers guessed that the crime was the work of what newspapers call a "sex maniac," and police all over America were notified. Before night a widespread hunt for violent sex deviates was on. All across the continent, in the next few weeks, unsavory characters were picked up, questioned, released. One newspaper estimated that at one time more than six hundred officers were devoting full time to the case. Possible leads poured into Kansas City. All, even the most unbelievable, had to be checked and double-checked. In Omaha, Nebraska, the sheriff took into custody a man who had served a prison sentence for a sex crime and whose record showed forty-two arrests in the Kansas City area. The man's face was bruised and scratched, and he claimed he had been hurt in a fight. A bus driver reported that the evening of the day after Mrs. Allen disappeared a man of about forty boarded his bus at Warrenton, Missouri, his clothing dirty, lips cut, left cheek deeply scratched. On the afternoon of Mrs. Allen's disappearance two teen-age boys had followed a convertible they were sure was hers on U.S. Highway 69. None of these leads proved fruitful.

The first break came Saturday evening, August 6. Late that afternoon Richard A. Taylor, a Kansas farmer, was

driving a tractor on Highway 69 some twenty-five miles
south of Kansas City when he saw a blue handbag in the
ditch. He did not stop. Later he read in a newspaper that
Mrs. Allen's handbag was missing, so he sent his young
son back to hunt for it. The boy found the bag, empty,
and Taylor notified the sheriff. The purse was quickly
identified as Mrs. Allen's. The next morning another
farmer, Clifford Erhart, and his son Milton were out in
their station wagon searching back roads for a strayed cow
and calf. On Tibbetts Road, about six and a half miles
from the ditch where the handbag was found, they saw a
pasture gate standing open. It led to a moist field hidden
from the road by brush and trees. They drove in, thinking
only of strayed animals. But as they bumped across the
field, young Milton pointed and cried out, "What's that?"

"It was some distance off," Erhart said later. "But I
knew right away. We didn't even stop, just drove to the
nearest telephone and called the sheriff. He came fast."

The body was nude. Mrs. Allen's hands were tied behind her with the striped scarf. She had been shot twice in
the back of the head. Her jewelry, even her wedding
band, was missing. Officers immediately roped off the
area, but rain had washed away all evidence. Not a foot-
print or tire track remained. Among early arrivals at the
pasture was an FBI agent. Now, with proof that the victim
had been carried across a state line, the crime became a
federal offense. Agents from several Midwest offices converged on Kansas City. Experts were flown in. Files were
restudied, in search of some related bit of information.

Yet, despite full coöperation among federal, state,
county and city agencies, officers could not find a single
clue. The frightened public was demanding a quick solution. Law-enforcement agencies worked feverishly—and
wholly in the dark. Medical examination of the body

threw doubt on the "sex maniac" theory. Then how explain the nude body and the ripped and bloody garments in the car trunk? Police asked psychiatrists for aid in forming a picture of the type of criminal involved. This led nowhere. As the search dragged on, day after day, night after sleepless night, newspaper headlines shrank to two oft-repeated words: "No Clues!"

Police in most cities have always coöperated with one another but until recent years this coöperation has been hit-and-miss. Now, with the vast network of the FBI covering the entire nation, with a central office through which pass all reports of serious crimes and wanted men, local officers rely more and more on its aid in solving their knottiest problems. Even when the FBI can't be called in on a case directly, its records and laboratory stand ready to help all law enforcers. For example: Details of Crime A in Seattle and Crime B in Miami are poured into the hopper in Washington, and probably at first seem to have no connection. But when Crime C in Chicago is added, a pattern may take shape and the assembled facts point to a solution. That happened in the Kansas City case.

On August 31, four weeks after the murder, a burglary suspect, identified as a thirty-year-old California parole violator named Arthur Ross Brown, twice shot and critically wounded a Wyoming sheriff as the sheriff was arresting him. The man got away. Brown, who came from a respected family, had been charged, when he was fourteen, with forcing a young girl into a car at gunpoint and driving her into the hills, where she persuaded him to return her to her home. There were other arrests on his record: another abduction—with a gun—of a woman, and twice he had been apprehended while stealing lingerie from women's bedrooms. However, nothing in his record showed that he ever had been in Kansas City. He was married, but his wife's whereabouts was unknown.

Shortly after the shooting Brown stole a car in Sheridan, Wyoming, and drove to Rapid City, South Dakota, where he robbed a liquor store. He was later identified from photographs. Thereafter he stole a series of cars, one of which was recovered with his fingerprints—but no palm print—on it. Next, a man answering his description held up liquor stores in Florida, Texas and Indiana. In each case a woman clerk, alone in the store, was the victim. Meanwhile, the FBI and California police kept close watch on the homes of Brown's relatives and friends. They still did not connect him with the Allen case. He was wanted for shooting the Wyoming sheriff.

Then, on November 9, a frightened householder called the Kansas City police and the local FBI office. A neighboring woman, the caller reported, had been visited by her estranged husband, who had forced her at gunpoint to accompany him in his car. The woman's name? Mrs. Arthur Ross Brown. A search was launched immediately—without result. Four hours later Mrs. Brown returned home, so unnerved that she was incoherent. Brown himself had escaped again. This time he fled to California, a move the FBI had anticipated.

Local officers and FBI agents interviewed all members of Brown's family, wherever they lived, and all persons who knew him. His mother, a God-fearing, law-abiding woman who lived in San Jose, California, was convinced that her son was mad, and begged officers to apprehend him before he could do more harm. She promised to notify the authorities if she heard from him. She did, on November 13. That evening she thought she saw a prowler outside, and a little later her son telephoned. He had tried to see her, he said, but had fled, fearing a trap. Now he would kill himself. He hung up. The frantic

mother called the FBI, which went into quick action.
Several agents rushed to keep a close watch on the
mother's house. Others went to an uncle's home in Oak-
land and to that of an aunt in San Francisco. A car parked
on a dark street near the aunt's house quickly drew their
attention. An agent approached it silently, saw a man, his
face hidden by a blanket, apparently asleep on the front
seat. Car windows were closed and doors locked. The
agent backed away. This might be Brown, or it might be
someone sleeping off a drunk. Just then a city police
cruiser rolled past, turned its spotlight on the house occupied by Brown's aunt, went on. The FBI agents overtook
it. Earlier, the police said, the aunt had reported a
prowler. They had responded, found nothing. Now they
were making sure he had not returned. The city police
called for a second squad car and, when it arrived, eight
officers—four local and four federal—quietly surrounded
the sleeping man. They turned two strong spotlights on
him, ordered him into the street. Groggily he obeyed.
They studied his sullen face. The hunt for Brown was over.

The agents sped him to their office, quickly made prints of his palms. Then the questioning began. He admitted some robberies, denied others, contradicted himself. The agents mentioned the Wyoming sheriff. At first Brown denied his guilt, then finally broke. Had he shot the sheriff in Wyoming? "Yes," he admitted. Then he added: "But where I'm really wanted is Kansas City."

Before morning he had told the whole horrible story. The motive in the Allen case, he insisted, had been robbery. He never had seen his victim until she walked out of the beauty shop. "I was looking for someone to rob," he explained. "She looked wealthy." As she got into her car in the parking lot, he climbed in beside her, gun in hand. He directed her on the long drive. She pleaded with him, talked of her children. He "just was lucky" in finding the open gate to the pasture. There he stripped her of her clothes—to prevent identification, he lamely explained— took her money and jewels. Then, as she cowered on the floor begging for mercy, he shot her in the back of the head. He dragged her out to the soggy ground, shot her again, tried to wipe away the blood in the car with the clothing, put it in the trunk and drove back to town.

In Kansas City, indicted under the Lindbergh Act for kidnapping, a capital federal offense, Brown refused to plead insanity, and psychiatrists appointed by the court found him sane. A jury of twelve men found him guilty. He was sentenced to die in the gas chamber of the Missouri State Prison. Shortly after midnight on February 24, 1956, the sentence was implemented.

Thus ended a classic case of coöperation among federal, state, county and city law-enforcement agencies. Working together, with the FBI coördinating their far-flung efforts, in 101 days they solved a mystery without clues and brought to justice a ruthless killer.

Baker Street Episode

By Ellery Husted

A FTER I'd been waiting around Ford Island three weeks, my orders finally came: "Report Cincpac [Admiral Nimitz, Commander-in-Chief Pacific] Advanced Intelligence Headquarters, Guam. Passage via Air Transport. Proceed without delay." An hour's paper work, fifteen minutes' packing, and I made it a minute before the plane took off. There was a two-day hop ahead, and I'd forgotten to pack a book. On my way through the hangar I saw on a chair a paperback volume with no visible owner. The cover said: *Six Adventures of Sherlock Holmes.* I stole it without shame.

After reading it twice I wondered what I could do to make my monotonous trip less depressing. I pictured Sherlock Holmes and Dr. Watson seated comfortably before their fire at 221B Baker Street, and since I was an architect in peacetime it was natural to speculate as to what their rooms had looked like. Suddenly a thought burned through the cloud of my ennui. I retrieved the *Six Adventures* and prepared for another reading with reawakened eyes. Scattered through each of the stories were disconnected but explicit references to the physical arrangements of the famed rooms. I began to copy all descriptions of them. When I'd finished and had sorted and assembled the architectural references, I found to my surprise that each fitted like a shaped piece into a picture puzzle. Then I reconstructed the plans and elevations of 221B. No line was drawn without clear confirmation from the text.

The complete work made a bulky package, and on landing at Guam I was about to throw it away when I thought of my friend Dick Clarke, another Navy man and a member of The Five Orange Pips, one of the Sherlock Holmes fan clubs that flourished in the United States. It might amuse him to receive this bit of literary archaeology. I put the papers in an envelope addressed to Clarke, gave them to a yeoman to send by air mail and forgot them in the more serious business of war.

Some months later the war ended, and I got my orders home. I was cheerfully destroying official papers when I was handed a large and familiar envelope covered with the ink of rubber stamps. It was my letter to Clarke come back to roost, and I assumed that it had been sent off with too few stamps.

Next morning on the plane back to Pearl Harbor a blond young ensign in the seat ahead turned around and said, "Your name's Husted?" I nodded.

"And how's Dr. Watson?" he asked with a grin.

I considered the question for a moment and realized the ensign must have been a Cincpac censor. "I suppose you censored that Baker Street letter."

"Yeah. *And did it give us trouble!* They put the best brains in Guam on it, but nobody could make anything of it. It was obviously in code, but we couldn't break it, so we sent it to Pearl. They spent some time on it and sent it on to

Washington, but it was no go. It came back to us, and we held it until the war was over."

I laughed and said, "You knew all about *me*. Why didn't you ask me about it?"

The ensign smiled. "Yeah, we knew all about you, but it wasn't that easy. We checked your handwriting with the letter and it didn't agree. Too jerky. And you'll agree that all that stuff about 221B Baker Street sounded queer. The letter didn't make sense." I thought of the wavy handwriting caused by the undulations of air travel, of my mysterious disconnected passages lifted from the text and especially of my enigmatic letter to Clarke:

Dear Dick: Tell your group of Peculiar Pips that 221B did exist, and that it has been resurrected by one who is not of you, but believes in you. I wish Holmes were with me to solve the riddle of the Empire. God bless you, and in the name of Holmes and Baker Street keep up the good fight.
Yours,
Husted

I could only agree that Cincpac's alert censors had had cause for their suspicions, and was ruminating pleasantly over the extent of the trouble I had probably caused, when the blond head before me revolved again to say: "And worst of all, my friend, Baker Street was the unofficial code name for OSS Headquarters, London."

The publishers of Mary Roberts Rinehart's books asked her to check her first three mystery novels, written some fifty years before, for reissue. Mrs. Rinehart, who never reread her books once they were published, was reading one of these early novels when her publisher stopped in to discuss them. "I'm having the most wonderful time," she said. "I'm reading *The Man in Lower Ten*, and I can't figure out who committed the murder!"
—*Stanley M. Rinehart, Jr.*

A Girl Named Lavender

Condensed from the book Dark Trees to the Wind

By Carl Carmer

"It's always seemed to me that legends and yarns and folk tales are as much a part of the real history of a country as proclamations and provisos and constitutional amendments."
—Stephen Vincent Benét

This is one of a number of rural New York ghost stories collected by one of the Empire State's most distinguished historians.

ONLY A few miles northwest of New York City, along the boundary between New York and New Jersey, lies a hilly wilderness through which flows the Ramapo River. A few years ago the postmaster in a village that lies beside its lonely waters talked often about a lithe, tawny girl with hyacinth eyes and wheat-yellow hair. The postmaster was a sophisticated, traveled and urbane member of a distinguished family in those parts. To atone for his sins, he said, he taught a boys' class in a Sunday school in a tiny, weathered church in the Ramapo hills.

The boys were a shy lot but wild as woods animals are wild, and they found the simple lessons in Christian ethics the postmaster was trying to teach difficult at best and impossible at those times when that girl was around. She went through his class, he said, like a slow pestilence. A boy would be gone for a month or two, and then he would come back on a Sunday, glowering and sheepish, and one of his schoolmates would be absent for a while. The postmaster would sometimes see him and the girl picking blackberries or walking the road to a country dance.

One Wednesday night the contents of three barrels of old clothes from a New York City church were to be distributed after prayer meeting. The girl came just as the preacher beat in the head of the first barrel. She was barefoot and wore a patched calico dress much too small for her. She sat in the back pew and paid no attention as the usual pathetic garments were displayed. There was a gasp when the preacher pulled from the second barrel a lavender evening dress covered with sequins that glinted like amethysts; it was cut low off the shoulders. No one spoke up for it, but without saying a word the girl dashed forward, grabbed the dress and raced out of the church.

From that time on no one ever saw the girl in other costume. Rain or shine, day or night, she was a brushstroke of lavender against the brown dirt roads, the green hillslopes, the khaki-colored shirts of whatever boys strode beside her. Mid-December brought a cold snap and the thermometer showed eighteen below zero when the postmaster opened his window for business. The people coming for mail were more eager to give him the news than to receive letters. The body of the girl in the lavender dress had been found frozen stiff a few miles up the road. The evening dress had proved too flimsy for such weather. The postmaster said that after this tragedy all the students in his class came regularly to Sunday school. That was the end of the story of the girl.

The girl froze to death about 1939, a fact attested to by

many witnesses, and for a decade nothing more was heard
about her. Then a strange report began its rounds of up-
state towns and, particularly, colleges. It had many var-
iants, but in none of them was it in any way connected
with the postmaster's account of the girl and her death—
facts known only in the vicinity of her Ramapo home.

As I heard it, one Saturday evening two Hamilton College juniors, motoring to a dance at Tuxedo Park on the
road that runs through the valley of the Ramapo River,
saw a girl waiting. She was wearing a party dress the
color of the mist rising above the dark stream, and her
hair was the color of ripe wheat. The boys stopped and
asked if they could give her a lift. She eagerly seated herself between them and asked if they were going to the
square dance at Sterling Furnace. The thin, tanned face
with high cheekbones, the yellow hair, the flashing smile,
the quicksilver quality of her gestures enchanted the boys,
and they persuaded her to accompany them to the dance
at Tuxedo. When they presented their new friend to their
hosts at the Park, she said, "Call me 'Lavender.' It's my
nickname because I always wear that color."

When the dance was over and they started home, she
was cold, so one of the boys helped her into his tweed topcoat. After directing the driver through dusty woodland
roads she finally bade him to stop before a shack so dilapi-
dated that it would have seemed deserted had it not been
for a ragged lace curtain over the small window in the
door. Promising to see them again soon, she stood beside
the road waving until they disappeared. The boys were
almost in Tuxedo before the coatless one realized that he
had forgotten to reclaim his property. They decided to
return for it on their way back to college next day.

When the boys knocked on the door of the shack, a
decrepit white-haired woman peered at them out of

piercing blue eyes. They asked for Lavender. "Old friends
of hers?" she asked, and the boys, fearing to get the girl
into the bad graces of her family by telling the truth about
their adventure, said yes. "Then ye couldn't a-heerd she's
dead," said the woman. "Been in the graveyard down the
road fer near ten years." The boys protested that this was
not the girl they meant—they were trying to find someone they had seen the previous evening.

"Nobody else o' that name ever lived round here," said
the woman. "'Twan't her real name anyway. Her paw
named her Lily when she was born. Some folks used to
call her Lavender on account o' the pretty dress she wore
all the time. She was buried in it." The boys started for
the highway. A hundred yards down the road the driver
jammed on the brakes.

"There's the graveyard," he said, pointing to a few
weathered stones in an open field overgrown with weeds,
"and just for the hell of it I'm going over there."

They found a little stone marked "Lily"—and on the
mound in front of it, neatly folded, the tweed topcoat.

THE
READER'S
M DIGEST
URDER
CASE

Condensed from the book of the same title

By Fulton Oursler

ONE SPRING afternoon in 1948, a lumbering, bushy-haired convict named Calman Cooper appeared before a parole board in Clinton State Prison at Danne-mora, New York. The prisoner had a violent history. After breaking probation for earlier crimes, he had been sentenced to Atlanta Penitentiary as an interstate automobile thief, but escaped from the prison within a year. At large in New York under an alias, he was next nabbed during a burglary, only to go free on a suspended sentence; no one seems to remember why. Finally he was caught red-handed during a Brooklyn factory robbery in which a night watchman was killed.

Although charged with murder in the first degree, Calman Cooper was sentenced to serve twenty years to life. One might suppose that he would be safely behind bars for at least twenty years. But not so. With more than a third of his term still to serve, Calman Cooper was paroled through some inexplicable tenderness.

On that same day in 1948 there was working in the home office of The Reader's Digest near Pleasantville, New York, a messenger named Andrew Petrini, a curly-haired, amiable young man with a wife and baby boy. For Petrini, the parole certificate of Calman Cooper was a death warrant. Andrew Petrini was murdered when Cooper and three companions held up and robbed a Reader's Digest truck in the April of 1950.

This is the story of how the job was planned, so carefully that at first it seemed a crime without a real clue, and of how, by tireless patience, through disheartening months of search, by astute detective work, the mystery of this cold-blooded outrage was solved and the killers brought to justice by the New York state police. But this is more than the story of a mathematically plotted outrage executed on a split-second timetable; more, even, than an example of modern detective work at its best. Overshadowing the crime and its solution, The Reader's Digest murder case is a shocking example of some of the gravest weaknesses in America's judicial and penological systems.

The record of the proceedings in Westchester County Court at White Plains runs more than four thousand typewritten pages. Although the evidence was plain enough, the trial, at burdensome cost to the taxpayers, dragged on from November 1 until December 23, 1950. The trial of the fourth bandit, Dorfman, in 1952 added a further burden to the community. And in all those weeks, under the benevolent protection the state extends to all criminals, not a whisper of the records of the murderers' vicious pasts, nor of their various prison terms, could be allowed to reach the jury. So far as the twelve women and men of the jury were concerned, the three highwaymen had never before been accused of so much as a parking violation.

This murder illustrates above everything else the danger that lies in the abuse, and the weakness, of parole standards and parole administration. No sooner had the case been given to the jury than one of the defense attorneys said to me: "The State of New York should have been indicted for ever turning my client loose on the community."

The scheme was hatched behind prison bars. When Calman Cooper was paroled from Clinton he still owed time for his break from Atlanta Penitentiary. On his way to finish out that sentence he was taken first to the Federal Detention House in New York City. There he made friends with another convict, who had been sent up for filching The Reader's Digest mail from a truck rented by the Pleasantville Post Office. Such is life in jail today that Cooper and his acquaintance played chess and hand-ball together while Cooper slyly asked questions about the handling of the magazine's mail and bank deposits. By the time Cooper was sent to the Lewisburg, Pennsylvania, prison—where once more his sentence was benevolently shortened—there was already glowing in his brain a plan for one grand haul to make him rich. For Cooper was bespelled with the false impression that The Reader's Digest received fortunes in cash from subscribers every day. "I'll work with Harry on this as soon as I get out," he promised himself. "Harry will plan a perfect job."

Harry Stein—beetle-browed, angry-faced son of a Russian peddler, never naturalized—was a Clinton crony. Another habitual lawbreaker, he knew more about legal loopholes than many an attorney. In the prison yard Cooper had heard Stein advise convicts so shrewdly that long-termers were "sprung" on technicalities that their own lawyers had overlooked. Years before, Stein had seemed on his way to the electric chair for choking to death Vivian Gordon, a blonde playgirl who had threatened to denounce him. Because an eyewitness changed his story Stein could not be convicted of murder. But soon afterward he was convicted of robbery and sentenced to a term of twenty-five years. Now Stein, too, was out on parole.

On a wintry dusk in January 1950, Calman Cooper and Harry Stein held a reunion in the lower slums of Manhattan. With a salesman's ardor, Cooper depicted to his pal a robber's fantasy of imaginary fortunes in cash, transported along lonely country roads, ready to be grabbed.

"It's a juicy pitch," agreed the dazzled Stein. "But we must have another man. How about Nattie?"

Nathan Wissner, another Clinton buddy, and also released on parole, was a bald, squat, bullnecked thief whose record was splotched with assaults, robberies, four homicide charges and other strong-arm jobs. Now he was running a downtown auto-rental agency. Within the hour the ex-convicts were huddled in Wissner's office. Later the unholy three called in moon-faced, bespectacled Benny Dorfman, partner of Wissner and small-time chiseler. That night the four of them conspired to rob a truck of The Reader's Digest carrying mail and the daily bank deposit.

From an agency where he was unknown Calman Cooper rented an old rattletrap truck. Why select such a piece of junk for a holdup? That incongruity was part of the plan; an old truck looked innocent. On three successive Mondays—because weekend receipts would be larger—the bandits prowled around the Digest grounds and nearby roads, but not until the fourth visit, on the squally, showering afternoon of April 3, did they decide to strike.

They came that day riding in two cars. In front, the hired truck was driven by Cooper, bringing with him lengths of cord, rolls of adhesive tape, three revolvers and an automatic, all wrapped in a towel. The second car, from Wissner's own agency, was a dark-gray, four-door sedan. In this new model they meant to flee the scene; the split-second timetable was scheduled to be completed in five minutes.

On Route 117, half a mile south of the entrance into The Reader's Digest grounds, the two cars halted. The sedan was parked by the side of the road, not far from a dirt lane, Old Farm Road, scouted in advance as the rendezvous for the climax of the crime. Meanwhile Stein distributed weapons from the truck; a gun for every man. Leaving Wissner walking on the open road, Cooper, Stein and Dorfman rode the truck to the Digest's private road and into the parking circle in front of the building, a place of green lawn, shade trees and peace. There the rented rattletrap was halted, and there, through misty showers, the criminals kept watch on the front door where a Digest truck was being loaded. Two men were riding in the Digest truck when it started for the bank and post office. At the wheel was William Waterbury, who was to live, and beside him was Andrew Petrini, very soon to die.

According to plan, the robbers' truck darted forward. First to reach the long private driveway, it began to weave and zigzag back and forth as if a drunkard turned the wheel. Baffled, Waterbury had to slow down until, not far from the exit on Route 117, he was forced to stop altogether, blocked by the battered carry-all halted diagonally in front of him. At that moment Petrini cried: "Look out, Bill!"

Turning his head, Waterbury beheld an extraordinary figure springing from the right side of the road; a red-faced, bullnecked man wearing large spectacle rims without lenses and a grotesque rubber nose. The masquerader was Wissner and in his right hand gleamed a leveled revolver. The intruder rattled the right-hand door, but he couldn't open it. There was only one second's delay—then the brief roar of a shot and Andrew Petrini, with one anguished gasp, crumpled in a forlorn heap, blood staining eyelids and cheek.

Instantaneously with the shot, Stein and Dorfman, brandishing revolvers, appeared at the left window. Waterbury held up his hands.

"Get in the back of the car if you don't want the same treatment as your pal," Waterbury was told, and he obeyed. Stein and Wissner clambered after him into the rear of the truck, tying him up and taping his eyes and mouth, while Benny Dorfman took the wheel. Slowly the Digest truck moved toward the highway, following the rattletrap driven by Calman Cooper. Up the Old Farm Road the three criminals halted behind a screen of trees and bushes. Then, carrying the bank deposit, they ran toward their parked sedan, joined by Cooper, who had been waiting near his hired truck on the edge of the highway. Behind them they left William Waterbury, tightly bound, face down on the floor of the Digest truck, and the dying Petrini.

In less time than all this takes to tell, the gray sedan was speeding away—Wissner driving and his confederates crouched on the floor. Soon, they knew, the police would be looking for a fleeing quartet, but all that was visible in the gray sedan was one man at the wheel. Along deserted side roads the robbers began, piece by piece, to toss away incriminating evidence. One by one they cast out their bullets—"pills," they called them. Guns, too, were chucked through the window; they even changed jackets before they reached the Bronx River Parkway. And also through the window went Benny Dorfman's expensive green fedora. Wriggling around on the jouncing floor, they stowed the bank deposit in a brown zipper bag. When all was done, they began to boast of the precision with which they had followed their plan. No one expressed regret for the murder. "For my sister-in-law Essie and her kids," Calman Cooper told the others virtuously, "I'd kill fifteen people."

By 4:30 p.m. the gang was in New York. Leaving the sedan by the road to be picked up later, they carried their bag to an elevated railroad station. They soon lost themselves—as they believed, permanently—among the 12,000,000 people of the metropolitan area. Before dark they were in the bedroom of Dorfman's flat, splitting the swag. And then came the great surprise. They had dreamed of fortunes. What did they find? While the bank deposit was more than $40,000 that afternoon, $35,143.26 was in checks—so far as the thieves were concerned, fit only for burning. The cash they split amounted to $4960.91—less than $1250 each. And for less than $1250 each of the four was legally guilty of the murder of Andrew Petrini.

In command of the manhunt was Captain Daniel F. Glasheen of the New York State Bureau of Criminal Investigation. With Inspector John J. Quinn as his field marshal, Captain Glasheen threw thirty trained men into the quest, all operating out of the ivy-covered barracks of Troop K at Hawthorne, New York, a few miles from the scene of the crime. For the next two months these men were working on the case night and day.

Without regaining consciousness, Andrew Petrini died that first night. His partner William Waterbury was removed with his wife from their home to a safe hiding place. As he was the only eyewitness, Waterbury's life was in danger. The rattletrap truck was soon found. But so many immediate details were clamoring for action that it was 11 p.m. before Joseph Sayers, John Manopoli and David H. Hardy, plainclothes sergeants from Hawthorne Barracks, appeared at the all-night offices of the Bureau of Motor Vehicles in Manhattan.

The owner of the rental agency was located by the license number and roused from bed in Staten Island. He referred the telephoning sergeants to his manager, Arthur Jeppesen, a chunky Virgin Islander, who a little

after midnight opened up the offices. There he produced
the rental slip on which the investigators were pinning
their highest hopes. The process of renting any vehicle
in New York is surrounded with police precautions. No
one can simply hire a car and ride off in it; the law
requires that the hirer must first produce a driver's
license, and that the renting agent must make a careful
transcript of the data from the license onto what is called
a "rental slip"; and that the hirer must also sign his name
to the slip. So it was with fervid interest that Sergeant
Sayers and his companions examined the rental slip, on
which they read: "Walter William Comins—gray-eyed,
brown-haired, 5 feet 10 inches tall, 39 years old, weighing 200 pounds."

The sergeants could not know that the very man they
were looking for was, at that moment, within pistol
range. Much later they would learn that two of the
bandits, Cooper and Stein, were hiding less than a block
away. As an afterflourish of perfection, they had come
back to break into the office and destroy the rental slip.

But they were too late.

The detectives carried away with them a specimen signature of "Walter William Comins." Their next goal was
the address he had given as his home on West 47th
Street. On the way, as a part of police protocol, they reported in to New York police authorities, and from then
on City Detective William Mulligan, one of the ablest,
worked with the state police until the finish of the case.
With Mulligan they drove to West 47th Street, only to
find that the address given by Comins was the Hotel
Edison. No "Walter William Comins" was living there.
However, a search of the hotel files showed that on
November 1, 1949, he had been registered. On that day
he had mailed in his application for a permit for a

driver's license, giving the hotel as his address. On November 3—five months before the crime, to the day—the permit had been delivered to him by mail. "Comins" had then departed, never to return; and no such person had ever been heard of in the Pennsylvania town that he wrote in the hotel register as his home.

At 2 a.m. the detectives were back at the Motor Vehicle Bureau. Was there any record of where and when "Comins" had taken his driving examination? There was, plus the license number of the car he had driven for the test. The address of the owner of that car was in Ossining, New York. The detectives drove to the Ossining house and waited until morning. But when the owner appeared to take in his milk bottle the lead collapsed. The man did run a driving school, but he kept no useful records. A blank wall—and it was not to be the last of many encountered in the weary months that lay ahead.

On the dirt road in Chappaqua other detectives had found the spectacles, rims broken, and the rubber nose, split as if crushed under heel. On another road they picked up a greenish-gray hat, with the dealer's name razored off the sweatband. When the hat was taken by Detectives Sweeney and Zimmer to Danbury, Connecticut, famous for its hats, one manufacturer identified the felt, another the leather band, and before long the investigators stood in a shop on New York's Lower East Side, talking to the clerk who had actually sold the hat. To whom? How could he remember? A laborious search of auto-sale files showed "Comins" had also bought a secondhand car. A Long Island dealer produced the bill of sale, according to which "Comins" lived at an address on Manhattan's Lower East Side. Odd as it seems, there lived in that tenement street several families with the unusual name of Comins—but every one of them was innocent and could prove it. Not one had ever heard of a "Walter William Comins."

Wherever the investigators turned, a dead-end street! It was clear that the crime had been the work of painstaking professionals. Out at Hawthorne Barracks, Captain Glasheen and Inspector Quinn faced the fact that every tangible clue had come to nothing. In their next move they would have to break new ground. And they did. That same day Sergeant Joseph Sayers entered the New York Post Office and put a question to Assistant Postal Inspector James Graham. Were there not possibly files of postal investigations in which the name of Comins might crop up? Inspector Graham was helpful. The records of tracing of lost addresses might prove useful, he suggested. It was possible that other persons had tried to find "Comins" on West 47th Street. The Post Office had always taken pride in getting mail to addressees even under great difficulties; every effort was made to trace persons who had moved. Records of such searches were kept for some years; perhaps they might show that "Comins" had already been located through persistent postal search.

Also, Graham suggested, it might be worthwhile looking through records of investigations of mail frauds. Of these, there was a wide variety—from filching government checks out of tenement-house mailboxes to swindling investors by selling fake gold-mine stocks. Moreover, Mr. Graham added, it might be wise to check over the "mail-drop" inquiries. What is a mail drop? It is an office where, by paying a small monthly fee, you can arrange to have your mail accepted and your telephone calls received and noted. The cost was then around $10 a month; for $20 a man could print letterheads, giving a mail-drop address, and appear to be in business at a good

Manhattan address. Because of fly-by-night swindling and general skulduggery, such places are rigidly supervised by postal inspectors. It was, finally, in the mail-drop records that Sergeant Sayers struck gold.

There were goose pimples on the sergeant's broad back when he discovered that on November 2—while still registered at the Hotel Edison—"Walter William Comins" had also applied to a mail drop known as the Reliance Business Service, in downtown New York. Right at this point fate seemed to have taken a hand in this will-o'-the-wisp game that "Comins" had been playing. All that "Comins" had wanted from the mail drop was telephone service; and for servicing such calls no signed documents are required, because the Post Office has no jurisdiction over telephones. All "Comins" had to do was pay his fee and leave his name. But, as luck would have it, the girl who regularly handled such matters was home sick that day, and a substitute dealt with "Comins." She insisted that he fill out the blank, including references required by the Post Office for mail clients of the place. "Comins" could have refused—but the girl did not know that and neither did he. Now Sergeant Sayers held in his hand two "Comins" signatures—one from the rental slip, another from the mail drop.

"Then we knew," says Inspector Quinn, "that there really was a man wandering around somewhere, signing the name Comins. That's where he had stumbled. I felt certain that if we kept right on doggedly working we'd land our man sooner or later. Because he was pretty sure to stumble again."

No one at the Reliance office remembered "Comins." But they had kept the list of references he gave them, all of which proved to be mere letterhead phantasms from other mail drops. This lead, too, might have seemed no more than just another will-o'-the-wisp, except for one potent fact. One of the men named as reference by "Comins" was being investigated on the charge of selling forged auto parts and accessories. Sergeant R. T. Barber and Corporal J. N. Dershimer set out on that trail. From the Federal Trade Commission the inquiry led to the office of the New York District Attorney. An investigation had been made into the forged-parts case but the mail-drop dealer's defense had been that he bought the forged stuff in good faith. From whom? From a man named Cooper—William Cooper. But William Cooper had not been found.

Hearing this report in the DA's office, Sergeant Barber became very thoughtful. Somewhere, once before in this investigation, he was certain he had heard the name of Cooper. But where? The detectives were on their way back to the Post Office before Barber remembered. Sergeant Barber had seen the name listed on the bulletins maintained at Troop K Barracks—a list of every name that was mentioned by anyone in connection with the case. On the night that Andrew Petrini died Inspector Quinn had visited The Reader's Digest building. There he had learned of a previous robbery of Digest mail. A thieving driver, employed by a contractor trucking mail for the Pleasantville Post Office, had been sentenced to two years but was now out on parole. Coöperating with the police, this man's parole supervisor carefully questioned him. Had he made any close friends while in jail? Had he talked to anyone about The Reader's Digest? Yes, to both the questions—and one of the names he mentioned was Cooper.

A search of the federal files produced a full dossier about Cooper, recently sentenced on an income-tax charge. He had gray eyes, brown hair, was of the same age and—although the name was different—the script of his signature was identical and unmistakable. Willie Cooper and "Walter William Comins" were one, the same man.

But in that moment of triumph Sergeant Barber's jaw dropped. There in the court papers before him he beheld an unthinkable, incredible contradiction. Cooper was innocent of The Reader's Digest murder. He had to be. He had an unshakable alibi. For soon after he had checked out of the Hotel Edison in November 1949 he had been arrested, and now he was serving a two-year sentence. On April 3, when Andrew Petrini was shot, William Cooper was behind the bars of a federal prison.

For a while this contradiction looked to be the blindest of all blind alleys. But with a study of Cooper's family history, the mystification began to fade. William Cooper had brothers who were also convicts. One of them, Calman Cooper, had been in the Federal Detention House when the Digest mail thief was also there—and Calman Cooper had been released from prison only a few months before the crime. As one brother went into prison, another came out. So the sequence of events was that William Cooper got a driver's license in November 1949. He went to prison in December, and his brother Calman came out of prison in January. Could Calman Cooper have used his brother's license to hire the robbery truck? Where was Calman Cooper now?

While prison and parole records were being consulted, the detectives carried Calman Cooper's "going-out" picture, taken the day he left Clinton, and showed it to the agency manager who had rented the truck. Arthur Jeppesen studied it dubiously; he could not be sure. Before long the detectives promised to bring him face to face with the suspect. Already through the parole-board records they had located him, and sentinels were watching, day and night, the front door of the man who once had escaped from Atlanta Penitentiary.

Cooper was living with his mother in a flat on West 120th Street. There were court-approved wiretaps on his telephone. Early and late, those warm June days and nights, listeners-in recorded every conversation, hopeful that by some unguarded word Cooper would give a clue to the whereabouts of his confederates. But Calman Cooper talked in cryptic monosyllables, and so did his friends. His most frequent caller was a man addressed only as "Harry," and one night Harry blurted out an invaluable clue: he was on his way to see his mother, who was in Roosevelt Hospital suffering from gangrene. Before he got there, the detectives were in hiding in the ward; before he left, they knew that he was Harry Stein, of the Vivian Gordon case, chronic evildoer, also recently out on parole. From then on there was a shadow at Stein's heels.

Two more bandits remained to be found, but the police sentries had to abandon their waiting game when they learned, by wiretap, that their birds were preparing to leave town. As it happened, a third brother, Morris Cooper, had just arrived in New York from Florida. He, too, had been paroled, although guilty of murder. But his presence in New York now was a violation of his parole; he was supposed to stay in Florida. The old father of the brood was with Morris, and it was his idea for the whole family to return together to Florida before Moe's parole violation became known. Hearing their talk, one got the impression that the patriarch of the Coopers doted on his boys. Plainly the time had come to act, and yet the troopers still needed identification. That night they took a new collection of police pictures of Cooper to Jeppesen, and

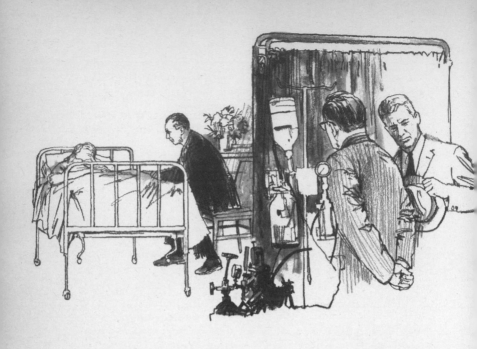

for a long time the rental manager pored over them. But the best he would say was: "I'm not sure! Maybe!"

So a trap had to be laid. Next morning Jeppesen was taken to 120th Street in a car. By now the watchers were well aware of Calman Cooper's habits. Around the same time every morning he emerged to go to a corner grocery. Later he would leave the house to go downtown, where he posed as a carpenter looking for work. Now the watchers were warned of his approach by signals from sentries along the way—one man took off his hat, and another used his handkerchief—and presently Cooper appeared, stalking toward them. The waiting car moved slowly forward, Jeppesen's face close to the window. As the car passed Cooper, the detectives turned to Jeppesen. Was that man his customer? Still the rental manager could not say; the car had passed too quickly.

Once out of sight behind a corner, the car raced around two blocks, once more to face the oncoming Calman Cooper, now walking south on Amsterdam Avenue. This time Jeppesen left the car and walked toward the suspect. If he could identify him, he was to greet him and shake hands. At any moment there might be gunplay; it was a hot spot for Mr. Jeppesen, but he started courageously up the street. Jeppesen never had to decide—because Calman Cooper saw him first.

The criminal's startled face betrayed his astonishment. One hand in his coat pocket, he rushed up to Jeppesen, grabbing his arm and demanding to know what he was doing in the neighborhood. Had the police been talking to him? Several detectives heard this; Calman Cooper had identified himself!

The heartbreaking search was over. Sergeant Sayers grabbed Cooper and held him against the wall of a house. He was taking no chances, for he knew Cooper's ferocity and the convict's hand was in his pocket. Actually, however, Cooper was unarmed. Taken utterly by surprise—he had believed his trail so completely covered that he could never be found—the astonished prisoner looked wildly around him, beholding more plainclothesmen approaching from every direction. In another moment handcuffs were on his wrists. At two o'clock the next morning other detectives surrounded a house on East Third Street— they knew that their quarry was also dangerous—and knocked on the door. Presently Harry Stein sat handcuffed between detectives as he too was driven back to Hawthorne.

For long hours the prisoners were questioned in the Hawthorne Barracks of Troop K by Captain Glasheen, Inspector Quinn and others. It was Cooper who broke

first. Eleven typewritten pages were filled with his confession, and at the bottom appeared these words:

> Q. This statement was made of your own free will, voluntarily,
> without force or threat being used against you?
> A. Yes.

Yet at the trial the lawyers of Cooper and Stein were to
assert that the confessions were extorted by police brutality; Cooper's attorney declared his client was "beaten by
twenty state troopers, working in relays over more than
two days; refused food and water and deprived of sleep."
Shopworn and mendacious, these stock-in-trade plaints
of professional criminals did not excite Presiding Judge
Elbert T. Gallagher, who pointed out that Cooper had
been examined in the county jail by Dr. Robert Vosburg
of Grasslands Hospital and found to be in excellent physical condition, except for a few superficial marks which
could have been self-inflicted.

Police have long been familiar with the practice of
criminals who beat themselves up, pounding stomach and
thighs, face and buttocks, with their own fists, in order to
simulate evidence of beatings that never took place. As a
matter of fact, Cooper confessed after exacting a promise
that his brother could go back to Florida and not be
returned to prison for four years. His brother had once
protected Calman from being implicated in a crime; this
was Calman's chance to return the favor. Stein flew into a
rage when he heard of Cooper's confession and promptly
told his own story, with full details. No brutality was
necessary; the only brutality in the case was the murder
of Andrew Petrini.

In their confessions both Cooper and Stein had named

Nathan Wissner as the triggerman. By 9:30 the following morning the gunman had been yanked away from breakfast in a hashhouse and brought to Hawthorne Barracks. On June 8 District Attorney George M. Fanelli confronted Stein with William Waterbury.

"Do you know this man?" Fanelli asked, and Stein blurted out: "He looks like the man who was the driver of the Digest truck."

This identification of Waterbury by Stein was of vital importance, because it supplemented Stein's confession. His identification of Waterbury was independent, indisputable evidence that he knew just what he was talking about. Waterbury just as promptly identified Stein as the man who tied him up. From a line-up of eight men, Waterbury unhesitatingly picked Wissner as the man who fired the shot. Rubber nose and vacant spectacle rims made no difference; the murderer's eyes had made an impression nothing could erase. While Wissner denied everything, the confessions of his confederates reeked with details which could be confirmed—as, for example, the role played by Benny Dorfman, fourth partner, still missing.

When Sergeants Barber and Manopoli knocked at the Dorfman apartment in Brooklyn, they were met by the runaway's wife, a sad little blonde with three small children. Late in the afternoon of April 3, she testified, her husband had come home with three other men. One she knew as his partner, "Nattie" Wissner; Stein and Cooper she later identified.

"Keep the kids in the kitchen," Benny ordered, and led the others into an inner bedroom of the flat. Presently Cooper and Stein departed, while Dorfman and Wissner carried a brown zipper bag down to the furnace basement. There, as the confessions made clear, the checks

were burned. When Wissner too had left, Dorfman could
not hold out against the questioning of his suspicious wife.
He admitted they had just robbed a Reader's Digest
truck. Later he left town for Florida.

Seeking for confirming evidence, Barber and Manopoli
squatted on the floor with the brown zipper bag opened
between them. At first it seemed empty—not even a fleck
of dust—but presently, there in one corner, they spied a
bright fragment of salmon-pink cardboard, a tiny sliver
torn off from some piece of printing. One under another,
these letters were visible:

"... now
"... ceive
"... sues"

Here was a tiny clue in the best tradition of detective
stories. "Ceive" might be part of the word "receive." And
might not "sues" refer to "issues" of magazines? In The
Reader's Digest offices there were found just such sub-
scription order forms, of which there had been many in
the stolen mail. It was explained to the sergeants that
currency was sometimes affixed to the order form with

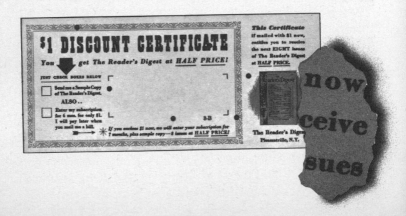

adhesive. Obviously, in this case, when the currency was removed, a fragment of the form had adhered to it. Later, it had fallen off into the bag. That salmon-pink fragment of cardboard linked the Dorfman flat with the scene of the crime, thirty-five miles away.

The pieces of the case were beginning to fall into place when suddenly, on June 19, a lawyer appeared in District Attorney Fanelli's office in White Plains to surrender his client, Benny Dorfman, who a few days later declared: "I want to tell the truth and get it off my chest."

A disillusioned and miserable man was Dorfman. The loot had been far less than he expected. He had been given less than the others. The money went to pay off debts. He'd had to pawn his only extra suit to run away. Dorfman was granted a separate trial from his partners, and both he and his wife testified against them. On November 1, when the trial began, the aisles and doorways of the courtroom were guarded by New York state troopers, visibly armed.

Throughout the seven weeks before the verdict, there were rumors about threatened delivery of the prisoners. Warnings came to the police from stool pigeons in the underworld that gangsters for whom Wissner had done many an unsavory job were plotting to kidnap him so as to kill him themselves later on. The reason for such a desperate scheme was the fear of the gangsters that Wissner, when all his legal appeals were exhausted, might offer to tell what he knew about various unsolved crimes in exchange for commutation of his sentence to life imprisonment. Whether these sensational rumors were true or not, it is certain that the three prisoners themselves were considering escape. The discovery of their plotting was a garish episode in this process of justice.

From the day of their arrest the holdup men were kept separated. Not until they were brought to court and sat together at the trial table did they have a chance to confer. One day it was noticed that even during the testimony of witnesses they were talking back and forth in Yiddish— a dialect no court attendants understood. That same day a Yiddish-speaking detective was called in. During the night, when the courtroom was empty, the trial table was moved to bring it nearer to where the new detective would sit among the reporters. Experiments were made to be sure that he could hear conversation at the table. From that time on the detective was listening to everything the defendants said to each other. In the midst of the droning testimony from the witness chair, Stein was heard roundly denouncing Wissner for not having seized the revolver of a state trooper at one careless moment and shooting a way out for all three. Thanks to the new listening post, the order was given to keep the felons handcuffed to their guards until they were seated at the table and surrounded. They must have guessed they had been overheard, for all talk of staging a break came to an end—and they engaged in no more talk in a foreign tongue.

The proceedings were prolonged by endless wrangles over technicalities, but the facts were so indisputable a jury found Cooper, Stein and Wissner guilty of first-degree murder as charged. On the first ballot the jury voted unanimously for a verdict of first-degree murder, but one woman wanted to recommend clemency (life imprisonment). Finally, after eight hours, she yielded.

As I watched the sentencing of these three men to death in the electric chair I still wondered skeptically if they would ever have to pay the penalty. Appeals and other legal devices still stood between them and punishment. All three had squirmed off the hook so many times before: would they do it again? Their records reeked with incorrigibility—Wissner's history alone would horrify any honest man:

Five years for attempted robbery in 1928 *but*—pardoned in 1930.

Charged with homicide in 1930 *but*—discharged.

Charged with homicide in 1932 *but*—discharged again.

Charged with assault and robbery in 1933 *but*—discharged again.

Charged with homicide in 1934 *but*—discharged again.

Charged with robbery in 1935 and convicted, sentenced to fifteen years, *but*—paroled in 1944.

How many undetected crimes he committed in the intervening years no one knew but himself. He admitted to Captain Glasheen that he had committed more than a hundred stickups.

Cooper, Stein and Wissner certainly tried their best to have their sentences commuted or reversed—appealing in vain for five long years. But on July 9, 1955, they paid their final penalty at Sing Sing. Benny Dorfman was allowed to plead guilty to manslaughter after he turned state's evidence. He was sentenced to ten to twenty years at Green Haven Prison, Stormville, New York—from which he was paroled on December 24, 1957.

J. Edgar Hoover has said: "Abuses of parole, probation and pardon contribute to the fact that a serious crime occurs in this nation every eighteen seconds, day and night, and explains, in part, why the cost of crime exceeds by many millions what we spend for our educational and religious institutions."

This also explains how, because of such abuses, good men often lose their lives. Like Andrew Petrini.

"A Mistake Doesn't Have to Be Final"

By Joseph Phillips

IT ALL began on March 15, 1955, when seventeen-year-old Truls Halvorsen's ship, the Norwegian freighter *Fernhill*, was anchored at Hong Kong. Early that morning several Chinese tailors boarded the ship to sell suits to the seamen. Halvorsen needed a suit, but on his pay of $50 a month he didn't have enough money. He asked a tailor to mend a pair of torn trousers.

On the way to Halvorsen's quarters the tailor eyed the lad appraisingly. He saw a handsome, well-built six-footer, blond, blue-eyed, with pink cheeks not yet shaved. He also saw a boy who needed money. Picking up the trousers, the Chinese said, "You want to make $1200?"

"Sure," Halvorsen replied. "How?"

"Smuggling. Opium. Many seamen do it. Easy." Taken aback, the young sailor said he'd think it over. The tailor promised to return in three hours

To Halvorsen, $1200 was a lot of money—two years' pay. If other seamen got away with smuggling, why couldn't he? "Opium" conjured up nothing more for him than some dimly lit den where Orientals lay around

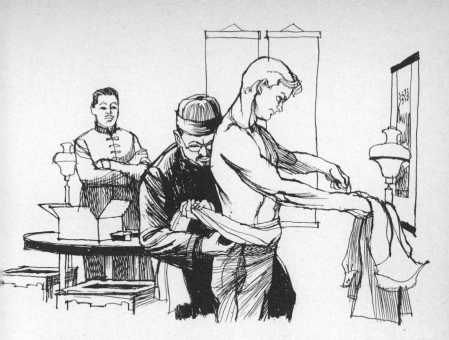

puffing pipes. When the tailor returned, Halvorsen said
yes. The tailor wrote out a Hong Kong address and told
him to be there at 6 p.m.

That evening, in a clean, sparsely furnished room,
Halvorsen was greeted by the tailor and his boss, a
stout, businesslike Chinese. Halvorsen's job, the boss
specified, was to hide the opium on ship, smuggle it past
Customs and deliver it in San Francisco, where he would
be paid his fee. The boss opened a cardboard box. It held
ten bags of opium, each weighing about half a pound.
The shipment was larger than customary, the boss said;
payment would be $1350 instead of $1200. After having
Halvorsen photographed so that the San Francisco receiver would recognize him, the boss showed him how to
smuggle the narcotics off the ship. He had Halvorsen
take off his shirt, folded a white silk sash lengthwise, tied
it around his waist, then concealed the bags in the fold.

He wrote down the San Francisco address for delivery— Lew Gar Kung Saw, 854 Clay Street—then gave Halvorsen half of a carefully torn Chinese coupon. The receiver would have the other half. "Nobody gets caught," he said. "We've done it many times."

Halvorsen knew that smuggling was a crime. But, as he slipped the opium into his locker aboard ship, "being the key man in a real-life mystery story seemed like a big adventure." The thrill vanished, however, when the *Fernhill* weighed anchor. Halvorsen's conscience nagged him. This was the first time he had touched trouble. Until the age of fourteen, when he went to sea, he had been an excellent student. On ship he had worked hard and learned fast. With his intelligence, he could look forward to steady progress in the Norwegian merchant marine.

During the long voyage to Suez, Halvorsen began thinking about other people—his parents, who ran a small hotel near Oslo; his girl friend; his pastor, John Henriksen. Halvorsen had met the pastor in Brooklyn on his first voyage, and a close friendship had developed. He began asking shipmates about narcotics—and soon realized that he was deep in a crime far greater than smuggling. If he made delivery, he would be helping to destroy the lives of hundreds of men and women, boys and girls. The enormity of the crime he had agreed to commit overwhelmed him. "For many days I kept thinking of Pastor Henriksen," he said later, "and finally I could not stand it any longer."

At Suez, Halvorsen sent an air-mail letter to Henriksen. Would the pastor present the entire opium matter to the authorities? Could Halvorsen help, perhaps, in getting the people in San Francisco jailed? In New York, Halvorsen's pastor rushed to the FBI with the letter, then to the Bureau of Customs. On May 7 the clergyman sent Halvorsen a cable: "All in order here."

The *Fernhill* was scheduled to stop at Boston and New York before going on to San Francisco. At Boston, Customs agents boarded her, picked up the narcotics and questioned Halvorsen. "We found him truthful and straightforward," the agents reported. "He took full blame for what he had done, and made no excuses. He kept worrying about the effect of the news on his father."

The heroin (an opium derivative) in Halvorsen's locker proved to be one of the most valuable illicit shipments known to have entered this country in the previous ten years. Government chemists determined that it was 97 percent pure. Cut and recut, it would provide hundreds of thousands of "shots." It would retail on street corners for about $3,000,000. Agents emptied the bags, refilled them with a milk-and-sugar powder, meticulously resewed them along the original thread-holes. Then Halvorsen and a Customs agent flew to San Francisco to make delivery. Halvorsen was intensively rehearsed for his role. He would be accompanied by an agent posing as a shipmate. The agent would do no talking, but if any problems arose in the meeting with the criminals, Halvorsen would pick up his cues from the eyes of the agent.

"The kid showed fear," said the agent who worked most closely with Halvorsen, "but he never hesitated. He felt he had to make amends for what he had done."

At 10 a.m. on May 27 Halvorsen and the agent walked into 854 Clay Street, in the heart of San Francisco's Chinatown. They climbed three dark flights of stairs without encountering anyone. In the fourth-floor hall they met a Chinese to whom Halvorsen showed the paper bearing the words "Lew Gar Kung Saw." The Chinese pointed to a kitchen at the end of the hall. There they were silently greeted by an elderly Chinese who glanced at the paper and made three telephone calls. "Come back twelve o'clock," he told them.

When Halvorsen and the agent returned, the same Chinese arose from a chair. "Five minutes he come," he announced, and left.

Halvorsen was tense. "The boy was on a spot," the agent said later. "If he blew his lines or made a mistake, anything could happen. The room had a big closet that could have concealed a member of the gang. We might have been under scrutiny through a peephole. The setup was dangerous."

After fifteen long minutes a thin, well-dressed, middle-aged Chinese, wearing thick-lens glasses and a hearing aid, entered the room. He was later identified as Lew Doo. Halvorsen extended the paper with the address and asked, "Are you this man?"

"Yes, yes," Lew answered.

"Show me the coupon and my picture." Lew took from his pocket the boy's photograph and a torn piece of coupon. The coupon fitted the piece in Halvorsen's hand.

Nodding toward the agent, Halvorsen explained, "This is the bosun from the *Fernhill*. He helped me. We got our ship's pay in New York and came here by bus." Halvorsen spoke in an unnaturally loud voice. The agent saw his jaw muscles pulsate. But Lew apparently accepted his nervousness as a sign of inexperience.

"You got the opium with you?"

"No, it's in a locker at the bus station. Have you got the money?" Lew pulled out a roll of bills.

"You come to my hotel room," Halvorsen said. "We'll pick up the opium and do business there."

Lew got excited. "No, no, no. This place very safe. Do

business here all the time. Hotel room no good." From the government's point of view, the ideal plan was to persuade the receiver to come to the hotel room where a tape recorder could record the negotiation. But a glance at the agent told Halvorsen to string along with Lew.

When Halvorsen and the agent returned with the "opium," Lew took out three bags, examined them without cutting them open and counted the remainder. Seeing only eight bags, he exclaimed, "But I pay in Hong Kong for ten."

Halvorsen explained that two bags had gotten wet in the hiding place in the hold of the ship and had to be thrown over the side. Lew nodded, stuffed the heroin into a brown-paper shopping bag. He refused to pay $1350 for only eight bags, however. Halvorsen haggled, then said he'd take $1200 plus his bus fare from New York. When Lew counted out the money, the agent casually picked it up, then quickly drew his gun, whirled Lew around and handcuffed his hands behind his back.

Lew Doo, alias Frank Lew, alias Lew Wah, arrested seven times since 1933 but never convicted, was turned over to Customs agents who had deployed around the building. Papers found in Lew's room revealed the names of the Hong Kong leaders and showed that Lew was the direct United States contact for one of the biggest narcotics rings in the world. On August 2 Lew was sentenced to four years in prison. In gratitude to Halvorsen for his coöperation, Customs awarded him $1000.

Shortly before he sailed for Norway in mid-July, the boy and his pastor had a last talk. "You've learned something we all need to know," the pastor said. "A mistake doesn't have to be final. When we have determination, we can change a mistake. It's worth the effort."

Britain's Most Baffling Crime

By Anthony Abbot

MR. JUSTICE WRIGHT lifted the black cap and fitted it on his head. "The murder of this woman," he declared, "is unexampled in all the annals of crime! William Herbert Wallace, for having killed your wife, Julia, I condemn you to be hanged by the neck until you are dead." On that rainy morning the judge of the Liverpool Assizes believed that the death sentence ended the case. But no jurist was ever more mistaken.

The monstrous killing of Julia, one winter's night in 1931, was unique because every circumstance that pointed to the prisoner's guilt could also be argued to prove his innocence. Famous authors have written about this crime. But in none of the writings can you find one mention of the secret hearing at which the prisoner's fate was really decided by what was truly a jury of his peers. Not even Mr. Justice Wright knew anything about that unprecedented process, which I tell here for the first time in print.

In appearance the soft-voiced insurance agent whom Mr. Justice Wright consigned to the gallows resembled that timid soul of caricature, Caspar Milquetoast. A lanky, bloodless fellow, William Herbert Wallace was taller than six feet; his hair was silvery. In neatly pressed suit and stand-up collar he peered at life quietly through gold-rimmed spectacles. Artistic and methodical, after eighteen years of married life he had remained patient with Julia's untidiness, rigid ideas and old-fashioned clothes. Whenever she got too much for him he fled to a chess club, where the dire history begins on the freezing evening of January 19, 1931.

There was to be a championship match in the warm, smoke-laden clubroom beyond the bar of the North John Street pub. But at 7 p.m., when the games began, the insurance agent had not arrived. A telephone call came for him and a barmaid answered. The caller said his name was "Mr. R. M. Qualtrough." Though his voice seemed far away, he was in a happy mood. It was his daughter's birthday and he intended taking out insurance in her favor. Would the agent call upon him next evening? Address: 25 Menlove Gardens, East. Fifteen minutes later, Wallace came in and was given the message. He then battled for two hours against a stubborn chess opponent, finishing as winner.

The next evening at 6:45 he set forth to find his unknown prospect. After a long ride on a tramcar he was seen by many persons wandering through the dimmish lanes of Menlove Gardens, North, South and West. Policemen, shopkeepers and others told him repeatedly that there was no such district as Menlove Gardens, East. Nor had they ever heard of any Mr. Qualtrough. Plainly he had been hoaxed. But why?

On the witness stand Wallace testified that alarm now entered his soul. Hurrying home, he arrived at 8:45, to find his front and back doors bolted. This is what he told

some neighbors who came out to watch him. Try the
back door again, they advised; and when he did, it
yielded. A low light was burning in the kitchen, but no
Julia was there. Upstairs he climbed. His wife was in
neither bedroom; there was no answer to his gentle calls.
Where else to look except in the front parlor, which they
almost never used? On its threshold the husband struck a
match and by its flicker saw his wife stretched on the
floor.

With some heavy implement, never found, Julia had
been pounded to death. More than a score of lethal blows
had been rained on her head. She was lying neatly with
her feet near a fireplace gas burner. A rolled-up mackintosh was tucked under her shoulders. The tail of the raincoat was partly burned; so was Julia's skirt, although the
burner was not lit. But there was blood on it. Indeed,
what object in the parlor had escaped the scarlet shower?
Sofa cushions and hearthrug were darkened with damp
stains; blood was on the walls, on the ceiling, on the
chandelier.

Not even in such a shambles did the self-controlled
insurance agent quail. Soft-voiced, he called in the neighbors, led them into the parlor. Then he led them out.
They lit a fire in the kitchen range and sat and talked.
When the police came the bereaved husband was in a
rocking chair, stroking a pet black cat and looking them
straight in the eye. Not all the questioning—days and
nights of it—could break his calm; not even when they
charged him with bludgeoning Julia to death.

In the view of most judges, circumstantial evidence is
far better than fallible human memory, but only if the
linked-up facts are overwhelming and complete. Were
they so in this case? The public was convinced of it and

already abhorred William Wallace as a monster. In theory it was Wallace who had made that telephone call, disguising his voice and leaving a bogus message for himself as an alibi. Quite by accident, telephone engineers were able to trace the call to a street-corner kiosk only four hundred yards from the prisoner's house, just at the time Wallace would have passed it when walking to the club. There had been trouble getting coin returns from that booth, and all calls were carefully recorded.

The rest of the crime, in the prosecutor's view, had been planned with the cunning of an expert chess player. Wallace was to be pictured by the jury as arriving home the next evening, going upstairs ostensibly to change but really to strip naked. Then he dons a mackintosh. He descends, enters the parlor and calls to his wife from the dark. He beats her to death, then carefully lays her out. Cold, he lights the gas burner, and Julia's skirt catches fire. He smothers the blaze with the mackintosh, turns off the burner, goes upstairs and bathes. At last, dressed and stainless, Wallace hastens out, making a great show of looking for a nonexistent man. After two hours he goes home to play-act some more. Where was the weapon? Thrown away on the journey to Menlove Gardens. A charwoman will swear there was, in the parlor, an iron rod fifteen inches long; and it is there no more.

The public antipathy to his client began to frighten Hector Monro, who had been appointed counselor for the defense. Wallace's life savings amounted to less than £400 and a proper defense would cost £1500 at least. No great trial lawyer, Monro wanted to call in a courtroom star who could give the accused man a fighting chance— but where was he to raise the money? Relatives could not help, nor would the officials of the insurance company.

Monro decided to appeal to the trade union of insurance collectors, to which Wallace belonged. When he arrived in London, however, the union officers rebuffed him.

"But you're condemning a fellow worker without a hearing. Why not be fair to him?"

"How?" asked the president of the union. An answer, like a conjurer's rosebush, suddenly bloomed in the counselor's brain.

"Put him on trial yourselves!" pleaded Monro. "Let me be prosecutor *and* defense attorney. You be the jury. I'll give you the whole case *against* him—and the case *for* him. Then you can decide." So, after closing time, in the offices of the insurance company there was held a murder trial unique in the history of bloodshed. Some twenty members of the executive committee of the union sat as a jury. As convincingly as he knew how, Monro set forth the police theory.

"That," he wound up, "is the worst the King's attorney can bring against my client. Now what can be said for him? Remember that you are not called upon to decide who killed the woman. The jury has only one thing to decide: Is it certain, beyond a reasonable doubt, that the husband did it? True, that bogus telephone call was made near my client's house. But that is a point in his favor. If he was plotting murder, would he dare to use that phone, when some neighbor might notice him? More likely the murderer, keeping watch on the house, would use the booth to throw suspicion on the husband. Remember, the waitress will testify that the telephone voice was unfamiliar to her.

"Was Julia still alive when the husband left the house at 6:45? Fifteen minutes before, a milk boy had talked with Julia on her doorstep. So, if you believe him guilty, this man had only about ten minutes for the whole horrible job. Can anybody believe that a man could rain twenty-one blows on a woman's head, put out a fire, compose her body, bathe off bloodstains, dress himself and get out of the house, all in ten minutes? A surgeon professor will testify that those blows were dealt in a frenzy of ferocity. Can anyone imagine that timid man in a frenzy? For fifty-two years he has lived without a blemish on his reputation. And since the murder was discovered not one of his statements has been disproved.

"Most important of all—if he did it, can you tell me why? Hatred of his wife? He and his wife got on like Darby and Joan. Some other woman? No; not now, not ever. Robbery? Of what—£4 in the house? His wife's insurance? She had only a small policy. This man gains nothing by his wife's death, except loneliness. I can assure you that the prosecutor will not advance one sensible reason for my client to have murdered his wife."

Wallace's twenty fellow workers heard the evidence fairly. In that quiet business office they put their heads together and brought in a verdict: Innocent! The whole unprecedented proceeding had to be cloaked in secrecy, for it could well have been held to be in flagrant contempt of British law. Not very long ago the editor of a London newspaper spent two months behind bars for discussing, in fictional form, a crime yet to be tried in court.

Convinced that there was not a rag of evidence to prove their associate guilty, the union members set out to raise money. Within a few days eminent counsel was engaged to conduct the defense. The trial lasted four days. Ten men and two women on the jury heard the prosecutor promise that although he could suggest no motive he would nevertheless prove the prisoner's guilt. Then came the parade of his witnesses. After that, for one full day the accused man himself stood impassive in the witness box, firm of voice as he denied everything. The jurors took but one hour to reach their unanimous verdict: guilty. And Mr. Justice Wright pronounced the death sentence.

What to do now? Never in British legal history had a Court of Criminal Appeal quashed a conviction for murder on the ground that the jury's verdict was unreasonable. But the union pushed the appeal on that ground alone. And one day three judges in scarlet robes listened to the arguments and decided there was a reasonable doubt. They unanimously set Wallace free.

Retiring to a tiny farm far from Liverpool, William Herbert Wallace installed in his lonely home a system of lights and burglar alarms. Guns were always at hand. He wrote that someone unknown was coming to finish him off, as Julia had been finished. After two years of terror he died a natural death. Was the fearful old fellow really a murderer? To this day you can have an argument on that in any pub in Liverpool. No one will ever know.

One of the legal cases which brought the late Senator William E. Borah into national prominence was the murder trial of one Paul Corcoran, whose alibi was that he was in the town of Burke, several miles away, when the killing in question occurred. Witnesses for the state swore that they saw Corcoran leave the scene of the crime on top of a boxcar, that he was carrying a rifle and that he jumped off the train at Burke. The conductor and brakeman of the train, called by the defense, testified that any man riding that train that day, at the speed it was going along the rough, grapevine track, would have been flung off and killed. "I will show them," Borah said. "I will ride that boxcar myself, under identical conditions." It was Borah's life against Corcoran's alibi. Somehow he stayed on, and at Burke he leaped from the top of the car, rifle in hand, and landed on his feet. It was the turning point of the case. —*Beverly Smith*

The Blaster

By J. Edgar Hoover

FOR TWO maddening years, by robbery, kidnap and murder, the Blaster gathered half a million dollars in plunder while no policeman laid hand on him. Informers were too frightened to betray his name; and we had not even a useful description, because his victims were invariably too confused—or too dead—to remember.

All that we knew was that some trigger-crazy hoodlum was at large in the Middle West. Around him he had raised his merciless and obedient crew. Like apparitions, they appeared in a bank lobby; with deadly and precise routine they leveled weapons and scooped up the cash; one false move by civilian or peace officer and the machine guns blazed. Then, in a plume of exhaust gas from a speed car, they vanished, untouched.

But the unknown mobster made his irretrievable error on January 17, 1934. Edward George Bremer, a banker, halted his car before a traffic light at a quiet intersection in St. Paul, and a stranger yanked open the door. "Move over!" he ordered, poking a gun against the rich man's ribs.

As the order was obeyed, the banker was pounded over the skull. When he regained consciousness, he was in another car. He did not see home again until all the demanded money was paid—an unparalleled extortion of $200,000!

Here was another job by the unknown bandit; resemblance to his previous crimes was unmistakable. Eagerly we questioned Bremer. We turned up one detail, seemingly trivial: "The kidnapers carried their own gasoline; several times I heard them fill the tank and throw away the used cans."

By teletype and telephone a call sped forth to local and state police and to our FBI agents throughout five states. Within twenty-four hours we recovered four discarded gasoline cans found by a farmer; from them we lifted clear fingerprints. The next day I held the gangster's prison picture in my hand—a short, slight man, with toothbrush mustache and rigid lips; from his hostile eyes perdition glared at the camera. He was Arthur "Doc" Barker, on parole from a prison in Oklahoma, where he had been serving a life term for a vicious murder.

Among all the human wickedness I have confronted in my many years as director of the FBI, the misdeeds of this one lawbreaker give me to this day the greatest concern—not because he was a genius of criminals, but because he demonstrated what mischief sheer mediocrity can do in an indifferent society.

Detailed reports gave us his background. Doc Barker was born in a small Missouri town in 1899. His father was a mechanic, his mother a blowzy, unkempt woman who henpecked her husband. Never was the family hungry-poor. They lived in respectable neighborhoods and, when they moved to Oklahoma, Doc was sent regularly to church and to public school. How did it happen, then, that this child grew up to commit crimes more atrocious than any done by Jesse James?

Did it not require intelligence and boldness to manage a long string of robberies and to engineer two major kidnapings? Yet in the classroom Doc was a dullard, and in any wrangle a sniveling mamma's boy. Every school year he failed, yet Ma Barker terrified the teachers into promoting him. She flooded the police with reproachful tears when they suspected his thieving. But over the backyard fence Ma boasted to neighbors: "I got great days ahead of me, when my children grow up. Silk dresses. Fur coats and diamond rings."

And the staring child she led by the hand lived for the day when he could grab from life the pretties his mother longed for. From his youth he knew two overmastering emotions—doglike devotion to Ma and contempt for all other authority. Ma Barker was, at last, to die in a Florida cottage during a machine-gun battle with law-enforcement officers, but the training she gave her son bore evil fruit. He was already an auto-stealing delinquent while still in the eighth grade. His first job, which Ma found for him, was with a glassblower whose secret avocation was coaching young thieves. Doc was only nineteen when he was first arrested for stealing a government car, and he was only twenty-two when he was involved in a brutal holdup killing and drew his life sentence.

Some years later an angry rumor came from the prison, "Doc Barker's sore." The word went around the poolrooms. "Not because his Ma left his Pa—he just don't seem to like what he hears about this new fellow Dunlop she went and married." It wasn't long before, by the dark shore of a lake, the new fellow Dunlop fell dead, his heart blown out by an expert shot. No one was ever arrested for the crime, but the underworld knew it was done by Doc's friends. Even before he left prison he earned his title of "the Blaster."

In spite of the gossip Doc was soon free on parole with the fantastic provision that he leave Oklahoma never to return. Out of the penitentiary he stomped with a chronic glaze of rage in his hard dark eyes. Soon he was in Minneapolis with a partner, a criminal called Alvin Karpis. Enlisting a disciplined gang of lawbreakers, he plunged at once into his two-year outlaw carnival, shooting or bribing his way out of every trap. Now, as I looked at his photograph, I resolved: "Barker, it won't be long! We're coming after you."

Doc's "wanted" pictures were hanging in post offices and station houses. To outwit us, he decided to change his face and fingerprints, enlisting the aid of Dr. Joseph P. Moran, then surgeon-extraordinary to mobsters. While serving a sentence at Joliet, Moran had helped in the hospital. Now, free, he had built up a practice among released convicts. One night the gangster and the surgeon locked themselves in a Toledo hotel room and, with only a nightclub girl as nurse, Moran carved away at Doc's nose, mouth, cheeks and fingertips. For days the bandaged crook cursed in agony, but at last the time came for the bandages to be taken off. The hard eyes of Doc Barker glared at this new face in the glass, then he roared like a wounded bull. The operation was a botch!

A few months later the Blaster and one of his henchmen smilingly escorted the drunken Dr. Moran out of a barroom in Toledo. Never again was the plastic surgeon seen by his friends. Apparently he was taken for a night sail on Lake Erie. His feet were placed in a bucket of cement.

When the mixture hardened the doomed surgeon was hoisted overboard.

Such brisk and businesslike vengeance was peculiar to Barker. When one of his associates was brought to trial the attorney was J. Earle Smith. In spite of a determined defense, the man was convicted. On the following morning the lawyer's riddled body was found on a country-club green. He had let the gang down. Even more shocking was the fate of William J. Harrison, another of Doc's minor satraps. Ma, from her winter home in Florida, had written to Doc that Harrison had indiscreetly disclosed confidential information to other members of the mob. On some friendly pretext Doc Barker amiably drove Harrison to an abandoned farm near Ontarioville, Illinois. There in the barn the garrulous underling was shot through the head; his body was soaked with gasoline, and then Doc set fire to the barn. The next day he wrote to Ma: "I took care of that business for you. It was done just as good as if you had did it yourself. I am just like the Standard Oil—always at your service. Ha! Ha!"

Even criminals began to feel unsafe if they had a speaking acquaintance with Doc; no one cared to be introduced to him; his bloodstained legend was growing. But now, with every police resource alerted, we were tracing Barker. We knew he had managed the kidnaping of William A. Hamm, Jr., St. Paul brewer, and had collected a ransom of $100,000. We learned that a cavalcade of his gangsters had then motored to Reno, to spend their swag, sheltered by political friends.

We soon found that the woman-shy son of Ma had suddenly taken unto himself a girl friend and was living with her in Chicago. Day and night he was watched; without suspecting, he led our operatives to the hideouts

of his companions, all of whom were cooling off after the Bremer job. At last, one dark winter morning, came the roundup. When our agents braced Doc Barker on the street, he made a dash, slipped on the ice and fell ignominiously on his face. Once again Barker was given a life sentence, this time in Alcatraz. It was there I finally met him.

He stared at me fixedly, hate shining in fathomless dark eyes. I see him now in memory as I saw him then in flesh; I can sense again the foul sprinkle as he spat at me through the bars. The hate on his face was a true reflection of an inner passion. Even then he was planning to get out.

And he did! The underworld boasts that he used a clever trick, telling guards about his love for music. Was there any reason why he could not be allowed a simple harmonica? Underworld gossip states that the harmonica that came to Barker concealed two small saws laid in under the instrument's metal strips. However he got the saws, on January 13, 1939, Doc Barker cut two metal bars from his cell and climbed out. Four other convicts did the same. They crossed the cellblock to a window of the outside wall, cut a steel railing and dropped to the ground. Soon the alarm sounded. At 4:10 in the morning, search lamps from a Coast Guard cutter and the Alcatraz launch located Barker on the shore by the Golden Gate. He refused to surrender, and as he frantically sought cover the machine guns and automatic pistols roared. . . . He who had lived by guns died by gunfire. At the prison hospital his last words were: "I am crazy as hell!"

Did he speak the truth? If so, was not society even crazier? Why did it not find out that Barker was mad—if he was—before he and his gang had committed thirteen murders? If his antisocial behavior had been noted by his early teachers, had there been a school psychiatrist to examine him, he could have been removed from the vicious influence of his mother. Perhaps his mental quirks could have been straightened out with proper care. If not, he could have been isolated in some decent institution. Some day, by such techniques, society will not only assist its misfits but protect itself.

Historian W. E. Woodward, writing about the Judd Gray and Ruth Snyder murder case, points up a small thing that played an important role in sending Gray to the electric chair. Among the witnesses was a taxi driver who remembered him on the night of the murder. Why? Because on a $3.50 fare Gray had given him only a five-cent tip.

"Five cents!" the taxi driver said. "I took a good look at his face, and I'll never forget him. There he sits, right over there." And he pointed to Judd Gray. —*Fitchburg Papers*

Things I Can't Explain

Condensed from the book My Story

By Mary Roberts Rinehart

HOURS after my husband died I went into his room alone and, after an old habit, sat down on the bed and took his hand. Only now there was no response, as there always had been before. I think it was then for the first time that I realized he had gone.

Dr. Rinehart had had a certain rather embarrassed belief—or perhaps a hope—not only in survival after death but in the possibility of communication. I myself had no faith in the ability to establish contact with those who had died, and an intense dislike of making the attempt. Nevertheless, we had together investigated all sorts of psychic phenomena and had made a compact to attempt to communicate with each other when one of us was gone.

So one bright morning not long after his death I sat in a dark hotel room, with the door locked and a pleasant young married woman from a Western city in front of me. I had searched the room, which was empty save for a table, a stand in a corner with a bunch of flowers on it and our two chairs. The medium did not know who I was, though that would not have influenced what followed. She did not go into a trance, and we sat talking quietly while I held her hands tightly and kept her knees between mine so she could not free either hand or foot without my knowledge. What followed, cut to a minimum, was like this.

I (calmly): "There is a hand on top of my head."

Medium: "Just sit still. It's all right."

I: "Now it has moved down my arm and is touching my wedding ring."

Medium: "Why don't you speak to whoever it is?"

I spoke to the darkened room. "If you are who I hope you are, do you know what I brought with me today? It belonged to you."

I expected nothing. Remember, I had both the medium's hands in mine, the opening of the door to admit a third person would have let in a blast of sunshine, and there were a dozen places where I could have hidden the object—in my bag, in a stocking, in my hair under my hat. Judge, then, my astonishment when something roughly pushed down inside the open neck of my dress and seized and shook the thing I had pinned at my waist—a caduceus, the insignia of the Medical Corps, from my husband's Army uniform. To say that I was startled would be an understatement.

Medium: "Did anything happen?"

I: "Yes." (Suddenly) "There is something among the flowers over in the corner. I can hear it. . . . The hand is back. It is putting something down the neck of my dress."

I let go of the medium then and investigated. Lying beside the caduceus was a fresh rosebud!

That ended the sitting. For fifteen years I have gone over it in my mind for fraud, for telepathy, even for hypnotism. I still cannot explain it. Nevertheless, for

years I carried the rosebud in the back of my prayer book. Only once since have I tried again to fulfill my promise. Two years later I had a sitting with the well-known English medium Eileen Garrett, with my three sons present. I had never met her before, and she had come in that afternoon for a cup of tea and a talk. In that sunny apartment, with the traffic of Park Avenue passing below, she unexpectedly put down her teacup and suggested she might "try for what she could get." She leaned back in her chair and was soon asleep.

There followed the usual preliminary palaver. Then something happened. The medium assumed Dr. Rinehart's voice, his mannerisms, even his little chuckle. The boys were on the edge of their chairs, staring and incredulous. Then once more occurred the incredible. The voice said, referring to his death: "I did not realize what had happened to me until you came in that night and sat down on the side of the bed and took my hand."

Never once in all that time had I told anyone what I had done. I had almost forgotten it myself. I have never tried since—for, no matter how much I believe of any psychic phenomenon, I cannot hold that belief long.

Yet I may be wrong. About a year before my husband's health began to fail, I went to a crystal gazer, a dreadful woman who called me dearie and needed a bath badly. We sat down on either side of a small table with a crystal ball on it. A piece of velvet covered the ball on my side while she peered into the other. Finally she looked up. "I see a military funeral for someone close to you," she said.

It seemed absurd at the time. Yet two years later I was standing in Arlington while a platoon of soldiers fired a salute over my husband's grave. I am still not a spiritualist. But, after all, the art of prophecy comes down to us from Daniel, and what about Nostradamus? In her small way, in her dirty house, that woman may have had a touch of it.

After an exhausting day with patients, Dr. S. Weir Mitchell, famous Philadelphia neurologist, had retired to rest. He was awakened by the violent ringing of his front doorbell, and at the door found a little girl, thinly clad and plainly in distress. "My mother is very sick, sir," she said. "Won't you come, please?"

The night was cold, with snow whirling before a bitter wind. Dr. Mitchell was very tired; he expostulated with the child, but something in the way the little messenger spoke made him relent. He dressed and followed her. Finding the mother very ill with pneumonia, the doctor arranged for proper medical care. Later he complimented the sick woman on the intelligence and persistence of her little daughter.

"But my daughter died a month ago!" cried the woman weakly. "Her shoes and shawl are in that cupboard."

Dr. Mitchell, amazed and perplexed, opened the cupboard door, and saw the exact garments worn by the little girl who had brought him thither. They were warm, and could not possibly have been out in that wintry night.   —*George K. Cherrie*

Death in the Arctic

By Arthur Train, Jr.

T HE MURDERERS had confessed. The public expected an easy conviction. What, then, had drawn the huge crowd to this session of the Supreme Court of Alberta at Edmonton on August 14, 1917? One attraction, certainly, was Inspector C. D. "Denny" LaNauze, handsomest and most popular officer in the North-West Mounted Police. But the real center of attention was the prisoner himself, for he was the first Eskimo to be brought to trial in a white man's court.

The culprit and his accomplice could not speak a word of English. They did not know the meaning of an oath, though they agreed, Eskimo-fashion, to "speak straight and not with two tongues." As stolidly as they would have recounted the killing of a seal, they told how they had slain two missionaries, hacked them up and eaten their livers. Inspector LaNauze had spent more than two years covering six thousand miles by dog team and boat to track down the culprits. His exploit is still a favorite story around campfires along the Mackenzie and in igloos far out on the polar ice. For LaNauze was the first officer to bring justice to the arctic and make its wild and desolate expanses safe for the white man.

Loneliest and most inaccessible of the rivers of the Canadian North, the Coppermine winds its way through several hundred miles of dreary tundra, passing the Dismal Lakes en route to the Arctic Ocean. In these forlorn reaches the missionaries met their death in November 1913.

Few white men will remain in these desolate wastes unless sustained by an ideal. But the Oblates of Mary Immaculate are the shock troops of the Catholic Church. Mission by mission, they had been pushing their way north. Several missions had tried to convert the Eskimos. Then in 1911 Bishop Breynat, head of the Oblates in Mackenzie District, selected for the task Father Rouvière, a rugged mountaineer from the Cévennes in France, and Father LeRoux, a scholarly young Breton. For a time things went well. Then the Eskimos, in their search for game, moved north to the Arctic Ocean. The missionaries went with them—and were never heard from again. In 1915, near the Dismal Lakes, one of the North's outstanding woodsmen, D'Arcy Arden, spotted an Eskimo wearing a priest's surplice. Examining the garment carefully, he saw a bullet hole.

To the almost hopeless task of finding the missionaries or their slayers the Mounted Police assigned Inspector Charles Deering LaNauze, a French-Irishman with immense vitality and vast knowledge of the North. With him LaNauze took a corporal, a constable and an Eskimo interpreter. At Fort Norman they loaded a shallow-draft boat with supplies to last two years and headed for Great Bear Lake. Against the swift, icy current of Great Bear River progress was so slow that at night they could

look back and see their last camp. There was one mile
that took them four days.

When the bitter arctic winter set in, LaNauze and his
men holed up along an arm of the lake. At the first hint
of spring they set out on dogsleds over a difficult terrain
cluttered with huge blocks of ice. Often it was necessary
to beat out a trail and then go back for the supplies. But
by the end of April 1916 they reached the Arctic Ocean.
There Inspector LaNauze met Corporal Bruce, who had
been sent along the coast from Herschel Island to work on
the case. Bruce had accumulated more evidence, including a cassock with Rouvière's name on it; but he had not
learned anything about a murder. Patiently LaNauze
and his interpreter went over the ground themselves, village by village, tent by tent—questioning the Eskimos
repeatedly, giving them a chance to trip themselves up.
But there was never a break in their avowals of ignorance
about the missionaries.

Then one day an Eskimo looked at Ilavinik, the interpreter, and said: "Didn't you work with the white man
Stefansson?"

"Yes."

"I heard about you from my cousin, who was with
him."

The atmosphere began to thaw. Ilavinik resumed his
questioning of the group. LaNauze, watching, saw that
he was beginning to tremble. Suddenly he turned to
LaNauze and said: "I got him. Priests killed by Eskimo
all right. These people very, very sorry. Write down these
names—Sinnisiak and Uluksuk."

Sinnisiak was busily making a bow when the Mounties
caught up with him. He shuddered with fear when his
eyes met those of tne police, as if he expected to be killed
on the spot. During his questioning, the tent filled with

tense friends and relatives of the culprit. For a time
LaNauze and his men feared they would suffer the same
fate as the priests. But when the Eskimos saw that the
white men were not going to wreak vengeance on Sinnisiak immediately, the elders spoke up. "It is right that
Sinnisiak should go back with the white men," they said.
Uluksuk, the accomplice, was picked up soon afterward.

Exactly what happened between the two Eskimos and
the missionaries? We have only the Eskimos' account. At
the beginning the Eskimos were kind and hospitable. As is
their custom, they shared what they had and expected to
share what others had in return. But, when the caribou
grew scarce, people were hungry, nerves were stretched
to the breaking point. The last page of Father Rouvière's
diary, picked up at the scene of the crime, contains the
despairing entry: "Disillusioned by the Eskimos. What
shall we do?"

The priests had shared a tent with Kormik, a medicine man, who resented their competition. Driven by hunger, Kormik's wife helped herself to the priests' dwindling stock of provisions. Then Kormik took Father LeRoux's rifle. In the North, taking a man's rifle when starvation threatens is tantamount to a death sentence. Father LeRoux demanded the return of the rifle, and the villagers became wildly excited. Enraged, Kormik leaped on the priest and tried to kill him. Wiser heads prevented this, but the Fathers were persuaded to leave. "Come back next year, when things are better," the elders called after them down the trail.

The Fathers were ill and weak from lack of food. They did not know the way back. Some twenty-five miles up the river, in a blinding snowstorm, they met Sinnisiak and Uluksuk. The Fathers told them to help pull the sled. But the Eskimos wanted to go back to their village.

"I had ice in my boots and I was freezing," declared Sinnisiak at the trial. "I did not know when I would see my people again. Every time the sled stuck, Father Le-Roux pulled out Father Rouvière's rifle.

"'I think they will kill us,' I said to Uluksuk. 'I will try to kill them.'" So, watching his chance, he stabbed LeRoux in the back.

"You finish off this one. I'll get the other!" he shouted to Uluksuk as Father LeRoux toppled forward. Reluctantly Uluksuk drew his seal knife and stabbed the priest again. Sinnisiak picked up the rifle and fired twice at Father Rouvière. The Eskimos hacked open the bodies of the priests and ate their livers, to keep the white men's spirits "from getting up again." So died Jean-Baptiste Rouvière and Gabriel LeRoux, a few miles above Bloody Falls in the Barren Lands, martyrs to their faith.

LaNauze took his prisoners and Eskimo witnesses out

by whaleboat from Herschel Island. From Peace River they traveled by train to Edmonton, where their arrival caused a sensation. At no time were the prisoners shackled. They looked on their Mountie guards as the only link with their life in the North and followed them around with pathetic devotion.

During the trial the people of Edmonton became convinced that these simple aborigines could not possibly understand the gravity of their crime. The tide of popular sympathy began to turn in their favor. By the time the three-day trial was over, half of Edmonton was clamoring for acquittal. Bishop Breynat gave an example of compassion by suggesting that after conviction the authorities show clemency. Although his own spiritual sons had been murdered, he pleaded, almost in Christ's own words: "Forgive them, for they know not what they do."

The jury was out a surprisingly short time and came in with the verdict: "Not guilty."

The first person to break the silence was Chief Justice Harvey. "Gentlemen," he informed the jury, "you have not done your duty."

Only one Eskimo had been tried for the murder of one priest. After a change of venue, the case was reopened in Calgary. This time the jury brought in a verdict of guilty, "with the strongest possible recommendation for mercy." The governor-general commuted the death sentence to imprisonment at Fort Resolution under the surveillance of the Mounted Police and the Oblate Fathers. They were released in 1919.

This example of the white man's fairness spread all over the arctic. But even today it is not generally known that it was Inspector Denny LaNauze who was mainly responsible for this happy outcome and for the pacifying effect it had on Eskimos throughout the North. LaNauze had given the natives a preliminary hearing on the Arctic Coast. He had obtained from the accused an account of the crime which by its frankness proved how little they understood its gravity. The record of this hearing constituted the main body of evidence at the trial and provided the basis for the merciful sentence and for the eventual clemency order from the government at Ottawa.

Anyone venturing into the Coppermine region a few years later would have found that LaNauze's fairness paid off. It was now safe for Oblate missionaries to carry on the work for which Father Rouvière and Father LeRoux had died.

How good a detective would you be? Here are problems taken from the files of actual homicide cases. For the answers, turn to page 482.

1. Would you expect to find that the fingerprints of identical twins match? (*Yes*) (*No*)

2. The slayer, slightly wounded, left his or her blood spattered at the scene of the crime. Can science ascertain the slayer's sex from the blood spots? (*Yes*) (*No*)

3. The widow is suspected of having poisoned her husband, who died three years ago, with arsenic. Can this be determined if the body is exhumed? (*Yes*) (*No*)

4. From all indications, the circus strong man committed suicide by choking himself to death. Is this possible? (*Yes*) (*No*)

5. When the body was brought to the lake surface, there was virtually no water in the lungs. Does this prove that death took place before the body was flung into the water? (*Yes*) (*No*)

6. You have just come across suspicious footprints in fresh snow, but they will soon melt. Can plaster casts be made of them? (*Yes*) (*No*)

7. In the victim's clenched fist is a strand of hair from the killer's head. Can the killer be positively identified from that alone? (*Yes*) (*No*)
                                                              —*Larry Roberts*

Impersonator Extraordinary

By Irwin Ross

Aᴛ ᴛʜᴇ United Nations, Stanley Clifford Weyman was known as a smooth-talking reporter with a far-flung international background. He had been at the U.N. for nearly two years before his colleagues discovered how really impressive was his background. Over a forty-year period simple Stan had been, among other things, U.S. consul to Morocco, Peruvian ambassador to the United States, Rumanian consul general in New York, Serbian military attaché in Washington, a medical technician in South America, a State Department protocol expert, an officer in the Air Corps, an officer in the Navy and an expert on prison reform. There was only one flaw: all his posts were self-appointed. For Stanley Clifford Weyman was one of the most imaginative and talented impostors ever to foist himself on a gullible America. The FBI, the State Department, the New York police knew him well— under many names, including his real one: Stephen Weinberg.

Weinberg did not look impressive: a faded little man, now sixty, with a faded face, in a faded suit. Soft-spoken, easygoing, he had none of the flamboyance of the confidence man. Throughout his career he seemed more interested in collecting honors than in filling his pocket. But he had boundless audacity—plus a flair for wearing a uniform. His facility as an impostor came from long practice: he seldom had any other profession. Born in a shabby section of Brooklyn and educated in the local schools, when he was eighteen he got himself elected the sole male delegate to a woman-suffrage group. He also acquired an education at the College of Political Tactics in Charleston, South Carolina—the existence of which has never been clearly established. He wore a Phi Beta Kappa key.

Soon he brandished documents attesting to his appointment as U.S. consul-designate to Morocco. But the new consul quickly came to grief: he was caught stealing a camera and was packed away to the New York State Reformatory in Elmira. Paroled in June 1913, by December he was back in the jug—for simultaneously impersonating the Serbian military attaché and a U.S. naval lieutenant! After his second parole in March 1915, he acquired a dazzling blue uniform, trimmed with gold braid and topped with epaulets, and an admiral's hat that sported a plume. Thus attired, he presented himself at the Hotel Astor as Lieutenant Commander Ethan Allen Weinberg, Rumanian consul general in New York. He wanted to hold a banquet. Preparations were far advanced before it occurred to someone that Consul Weinberg seemed a little too young for his role and his shoes looked shabby. The banquet was canceled.

The lieutenant commander next appeared aboard the battleship *Wyoming*, lying in the Hudson River. The ship's captain took the Rumanian diplomat on a tour of the vessel, and Weinberg grandly repaid the gesture with a banquet for the officers at a New York hotel. However, a detective crashed the party; Weinberg was soon returned to jail, not to emerge until the end of 1916.

On the United States' entry into World War I, Weinberg commissioned himself Lieutenant Royale St. Cyr of Army aviation. He also discovered the joys of the press release—bombarding the newspapers first with the announcement that he was marrying a celebrated movie actress, and later that they were planning a divorce so that they could adopt each other. But St. Cyr got himself involved in a small matter of forgery. When the cops caught up with him he was conducting a formal inspection of the 47th Regiment armory in Brooklyn. He was soon in Blackwell's Island jail.

Weinberg's major phase opened in 1920, when he was twenty-nine years old. A New York development company was seeking a doctor to go to Peru to supervise sanitation projects. Among the applicants was Dr. Clifford Wyman, who sauntered in dressed in a naval uniform. Applicants were told that a physician at a well-known university would interview them and advise the company whom to hire. Three days later the doctor urged the appointment of Dr. Wyman, who was immediately hired.

The university man later related what had occurred.
Wyman had rushed up to him, wrung his hand and assured him that he was a great admirer of his work. The
good doctor thought that Wyman had been one of his
students. Wyman certainly *talked* like a doctor, he recalled. (Weinberg had long been a medical fan around
the university.)

Wyman sailed for Lima with a Mrs. Wyman, whom he
had acquired somewhere along the way. He installed
himself in a palatial home (but neglected to pay the rent),
bought a car and went about his duties. He was admi-
rably successful—through the simple expedient of approv-
ing existing conditions and avoiding technical discussions. He was a lavish entertainer and a popular figure—
until the company discovered Dr. Wyman's identity. His
wife persuaded them not to call the cops.

In July 1921, Princess Fatima of Afghanistan and her
three sons arrived at the Waldorf-Astoria. The princess'
bizarre attire, the jewel in her nose and her 42-carat
"River of Glory" diamond captured the imagination of
a jaded town. Among the dignitaries who called to pay
their respects was Dr. Sterling Clifford Wyman, lieutenant commander in the American Navy, emissary and protocol expert of the U.S. Department of State. Dr. Wyman,
it developed, had a dual mission. He was detailed by the
State Department to be the princess' secretary—an assignment that involved her paying his expenses—and he
was also interested in peddling the "River of Glory"
diamond. Wyman indicated impressive business affilia-
tions, and he was given a power of attorney to sell the
diamond. A few days later the entire party entrained for
Washington, Dr. Wyman having assured the princess that
President Harding was eager to receive her. Wyman arranged the meeting by calling the State Department.

Later, resplendent in the white uniform of a lieutenant commander in the Navy Medical Corps, he grandly performed the introductions at the White House, posed for newsreel pictures, then took the party to meet Secretary of State Charles Evans Hughes. Wyman handled all the details of the junket—including honorariums for the reporters and newsreel photographers, which he told the princess were customary in this country. The commander also received money to pay the Willard Hotel, a detail he overlooked. Back in New York, the princess unaccountably balked at allowing Wyman to take the diamond to Atlantic City, where he claimed he could sell it. Commander Wyman made a quick exit.

Wyman (now Captain Rodney Sterling Wyman) next turned his attention to politics. At the height of the New York mayoralty campaign he was ensconced at a desk in Democratic campaign headquarters. He had not been appointed to his post. As the story was reconstructed, Weinberg had sauntered into the office behind Mayor Hylan's campaign manager. Seeing the two men together, underlings concluded that Weinberg had been recruited by the boss, and they made no objection when he took over a vacant desk and went to work. Weinberg was an assiduous volunteer, arriving at the office before the other staff members and going through the mail, which often contained campaign contributions. Someone got suspicious, and Weinberg's political career ended.

A few weeks later, Dr. Adolph Lorenz, the famed "bloodless surgeon" of Vienna, arrived in the United States. "Dr. Clifford Weyman" called on him at once, explaining that Dr. Royal S. Copeland, U.S. Commissioner of Health, had delegated him to be Dr. Lorenz's secretary and to "look after his affairs." Dr. Lorenz was delighted with the gracious offer, and Dr. Weyman was shortly installed at Dr. Lorenz's free clinic at the New York Hospital for Joint Diseases. An anonymous phone call led to the discovery that Dr. Weyman was soliciting gratuities before allowing the impoverished patients to see the great doctor, and he was precipitously retired. When this story appeared in the newspapers, one of Princess Fatima's sons recognized Dr. Weyman's picture. Weinberg was arrested for impersonating a naval officer and sentenced to serve two years in the penitentiary.

His incarceration left him with an abiding sense of civic duty. In 1925 he appeared at Sing Sing as a prison-reform expert, protesting the execution of a prisoner. Weinberg created quite a stir—until Warden Lewis E. Lawes recognized him.

In 1926, when the newspapers reported that Pola Negri had collapsed with grief at the death of Rudolph Valentino, the ever-helpful Dr. Wyman appeared at her hotel as an old friend of Valentino and was promptly engaged as Negri's physician. From there it was a short step to taking a hand in the funeral arrangements. When the big day came, Dr. Wyman's car—with a police siren—was the first behind the hearse. Soon after the funeral the city's newspapers received a letter from Valentino's business manager asking that publicity be given to a medical report on Valentino's preoperative condition in order to squelch rumors of foul play. At the bottom of the letter was penned a note: "This report was concurred in by three reputable surgeons and by Sterling C. Wyman, medico-legal expert, who was a dear friend of V." A reporter got curious about Dr. Wyman, and the Valentino hoopla ended.

He appeared at Middlesex University, a new medical school in Massachusetts, as a New York State Lunacy

Commissioner and read a learned paper on "Insanity as a Defense in Crime." In 1927 he was driving around New York in a white car labeled "Third Pursuit Squadron" and was wearing a uniform remarkably similar to an Air Corps officer's—but not enough like one to warrant prosecution. When he set himself up in the practice of law without troubling to become a member of the bar, however, he let himself in for a stretch behind bars.

The 1930's were a relatively quiet period for Weinberg. But with the outbreak of World War II he installed himself in a New York hotel and, as a "Selective Service consultant," ran a school for draft dodgers, teaching how to fake deafness, feeblemindedness and other ailments. When tracked down by the FBI the students spilled the story, and nine were convicted with Weinberg, who was sentenced to seven years.

With time off for good behavior, Weinberg was out in 1948. As Stanley Clifford Weyman, he asked Robert Erwin, head of the Erwin News Service, for a job. The agency, which specializes in Washington coverage for small-town papers and radio stations, was starting a Latin-American service, and Weinberg proposed to furnish feature material from the United Nations. He said he was a former newspaperman, publicity man and student of Latin-American affairs. Mr. Erwin was so taken with Weinberg's knowledgeable and breezy charm that he did not bother to ask for references but quickly accredited him at the U.N. and set him to work on a part-time basis. Weinberg worked out well. "He wasn't a brilliant writer," Mr. Erwin reported, "but he had good news sense—and he seemed to know everybody."

Once he had accreditation, it was relatively easy for him to find employment with the London *Daily Mirror* on a piece-rate basis, and to become U.N. correspondent for the FM station WFDR, on which he delivered a five-minute daily commentary. Once a week he also brought U.N. luminaries to his microphone to be interviewed by a panel of reporters; the delegation chiefs of Greece, Egypt, China, Thailand, Haiti were all squired to the WFDR microphone by him. Weyman became a special favorite of the Thailand delegation, having persuaded them that he had been an OSS operative in their country during the war. Ambassador Wan Waithayakon was about to employ him as a press officer, giving him diplomatic status in the bargain. For Stanley Clifford Weyman it was a lifelong dream come true.

He then made his fatal error. He wrote to the State Department on March 7, 1951, inquiring about the effect on his American citizenship if he took such a post. The State Department looked up its file on Weyman, and the wires buzzed between New York and Washington. By the time the dust had settled, Weyman was disaccredited by the Erwin News Service, his probation officer had directed him to get a job in nondiplomatic circles and the Thailand delegation was looking sheepish. And everybody was a little sad, for good old Stan had been a pleasant fellow with a remarkable talent for influencing people.

One reason for our high crime rate is that the long arm of the law is often shorthanded.   —*Hal Chadwick*

A Chicago girl sued for annulment of her marriage on the grounds of fraud. She said her husband pretended to be a forty-dollar-a-day bricklayer when he was, in reality, only a banker.
                                                            —*Swing*

Bluebeard of Paris

Condensed from the book I Found No Peace

By Webb Miller

THE MOST monstrous criminal character in modern annals was probably Henri Désiré Landru, whose head
I saw chopped off at dawn on February 25, 1922. He was
convicted of the cold-blooded murder of ten women and
one boy, whom he had hacked to pieces and burned in his
cookstove at Villa Ermitage in Gambais, near Versailles;
he had been the lover of 283 women.

Over a period of five years Landru had pursued the
grim business of systematic lovemaking and slaughter.
Relations duly reported the mysterious disappearances of
his "fiancées" to the police, but each time the circumstances and the name of "the man in the case" were different; the police found no clue and did not connect the
disappearances as the crimes of one man. The disorgani-
zation of civilian life during the war favored Landru's
schemes. The husbands of many of the women were at
the front; others, whose husbands had been killed, were
only too anxious to listen to offers of marriage. Then, by
pure chance in April 1919, the sister of one of the missing "fiancées" caught a glimpse of Landru in Paris, fol-

lowed him to his apartment and informed the police. Without realizing they had made one of the greatest catches in Parisian criminal history, the police took him into custody.

The whole fantastic story began to come out when, on the way to the station, detectives caught Landru attempting to throw away a little notebook. It was the famous *carnet* containing the key to the entire series of astounding crimes. The entries look like notations of business transactions and remained a mystery until police compared the names of women in the *carnet* with the names of scores of women missing since 1915 and found that ten tallied.

Then the police pieced together a bizarre drama. They learned that Landru had lived in eleven different places in Paris, under at least fifteen names (he sometimes adopted the name of his previous victim). He was the son of a respectable Parisian businessman who had become insane in later life and committed suicide. In youth Landru was studious, bright and normal; but as he attained manhood criminal tendencies asserted themselves. He served two brief prison terms for petty fraud and about 1914 hit upon the unique idea of wholesale lovemaking as a business. By matrimonial advertisements and offers to purchase furniture, he came in contact with hundreds of women and made violent love to every one of them. At first he seems to have confined his operations to swindling his enamored victims.

Henri Désiré's courtships were so skillfully ardent that he was able to propose matrimony at the second or third meeting. His diary revealed him at times courting seven women simultaneously, maintaining a passionate correspondence and turning out love letters by the score. A bundle of such letters was found in his villa, ready for use.

During this time Landru maintained a separate home for his wife and son and was a good husband and family man. He explained his frequent excursions to the villa as "business trips." Neither wife nor son knew the nature of his business and often unknowingly helped dispose of the property of his victims.

Landru's unforgettable trial, in the fall of 1921, was better than anything the *Folies-Bergères* ever put on. All Paris stormed the doors. Landru maintained an imperturbable dignity; under questioning he would smile deprecatingly and say, "It's an affair of honor. I do not kiss and tell." One day he sent for the judge, saying he was remorseful and wanted to talk. At last, buzzed the prosecution, Landru is going to confess. But to the judge Landru sighed and said: "I must tell you. I am remorseful about all the 283 infidelities to my wife." The prisoner's story ricocheted around the courtroom to roars of laughter.

But day by day the prosecution unraveled the cryptic entries in the "death *carnet*." The first was the name of the widow Cuchet, whom Landru met through a matrimonial advertisement. After a whirlwind courtship she went to live with him at the fateful Villa Ermitage (railroad station, Vernouillet), under promise of marriage. Then came the stark inscription: "One round-trip, two single tickets to Vernouillet," with the cost. Mme. Cuchet and her seventeen-year-old son disappeared from the face of the earth from that day forth. Some of her furniture later turned up in the apartment of Landru's wife. Landru's wife and her son's sweetheart were found to be wearing some of Mme. Cuchet's jewelry when Landru was arrested.

Entries in the *carnet* marked with monotonous regularity a fatal jaunt to Vernouillet and the disappearance of one more victim. The majority were widows, but one was a nineteen-year-old girl; and at the time of Landru's arrest Fernande Segret, an attractive girl of twenty-nine, was wearing the "death ring"—the engagement ring Landru had used for ten other "fiancées." At the same time he was engaged to Jeanne Falque, from whom he had borrowed 2000 francs. Despite Mlle. Segret's knowledge that she had narrowly escaped the fate of ten predecessors, she refused to testify directly against him. "He was always affectionate and respectful to me," she said. "I loved him and would have married him." At the trial she avoided his gaze. When she finally looked at him she swooned in the witness box.

As climax to a crushing array of circumstantial evidence, a celebrated criminologist produced 256 fragments of human bones from the ashes of the cookstove at Villa Ermitage and testified that they came from at least three bodies. Another expert testified that the soot in the chimney contained a high content of fat. An ashcan yielded bits of half-melted corset ribs and buttons from women's clothing. One closet contained scores of bottles that had contained tissue-destroying fluids. Neighbors testified they had often seen dense clouds of nauseating smoke coming from the mysterious villa.

Alienists and scientists who examined Landru confessed they could not understand his uncanny attraction for women. Except for his extraordinary eyes, which were large and serpentlike in their fixity and brilliance, he had no outward feature to account for it. He was fifty-five years old, of medium build and sallow complexion. At first glance his only unusual features were his remarkably shaped bald head and his Assyrian beard, of which he was inordinately proud. Parisian men about town tried to elicit Landru's system of winning women. But he smiled mysteriously and said: "Our relations were mostly of a business nature, and those of a private nature are a matter between them and me."

Henri Désiré Landru was sentenced to have his head cut off in front of the Versailles jail at dawn on February 25, 1922.

About 4 a.m. that morning, word came that Anatole Deibler, the famous executioner, had arrived with his guillotine, and we hurried to the prison. Four hundred troops had drawn cordons at each end of the street and permitted only possessors of little mimeographed tickets to pass. The only light came from the few electric street lights and the flickering candles in the workmen's old-fashioned lanterns as they bolted the grisly machine together.

Nearly a hundred officials and newspapermen gathered in a circle around the guillotine; I stood fifteen feet away. News arrived from the prison that Landru, whose long black beard had been cut off previously, had asked that he be shaved. "It will please the ladies," he said. He wore a shirt from which the neck had been cut away, and cheap dark trousers—no shoes or socks.

Just as the first streaks of chilly dawn appeared, a large horse-drawn van arrived and backed up within a few feet of the guillotine. Deibler's assistants pulled two wicker baskets from it, placed the small round one in front of the machine where the head would fall and the large coffin-shaped one close beside the guillotine.

Suddenly the great wooden gates of the prison swung open. Three figures appeared, walking rapidly. On each side a jailer held Landru by his arms, which were strapped behind him, supporting him and pulling him forward as fast as they could walk. His bare feet pattered on the cold cobblestones and his knees seemed not to be functioning. His face was waxen and, as he caught sight of the ghastly machine, he went livid.

The jailers hastily pushed Landru face downward under the lunette, a half-moon-shaped wooden block, which clamped his neck beneath the suspended knife. In a split second the knife flicked down, and the head fell with a thud into the basket. As an assistant lifted the hinged board and rolled the headless body into the big wicker basket, a hideous spurt of blood gushed out.

An attendant standing in front of the machine seized the basket containing the head, rolled it like a cabbage into the larger basket and helped shove it hastily into the waiting van. The van doors slammed, and the horses were whipped into a gallop. Since Landru had first appeared in the prison courtyard, only twenty-six seconds had elapsed.

Answers to questions on page 468.

1. *No.* Fingerprints of identical twins may be more dissimilar than total strangers'.

2. *No.* Laboratories can find no sex differences, *per se*, in blood.

3. *Yes.* Arsenic is readily recovered years after death.

4. *No.* The would-be suicide's stranglehold would relax when he became unconscious.

5. *No.* Death by drowning is caused by asphyxia when the windpipe is clogged with water and mucus, rather than by water in the lungs.

6. *Yes.* Footprints in fresh snow can be cast in plaster after preliminary dusting with talc and spraying with shellac.

7. *No.* Although hair may be important corroborative evidence, it alone is insufficient proof.   —*Larry Roberts*

Our Travels with Ho-tei

Condensed from the book Together We Wandered

By C. J. Lambert

IN 1928 MY WIFE and I sold our home in Somerset,
England, and set off to see a bit of the world. Japan was
our first target. In Kobe we spied in a junkshop window
an ivory figurine which we immediately coveted. It was
a carving of Ho-tei, the ancient Japanese god of good luck.

A tiny figure about an inch and a half high, with a
laugh of blissful content on his pudgy old face, he sat
tailor-fashion on an ivory cushion. This cushion, on which
his overflowing tummy rested, was ornamented with
sprays of flowers, and his kimono was covered with chry-
santhemum embroidery. We entered the shop and asked
his price. Incredibly, it was less than five shillings. Overwhelmed with our luck, we returned to our ship to study
the god more closely, for at that price it seemed there
must be something wrong with him. Examination showed
that we were even luckier than we had thought. The

figure was certainly very old, for it had the deep, creamy luster peculiar to old ivory, and the carving was truly exquisite. There was only one curious thing. Apparently the carver had started a fraction too low in the elephant's tusk, for centered in the underside of the cushion there had been a hole where the nerve of the tooth had ended. But this was plugged with an ivory peg, and we thought nothing of it at the time. We were to ponder deeply on it later.

Meanwhile, with Ho-tei carefully tucked away in Marie's dressing case, we embarked for Manila. On the second day out Marie began suffering from a nagging toothache. The ship's doctor gave her some stuff to deaden the pain, but it did no good and she had a wretched twelve days. We were very glad indeed to reach Manila. However, both of us were immediately struck down with dengue fever, an unpleasant malady marked by high temperatures and racking pain in every joint, and it was weeks before Marie was able to stagger out to a dentist. He proceeded to drill one of her teeth straight through to the nerve, and I thought she would go mad with the pain on top of the aches and pains left by dengue. We concluded that the Philippines were not for us, obtained passage to Sydney and crept on shipboard more dead than alive.

When I unpacked I noticed that Ho-tei had somehow been swapped over to my baggage. Naturally I laid no stress on this, but the following day I started the most appalling toothache. There was no doctor on board, and I lived almost entirely on aspirin. I was nearly desperate when we reached Cairns, our first port in Australia. A dentist there tinkered with my teeth but said there was nothing wrong. Within minutes of our return to the ship they were aching as badly as ever, so I saw another dentist at the next port, two days later. He too found nothing wrong, but the fact remained that my teeth started aching as soon as I got back to my cabin.

At Brisbane, after another two days, I told a dentist to start pulling my teeth, and to go on pulling them till I told him to stop. Immediately the first one was out—within ten minutes after coming ashore—I felt such relief that I was certain it had been the culprit. The dentist said the tooth should have given me no trouble at all. But I was sure my miseries were over—until we boarded the boat, when I started living on aspirin again. In Sydney we left most of our luggage in bond, so Ho-tei was parted from us for several weeks. After a delightful pain-free time we made a four-day voyage to New Zealand. Both of us had toothache on only one day during the journey—when we had our heavy luggage brought into our cabin for repacking. Then Ho-tei went back in the hold and our teeth behaved again.

After a wonderful six weeks in New Zealand we sailed to Panama, then caught another boat down the west coast of South America to Chile, where we were to visit my mother. The entire trip was uneventful as far as our teeth were concerned, except for one day: when we repacked our luggage in the baggage room. So far we had no suspicion that the little god was the cause of our intermittent tooth trouble, and if we had we would have laughed scornfully. I should have got a clue when we reached my mother's, for she fell in love with Ho-tei and Marie presented him to her. She had good teeth, but within a few hours they started aching wholesale. We were surprised and a trifle hurt when my mother handed him back and said she felt he was "bad medicine." But we put him back in our luggage in the storage room, and the incident was forgotten until we were back on shipboard—bound for England.

One day we mentioned the glory of Ho-tei's carving to some friends who were interested in ivory. Marie fetched the god from the baggage room and gave it to one woman to show her husband. We saw no more of the woman that day, which we thought strange; but next morning she and her husband came up to us, looking very far off color. They had both been ill with toothache.

Suddenly a great light struck us. We went over dates and symptoms carefully all the way back to Japan, and our hair rose in horror. We couldn't believe, and yet we had to; such a sequence of events could not be a simple coincidence. Marie was all for chucking the little devil overboard, but I was so alarmed at his seeming power that I wondered if he would retaliate by rotting every tooth in our heads. The best thing seemed for us to return him to his countrymen on our arrival home.

Soon after we reached London, I went to a famous Japanese art shop on Bond Street, placed the god in front of the suave little Japanese manager. He examined the figure and said they would be delighted to buy it, for the carving was as exquisite as anything he had ever seen. Feeling rather silly, I replied that I could not take money for the god and related some of our troubles. A strange expression came over the man's face. He rapped out an order in Japanese, and a few moments later an assistant brought in an aged Japanese in national costume.

The moment the old man sighted Ho-tei he gasped, extended both hands in a kind of supplication, then picked up the little figure and immediately examined the bottom of the cushion. Ignoring me utterly, the three men then passed the carving from one to the other, each examining the bottom of the cushion, and exchanging short sentences in Japanese. They were completely absorbed in this queer business. Later, from people who had lived in the East, I learned that some Japanese temple gods were given "souls": tiny medallions were engraved with characters, and this strange "soul" was hidden in the body of the god. Be that as it may, the old Japanese carefully placed our smiling Ho-tei on an ornate lacquered shrine at one end of the shop and lit a row of joss sticks at his feet. As the heavily sweet smell of their burning filled the room, not another word was spoken. When the manager bowed me out of the shop, there was an expression of awe, almost of fear, on his face. I stepped out into the roar of London's traffic with a great sense of freedom.

I never returned to that shop in Bond Street; I do not know even if it is still there. I do wonder sometimes what has happened to that tiny ivory figure, but I have no intention of finding out.

As I entered the police station the other evening to pay a parking fine I noticed that an old lady just ahead of me was trembling all over. I paid my $3 and was about to leave when I saw the lady sitting on a bench in the corner absorbed in a book. "What's the trouble?" I asked. "Is there anything I can do?"

"No, thank you," she replied sedately. "You see, I was sitting at home all alone reading this mystery story, and I got so scared that I came down here to finish it under police protection."

— *Wayne Gray*

In Chicago, a woman won a divorce when she complained that her husband, a murder-story fan, took up most of her evenings making her lie on the floor as the "corpse" while he tried to reconstruct the crime.

— *Time*

Who Killed Les Wilson?

By Joseph P. Blank

SILENTLY the murderer crept across the porch of the house in Crestview, Florida, and raised his shotgun to the glass pane in the door. It was 8:05 on the night of March 15, 1940. Six feet away sat Les Wilson, father of six children and leading candidate in the Okaloosa County sheriff's race. He was listening to the radio. Across the room sat his wife, Bama, and her father. In an adjoining bedroom was twelve-year-old Ray. The murderer fired.

With the roar of the gun Ray ran into the living room, to see a terrible thing: his father's shattered body lying on the floor. Later that night, in a cousin's house, the boy lay awake, crying and shaking—and making plans. He promised himself that some day he would do what his father would have done: clean up Okaloosa County. That night young Ray Wilson began running for county sheriff.

Located in the northwest corner of the state, Okaloosa County (1940 population 12,900), with Crestview its seat, was notoriously rotten. Slot machines were displayed in many ordinary places of business; nearly every bar, beer

joint and pool hall boasted a gambling room. Illegal
whiskey was openly sold. The machine that ruled these
operations largely controlled the law. Thugs beat up
citizens on the street. Each year murders and mysterious
disappearances went unsolved.

Why didn't the law-abiding people of the community
do something about it? A leading Crestview businessman
says: "There was fear here. If you sounded off against the
machine you were picked up and brought in to see one of
the leaders. He looked you in the eye and put his hand on
the butt of his gun and told you not to cause any trouble.
You damn well didn't."

Ray's father had been the exception. A small, bespectacled man, Les Wilson did cause trouble. He despised
the gamblers and the thugs, and everyone knew where he
stood. In the early 1930's he had been police chief of
Crestview, and criminals stayed out of his jurisdiction.

The crooks hated him, but his belief in the law won him a multitude of friends. Scores of men and women remember, even today, favors he did for them. Les operated a taxi business, and when people were sick he brought them food and medicine and drove them to the doctors, refusing payment.

In 1940, when Les Wilson announced his intention to run for sheriff, most people conceded that his victory was inevitable. Soon rumors began to spread that he would never live to take office. One warning came to his brother, Fox Wilson. "Two weeks before the murder a fellow I knew walked up behind me on the street and whispered, 'Tell your brother they're fixing to kill him,'" Fox later recalled. "I told Les about it and asked him if he didn't think he should drop out of the race and move away. He thought for a while and said, 'No, this is my home. I'm going to live and die here.'"

For a week after the murder twelve-year-old Ray couldn't get the tears out of his eyes. At night his mother sat in the darkened living room, crying to herself. "And all I could do," Ray recollects, "was wait for the time when I would be old enough to run for sheriff."

While Ray was growing up, Fox Wilson searched for clues leading to the murderer. Most of the scanty evidence, including empty shotgun shells and wadding, mysteriously disappeared. In October 1940 Governor Fred P. Cone sent an investigating team to gather evidence. But it achieved nothing. In 1949 Governor Fuller Warren decided that the case was hopeless; no more of the state's money would be spent on it. But Fox could never stop thinking about the case. He often awoke Ray in the night to drive with him to a corner of the county where, he had heard, a man "knew something."

After graduation from high school in 1946 Ray went into the Army, serving two years with the infantry in Korea. He returned to Crestview, worked a year for a dry cleaner, then moved to Port St. Joe, where he took a job in a paper mill. When he married his wife, Virginia, in 1950, he told her that his decision to run for sheriff someday was part of their marriage vow.

Intelligent and hardworking, Ray advanced rapidly in the paper company. He could look forward to a good, secure life for himself and his family. "But he wasn't content," Virginia reported. "Nearly every weekend we drove 148 miles to Crestview. Finally I told Ray, 'You'd better make up your mind to tell your manager that we're going back to Crestview. You won't be happy until you run for sheriff.'"

They settled in Crestview with their child in 1953. Borrowing money, Ray went into a dry-cleaning business and built up the most successful one in the area. Early in 1956 Ray figured the time had come to run for sheriff. To the consternation of his friends, he put his business up for sale to raise the money for his campaign. At the outset not a single politician, civic leader or important businessman supported him. For two months he campaigned from early morning till late at night. His platform was based on efficient, impartial law enforcement. He made no public issue of his father's murder.

As Ray gathered voting strength his family and friends worried about him. Several times he was warned to "watch his step." He was offered $10,000 to quit the race. In the first Democratic primary Ray and the incumbent sheriff captured the most votes. Then people began to abandon their fear and announce openly that they were voting for Wilson. In the second primary—a runoff be-

tween the two leaders—Ray won a crushing victory, taking thirty-three of thirty-six precincts. At twenty-eight he
became the youngest sheriff in Florida.

He immediately started to clean up the county. His
policy was simple: if you broke the law, you were going
to be arrested. The night before he became sheriff the
largest gambling establishment moved out of the county.
Several gamblers and moonshiners tried offering him
bribes—then quickly folded their operations. For six
months Ray worked furiously, reorganizing the ten-man
sheriff's department, jerking out every slot machine, shov-
ing the thugs out of the county and setting a record for
the destruction of illegal stills. The once infamous county
became as law-abiding as any in the state. Then Ray
turned to the question he, his family and the people of
the county had long wanted answered: Who killed Les
Wilson?

Finding the answer loomed as a big task. Ray's job as
sheriff came first. Although the hunt was official business,
it would have to be conducted during nights and weekends. Ray asked Walter R. Steinsiek, Jr., superintendent
of identification at the nearby Pensacola police department, to help him. "It looked hopeless to me," Steinsiek
said later. "Seventeen years had passed. But Ray had a
hunch that time had made the killer feel secure and that
he was still around. He convinced me."

The two men read and reread the old files on the case.
They checked out and discounted all the previous rumors
and leads. For months Ray searched in vain. Then he
picked up a trail that led toward Jesse and Doyle Cayson,
brothers whom Ray had known since his boyhood. Sig-
nificantly, Ray found that soon after the murder both
men had become more prosperous; the local suspicion

that they had been the hirelings of the machine was strong.

But frustration followed frustration in Ray's search for the necessary proof. He and Steinsiek drove nine thousand miles in six months, seeking witnesses. Many were afraid to talk; others knew nothing. By July 1957, Steinsiek felt they had reached a dead end. "We had talked to more than a hundred people," he said, "and we still didn't have enough evidence for an indictment."

Ray refused to give up. While he searched for evidence he saw the Cayson brothers frequently, but he never betrayed his feelings or changed his attitude toward them. "I felt sure that they knew what I was doing and were sweating it out but trying not to show it," Ray says. "I wasn't afraid of their taking off. Running away would have been the same as a confession."

The first hopeful piece of information concerned a woman named Jane, who allegedly had been close to the murderers. She had vanished shortly after the murder, but Ray and Steinsiek managed to get the address of her mother. Through her they learned that Jane had twice changed her name and now lived in San Antonio, Texas. When Ray and Steinsiek confronted Jane, she refused to testify. "I'm afraid," she said. "It will get me into terrible trouble."

She said that she had been with Jesse Cayson in a café about half an hour before the murder and that Doyle had rushed in, saying, "The plans have been changed. Come on. We're doing the job tonight." She saw them leave with shotguns. Afterward she was ferociously beaten with a tree branch—a warning to keep her mouth shut. A few years later, while driving, she and her husband were fired on. She left Crestview then, and tried to disappear.

Ray appealed to her. "With your testimony we can bring my father's killers to trial. I'll protect you."

She finally agreed. "I'll testify. I'm scared, but I've been waiting all these years to clear my mind of what happened that night."

They tracked down another essential witness, a woman who shortly after the murder had heard Jesse Cayson admit that he had told several people he shot Les Wilson. And when he was asked whether he had, he broke into tears of remorse and could not answer.

They located—after a full year's search—the switchboard operator who, it was rumored, had recognized the voice and overheard the questions of one of the suspects when he telephoned a café near the taxi stand to find out if Les was driving a taxi that night. They got her to agree to testify. In all, they located more than twenty people who could testify for them.

During the investigation several men approached Ray and asked pointedly if he wasn't afraid of a repetition of what had happened to his father. To avoid an attack, Ray let it be known that copies of the information and evidence were filed in several places.

In June 1958, after eighteen months of work, twenty thousand miles of travel and interrogation of more than two hundred persons, Ray appeared before a grand jury in the Crestview courthouse and said, "I'd like to present evidence in the murder of Les Wilson." In secret meetings the grand jury heard Ray, Steinsiek and more than a score of witnesses. They considered the case for two weeks, then ordered the two Caysons to stand trial. In November the accused were found guilty of first-degree murder. In answer to their appeals the Florida Appellate Court in February and the Florida Supreme Court in April 1960 upheld the conviction. (The Caysons are now serving life sentences.)

"It's over," Ray said. "Getting it finished gives me no joy. I just feel at peace." So do the other good people of Okaloosa County.

San Francisco detectives who ate their lunch at a Kearney Street bakery back in the 1870's all liked soft-spoken old Charley Bolton. Charley, a Civil War veteran who lived in a nearby rooming house, often sat at the detectives' table and chatted with them, sometimes about Black Bart, the bandit nemesis of Wells Fargo stagecoaches.

"Those upcountry sheriffs are no good," Charley Bolton would say. "Too bad they couldn't send a few of you up into the hills to get hold of that Black Bart."

Black Bart was not the first man to snatch a Wells Fargo treasure box, but he was far and away the most dashing. Wearing a flour sack with cutout eyeholes over his head and a long linen duster, he pulled his first job one sunbaked day in July by stepping out from behind a rock on a Calaveras County road and waving a sawed-off shotgun at Billy Hodges' stagecoach. "If they dare to shoot, give them a solid volley, boys," Black Bart shouted toward the rocks alongside the road. Driver Hodges, able to see half a dozen gun barrels covering him, eagerly threw down the green, ironbound Wells Fargo treasure chest. Next day an investigating party discovered that the "guns" Driver Hodges had seen among the rocks were only sticks.

Working alone and on foot, Black Bart held up twenty-eight stagecoaches in eight years. While Californians built legends around his name, Wells Fargo detectives scoured the mountainsides for clues. They found little.

Finally Black Bart slipped up. Hurrying away from a stage robbery near Sonora in 1883, he dropped a handkerchief bearing the mark of a San Francisco laundry. That was all his pursuers needed to track him down. He turned out to be a fifty-five-year-old man who lived in quiet "retirement" and often ate his lunch at a Kearney Street bakery. His name: Charley Bolton.

—Time

Seeds of Treason

The Story of the Hiss-Chambers Case
Condensed from the book of the same title

By Ralph de Toledano and Victor Lasky

This is more than the story of a famous trial. It is more than the account of two men caught in what one of them called "the tragedy of history." It is, in a way, the biography of an era, an anatomy of the period when gilt-edged Communism was both a fashionable avocation and a negotiable bond, and when—under the cover of smart cocktail parties and fancy fronts—the real Communists were systematically betraying the United States.

IN THE late summer of 1934, according to Whittaker Chambers, four men met in a Washington restaurant. They arrived separately, by prearrangement, and drifted casually to a secluded table well out of earshot of other diners. To their waiter they must have seemed a strangely ill-assorted quartet.

There was the heavy-set J. Peters, looking like a tame government clerk; Harold Ware, in appearance a cross between professor and racetrack tout; the tall, thin Alger Hiss, correctly dressed, the very model of a rising young government lawyer; and finally Whittaker Chambers—introduced to Hiss as "Carl"—a short, plump young man, uncomfortable in his first white suit. It was Peters, known to the others as the top Communist International representative in America, who took the lead, speaking with a slight foreign accent. The Party, Peters explained, had exciting plans for some of its Washington adherents. A new "apparatus" would be set up, consisting of comrades who seemed to be going places in the government.

Alger Hiss was one such man, he announced. Why waste him on open Party activity, eventually destroying his usefulness by marking him as a Communist? He was to detach himself immediately from Hal Ware's "cell" in the AAA (Agricultural Adjustment Administration) and keep himself henceforth strictly aloof from any left-wing activity. His home must be cleared of all telltale books or pamphlets. Only his comrades in the secret apparatus would know that he was anything but a rather conservative New Dealer. Carl (Chambers) would be his immediate "contact" and superior, whose orders were to be followed without question. This, said Chambers, was when the lines of his own destiny and that of Hiss first crossed. They were to remain entwined, first in the twilight of common underground work and fourteen years later in the blazing limelight of a public drama.

The man Whittaker Chambers was born J. Vivian Chambers in 1901 of mixed Dutch, German, French and English—or briefly, American—stock. Shortly thereafter his family moved from Philadelphia to Lynbrook, then a rural Long Island community. Jay Chambers, his father, a moderately successful commercial artist, was an agnostic. But his mother, Laha Whittaker Chambers, insisted that the children—including Whittaker—be baptized as Episcopalians. In an amorphous atmosphere of genteel culture young Whittaker grew up a quiet, intense boy who lived closely within himself. He had some of his father's vague rebelliousness, clashing with his mother's conservatism. A job in the Lynbrook bank, when he was seventeen, bored him. His mother's insistence that he go to college irritated him. There was a domestic explosion, and he ran away from home.

Under the assumed name of Charles Adams the boy worked for months as a common laborer repairing car tracks in Washington. Then he hitchhiked to New Orleans, where he lived in a miserable dive in the French Quarter. After that he worked his way west as an itinerant laborer. Finally, chastened by his wanderings, he was ready to go to college. It was at Columbia that Whittaker's undefined rebellion began to focus on radical ideas. He was thrust into a group of campus intellectuals, bright, cynical, iconoclastic. The adolescent urge to remake the world seethed within him and found expression in high-pitched poetry and prose. Impatient with collegiate life, he ran away again, with a school chum, this time to Europe. This journey, more than anything else, pushed him into the Communist orbit. To the impressionable young American, Berlin in that summer of 1923 was a paranoid city. If a bushel of marks would not buy a loaf of bread, a cigarette could buy a woman. Communist students surged through the streets intoning the tender Marxist anthem: "Grease the guillotine with the fat of tyrants. . . . Blood, blood, blood must flow!" War-torn France and Belgium only added to his inner despair and left him with a compulsive conviction that he must do something about it all. Returning to New York City, searching desperately for solutions to the world's problems, Chambers resolved to join the Communists.

"No one recruited me," he said, testifying in Washington many years later. "At the crossroads the evil thing, Communism, lies in wait with a simple answer." He sought out a neighborhood branch. In a cold, dirty loft in Hell's Kitchen, Chambers got his first view of the revolution in action. He had expected to find tough-minded and dedicated Leninists but found instead a noisily squabbling group, the dregs of discontent, more concerned with factional battles than revolution. But, refusing to be disillusioned, he plunged hopefully into Party activities, performed the lowly chores exacted of novices and finally landed on the staff of the *Daily Worker*.

In October 1926 his revolutionary zeal was blunted by a personal tragedy. His moody, confused younger brother, Richard, committed suicide. The shock left Whittaker with a kind of paralysis of the will. But ultimately he found release in intensified Communist work. He was appointed foreign editor of the *Worker*. Because the official editor, Robert Minor, was preoccupied with factional struggles, Whittaker in effect ran the paper. As a marked intellectual, however, he was suspect and the target for gibes and intrigue. Eventually he threw over his job in disgust, though retaining Party membership. Having translated the German best seller *Bambi*, he easily obtained another such assignment: Franz Werfel's *Class Reunion*. Meanwhile, he continued to pour out his own poems and short stories. At this time he married Esther Shemitz, whom he had met while covering a textile strike in Passaic, New Jersey, for the *Worker*. She had been one of the strike leaders.

In his love of writing, Chambers might have drifted away from "the movement" had not a Moscow journal, *International Literature*, hailed him as the literary find of 1931 for his short stories in the Communist *New Masses*. Instantly the obedient literary commissars of Union Square made him editor of the *New Masses*. One spring day in 1932 he was called to the phone by a high-level Party functionary. Twenty-four hours later he was in the Communist underground, a Soviet agent—in his own phrase a "faceless man." Chambers was never informed why he had been selected for the role. "You are going into the underground," he was told. "If you refuse, you will be expelled from the Party." Chambers was distressed. He would have preferred to remain an editor. But having preached Bolshevik discipline and sacrifice, he could not flinch from the personal test. After that, none of his Party friends knew what had become of him. He turned into a man of many names and no name, moving about the country as ordered by the Hungarian Peters and other superiors.

As an apprentice spy, his first work was that of courier. Periodically, when German liners docked in New York, Party liaison men met Communist stewards and collected innocent-looking letters and cheap mirrors. These "transmissions" Chambers would carry to secret headquarters. Treated chemically, the letters revealed underground messages written in invisible ink; the backs of the mirrors,

pried open, gave up strips of microfilm. Chambers rose
rapidly in his apparatus by dint of brains and zeal. One
of his tasks was to recruit agents, not only for operations
here but for assignments in foreign lands. With the help
of a literary agent he set up a bogus "feature syndicate"
in Tokyo, for instance, as "cover" for a spy. One time he
traveled to San Francisco, where he delivered a money
belt stuffed with $10,000 to two Russian agents for espio-
nage in the Pacific islands.

Concurrent with his other work, Chambers was soon
given a major assignment, the one that was to fix the
pattern of his life. Moscow, frightened by Hitler's rising
strength, had decided on its famous Trojan-horse policy.
It was beginning to organize that worldwide seduction of
liberals misnamed the Popular Front. Washington, feverish with the fresh and honest ardors of the New Deal,
ranked high on its targets. To begin unlocking the doors
for the Trojan horse in the U.S.A., Chambers met Peters
in the national capital and conferred with Harold Ware.
It was at this rendezvous that he first heard the names of
the dynamic young radicals in government service whom
Ware had already forged into a Party "cell," among
them, said Chambers, Alger Hiss. The year was 1934.

Alger Hiss was born in 1904, the fourth child of a deter-
minedly middle-class family in Baltimore. His father was
a fairly well-to-do dry-goods merchant, and Alger's problems were not primarily economic. There were unsettling
events in his life which could have colored his outlook.
When he was two and a half, his father slashed his own
throat with a razor. Many years later one of his sisters
committed suicide. Yet, by and large, Alger lived the life
of a normal Baltimore boy. At Johns Hopkins University,
his quiet good looks and indefatigable charm made him a

favorite with students and faculty alike. He was a great joiner—taking part in a socially superior fraternity, the campus paper, dramatics, college politics. In 1926 the senior class voted him the "most popular," the "best all around," the "best handshaker."

From college he moved on to Harvard Law School. Ambitious, keen and hardworking, he stood out among the brilliant young men in his class. His teachers included men like Felix Frankfurter and Francis B. Sayre, and Hiss absorbed their embattled liberalism. Among his classmates were Lee Pressman—destined to become a pro-Communist big wheel—and others who affected a kind of Fabian socialism that Alger found congenial. Graduating *cum laude*, he stepped into one of the most coveted jobs open to a Harvard lawyer. On the recommendation of Frankfurter he was made secretary to the great Supreme Court Justice, Oliver Wendell Holmes. Hiss had reason to be pleased by this professorial compliment. He knew that other Frankfurter favorites—Francis Biddle, Tommy Corcoran, Dean Acheson—had risen to eminence.

But fate was to deflect the course of Alger's career. It took the form of Priscilla Fansler Hobson, a primly attractive, headstrong young divorcee, whom he married in December 1929. Alger's one-year term with Justice Holmes completed, the Hisses moved to Boston and then to New York, where Alger was able to attach himself to the Wall Street firm of Cotton and Franklin.

Socialism attracted Priscilla, and she and her husband began attending political lectures. In 1932 she joined the Socialist Party's Morningside Branch, at that time drifting rapidly into the Communist periphery. But probably the most important consequence of the move to New York was the resumption of a Harvard friendship. Lee Pressman picked up his old ties with Hiss. Pressman was to become a significant national figure—"the Big Brain of the radical wing of the New Deal . . . brilliant, magnetic, domineering," columnist Tris Coffin would call him in December 1948. At this time he was on the legal staff of the Agricultural Adjustment Administration in Washington. He began to fill the division with clever and energetic friends, all destined to rise quickly in the New Deal hierarchy: Nathan Witt, Charles Kramer, John Abt—and Alger Hiss. From the teeming agencies, but mostly from the AAA, Pressman had drawn together a group of like-minded lawyers and administrators galvanized by political ambition and loyalty to himself.

Communist doctrine could be very stimulating in those Depression days. It offered an "inevitable" solution to the world's muddle, backed by a powerful nation, embodied in a "tough" movement that made a fetish of success no matter how ruthlessly achieved. From the Communist outskirts, Chambers later testified, these men were drawn to its miasmic underworld by the timely arrival of Harold Ware, a man with an uncanny soundness of judgment and a tutored devotion to the Soviet Union. Ware was the son of Ella Reeve Bloor—"Mother" Bloor to all Communists. In the early twenties he had organized a Russian-famine-relief society, the first Red front in the U.S.A. As an agricultural expert, he made repeated trips to Russia. He married Jessica Smith, editor of *Soviet Russia Today*.

On his last journey to Moscow, Ware was aligned with the new Trojan-horse strategy. Like all Comintern agents, he was ordered to create Communist cells wherever possible. Because of his seven-year tenure (1925–32) as a dollar-a-year man for the Agriculture Department, he was assigned to operations in Washington. The idea—at first—was not espionage but infiltration: the faithful must

win the confidence of those who directed government
policy. Specifically it was Ware's task to seek out service-
able Party material from the wilderness of confused liberalism and set up a master cell. In the fulfillment of that
assignment he found the Agriculture Department coterie
invaluable, a ready-made nucleus. So well did he do his
job that when he was killed in an automobile accident in
1935, Mother Bloor could declare in pride: "I find his
boys and girls everywhere. It's my comfort."

Ware's efforts were not limited to Agriculture. In time
he set up at least half a dozen other cells, each counting
from seven to ten carefully selected comrades. And it was
he, according to Chambers' testimony, who first realized
the potentialities of Alger Hiss. With great astuteness, he
is said to have permitted the young lawyer to remain a
silent partner, kept above suspicion. From AAA, Hiss
moved in as counsel to the Nye Committee, investigating
the munitions industry, then briefly to the Justice Department's legal staff. It was shortly before this, in the summer
of 1934, said Chambers, that Ware, acting on orders from
J. Peters, brought Hiss together with Chambers at the
restaurant meeting already described.

Alger and Carl (as Chambers then called himself)
became very good friends. Chambers, a middle-class intellectual himself, liked Hiss's agile mind. Moreover, like
most underground workers, he felt contempt for the
"safe" Communist. Though Hiss was coldly calculating,
not emotion-motivated like himself, Chambers saw in
him another bold Bolshevik. Carl saw the Hisses at least
once a month, sometimes as often as once a week. He
introduced Mrs. Chambers to them, under the code name
"Lisa." The two couples soon shared a warm relation-
ship. They discussed Party matters, common interests in

literature, ornithology, their children's schooling. Lisa painted a portrait of Timothy Hobson, Priscilla's son by her earlier marriage; once Priscilla "sat" with the Chambers baby in Baltimore when Lisa had to go to New York.

On their part, the Hisses were proud of the close association with an important Party functionary. When Priscilla chafed over the restraints of hidden Party affiliation, Carl would argue that open activity was minor compared to the important work the Party had assigned to Alger.

Chambers testified later that in this early period Peters brought him together with David Carpenter, a Communist also engaged in secret work in Washington. Through Carpenter, a State Department official named Henry Julian Wadleigh was added to the Chambers ring, as well as Vincent Reno, a mathematician working at the Aberdeen Proving Ground. Wadleigh also testified concerning this. Through George Silverman, research and information director in the U.S. Railroad Retirement Board, Chambers met Harry Dexter White, whom he attached to the apparatus. White was the trusted monetary adviser of Secretary of the Treasury Henry Morgenthau and would later be credited with fathering the Morgenthau plan to pastoralize defeated Germany. Lee Pressman, meanwhile, dropped out of the ring when he left government service in 1935 to become chief counsel for the CIO.

The importance of the Carl (Chambers) group was immense. Each man enlisted became an entering wedge for comrades filtering into once sacrosanct departments and bureaus. For the Party it provided a magnificent patronage machine, for Moscow a wonderful set of eyes and ears in the American government. But to influence policy or slip into official positions had been only a way station. The next stage was espionage. Some who had swallowed Lenin uncritically were enticed into it by the argument that noble ends justify vile means. Alger Hiss, hardheaded, determined, needed no "moral" blandishments. "Hiss always knew perfectly well what he was doing," said Chambers. "He was a thoroughly developed Communist."

Peters was eager to obtain fairly important State Department documents to send to Moscow "as a token of possibilities," to convince his distant chiefs that underground funds could be well spent here. As temporary counsel for the Nye Committee, Hiss was in a position to extract such documents. A little doubtfully, Chambers suggested the scheme, and Hiss readily agreed. The papers were forthwith requested "by the Nye Committee," photographed by Chambers with a Leica in the Hiss apartment and transmitted to Moscow. The success of this gambit delighted Peters. Soon Chambers was feeding the cream of such secret materials, as well as data purloined by Wadleigh, White and others, to a Russian contact in New York known to him only as "Bill."

Carl's group, of course, was only one of several— "parallel apparatuses," in the technical phrase. In the interest of safety they were kept strictly apart. Only once did Chambers collide with another ring. That was when Hiss tried to draw in a "sympathetic" State Department official, Noel H. Field. Field informed him that he was being recruited by another underground agent, a Mrs. Hede Massing, whose first husband had been the famous Comintern agent Gerhart Eisler. To adjust the conflict, Hiss met Mrs. Massing for dinner at Field's home. She made clear her intention to hold on to Field, whom she had been "cultivating" for almost a year. On orders from Chambers, Field was relinquished to the Massing outfit. But the intimate friendship between Hiss and Field persisted at least until 1948, long after Field's espionage involvement was common knowledge.

In September of 1936, Hiss's former law professor Francis Sayre invited him to become his assistant in the trade-agreements division of the State Department. Intending to turn down the bid, Hiss nevertheless told Carl about it. The latter ordered him to accept. His presence in the highly sensitive American foreign office would be invaluable to Russia. The late Hal Ware, a good judge of character, had picked a winner in Alger. At this time J. Peters turned Chambers over to a Colonel Boris Bykov, an important NKVD (Soviet secret police) agent. Bykov was a small, red-headed man, with saturnine features and a brutally sardonic manner. From their first meeting, Chambers hated him but, as a disciplined Bolshevik, followed his orders.

His own major job by now had fallen into a pattern. He collected documents from his agents, photographed them and transmitted the films to Bykov. Hiss's materials he picked up at weekly or ten-day intervals at Alger's home, now in fashionable Georgetown and, ironically, opposite a police station. Transferring them to his own briefcase, he would rush to Baltimore, where they were microfilmed at his home. By midnight Chambers would be back in Washington, and the following morning Hiss would return the originals to the files. After a time, as the volume and importance of Alger's contributions grew, it was decided to reduce the risks by having the documents copied on a typewriter, the copies then being photographed. In this way the originals did not have to pass through another set of hands. The suggestion came from Bykov, and Priscilla agreed to do the typing.

Soon after taking charge of the ring, Bykov informed Chambers that he wanted to pay the Washington boys.

This was not generosity. In accepting money they would be more deeply incriminated. Chambers opposed the plan, insisting that White, Hiss and the others were "idealists" who would be horrified by a cash offer. "Very well," Bykov smiled, "we will buy them some rugs and tell them they were made by the hands of the Soviet workers." Chambers later testified that in December 1936 he got a friend in New York to purchase four rugs and ship them for distribution to George Silverman, who had been in contact with Harry Dexter White of the State Department. Silverman kept one for himself, gave one to Harry White and passed another on to Carpenter for Wadleigh. The fourth rug Chambers delivered to Hiss. Thus for over a year Chambers continued to drain some of America's most precious diplomatic and military secrets through his inside agents. But though he had tried to wall in his Leninist faith against the assaults of conscience and reason, in the end doubts beset him. His convictions were shaken—and finally destroyed.

For the honest Communist there comes a time when he must come to grip with doubts that have been put aside but not quieted. What follows is a dark night of the soul. He emerges from the struggle cold and cynical, his moral scruples atrophied—or he experiences a complete revulsion. Whittaker Chambers reached that crisis in 1937. He had closed his eyes to such crimes as the "liquidation" of the kulaks and the man-made famine that took millions of Russian peasant lives, as harsh means to good ends. But the Moscow purge trials forced him to confront his conscience. If the fathers of the Soviet state, almost without exception, had been traitors as charged, something was wrong with Communism. If the trials were a frame-up, something was wrong with the Soviet state. The impact of these conclusions shook him to his depths. Eventually he became certain "that Communism is a form of totalitarianism, that its triumph means slavery and spiritual night to the human mind and soul."

He knew it would be suicide just to announce, "I'm quitting." If he were to "disappear," no one would be the wiser. He needed time for a threefold task. He must hide himself and his family from the wrath of Moscow. He must reestablish his identity in the world as Whittaker Chambers. Most important, he must devise some form of "life insurance" to make his death more dangerous to the Party than his survival. To establish his identity, he obtained from Longmans, Green & Company another book to translate. Now if he disappeared, the publisher would make inquiries. Furthermore, he convinced Peters that he needed a government post as cover for his Washington activities. Within twenty-four hours of applying for it, he had a boondoggling job in the WPA, where he remained on the payroll, as J. V. Chambers, until a few weeks before his final break. In November 1937 he also borrowed $400 from the Hisses to buy a secondhand car—for his planned flight.

He already had a pretty good hideout. In driving through Maryland with Alger Hiss, in 1936, they had come across a small farm near Westminster. Hiss put up a deposit on it but later decided not to buy it. Some time after this Chambers had secretly purchased the place. As for "life insurance," his best hope, he figured, would be concrete evidence of the ring's existence and spying. If, as he feared, the Russians should kidnap his wife or children, at least he would possess some bargaining power. So, in the following months, he retained copies of many microfilmed documents. He also saved five long memoranda written by Harry Dexter White and four short ones in the handwriting of Alger Hiss. He did not keep these as potential evidence against Hiss, as was widely believed in subsequent years, but as evidence against his Soviet superiors.

By April 1938 he was ready for the terrifying break. Having picked up the last batch of State Department papers transcribed by Priscilla, he had them microfilmed. Then, instead of going to New York, he gathered up his family and installed them in an isolated shack he had rented about four miles outside Baltimore. After making sure he had not been followed, Whittaker made a trip to New York with a bulky package of the documents, memos and films he had accumulated. This he delivered to his wife's nephew, Nathan Levine.

"Put it in a safe place," he told him. "If anything happens to me, give it to Esther. . . . If anything happens to both of us, open the package. You're a lawyer, you'll know what to do." Nathan Levine stowed the manila envelope in the shaft of a blocked-up dumbwaiter in his mother's home in Brooklyn—and forgot all about it.

Chambers then drove his family to Daytona Beach, Florida, where they hid for another month. By day, Whittaker slept while Esther kept watch. At night, he remained on guard. Believing that at least temporarily he had eluded the NKVD, he drove back to Westminster, Maryland, stopping on the way to buy a shotgun. On the farm he continued to live like a hunted man, he recounted later, "sleeping by day and watching through the night with gun or revolver within easy reach. That was what underground Communism could do to one man in peaceful America in the year 1938."

Just before Christmas he faced up to another moral challenge: what to do about friends still in the ring. "It always seemed to me proper that they should have a chance to break away themselves," he explained much later. Despite the risk, he came out of hiding to make the attempt. With Harry White the effort was perfunctory; his loyalty to the cause made Chambers' words futile. But Alger was another matter, for Chambers considered him "the closest friend I ever had in the Communist Party." At the Hiss home on Volta Place the discussion was long and intense—but both Priscilla and Alger remained adamant in their Communist faith. There were tears in Alger's eyes when they parted.

Early in 1939 Whittaker looked up an old friend, an editor on *Time*, and was hired as a writer, thus picking up the career he had dropped in 1932. Almost a year having passed since his defection from Communism, he felt he could rejoin the community of free men with reasonable safety. And though he remained wary of Communist retaliation, he hoped somehow to square the circle: to warn the country against espionage without destroying men who had been his friends.

What followed was perhaps the most bizarre chapter of all. For Chambers—and others—sought to lay this story of Red skulduggery before the American people, and no one would listen! At least three times the Chambers charges were brought to President Roosevelt by men who were the President's friends. Detailed circumstantial evidence linking Hiss and others in government with the Communist underworld reached top State Department officials. Among people who specialized in the Communist problem the basic facts became fairly familiar. But no one in authority took any action.

In May 1939 Chambers hesitantly approached Isaac Don Levine, an anti-Soviet journalist. Levine, who was

then collaborating with General Walter Krivitsky on the
latter's revelations of Soviet espionage in Europe and
America, brought the two men together. Continuously for
twenty hours the ex-spies talked their hearts out. It was
the talkfest which determined Chambers to tell his tale
to the authorities. But the clincher was the Hitler-Stalin
pact of August 24, 1939. He realized in horror that henceforth the Gestapo, too, would have access to the information gathered by Communist spies in the United States.

Chambers was ready for a full revelation, but only to
the one man with full power of drastic action, the President of the United States. Marvin H. McIntyre, the
Presidential secretary, was approached. He was friendly
but suggested that Levine first speak to Assistant Secretary
of State Adolf A. Berle, Jr., then in charge of State Department security. On September 2 Chambers and Levine
dined with Berle at his Washington residence. Hitler had
invaded Poland the day before, Britain and France were
momentarily expected to declare war. Against this lurid
background the former spy told his story to a high official
who was a confidant of the President. Berle, visibly agitated, made copious notes. Even before his guests were
out of the room he picked up the telephone, apparently
to call the White House.

Chambers returned to his desk at *Time*, confident that
quick action would follow. The statute of limitations that
later would shield him and former colleagues did not yet
apply. He waited to be arrested, along with the whole kit
and caboodle of agents still in the government. He waited
in vain. Berle did go to the President and was told, in
effect, to go jump in the lake. In his eventual testimony
before the Un-American Activities Committee (August
30, 1948), Berle attested that he was greatly "worried" by
Alger's "pro-Russian point of view" and "pretty con-

sistent leaks whenever anything went through that
[Hiss's] office." He "checked on the two Hiss boys" with
Dean Acheson and Justice Frankfurter, both of whom
"could vouch for them absolutely." "Schematically, however," Berle testified, "I believed Chambers was telling
the truth as he saw it, so I caused the Department to establish very close relations with the FBI." Inexplicably,
however, Berle did not give the FBI his notes on Chambers' disclosures until four years later.

In any case, having conveyed the facts to the State Department as suggested by the White House secretary,
Chambers did nothing more. But Isaac Don Levine was
not so patient. Realizing that Berle did not—or could
not—effect a housecleaning, he pressed the issue in other
directions. He regards the record of his futile efforts as an
indication of powerful forces blocking a full investigation.
He conferred with Loy Henderson, chief of the Russian
section of the State Department and a staunch anti-Communist. Henderson was powerless to act singlehandedly in
what can only be described as a conspiracy of silence.
Early in 1940 Levine furnished sufficient evidence to
Martin Dies, then chairman of the Un-American Activities Committee, to warrant a full-scale investigation. But
the Dies Committee lacked funds to carry it out.

When William C. Bullitt, former Ambassador to
Russia, heard what both Chambers and Krivitsky had revealed to Levine of Soviet spying in the government, he
went straight to the White House. President Roosevelt
laughed and told him not to worry. Still trying to get action, Levine in March 1941 called on columnist Walter
Winchell at the Roney Plaza Hotel in Miami Beach.
Winchell, aghast, promised to take the facts to the President. According to his own subsequent statement, he
promptly did so. Another journalist, Will Allen, then

labor editor on the Washington *Daily News*, stumbled on
the information independently. While working on an
exposé of Red infiltration in government, he heard about
Chambers and cornered him.

"What's the good of telling you what I know?" Chambers asked. "You won't be able to do anything with it."

By way of test, he gave Allen the names of "four NKVD
men now operating in Washington." Delighted, Allen
hastened to pass the four names to the FBI, which, to his
surprise, was dubious. "You'll have to clear this with the
State Department," he was told. Luckily the security official at State was a friend of his. Without revealing his
source, Allen told him about the four Soviet operatives.

The friend smiled. "I see you've been talking to Whittaker Chambers," he said. Then he added, "You might as
well forget about the whole thing, Will. The Department
doesn't want those men arrested. Knock them out of the
picture and the Russians will send four more." So Allen
never got the big story for his paper.

In 1944 another reporter obtained a copy of a confidential FBI report which linked Hiss and twenty-one
others. He learned that the report had been submitted to
the State Department in 1943 but that it had been ignored. Thus for nine years the Chambers revelations were
kicked around, made table conversation in many a Washington home, were hinted at in anti-Communist periodicals. But the government did nothing, and some of the
names involved remained on Uncle Sam's payrolls.

The public and private lives of Hiss and Chambers,
once they had taken separate ways, were similar in two
respects only. Each man rose to great heights in his chosen
profession—and each hugged a secret which eventually
would destroy his brilliant career.

Chambers' rise in the *Time-Life* organization was, in its own way, as spectacular as that of Hiss in government service. His repeated warnings against Stalinists were brushed off as eccentricities, but no one could minimize his abilities. Even in so stylized a magazine as *Time*, his writings stood out. Slowly but steadily he climbed in the shifting hierarchy of the publication, until he attained a rung near the top as senior editor at $30,000 a year. Eventually he was able to buy a three-hundred-acre Maryland farm not far from his old one. His past caught up with him only casually. Not until 1943 was he visited by FBI agents. He told them part, though far from all, of his story. "You interest me greatly," one of the agents said. Nearly two years passed before there was any evidence of this interest. In 1945 the Bureau sent another man with a photo of Peters for Chambers to identify. Thereafter the FBI bothered him only when it needed information on specific Communists.

From the moment of his break with Communism, Chambers had felt the need for religion. For a while he renewed his baptismal Episcopalian faith. But he was moving gradually toward Quakerism, the religion of his grandmother. And in 1941 he became a Friend. His acceptance of a Quaker philosophy is crucial in this narrative. It was to be a strong force in guiding his subsequent actions. An uncompromising enemy of Communism, he yet felt bound to respect the human beings involved in it. When the test came he would choose deliberately to withhold evidence of espionage to shield Hiss, White and the others—and thus commit perjury.

"My purpose," he would explain to a jury, "had been to destroy and paralyze the Communist conspiracy in the government. At the same time I wished to do as little injury as possible to the human beings involved. . . . In my own case, I had been given time to work out a new life. I wanted to give these people the same opportunity I had."

So Chambers initiated no further move to expose Hiss, as he watched the man's phenomenal rise to power. And by 1939 Alger was definitely on his way. In that year Francis B. Sayre left the State Department to become high commissioner of the Philippines. Sayre consulted his assistant about a legal adviser in the new post. Glowingly Hiss recommended Noel Field, then with the League of Nations in Geneva and neck-deep in the Soviet spy network. Alger's next job in the Department was as assistant in the vital Far Eastern Division.

Shortly after becoming Assistant Secretary of State in 1941, Dean Acheson requested Donald Hiss, Alger's brother, as an aide. Berle was sufficiently disturbed to warn him about the Hiss brothers, pointing out that his information was "unconfirmed." Questioned, Donald denied he had any Red associations, whereupon Acheson told Berle "the matter was closed." The same year the FBI made a check of Alger Hiss under the Hatch Act. By 1942, when Hiss got another promotion, there was no longer need to be touchy on the Communist question. Uncritical acceptance of Russia after she became an ally was virtually official. Creation of the Office of Special Political Affairs in 1944—a sensitive and key area—was another stepping-stone for Hiss. Within seven months he was its assistant director, and later director.

In August of 1944 Hiss served as executive secretary of the Dumbarton Oaks conference. With Cordell Hull, Harry Hopkins and others he worked on the first draft of the United Nations charter. On succeeding Hull, Edward Stettinius found Alger's quick, retentive mind invaluable.

Thanks to his good opinion, Hiss was appointed a Presidential adviser and in that capacity attended the fateful Yalta conference. According to his own statement he "to some extent" helped formulate the Yalta agreement. Certainly by the mute testimony of the telephone directory published for the American delegation his status was impressive. At a meeting so star-studded with top figures—General Marshall, Admiral King, Stettinius, Hopkins, etc.—protocol was important. President Roosevelt's phone number was "1." Alger Hiss's was "4." When the conference adjourned, Hiss had been approved by the Big Three as general secretary of the upcoming San Francisco conference. At that historic gathering a few months later he proved that he was an organizational wonder.

But there were grumblings too. The American Federation of Labor accused Hiss of favoring the then Communist-infested CIO and charged that the U.N. was being used to promote the Soviet-dominated World Federation of Trade Unions, conceived in San Francisco. So pressing were these rumors that Stettinius, according to Senator Vandenberg, summoned some members of the American delegation to reassure them in the matter. Hiss even survived an indirect but unmistakable accusation by Igor Gouzenko, the Russian who had exposed the Soviet atomic-espionage ring in Canada. A fifty-one-page report for the use of sensitive Washington departments, in November 1945, included some startling information. Interviewed by the FBI and Canadian police, Gouzenko referred to four spy rings operating in the U.S.A. Moreover, he "stated that he had been informed by Lieutenant Kulakov in the office of the Soviet military attaché that the Soviets had an agent in the United States in May 1945 who was an assistant to the Secretary of State, Edward R. Stettinius."

Hiss, of course, had been Stettinius' assistant in Yalta, and the only assistant ever accused of Communist involvement. The most casual investigation would have turned up Berle's notes. But again nothing happened. Early in March 1946 Secretary of State Byrnes was tipped off that Hiss might be mentioned as a Communist in Senate attacks on the secret concessions made at Yalta. He summoned Hiss and asked point-blank, "Are you a Communist, Mr. Hiss?" He got a point-blank denial. Nevertheless, on Byrnes's suggestion, Hiss contacted the FBI. There he denied—though the FBI from its own files knew he was not telling the truth—that he had ever been associated with individuals or organizations which "might lend credence" to charges against him.

Hiss had now been sounded out by John Foster Dulles about becoming president of the Carnegie Endowment for International Peace, at $20,000 a year. Acheson agreed to release him. Even before Alger assumed this office, Dulles received urgent warnings on his Communism. Dulles telephoned Hiss, who contrived to set Dulles' mind at ease. He had "particularly" and "specifically checked" with Mr. Byrnes about the rumors, he explained, and the Secretary had told him they had been "laid to rest." There had been no such direct check. More significant in explaining Mr. Dulles' later testimony against Hiss, the new Carnegie president did not mention that he had been under periodic FBI investigation, that he had been the subject of a quiet Congressional scrutiny and that Byrnes himself had been alarmed by reports that would not down. On Alger's withdrawal from the government, *The Christian Science Monitor* could state: "More than one Congressman, whenever the subject of leftist activity in the State Department was mentioned, pulled out a list of suspects that was invariably headed by Mr. Hiss."

For all his surface calm, Hiss must have known that his fate was in the balance. In May 1947 the FBI called on him again to inquire whether he was a Communist—and if he knew Whittaker Chambers. Then, in February 1948, the noose tightened. Dulles, unable to ignore further the piled-up stories, "searchingly questioned" Hiss. Along with the usual denials, Hiss now admitted that he had been subpoenaed and interrogated by the federal grand jury probing espionage. He "reassured" Dulles that it was merely a "routine appearance." But time was running out for both the president of the Carnegie foundation and the senior editor of *Time*. One day newspaper headlines blazoned the confession of a former Russian spy, Elizabeth Bentley. The eleventh hour had struck.

The Depression was at its worst when Elizabeth Bentley, daughter of an old and conservative Connecticut family, graduated from Vassar in 1930. In postgraduate studies at Columbia she fell in with an active group of Communists and in March 1935 joined the Communist Party. In time she was ordered to destroy her Party card and enter the Communist underworld. Thereafter her contact with the movement would be solely through a mysterious "John." For a long time she was unaware that John was Jacob Golos, a Russian, president of World Tourists, Inc., or that this "respectable travel agency" was a front for Soviet spy operations.

Miss Bentley became courier and intermediary for the immense network of Washington spies. Her main contact, she later testified, was Nathan Gregory Silvermaster, who was with the Farm Security Administration. She visited him every two weeks and carried back to New York the material gathered by his ring. Much later she began picking up documents from the ring which she testified was headed by Victor Perlo, a Chambers alumnus. In all, she was the go-between for Russia with about twenty people in two groups and about ten more free-lance individual contacts. The material grew so voluminous that she had to carry it in a shopping bag. All this time, though she was betraying her country, she just "didn't think about it." But a turning point came with the sudden death of Golos, on Thanksgiving Day 1943, in her own apartment. She had been devoted to him. Now—though she continued her espionage—as she put it, "the effect of Golos was wearing off." Sensing a growing cynicism in her, Russian superiors tried to buy her off with offers of fat presents. Threats were added to blandishments. "Nobody ever leaves the service," she was warned by Anatol Gromov, first secretary of the Russian Embassy.

After wrestling with an aroused conscience, Miss Bentley in late August 1945 went to the FBI. The names she recited staggered her questioners: a White House adviser, a high Treasury official, a State Department employe, etc. Wary that she might be a "plant," they refused to take her seriously. For months she lived in frustrated suspense, despairing because no one seemed to believe her. Finally the FBI decided to put her to a test. She must return to the network and bring concrete evidence of her story. Reluctantly she consented. In October she notified the FBI that she had an appointment with Gromov. Apparently he, too, was testing her. On the deserted Hudson River docks he pressed her to incriminate herself by accepting money. In the end she accepted it. Gromov could not know that this transaction was witnessed by FBI agents or that his envelope, containing $2000, landed in an FBI safe.

Eighteen months after she had gone to the FBI, the government decided to move. With the approval of

President Truman, a federal grand jury was secretly empaneled on March 27, 1947, to hear Miss Bentley and to question the people she named. She began a piecemeal recital of her long activities. The jury, meeting for a few hours weekly, issued dozens of subpoenas. Interesting—and puzzling—is the fact that Alger Hiss was called but Whittaker Chambers, whose accusations were well known to the FBI, was not. With few exceptions the witnesses refused to talk, on the grounds that they might incriminate themselves. Veiled stories about the secret investigation began to appear in the press. Quite suddenly, in April 1948, Federal Attorney John F. X. McGohey was called into the proceedings. Evidently the Justice Department at this point—a Presidential election was in the offing—chose to shift emphasis. The espionage angle was forgotten and McGohey began to prepare an indictment of the Communist Party leaders under the Smith Act. The changeover was an open secret among newspapermen. The more cynical among them took it as a face-saving device or, worse, a tacit whitewash. To Miss Bentley, who for a year had given almost continuous testimony concerning espionage, the new turn came as a stunning shock. She sought out a reporter of the New York *World-Telegram*. As long as she was under subpoena there was little any newspaper could do. But sixteen months after it convened to probe espionage, the grand jury handed down an indictment against twelve members of the American Communist "Politburo."

If it had not been for the American press, the Bentley story—and the Chambers story which it accidentally opened up—might have been dead and forgotten. Under the joint by-lines of Nelson Frank and Norton Mockridge, the New York *World-Telegram* now published the ex-spy's startling information. The long-dormant Un-

American Activities Committee thereupon leaped to secure her testimony. On July 31, 1948, she took the stand, and her disclosures rocked the nation.

First on the Bentley list of confederates in the government was Silvermaster. Other names came thick and fast. Several of them—Silverman, Kramer, John Abt, Harry White—had been mentioned by Chambers. The Committee began summoning the men listed. Their behavior quickly fell into a pattern. Each denounced the Committee, made a flat over-all denial of charges, but on point-blank questions retired behind the Constitution: "I refuse to answer on the grounds of self-incrimination."

Harry Dexter White had been named in the past by Chambers, now by Bentley. In 1942 he had been casually listed in a Civil Service Commission report as a "known Communist." He had been charged with Communism on the floor of Congress in 1945. Of the people named by Chambers and Bentley, almost half were his friends and people whom he had employed. But he now professed that he knew no Communists and was wholly guiltless. A few days after his interrogation he died of an old heart ailment—and his death was promptly blamed by some upon the Committee.

Chambers had not been mentioned in the Bentley uproar. But Ed Nellor, Washington correspondent of the New York *Sun*, recalled having heard a version of his story. He urged the Committee to call Chambers. On August 2, 1948, Whittaker learned that a subpoena had been issued for him. "I'd always feared I'd have to cross this bridge," he told his friend and colleague at *Time-Life*, John Chamberlain, "but I hoped not to." Chamberlain has written: "The popular picture of Chambers rushing to Washington to 'get' Hiss just doesn't square with his behavior." In fact he was distressed and unhappy. In the New House Office Building, on August 3, 1948, Whittaker Chambers at last told his story in public.

"Almost nine years ago," he declared, "I went to Washington and reported to the authorities what I knew about infiltration in the United States government by Communists. . . . At that moment in history, I was one of the few men on this side of the battle who could perform this service." Then, having described his entry into the Party, he came to the underground group. Its Washington head at first, he said, was Nathan Witt, an attorney for the National Labor Relations Board. Later, John Abt took charge. Lee Pressman had been a member of this group, as he himself later testified in 1950 before the House Un-American Activities Committee, though he did not name Hiss. Chambers named Donald and Alger Hiss. (Donald Hiss later denied his part under oath.) Its purpose at the time was primarily "the Communist infiltration of the American government; but espionage was certainly one of its eventual objectives." Consciously, carefully, Chambers avoided the charge that any of these people had engaged in spying.

So far, Hiss was still a minor character in the drama. His name had been mentioned only in passing, along with half a dozen others. This was on Tuesday. By Wednesday the hue and cry against Chambers for "smearing" Hiss and Harry White had begun. Both men had powerful friends in government and press. Here started the fiction that a vindictive Chambers had sought the limelight by irresponsibly accusing prominent officials.

On August 5, Alger Hiss, a slim, smiling man of forty-three, took the stand amid cameras and klieg lights. With the exception of White and a very few others, he was the only topflight witness who did not hide behind Constitutional privilege. Instead he went on the offensive.

"I am not and never have been a member of the Communist Party," he attested. "To the best of my knowledge none of my friends is a Communist." So far as he knew, he had "never laid eyes" on Chambers but "should like to do so. . . . the statements made about me by Mr. Chambers are complete fabrications. I think my record in the government speaks for itself." Shown photos of Chambers, he failed completely to recognize the man. There seemed to be no question about the subversive activities of six others named by Chambers, said Representative Mundt; he wondered "what possible motive a man who edits *Time* magazine would have for mentioning Alger Hiss in connection with those other six."

"So do I, Mr. Chairman." Alger smiled as he said it.

By the time the hearing ended, most Committee members except Richard Nixon were busy making amends to Hiss for the inconvenience. In executive session the same afternoon they were inclined to drop the case. Only Nixon objected strenuously. "I felt," he said afterward, "that Hiss was much too careful a witness. . . . I noted that throughout his testimony he never once said, 'I have never known Whittaker Chambers.' He always insisted on using the qualifying phrase, 'I have never known a man by the name of Whittaker Chambers.'"

So Nixon insisted that a subcommittee go immediately to New York to question Chambers. "Let's get him to tell us everything he knows about Alger Hiss. Then we can see whether his story is a fabrication or not."

The effect of Hiss's denials had been electric. The cry of "Red-baiting," somewhat stilled since the cold war began, was again heard in "liberal" circles. The President's charge that it was all a "red herring" to cover up the sins of Congress sounded plausible. But, unruffled by the turmoil, Nixon was prodding the two men. His sub-

committee met with Chambers on Saturday, August 7.
True, the witness said, Hiss and the others had known
him only as "Carl." But Alger was a Party member; he
had paid his own and Priscilla's dues regularly through
Chambers. Most important, Chambers showed an intimate, detailed knowledge of the Hiss family, their homes,
their intimate nicknames, the makes and looks of their
cars. He had stayed at the Hiss home for as long as a week
at a time—it had been his informal Washington headquarters. They had a cocker spaniel, were amateur bird
watchers: "I recall once they saw, to their great excitement, a prothonotary warbler."

Chambers described an old Ford Hiss had possessed
before acquiring a Plymouth and told how Alger had
insisted that "the car be turned over to the open Party so
it could be of use to some poor organizer in the West or
somewhere." Much against Chambers' and Peters' better
judgment, he was finally permitted to make the transfer,
through a local car dealer. "Would you be willing to
submit to a lie detector on this testimony?" Nixon suddenly asked. "Yes, if necessary," Chambers replied.

Nine days elapsed between this session and Hiss's second appearance before the Committee, now in secret
session. In the interval investigators feverishly tried to
check statements of simple fact in Chambers' testimony
and in instance after instance he was corroborated. In
addition, Nixon visited him twice on the Westminster
farm. "I realized in my conversations with him," Nixon
has told the authors, "that when he discussed Hiss he
was talking about a man he knew rather than a man
whose life he had studied."

On the afternoon of August 16 Hiss arrived with a
slight chip on his shoulder. Nixon began by summarizing
the purpose of the session: to determine which of the two

men was a perjurer. Picking up two pictures of Chambers, he asked the witness whether he could identify them in any way. The witness was voluble if not forthright. "Actually the face has a certain familiarity," he conceded. "It is not, according to the photograph, a very distinctive face. I would like very much to see the individual. . . ."

When the questioning turned to details mentioned by Chambers, Hiss began to bargain and to argue. He feared that his accuser might learn of the answers and use them to bolster his claims, he explained at immense length. Presented with another photo of Chambers, he muddied confusion with a double negative: "The face is definitely not unfamiliar." But suddenly he took a new tack. He had cudgeled his brains, he said, as to who could have known details of his private life. "I have written a name on this pad in front of me," he said, "of a person whom I knew in 1933 or 1934, who not only spent some time in my house but sublet my apartment. . . . I do not recognize the photographs as possibly being this man. If I hadn't seen the morning papers with an account of statements that he knew the inside of my house, I don't think I would have thought of this name."

But still he refused to give details about the "subletting." Congressman Hébert intervened. "Up to a few minutes ago you have been very open, very coöperative," he said. "Now you have hedged. . . . Mr. Chambers did not have any indication as to the questions we were going to ask him, and we probed for hours. . . . He could not have possibly by the farthest stretch of imagination prepared himself to answer because he did not know where the questions were coming from. . . ."

The name on his pad, Hiss finally revealed, was George Crosley—a free-lance writer who had come to him for information, a man with "very bad teeth," who had stayed in his home several times and even sublet his apartment. He had "sold him an automobile," Hiss volunteered, "an old, old Ford we had kept for sentimental reasons." Having already bought a Plymouth, he did not need the Ford. Then he amended the statement—not exactly sold but thrown in free with the apartment lease, the rent for which "Crosley," being "a sort of deadbeat," never paid. No, he had not given title to the car, "just simply turned it over to him." Almost casually he added: "He gave me a payment on account once. He brought a rug which he said some wealthy patron gave him. I have still got the damned thing."

Further interrogation extracted startling, point-by-point corroboration of many of the details provided by Chambers: the family nicknames, the vacations, the cocker spaniel, even the prothonotary warbler. Moreover, Hiss recalled having driven "Crosley" to New York. He would not as yet say positively, however, that "Crosley" was Chambers.

Toward the windup Nixon asked whether the witness would be willing to take a lie-detector test, apprising him that Chambers had consented to do so. Alger's answer was long and oblique. He discussed the pros and cons of the instrument and questioned its scientific accuracy. In the end, without saying no, he declined to say yes.

At this point Robert Stripling, chief Committee investigator, raised a disconcerting point. Was it reasonable, he asked, that so acute a man as Hiss could have associated closely with so many notorious pro-Communists without having the slightest idea of their politics? As the hearing ended, the big curtain line for the press was there: Hiss and Chambers would be brought face to face.

Fortified by Hiss's lame recollection that he had perhaps known Chambers as George Crosley, the Commit-

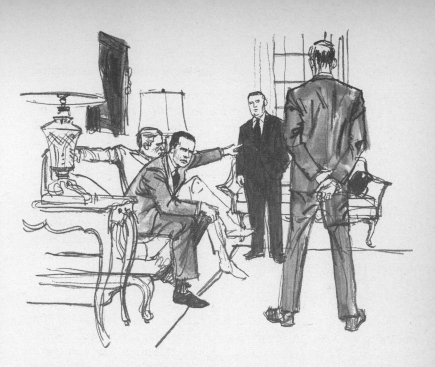

tee decided to move quickly. At 5:35 p.m. on August 17, in Room 1400 of the Commodore Hotel in New York, the great confrontation scene began. A highly perturbed Alger made his greeting and stated: "I would like the record to show that on my way downtown from my up-town office I learned from the press of the death of Harry White, which came as a great shock to me, and I am not sure that I feel in the best mood for testimony."

Chambers walked through the front door. Hiss, who had his back to the entrance, did not move or turn his head. Chambers walked around his chair and sat down on a divan opposite. The two men were face to face at last. They were asked to stand up.

Nixon: Mr. Hiss, the man standing here is Mr. Whittaker Chambers. I ask you now if you have ever known that man before.

Hiss: May I ask him to speak? Will you ask him to say something?

Chambers: My name is Whittaker Chambers.

Hiss (approaching Chambers): Would you mind opening your mouth wider? I said, would you open your mouth? You know what I am referring to, Mr. Nixon. Will you go on talking?

Chambers: I am a senior editor of *Time* magazine.

Hiss: May I ask whether his voice, when he testified before, was comparable to this? Or did he talk a little more in a lower key?

Representative John McDowell: I would say it is about the same now as we have heard.

Hiss: Would you ask him to talk a little more? . . . I think he is George Crosley, but I would like to hear him talk a little longer.

Chambers read a passage from *Newsweek*. Hiss listened gravely, then pronounced his scrambled verdict:

> *Hiss:* The voice sounds a little less resonant than the voice that I recall of the man I knew as George Crosley. The teeth look to me as though either they have been improved upon or that there has been considerable dental work done since I knew George Crosley, which was some years ago. I believe I am not prepared without further checking to take an absolute oath that he must be George Crosley.

Chambers declared that he had, in fact, had his upper front teeth fixed in the period since his earlier contacts with Hiss. That, Hiss said, "would tend to substantiate my feeling that he represented himself to me in 1934 or 1935 or thereabout as George Crosley, a free-lance writer of articles for magazines."

But, though "Mrs. Crosley" had stayed at the Hiss home, he did not remember the name of Crosley's wife. He had known the Crosleys for five or six months when he rented the apartment to them; together with their infant child they had camped in the Hiss home from two to four days before taking over the apartment; he had seen Crosley a number of times afterward, including the time Crosley had brought the Hisses a rug.

Stripling: Mr. Hiss, you say that person you knew as George Crosley, the one feature which you must have to check on to identify him is the dentures?

Hiss: May I answer that my own way, rather than just "Yes" or "No"?

Stripling: I certainly gathered the impression, when Mr. Chambers walked in this room and you walked over and examined him and asked him to open his mouth, that you were basing your identification purely on what his upper teeth might have looked like. Now, here is a person that you knew for several months at least. You knew him so well that he was a guest in your home . . . that you gave him an old Ford automobile, and permitted him to use or you leased him your apartment, and in this, a very important confrontation, the only thing that you have to check on is his denture; is that correct? There is nothing else about this man's features which you could definitely say, "This is the man I knew as George Crosley" . . . ?

Alger's answer was typically involved. From the first, he said, he was "struck by a certain familiarity in features." He was not given to "snap judgments or simple, easy statements." He remembered Crosley's bad teeth and wished to check. But he still was "not able to take an oath that this man is George Crosley." Then he was allowed to direct questions to Chambers, who denied subleasing the Hiss apartment but affirmed decidedly that he had lived in it for some weeks. "I was a Communist and you were a Communist," he said at one point. " . . . I was connected with the underground group of which Mr. Hiss was a member. Mr. Hiss and I became friends." His recollection was that he lived in the apartment at least three weeks, having been invited by Alger to do so.

"Mr. Chairman," Hiss thereupon announced, "I don't need to ask Mr. Whittaker Chambers any more questions. I am now perfectly prepared to identify this man as George Crosley." Chambers' admission that he had lived in the Hiss apartment for weeks, Hiss insisted, was what at last enabled him to make the identification "positive." (Of the many people who acknowledged having known Chambers in the underground period, Hiss was the only one who claimed not to recognize him. Pictures show that, except for a little more weight, Whittaker had not changed notably in the intervening years.)

Hiss had begun his testimony with relative calm but had grown more snappy, less tactful, as the hearing proceeded. Suddenly, white-faced with anger, he arose and strode toward Chambers.

"May I say for the record at this point," he burst out, "that I would like to invite Mr. Whittaker Chambers to make those same statements out of the presence of this Committee without their being privileged for suit for libel." Looming threateningly over Chambers, he shouted, "I challenge you to do it, and I hope you will do it damned quickly."

Alger Hiss did not realize that he was self-trapped. The Committee had let him know that Chambers had made some damaging disclosures, and Hiss had tried to pattern an innocent story to guilty facts. But since he did not know just what Chambers had said, he had been forced to work in the dark. He had guessed pretty well, but not well enough. He had forgotten that records existed— apartment leases, bills of sale on cars, etc., and these trivia entangled him hopelessly.

An open session of the Committee followed on August 25. The moment was supercharged with emotion. Hiss, accompanied by counsel, was in a fighting mood, ready to put on a superb exhibition of broken-field running. As he must have suspected, the Committee had used the intervening eight days to check records. It had found that, in all cases where Chambers' story was verifiable, it was corroborated, and where Hiss's counterstory was matched with records, it fell down. Hiss readily admitted that his recollection of dates, with reference to the apartment, the Ford and other matters, had been faulty. He still insisted that he had given the old car *after* he possessed the new one. The Committee thereupon produced sales documents which showed that he had not owned the two cars simultaneously during those months, as he claimed. Then Hiss did a shocking thing, completely out of character. He began denying the record of his previous testimony, revising his memory to fit the new evidence. He was no longer sure he had "thrown in" the car with the lease; perhaps he had given the car to Chambers *after* the "deadbeat" had welshed on the rent—a long time after, that must be it.

Then the revised memory, too, was exploded. A bill of transfer bearing Hiss's signature was introduced showing that the Ford was transferred to the Cherner Motor Company, which in turn transferred it to one William Rosen. (The following day Rosen, before the Committee, declined to "incriminate" himself on the subject of the car and on his membership in the Communist Party.)

As Alger's contradictions and palpable misstatements piled up, the pro-Hiss section began to melt away. If he had lied on so many minor matters, might it not be that he was lying on the major issues? Hiss did not help matters by presenting a long list of questions he wished Chambers to answer: his names, residences, writings; whether he had ever been treated for mental illness, or been convicted of crime. As he listed these questions, Hiss's lawyer began handing out copies to the press. For perceptive listeners it was a combined fishing expedition into Chambers' past and a calculated smear. Whittaker had never been treated for mental illness, had never been arrested. But the questionnaire provoked lurid rumors that echoed through pro-Hiss arguments from then on.

When the session adjourned, it had come to no official conclusion. But, whereas in the first public hearing newsmen and spectators had rushed to shake hands with Hiss, he left this hearing alone, under lowering clouds of suspicion. There the affair might have rested, as futile as the Bentley revelations, had not Chambers dared to court libel as challenged.

Chambers appeared as guest on the "Meet the Press" radio program on August 27. Referring to the Hiss challenge, one of the questioners asked: "Are you willing to say now that Alger Hiss is or ever was a Communist?"

"Alger Hiss was a Communist and may be now."

"Are you prepared to go to court to answer a suit of libel or slander?"

"I don't think Hiss will go to court," Chambers answered.

The newspapers blazoned Chambers' defy. Would Hiss sue? As weeks went by that question built up to a crescendo. Hiss was in a cleft stick. As president of the Carnegie Endowment he was responsible to a conservative group. If he did not sue, it would be taken as tacit admission of guilt. One month after the broadcast Hiss finally filed a $50,000 libel claim in a Baltimore federal court, later raised to $75,000. In mid-November 1948 Chambers had his first pretrial examination.

Back on his farm that night he realized that he had reached another point of crisis. He had sought to destroy Communism without hurting the people who espoused it, and had concealed information to shield them. Yet he also owed a debt of protection to his wife and children. For the first time in ten years he now thought of the "life insurance" he had put up against Communist vengeance. Reluctantly, with a heavy heart, he decided to disinter the evidence of his past. The bewildered nephew, Nathan Levine, had some trouble remembering where he had put the manila envelope. But together they found it, coated with a decade's dust.

"It's a strange thing," Whittaker remarked not long afterward. "But I no longer recalled what was in the package. I thought there were just a few memos in Alger's handwriting. When I saw what I had, I was amazed."

On November 17 he was in the book-lined office of the Hiss attorney, William L. Marbury, for the second pre-trial hearing. Marbury again challenged: "Do you have any documentary proof of your assertions?"

"Only these," said Chambers blandly, laying a thick sheaf of papers on the table. These were copies of forty-seven State Department documents, and four memos in Hiss's handwriting. A poet sitting in the room might have heard faintly the flapping wings of the Furies. The simple fact, obscured by thousands of pages of evidence and hundreds of irrelevant issues, is that Chambers had been compelled by a libel suit to reveal clinching proofs of espionage. His previous denials under oath that he had such proofs were all the perjuries he had committed.

The judge sitting on the case and both sets of lawyers, having examined the documents, decided at this point that the Justice Department should be called in. The papers were turned over to Alexander Campbell, chief of the Criminal Division, and everyone concerned was pledged to secrecy. A few days later the grand jury which had been sitting in New York was ordered to reconvene December 8. But there were rumors and leaks—enough of them to cause a top-notch reporter, Bert Andrews of the New York *Herald Tribune*, to alert Representative

Nixon, on a ship bound for a Central American vacation. His cable alluded to a "new bombshell . . . indications that Chambers has produced new evidence," and asked whether the Committee would reopen the case.

On Nixon's cabled request, Stripling hastened to see Chambers, who conceded only that he had in fact withheld evidence from the Committee. This was enough for Nixon. He commandeered a Coast Guard plane to fly him back to the capital. Chambers was served a subpoena calling for all documents in his possession. That night Committee agents followed Chambers' car up a long, winding approach to his farm. By the light of the electric bulb on the back porch they noted that a number of squash lay with their necks pointing to a pumpkin. "Here's what you're looking for," Chambers said. From the hollowed-out pumpkin came three rolls of microfilm in metal cylinders.

Prowlers had been near the farm and Chambers had decided on a unique hiding place. "The pumpkin," he said afterward, "was the last flare-up of my conspiratorial nature." He could not guess that hostile commentators would guffaw about the "pumpkin papers," as if ridicule could make the damning evidence evaporate. Carefully developed at the Veterans' Administration laboratory, the prints made a pile over four feet high—this in addition to the documents already in the hands of the Justice Department. Nixon and his colleagues checked the precious films through Eastman Kodak and learned that they had been manufactured in 1937.

The nationwide excitement forced the Justice Department's hand. The grand jury was summoned for the following day, December sixth, instead of the eighth. Subpoenas were issued to the principals in an effort to forestall their appearance before the Un-American Activities Committee. But Nixon, frankly distrustful of the Justice Department, would not be deterred, and the two investigations unfolded simultaneously. Whatever one may say about the Committee, it was the first to expose what was then the most serious case of espionage in American history.

When the grand jury reconvened, the mere names of the witnesses made news. But the real show began the next day when the House Committee resumed its sessions in Washington. The most damaging testimony against Hiss came from three of his former associates. Sumner Welles made it clear that "under no circumstances whatever" could such documents be removed "for any purpose from the [State] Department." John Peurifoy, chief security officer, testified that removal of the documents would be prima-facie evidence of a purpose detrimental to the U.S.A. The handwritten notes, if taken out of the

Department, he declared, would violate "all the security regulations." And Assistant Secretary Sayre attested that only he, two loyal office secretaries and Hiss had access to the files from which so many of the documents came. Sayre pointed out, moreover, that since some of the documents had been transmitted verbatim in highly confidential codes they would have served as keys to break those codes, an eventuality which he found "indescribably horrible."

Two days later, Henry Julian Wadleigh, a slender, studious-looking man, appeared before the Committee. Though he retired behind the "incrimination" formula, his nervousness led observers to believe he would crack. He did, forty-eight hours later, giving the grand jury a detailed account of how, while in State Department service, he had delivered hundreds of documents to Chambers and David Carpenter for photographing.

While the grand jury tried to extract admissions from recalcitrant witnesses, the FBI was at work digging up evidence. An examination of the Chambers documents revealed that they had been typed on an old-model Woodstock. State Department procurement records showed that no Woodstocks had ever been used in Hiss's office. It was also established that just such a Woodstock had been owned by the Hisses until 1938. But between *a* Woodstock and *the* Woodstock there was a crucial gap. Failing to find the typewriter, the FBI sought letters or papers typed on the Hiss machine at the time of the espionage activities. The Hisses claimed they had no old specimens. One morning, with dramatic suddenness, the FBI turned over to the jury two papers typed by Priscilla in 1937, letters found in the files of an insurance company and a school. Beyond doubt the typefaces and peculiarities matched those of the documents; the Hiss defense would never question this expert finding. That day Chambers resigned his editorship of *Time*, Hiss resigned from the Carnegie foundation post. Their brilliant careers lay in ruins.

Among the witnesses subpoenaed by the grand jury was Mrs. Hede Massing. She testified how, late in 1935, she had met Hiss at the home of Noel Field to settle whether Field should work for Hiss's espionage apparatus or her own. On emerging, she approached Alger in the witness room and pleaded with him to recall that rendezvous. "Very interesting," he said, smiling. "Thank you for coming. No doubt you think you are doing the government a service, but I never saw you before."

The trap ready for springing, Alex Campbell called in Alger and one of his lawyers. "I'm convinced you committed espionage," he told the ex-official. "You've seen Chambers, Wadleigh and others go in and confess. If you do the same, it will go easier with you." Hiss denied everything. Ominously Campbell continued, "I'm also convinced that you committed perjury—"

"What you say doesn't interest me," Hiss interrupted. "I've nothing to confess. I told no lies. I just don't know what you're talking about."

Before the jury, Hiss was asked the familiar questions and made the familiar denials. Moreover, he did not believe he had ever seen Chambers after joining the State Department, although "I cannot swear that I did not see him sometime, say, in the fall of '36. . . ."

"Can you say definitely that you did not see him after January 1, 1937?"

"Yes, I think I can say that," Hiss replied. The perjury trap snapped shut.

Upon being faced with the two hundred pages of typescript copied on his Woodstock, Hiss said quickly: "I am amazed; and until my dying day I shall wonder how Whittaker Chambers got into my home to use my typewriter." The jurors laughed out loud.

In the last hours of its legal life the grand jury handed down an indictment. The statute of limitations prevented espionage charges against Hiss. The jury did the next best thing, charging perjury on two counts. Hiss was accused of lying under oath (1) in denying that he had transmitted copies of secret documents to Chambers, and (2) in claiming that he had not seen Chambers after January 1, 1937. Conviction would thus be tantamount to proven guilt of espionage. The following day a sober-faced Hiss stood before a federal judge and pleaded not guilty on both counts. He was duly photographed and fingerprinted as a condition of bail. In Washington, Congressman Mundt said, "I hope that nobody anywhere will ever refer to this case again as a red herring."

After six postponements dragged out through half a year, the Hiss perjury trial got under way on May 31, 1949. Judge Samuel H. Kaufman, a sharp-faced little man sitting on his first important case, presided. Conducting the government's case was Thomas F. Murphy, six feet four inches and proportionately broad, soft-spoken and deliberate, an outsize mustache shielding a gentle face. The defense battery was commanded by Lloyd Paul Stryker, crop-haired, ebullient, noted as a brilliant cross-examiner.

He would prove, Murphy promised in the opening statement, that Hiss had taken documents wholesale from the State Department and transcribed them in his home for transmittal to Soviet spies. Stryker flamboyantly pictured the virtues and official connections of his client, invoking the shades of Oliver Wendell Holmes and Franklin D. Roosevelt. For contrast he limned Chambers as a "thief . . . moral leper . . . perjurer . . . furtive, secretive, deceptive. . . ."

For several days, under Murphy's guidance, Chambers reiterated his underground Communist career, the defendant's years of collaboration in espionage, and the long intimacy of their two families. He recalled that in November 1937 he had borrowed $400 from Hiss to buy a car. He told how on orders from Colonel Bykov he had given Alger a Bokhara rug in 1937—not in 1935 as claimed. In immense detail he described trips taken with the Hisses and the interiors of their several homes.

When Stryker took up the cross-examination, he was aided by the witness himself. For Chambers was in a penitential mood of self-accusation. Meekly he agreed that as a Communist he had lied and cheated, and that in withholding his proofs of espionage he had repeatedly perjured himself. "Chambers Confesses Perjuries," the press was able to headline the news. But on redirect examination he made clear the why of it. "There are degrees of injury," he said slowly, "and I sought to keep [Mr. Hiss] from the ultimate consequences of what he had done. . . ."

Perhaps the crowning indignity for Chambers was the presence of Dr. Carl A. L. Binger, a psychiatrist friend of the Hisses. He had offered to testify on Chambers' mental state before the grand jury, even before he had observed the man. Now he made copious notes as he stared at Chambers.

Esther Chambers confirmed her husband's account and added dozens of small, domestic memories of past intimacy with Priscilla and Alger. Her toughened hands gave a clue to her present occupation as manager of a three-hundred-acre farm. She spoke softly, but with obvious sincerity. For two days Stryker tried to shout her down. Though she wavered on dates, the body of her testimony—that the Hiss and Chambers families had been close friends—remained undamaged.

Several days were consumed by the reading of documents, one of which was kept from the jury on the request of the State Department. An FBI expert testified categorically that all but one document had come from the Hiss typewriter, that the four memos were in Alger's hand—facts the defense conceded.

The basic story of the Soviet spy ring was corroborated by Henry Julian Wadleigh. Like Hiss, he came from a highly respectable background into government service. "I began to take documents and give them to unauthorized people as soon as I joined the State Department in 1936," specifically to Carpenter and Chambers. But none of the papers in evidence was his; they were "rich finds" and he would have remembered them. He had received a Bokhara rug from Carpenter, he attested, in January 1937. A Washington bank executive testified that Mrs. Hiss had withdrawn $400 on November 19, 1937. An automobile salesman confirmed that Mrs. Chambers bought a car from him four days later, paying $486 in cash. Professor Meyer Schapiro testified to buying four Bokhara rugs for Chambers and shipping them to Washington; the rug dealer brought a sales slip fixing the purchase date as December 23, 1936.

Stryker acquitted himself superbly in chipping away at the prosecution case. Dramatically he produced the Woodstock the FBI had failed to locate; actually this did not affect the picture, since identification of the typescripts was not disputed. Then he advanced a brand-new theory: that the machine had been in possession of a former Hiss servant, Raymond Catlett, since early 1937. (The documents on display had been transcribed in 1938.) Raymond's mother, who had spontaneously recognized Chambers at FBI headquarters the previous February, now would admit only that she had seen him once, in 1936, as "Crosby, like in Bing." Raymond himself rattled off names and dates with ease, but under Murphy's hammering admitted that he did not know when he got the machine. His brother Perry under cross-examination knocked an even bigger hole in the theory. When he and Raymond received the typewriter, he said, they took it to a Woodstock shop on K Street and Connecticut Avenue to be repaired. The shop, it was proved, had not opened for business until September 1938.

The highlight of the proceedings, of course, was the testimony of Alger Hiss. He went into great detail about his contributions to the government. His sharply delineated face was calm. Only in the way he clenched his fist, gripped the arms of the chair, crossed and uncrossed his long legs did he betray the inner tension. Now Hiss insisted that he received a rug not in 1937 but in the spring of 1936. The four-hundred-dollar withdrawal, he said, was made to buy furniture for a new house; he did not attempt to explain how Chambers could have known about the precise sum. He rescinded previous testimony that the Woodstock had been in his house in 1938, the Catlett testimony having "refreshed his recollection." He had given the old Ford to "Crosley," he now recalled, long after the alleged subletting, though the tenant had failed to pay the agreed rent. For two days Murphy grappled with the nimble-witted Hiss. He moved slowly, ponderously, after a witness who usually eluded him. He lined up a long list of inconsistencies and "refreshed" versions in the Hiss accounts, but the defendant simply insisted that his current recollection was better than his past recollections.

Priscilla Hiss, by general agreement of spectators, did not help the defense. Point by point she denied Esther Chambers' narrative of interfamily intimacy. But she fell into a number of serious contradictions. She denied Socialist Party membership, whereupon Murphy produced photostats of her 1932 registration as a Socialist. Esther had testified that in 1937 Priscilla had planned to take a nursing course at Mercy Hospital in Baltimore. This Mrs. Hiss firmly denied. When Murphy produced her letter to the University of Maryland, dated May 1937, applying for enrollment in a chemistry course as a prerequisite to the Mercy Hospital course, the shock was as great to Stryker as to Mrs. Hiss. If, as she swore, Mrs. Hiss had last seen the Chamberses in 1936, how could Esther have known? Murphy had other puzzlers for Priscilla. Why had she told the grand jury that Mrs. Catlett was dead? Why, when she had charge accounts and an active checking account, did she draw out $400 in cash—for furniture in a house to be occupied many weeks later? Why had she said the Woodstock was in the house in 1938, then claimed to have given it away in early 1937? When she stepped down, Mrs. Hiss seemed on the verge of hysteria.

The defense brought eminent witnesses to attest to Hiss's reputation for loyalty and veracity. Among them were Supreme Court Justices Frankfurter and Stanley Reed, "taking a day off from Mount Olympus," as one reporter cracked. Judge Kaufman rose from the bench, visibly impressed, to shake hands with the Justices in the jury's presence. But neither man could give any information directly related to the evidence in the case. When

Murphy asked Frankfurter whether he ever put his stamp of approval on Lee Pressman, Judge Kaufman intervened and no answer was given. Before the defense rested, it called Dr. Binger. The bench allowed Stryker to read a forty-five-minute "hypothetical question"—one that accepted as fact even the most far-fetched defense allegations against Chambers—then refused to allow the physician to answer. "A grave injustice has been done to the government," Murphy roared. The prosecution's attempt to place Mrs. Massing on the stand was blocked by a bench ruling.

Four times the jury reported that it could not arrive at a unanimous verdict. As the hours of deadlock passed, Hiss put aside a statement he had been writing, to be issued following his acquittal. Frayed and weary—split eight for conviction and four for acquittal—the jury was discharged on the evening of its second day's deliberations. The long ordeal for the Hisses and the Chamberses thus ended after twenty-seven days and 803,750 pages of testimony. Alger, gray-faced and grim, stalked out of the courtroom without a word or handshake for Stryker. Down on his Maryland farm, Chambers said only: "I did what I had to do. . . . Time will bring out the truth."

Judge Henry W. Goddard, a veteran of twenty-three years in the federal courts, sat on the bench when the second Hiss trial opened on November 19, 1949. In his preliminary statement prosecutor Murphy this time stressed the importance of the concrete evidence—the "immutable" documents, memos, typewriter. A new chief counsel, a Boston lawyer of high reputation, Claude B. Cross, conducted the defense.

In his opening remarks Cross undertook to prove that the documents had been purloined by Wadleigh and another State Department official. Throughout the trial the press waited in vain to learn the identity of the second official. As for Wadleigh, besides his explicit denial that these had been among the four to five hundred papers he conveyed to the spy ring, it was proved that he was abroad during part of the period involved.

For those who had attended the initial trial, the second was largely the unreeling of an old film. Yet there were on both sides new facts and claims to round out the picture. The testimony of Whittaker and Esther was richer in detail and therefore more convincing. To an extent Chambers had overcome his former tendency to self-accusation. He fought back, and often his cross-examiner retired as loser in exchanges. Once, for instance, Chambers blandly invited Cross to press him on a point— what one of the Hiss maids had said when they were confronted by the FBI. Cross bit.

"She said she didn't remember me," Chambers said, "but that Lee Pressman and Nathan Witt were frequent visitors at the Hiss home."

The defense had subpoenaed a passport obtained by Chambers in 1935 under the name of David Breen. The document showed "Breen"with a bushy mustache. Cross tried to make much of Chambers' failure to mention this embellishment. All he proved, however, was that the Hisses had not mentioned it either, though Chambers had worn the mustache during the entire period in which Hiss admitted knowing Crosley. On the stand Esther Chambers alluded to a New Year's celebration with which the two families greeted 1937. Cross triumphantly produced a letter, postmarked December 30, 1936, from Alger to his wife, then visiting in Chappaqua, New York. Priscilla testified she had remained in Chappaqua with her son Timmie "about two weeks after the New Year."

For once the Chambers recollection seemed thoroughly demolished; obviously the celebration could not have occurred. Then Dr. Margaret Mary Nicholson, a prominent Washington pediatrician, brought her records to show that Mrs. Hiss and Timmie had visited her office on January 2, 1937, when Priscilla claimed to have been in Chappaqua. When this point boomeranged on the defense, the effect was devastating. Dr. Nicholson's records bolstered the government's case in another respect. To disprove that she had taken an automobile trip to Peterborough, New Hampshire, with the Chamberses during the summer of 1937, Priscilla had sworn that she had not once left Chestertown, Maryland, that summer. According to the Nicholson books, she had visited the Washington office repeatedly that summer.

Judge Goddard this time permitted Mrs. Massing to testify. Her account of her meeting with Hiss at the home of Noel Field made a deep impression. She was the first witness to corroborate the Chambers story directly.

There was little change in the defense case. A series of nineteen character witnesses—the two Supreme Court Justices conspicuously not among them—agreed that the defendant's reputation had been excellent. But Stanley Hornbeck, Alger's chief in the Far Eastern Division, admitted that on two occasions he had been warned of doubts about Hiss's loyalty by Ambassador William C. Bullitt. Francis Sayre volunteered that there was a difference of opinion as to Hiss's character; especially damaging was his testimony that Hiss had urged him to hire Noel Field.

Hiss himself, on the stand, was as suave as in the first trial. Eloquent on all immaterial matters, he became cagey and the tutored lawyer when faced with the mounting array of his discrepancies and revised recollections under oath. He played variations on the theme of refreshed recollection. But his wife shriveled up under cross-examination. She claimed that the four-hundred-dollar furniture purchases for a new house had been made in November 1937—though they did not move in until December 29—because she had the key to the place. Later, records were introduced proving that she first saw the house on December 5 and rented it on December 8. Though she had again and again stated that she was "not a typist," the government brought Columbia University records proving that she had passed a typing course. And so it went.

Dr. Carl Binger finally had his inning. This time the "hypothetical question" ran sixty-nine minutes. On this basis the doctor diagnosed "a psychopathic personality." He seemed so eager that at one point Judge Goddard interjected: "You are here as a witness, not as an advocate." A rare note of comedy was injected when Murphy pointed out that Dr. Binger had himself betrayed some of the "symptoms" he had cited against Chambers, such as staring at the ceiling. Did Dr. Binger know that in fifty minutes he himself had looked at the ceiling fifty-nine times? Murphy asked. There was a roar of laughter.

Possibly the most dramatic single witness appeared in the prosecution rebuttal near the end of the proceedings. She was Mrs. Edith Murray, the Chamberses' maid in 1936. For six months the FBI had sought her, with only her first name and a small portrait painted by Esther to go on. Finally they had located her. Now in a clear, quiet voice she told the court that she had been with the Chambers family (then living under the name of Cantwell) in Baltimore. They were "very nice people to work for," she volunteered, and Chambers "a very nice man."

Her unstudied honesty seemed to wash out the week-long psychiatric confusions. Mrs. Murray stood up and identified Priscilla and Alger in turn as people who had visited the Chambers house. Once, she said, "Miss Priscilla came and stayed overnight . . . when Mrs. Cantwell was pregnant and had to go to New York." Both Alger and Priscilla had testified that they had never been to the Chambers home. Cross-examination did not dent Mrs. Murray's account.

The final government rebuttal witness was Senator John Foster Dulles, who had helped make Hiss president of the Carnegie Endowment. Forthrightly he put his finger on five lies the defendant had told under oath about their relations. In addition he disclosed that Hiss had been virtually requested to resign in 1948 but had stalled until the "pumpkin" documents were produced.

No summation can do justice to the three million words of testimony in two trials. It was not, as a widespread fiction has it, a matter of one man's word against another's. The decisive element was physical proof—the documents, the typewriter, the records of the Ford transaction, apartment leases, medical records. This proof in turn was set in a framework of testimony that in substance confirmed the Chambers story while leaving the Hiss counterstory in a mass of splinters. The jury took just under twenty-four hours to reach unanimity. The woman foreman announced, "I find the defendant guilty on the first count and guilty on the second count."

"You have rendered a just verdict," Judge Goddard told the eight women and four men. The following week, on January 24, 1950, he sentenced the former Presidential adviser to five years' imprisonment on each count, the two terms to run concurrently. Alger Hiss rose to his feet. In a loud, clear, angry voice he declared: "I am confident that in the future the full facts of how Whittaker Chambers was able to carry out forgery by typewriter will be disclosed."

In the audience a sentimental woman wept. On the Westminster farm, where he had remained through most of the trial, Chambers said, "My work is finished. . . ."

But was it finished? Even as the last stories of the conviction and sentencing were appearing in the newspapers, an atonal shouting began as Hiss's supporters retired to prepared positions. Here was the chorus of innocents; here were the billowing skirts of know-nothing sentiment behind which the cynical and the perfidious can hide. There was still an appeal to the higher courts, some argued. But the courts, of course, would deal only with legalities; their findings would be irrelevant to the edifice of fact on which the jury had found Hiss guilty.

In two lengthy trials the tally of treason had been made. The accused had the benefit of able and expensive lawyers, support by eminent Americans, a public opinion which in the earlier stages was overwhelmingly on his side. But the evidence had been damning.

The meaning and the message of the Hiss-Chambers drama are that there is a "concealed enemy" in America's midst. The open and closed hearings, the three million words of the trials, exposed only a tiny corner of the vast Soviet netherworld. Hiss was one man, caught in a tragedy of arrogance and self-deception. But there are those—and their name is legion—who in their innocent blindness abetted him and his ilk in sowing the seeds of treason in the good American earth. Even afterward they refused to see, and this was the greater tragedy. Before it, the fate of Whittaker Chambers, the accuser, and Alger Hiss, the accused, paled into insignificance.

Evidence of the Unseen

By Archibald Rutledge

A FEW YEARS ago I wrote a magazine article in which I described a number of occult experiences—things that had happened to me or to persons of my acquaintance. After it was published I received hundreds of letters and also several visitors, all reciting similar psychic occurrences. The following accounts of contact with the shadowy world, which I am sure exists somewhere beyond our ordinary senses, are the most striking.

One day a dignified, white-haired gentleman—who, I learned later, was a judge of the Supreme Court of Pennsylvania—called on me. "Perhaps you will be interested in something that happened to me thirty years ago," he said. "Those to whom I have told it listen incredulously, yet nothing in my entire life is more vivid.

"During my practice as a country attorney I was making a long drive with horse and buggy over a country road one afternoon. The route was unfamiliar to me. As twilight fell I was driving down a country lane, on the right of which was a stone wall. There was no house in

sight. Not being sure I was on the right road, and therefore anxious to inquire, I was relieved to see a man sitting
on the stone wall ahead. When I came within fifty yards
of him he slipped down from the wall, moved toward the
road, then suddenly fell, face downward, and I saw him
lying in the road as plainly as I see you now.

"I thought the poor fellow had fainted, so I got out to
give what aid I could. The figure in the road never
moved, but as I advanced it faded from sight. When I
reached the spot the man was not there. I had not for one
second taken my eyes from him. And, I might add, I
was young, vigorous, had good eyesight and had had
nothing to drink.

"Greatly puzzled, I walked back to my horse. To my
amazement the animal, an old and phlegmatic one, was
in a state of terror. Its eyes were wide with fear, it was
breathing hard, it was in a profuse sweat, and when I
laid my hand on its back it trembled violently. It was all
I could do to get the creature past the place; once past, it
broke into a gallop, snorting with every bound.

"A half mile down the road I stopped at a house and
casually inquired about the place marked by the stone
wall. The woman to whom I talked eyed me curiously.

"'Oh, that place,' she said. 'Nobody ever likes to go by
there. The house burned down years ago. That was
where the awful murders were committed. You saw
something, didn't you? Things have been seen there.'

"Well, that is the story, corroborated by the woman's
statement that others had seen ghosts there. And there
was the frantic fright of the horse. I sometimes think
animals have a sixth sense about such things. Do you
believe what I have told you?" I told him that I did,
for I am convinced that there is an unseen realm whose
inhabitants sometimes become visible to some of us.

It is often suggested that animals have a sixth sense by which they apprehend what many people scorn as mere imagination or superstition. One of the letters I received told the story of a dog's peculiar behavior.

"Our setter dog, Marcella," this letter said, "was passionately fond of my husband. His business took him away from home frequently, and in his absence she slept on the floor of my bedroom. Once when my husband was away I was awakened by Marcella's growling. I turned on the light, thinking that some intruder was in the house. The dog's hair stood out stiff, her growls were deep and hoarse and very strange. Then she began to howl mournfully, after which she ran into my closet and lay there whimpering. Downstairs I found everything locked and safe. My two children were quietly sleeping.

"Within an hour a long-distance message informed me that my husband had been killed in a motor accident. I believe Marcella saw it, or saw him."

From Connecticut came this story:

"One evening my brother's wife and her three-year-old girl were alone in the brightly lighted bedroom of their apartment. The little girl was on her knees beside the bed, saying her prayers. Her mother stood nearby, listening. Suddenly she had a curious feeling that someone had come into the room, but she saw no one and said nothing of her feeling.

"When the little girl had finished she looked up and said, 'Mommie, who is that old man standing by you?' Her further description fitted perfectly her grandfather in Sweden, whom she had never seen. The very next letter received from Sweden contained the news that this grandfather had died on the night the child said she had seen him."

From a correspondent in Illinois came this story of a remarkable occurrence.

"My mother went with my sister to live in Richmond, Virginia, while my brother was studying there for the ministry. They rented a large, rambling old house. During the two years of her residence in this house there frequently appeared before my mother an officer of the Confederate Army whose left sleeve had a band of crepe on it. She told my brother and sister of seeing this figure, but they teased her about it. Later she told me, a more sympathetic listener. She said that one day, tiring of his repeated appearance, she remarked, 'Oh, why do you bother me so? I wish you would go away and leave me alone.' He looked up at her, sadly shook his head, vanished out the dining-room door and never returned.

"Several months later, in some museum or art gallery, my sister was looking over the catalogue. Suddenly she said to my mother, 'Here is a picture of your ghost.' My

mother's description of the apparition had been so accurate that my sister had recognized it immediately; and there, too, on the left sleeve, was the band of crepe. The catalogue said that the soldier in the picture was Dr. Hunter Holmes McGuire. They told the whole story to their hostess at a luncheon, and this lady said, 'Why, don't you know who Dr. McGuire was?' Mother declared that she had never before seen his picture or heard of him.

"'Well,' said her hostess, 'he was a surgeon in the Civil War. He attended Stonewall Jackson when the latter was mortally wounded. The crepe band covers a spot of Jackson's blood. Dr. McGuire remarked that since an officer must have a spotless uniform he had covered his beloved general's blood. The house you are living in was built and lived in by Dr. McGuire.'"

"Coming home late one night," wrote the editor of a financial publication, "I walked by a friend's house. His little son had diphtheria and was at the point of death. As I passed the house a little boy, very wan and pale, was standing on the sidewalk. Immediately I recognized him as the sick child and thought that in his delirium he had escaped the nurse. I spoke to him, and was about to take him in my arms and carry him into the house, when he simply wasn't there. I heard the next morning that he had died at the same hour that I had passed the house."

I cannot prove the truth of any of these stories, but I know some of the persons who related them and have complete confidence in them. In the case of the others, I can say only that their accounts seem to have the note of authenticity. Is it reasonable to call such strange occurrences spurious because they cannot be proved by any of our ordinary tests?

The Manufactured Clue

Condensed from the book Murder! Great True Crime Cases

By Alan Hynd

ON NOVEMBER 9, 1910, in Asbury Park, New Jersey, a nine-year-old schoolgirl named Marie Smith was beaten over the head, probably with a hammer, strangled and ravished. The child's body was found in a stretch of woods not far from where she had last been seen. For two weeks local sleuths frantically searched for clues. They called on the Burns Detective Agency of New York City. Raymond Schindler, who was then the manager of the agency's New York office, was assigned to the job. Young Schindler tackled the case with a brand of sleuthing that remains to this day a classic of investigation.

Marie Smith had last been observed on a semidesolate road at 3:10 in the afternoon, on her way home from school, but had failed to reach home at her usual hour of 3:15. The time and geographical elements of the crime were thus fixed. The trouble was that there were more than a dozen men living in what Schindler called the "suspect area" who could have committed the crime.

The young detective's first move was not too original. He soaked a hammer in chicken blood, then showed it to all the suspects, saying he had found it near the body and asking if they had seen it before. Of course they hadn't, but what Schindler wanted was a reaction from one of the human guinea pigs. He got it. A florist named Frank Heideman—a mild-mannered, good-looking young German who worked in a greenhouse within the suspect area—displayed signs of nervousness. Schindler then planned his next move.

One thing was obvious. Frank Heideman, though pleasant enough on the surface, was cold and resourceful. If this *was* the man who had committed the murder, a confession would not be easy to obtain. With no physical clues, Schindler knew that his problem was to trick him into talking about the crime. His opening gambit came right out of Conan Doyle's *The Hound of the Baskervilles*. In that famous story of Sherlock Holmes, the baying of a hound at night had a terrifying effect on the countryside in general and on several individuals in particular.

There happened to be a large dog near where Heideman, the suspect florist, lived. The dog, a particularly nasty customer, was fenced in. Schindler had another operative sneak up three times a night—at midnight, at 2 a.m. and at 4 a.m.—and throw stones at the dog. Thus, for more than a week, at the appointed hours, the dog would let out seemingly inexplicable howls that could be heard for miles. Each morning the suspects were looked over to see what effect the dog's howling had had on them, Schindler paying particular attention to Heideman. Ten days later he was tailed to a doctor's office. Schindler prevailed upon the medico, in the interests of justice, to tell him what Heideman had wanted. "He complains of a cold," said the doctor, "but he's jumpy as a grasshopper and won't say what's bothering him."

"What did you prescribe?" Schindler asked.

"A change of scene."

Heideman was followed to New York City, where he took a room on Sixth Avenue near 14th Street. Apparently a creature of habit, he ate all his meals in one restaurant at the same time each day. It was Schindler's hunch that Heideman would welcome companionship, particularly that of another German. From within the Burns organization Schindler dug up a young operative named Karl Neimiester. The young operative began to eat in Heideman's usual restaurant. He read a *Staats-Zeitung*, the New York German-language daily, while he ate. One day Heideman spoke to him. "I see you are a German," he said, extending his hand. "My name is Frank Heideman. What's yours?"

"Karl Neimiester."

The two men went to a movie. They saw each other frequently. Heideman, living on his savings, wasn't working, so it was necessary for Neimiester to invent a logical explanation for his own idleness. "I don't have to work, Frank," he explained one day. "I get $75 a week from my father's estate in Germany while it's being settled. A bank here in New York handles everything."

The first stage of the drama now successfully accomplished, Schindler decided to get a psychological reaction out of Heideman. Since the two friends were frequent moviegoers, Schindler, a man of many contacts, talked the proprietor of a little movie house on the East Side into sandwiching a sex-crime picture into his regular program for just one performance. Heideman and Neimiester were at that performance, as were several Burns men. As the film progressed, Heideman began to shift in his seat. His breathing became labored. He stiffened perceptibly when the murder was committed, and when the close-up of the body appeared on the screen he put his hands over his eyes, gasped and got up. "I'll see you tomorrow, Karl," he explained. "I've got a bad headache."

Schindler was now convinced that the German florist was *it*. He was trying to decide on his next move when Heideman decided for him. "Why don't we room together, Karl?" he suggested to Neimiester. And so the detective moved in with Heideman. That opened up an entirely new field for Schindler. He gave Neimiester his instructions. In the middle of the first night Neimiester shook Heideman into wakefulness. "What's wrong, Frank?" he inquired solicitously. "You've been raving in your sleep for almost an hour."

Heideman bolted upright in bed, his eyes wide with terror. "What did I say?" he wanted to know.

Neimiester shrugged. "I don't know exactly," he said. "You kept mumbling about a little girl."

Heideman sat in a rocking chair at the window for the rest of the night, smoking. This was repeated many nights. But by now the officials wanted results. Schindler and his boss, William J. Burns, pleaded for more time: to hurry a thing like this might ruin everything.

Schindler then arranged with Lyle Kinmouth, editor of the Asbury Park *Press*, to print a story saying the authorities had found a hammer believed to be the one used in the murder. Furthermore, the story continued, they planned to show it to Frank Heideman, the florist who was off somewhere for a rest, to see if he could identify it. Heideman, Schindler knew, would see the story, for the young German bought the Asbury Park paper every day.

Heideman began to chain-smoke after he read the *Press* in his room. Later, Neimiester picked up the paper and appeared to go through it casually. "Say, Frank," he said, "your name's mentioned here. Are you from Asbury Park, Frank?"

Heideman glowered at his friend. "Yes, I worked there for a couple of years. Where does it mention my name?"

Neimiester showed him.

"Oh," said Heideman, "they'll never be able to solve that murder down there. That hammer they found isn't the murder hammer because—" Heideman stopped short. Neimiester played it dumb. "Let's go to a movie," he suggested.

There was no doubt now that Heideman was the killer. He had almost let slip an admission of that fact. Schindler began maneuvering him now toward a full admission. One day Heideman and Neimiester, at the latter's suggestion, hired a horse and buggy and went for a drive through a lonely section of Yonkers. A hitchhiker—a desperate-looking character—asked for a ride. Neimiester, at the reins, refused and the man called him a name.

Neimiester jumped to the road and began to tangle with the man. The hitchhiker hurled a rock and the detective ducked just in time. Then Neimiester whipped a revolver from his pocket and fired twice. The hitchhiker dropped to the ground, face downward. Neimiester leaned over him and fired several more times. He rolled the body to the side of the road, ran back to the carriage, whipped the horse and took off. Heideman's first words were, "Karl, you should not have done that."

"Why not?" asked Neimiester, simulating a combination of rage and fright.

"Because," said Heideman, "you'll never be safe as long as you live. You have killed somebody and you'll always be afraid that the police will find out."

"I don't want to talk about it!" snarled Neimiester. The murder, of course, was phony. The hitchhiker had been a Burns operative, and Neimiester had fired blanks.

Now Schindler cooked up another fake news story for

the suspect's benefit. The publisher of the Yonkers *Herald* ran off one copy of a paper reporting that a hitchhiker had been slain and that the Yonkers police had a good description of the killer. Neimiester showed the paper to Heideman and announced that they would have to leave town. They went to Philadelphia and then to Atlantic City. Phony correspondence between a banker and Neimiester indicated that the mythical estate in Germany was about to be settled. "When I get the money," Neimiester said, "we'll go to California, or some place far away. I'll set you up as a florist. How does that sound?"

It sounded great to Heideman. The stage was all set now for the denouement. Schindler had terrified Heideman, shocked him, surprised him. Nothing had brought about a confession. His next move *had* to pay off: almost four months had elapsed. The two young men were staying at Young's Hotel. Schindler and other Burns operatives were in an adjoining room with a listening device. One day Neimiester received a letter that he acted very secretive about, though he had always been free in discussing his affairs with Heideman. Neimiester went down to the lobby for a pack of cigarettes and left the letter lying on a desk. When he returned, Heideman was blazing mad. He held the letter in his hand. "So you planned to double-cross me, eh!" he demanded.

The letter, written on North German Lloyd stationery—by Schindler—confirmed a reservation on a liner to Germany two days hence. "You and your big talk!" shouted Heideman, while Schindler and others listened in the next room. "You were going to set me up in business—*you*, my *friend!* And instead, what do you do? You make plans to go back to Germany and leave me here!"

Neimiester summoned up all the spurious warmth at his command. "Frank," he said, "you know how much I like you. But people are funny, Frank—you and me, *everybody*. People change. They are friends today and enemies tomorrow."

"What are you getting at?" Heideman demanded.

"Suppose that sometime you and I, as good friends as we are, quarreled. You would always know I killed that man in Yonkers, and you could always tell the police."

"So *that's* it!" said Heideman, relief in his voice.

"Yes," said Neimiester, "that's it. I'm going back to Germany because I'm scared. Wouldn't you do the same thing if you were in my place—if you knew that somebody knew *you* had committed a murder?"

"No," said Heideman. Neimiester looked at him. "I wish I could believe that, Frank."

"You *can* believe it," said Heideman. "I would never tell the police you committed that murder, *because I committed a murder, too*."

Neimiester scoffed. "*You* committed a murder? Who did *you* ever kill?"

"I killed that little girl down in Asbury Park. Remember the time it mentioned my name in the paper?"

"You're only making all that up to change my mind."

"But I'm not, Karl. I killed her. I killed her on the ninth of November. I hit her on the head with a hammer, and then I strangled her." Neimiester continued to simulate doubt. In his effort to convince Neimiester, so that his friend would remain in this country and finance him in the florist business, Heideman spilled the whole story.

On a night in May of the following year Frank Heideman was electrocuted. He had but one regret. He had been unable, after learning the truth about his friend, to murder him too. Young Raymond Schindler had no regrets. He was on his way to wealth and renown as head of his own agency.

The Millvale Apparition

Condensed from the book My America

By Louis Adamic

AUTHOR'S NOTE: *I decided to write this article partly because I didn't want the story to get first into the daily press, where it might be dealt with hastily and superficially, to the possible detriment of the Croatian people and Maxo Vanka's murals; and partly to call the Millvale "ghost" to the attention of reputable groups engaged in scientific investigations of psychical phenomena.*—L. A.

Maxo Vanka came to America in 1934. He had been for years professor of painting at the famous Zagreb Academy of Art in Yugoslavia and, as a recognized artist, he had pictures in museums and galleries all over the Continent. I saw a good deal of him and found him an extraordinary person, possessing such a sensitive temperament that he repeatedly anticipated my thoughts or words and began to respond to my remarks or questions before I finished uttering them.

Maxo found it hard to sell his pictures in this country and had become discouraged when, in April 1937, he was engaged by the Reverend Albert Zagar, pastor of the

Croatian Catholic Church of St. Nicholas at Millvale, an industrial suburb of Pittsburgh, to paint a series of murals for the church. Father Zagar hoped to have it completed in time for a mid-June celebration. By painting every weekday from nine in the morning till two or three the next morning, Maxo accomplished the work in two months—superb artistry that would have taken most artists a year. The murals attracted much favorable attention. One art critic called them "the best church murals in America." *Time* devoted a page to them, with reproductions. Streams of visitors have visited the little Croatian church to see them. But they were unaware—as was I when I first saw the murals—of the extraordinary, really fantastic circumstances under which Maxo had worked.

One day in August, Maxo told me the weird story. "When I got to Millvale," he began, "I knew that if I was to complete the job in two months I should need every minute I could get, without distraction; and therefore I persuaded Father Zagar to let me lock myself alone in the church every weekday from nine o'clock on. I saw no one until I returned to my room in the parish house, where I regularly found Father Zagar waiting up for me with coffee and cake.

"While I was working by my single powerful lamp on the creaky scaffolding the second or third night, a sudden long sound came out of the organ in the back of the church. It startled me, but I thought it was due to the vibrations from the motor traffic below the hill or from the nearby railyard. On the fourth night, while mixing paint, I glanced at the altar beneath me, which was rather fully illumined by my lamp's downward flood of light . . . and there was a figure, a man in black, moving back and forth in front of it, raising his arms and gesticulating. I thought, of course, that the man was Father Zagar and went on mixing the paint. I told myself he was probably practicing ritualistic gestures. As I entered the parish house that night, there was Father Zagar as usual. But he said nothing about having been in the church, and I didn't ask him about it, as I was tired and didn't want to start any long conversation.

"On the eighth night I happened about midnight to look down from the scaffold, and there was the figure again, the man in black, who, I assumed once more—without looking carefully—was Father Zagar. For almost an hour I heard him pacing the aisle, mumbling rhythmically. 'Well,' I thought, 'he's praying.' Then—all quiet; only the barking of dogs outside.

"Entering the parish house shortly afterward, what did I see but Father Zagar asleep on the couch in the living room! Waking with a start, he jumped up and said, 'Oh, my, it's past one o'clock. Why didn't that woman wake me?' He was angry, explaining that he had lain down about nine, having instructed his housekeeper, Mrs. Dolinar, to wake him at eleven. Then I told him I thought I had seen him in the church, but if he had been asleep ever since nine, I was impelled to think he was a somnambulist.

"'Believe me,' Zagar said seriously, 'I am not a sleep-walker.' He hesitated an instant, then asked, 'Tell me, have you since coming here heard of the tradition that this church is occasionally visited by a ghost or some strange phenomenon?'

"I answered, 'No.'

"'I have never had any experience with him or it myself,' Zagar went on, 'but listening to several people who say they have, I have admitted there might be some phe-

nomenon which we don't understand. . . . The reason
you always find me here so late when you come out of the
church is that I have stood watch outside the door between eleven and one every night since you began to
work, except today. I intended to rush in if I heard you
cry out or start hastily to climb down.' We decided that
hereafter Father Zagar would come into the church at
about eleven every night and stay until I stopped work.

"The following night he came in at about quarter to
eleven; he climbed up on the scaffold, bringing me a pot
of coffee; helped me with paint-mixing—something he
did regularly thereafter—then went down again lest he
distract me. . . . Suddenly there was a strange click or
knock at the back of the church, beneath the choir.

"'Hear that, Father?'

"'Yes, but wasn't it a creak in the scaffolding?'

"'I don't know,' I said. 'I don't think so.'

"Then—another click, but in another part of the
church. It sent a chill through me, and at the same time
sweat broke out of every pore of my body. Father Zagar
faced the rear of the church and in a tense, sharp voice
challenged, 'Come on, show yourself, whatever you are,
or speak if you can—'

"I interrupted him with a yell, for just then I saw
him—the 'ghost'—moving down the aisle toward the
altar: an old man in black, with a strange, angular face
wrinkled and dark with a bluish tinge.

"'Look, Father!' I shrieked. 'There he goes—to the
altar—*he's blown out the light!*'

"Shaking with terror, I started down from the scaffold,
and barely managed not to fall off the ladder. The light
was the 'sanctuary lamp,' which is *never* allowed to go out.
The glass bulb around the flame is so arranged that no
draft can touch it; besides, all doors and windows were

closed. Rushing to the altar, Father Zagar found that the wick in the lamp was still smoking. He touched the lamp; it was hot. The flame had, obviously, just been extinguished. Outside, the dogs were yelping and squealing.

"After that experience, whenever I got the 'signal,' as I called the sudden chill, I was impelled to rush out of the church as fast as I could. The sensation was stronger than fear. I tried to ignore it a few times and worked furiously. I put blinders, made of newspapers, on either side of my face. I stuffed cotton in my ears. At the end I would always have to go—the feeling of horror was intolerable.

"This went on for two months, usually between eleven

and twelve o'clock. Once 'he' came earlier in the evening, but the 'signal' was weak. I put on my newspaper blinders and worked. 'He' burned candles in front of the little altar on the right from the time 'he' came till Father Zagar entered the church at eleven, accompanied by Mrs. Dolinar.

"'What's this smell?' demanded Father Zagar.

"'He's been burning candles all evening,' I said. They found the chandelier full of molten tallow, while one wick, burned almost to the bottom, still flamed.

"This is my story," concluded Maxo. "I don't think I'm crazy. Nothing so intense, so terrific has ever happened to me. A ghost? I think so—something that is not substantial with flesh and bones and blood—call it what you like."

The matter of the "eternal light" going out was hard to explain, but I was inclined to believe that Maxo's experience was largely his own creation. The "ghost," I theorized, was a creature of Maxo's subconscious mind. Perhaps, deep down, Maxo doubted he could complete the job on time, and his subconscious mind, getting wind—via his acute, penetrating intuition—of the ghost tradition, had created the "ghost" to have in case of failure. I told Maxo my theories. He complimented me as a psychologist but shook his head: I was all wrong.

"There are several Croatians in Pittsburgh," said Maxo, "who have had 'experiences' with 'him.' The popular belief is that 'he' is a dead priest who while alive took money from parishioners for Masses which he never read, and who neglected his other priestly duties, and is now coming to the church to make up for his sinful negligence. The dogs seem to feel 'him,' for they barked violently nearly every time I saw 'him.'"

The story fascinated me, so, in mid-August, Maxo and

I drove to Pittsburgh and spent two days with Father Zagar at Millvale. The priest and Mrs. Dolinar, both of whom impressed me as being utterly incapable of any charlatanry, corroborated Maxo's story in every respect. They both insisted that on the occasion when "he" had burned candles all evening no living person could possibly have got in to burn them, for all the doors had been locked and the keys—except Maxo's—were in the parish house. Joking, I accused Maxo of burning the candles nimself. He laughed; he had too much to do to bother lighting candles.

I looked up a number of persons who had heard the strange knocks, had felt the chill, had heard the organ (which is electrically operated and therefore not subject to vibrations from the traffic). None had actually seen "him," but some had heard of persons who claimed they had seen "him" and that "he" looked like a priest. The majority of parishioners, however, seemed skeptical of "this nonsense." None of the latter knew of Maxo's and Father Zagar's recent "experiences" and thought the less said of the so-called "ghost" the better.

Father Zagar and I went into the church at midnight on Tuesday, August 17—Maxo did not want to come with us—and stayed there about an hour. But there were no knocks or clicks, we felt no chills and we saw nothing unusual. I was told that sometimes apparently "he" did not come for weeks or possibly months at a time. The dogs had been very quiet at night now for many weeks.

I left Pittsburgh not as definite a skeptic or scoffer as I had come there, but certainly an agnostic. There seems to be *something* in that church, but what it is I don't know. I can only say this: if there *was* "something" to see and experience, Maxo Vanka, if anyone, would see and experience it.

Ponzi's Monumental Swindle

Condensed from the book Strange Tales of Amazing Frauds

By Henry Thomas and Dana Lee Thomas

IN 1901 CHARLES PONZI, a restless, thin-faced youth in his late teens, left his native Italy for America with $200 in his pocket and a dream of wealth in his eyes. By the time he landed in New York he had $2.50 in change—he had lost the rest at the card table. It was an unpromising start for one who was to become the most amazing swindler of his day. Ponzi got a job as dishwasher in restaurants off Broadway. When he rose to be a waiter he got his first tuxedo. He liked the feel of it and made up his mind that he would always have one—and wear it, not as a waiter but as the man who pays the tips.

He went to Montreal and became a clerk at the Zrossi Bank, where he handled bundles of cash, dreaming it was his. Soon the line between dream and reality was obliterated. Ponzi was detected signing other people's names to checks and sent to prison for three years. He came out with his dream still big, beautiful, undiminished.

In 1917 he took a job as stock boy with J. P. Poole, Boston import and export brokers. Then came his big opportunity. Promoted from stock boy to clerk, he entered into business correspondence with a Spaniard who mailed him a postal-reply coupon to pay for the remittance of a certain article. In exchanging it for stamps Ponzi made a fascinating discovery: the coupon, bought in Madrid for one cent in American money, was redeemable in the United States for a nickel. This discrepancy came about because postal-reply coupons were redeemed at a rate fixed by treaty which did not reflect the actual rate of exchange. Why couldn't a smart fellow make millions just by buying postal-exchange coupons abroad with American money and redeeming them here?

Magnanimously, Ponzi decided to let a few friends in on the scheme. He quit his job and rented a one-room office at 27 School Street. On the first day of business, December 20, 1919, he collected $250. A few weeks later he turned over to his charter clients $375. News of this golden opportunity spread quickly: "Fifty percent profit on your money in forty-five days—double it in six months." Agents began to work for Ponzi, whispering the glad tidings to workers in offices and factories. The stream of investors swelled into a torrent. Clerks, stenographers, immigrants, small businessmen—all hurried up School Street and through an entrance marked by a sign: "To Charles Ponzi, Head of the Securities Exchange Company." At a teller's desk in a simple room a young man paid out greenbacks, while close by an armed comrade watched every movement. Free coffee and frankfurters were served to the eager people as they waited in a line that extended along the street to invest their money.

Ponzi's dream had come true. By the spring of 1920 he was collecting $250,000 a day. His chief assistant, an ex-butcher's helper, was earning $7000 a week. The money flowed in so fast that it filled all the desk drawers and spilled over into a dozen wastepaper baskets. Stacks of it reached the ceilings of the closets; sixteen clerks were hired merely to keep an eye on the cash. So great was the hysteria to get rich quick that people sold their Liberty Bonds and borrowed from loan sharks to invest with Ponzi. Bankers looked on with consternation as their savings accounts diminished. Ponzi claimed to have agents all over Europe. "I buy millions of postal coupons," he announced to the press. "My scheme can be tried by anyone, except for one little thing. How I exchange these coupons for cash in America is my secret."

In less than eight months this ex-dishwasher collected $10,000,000, and his name had become a byword from coast to coast. He acquired large holdings of Boston real estate, purchased the controlling stock of the Hanover Trust Company and bought out the brokerage firm which had employed him as a stock boy three years before. He had a showplace estate, spent $500,000 on furnishings, stocked his cellar with rare wines. The basement was lined with vaults containing millions of dollars. Guards patrolled the grounds with orders to shoot any prowler on sight. Ponzi drove around town in a custom-built limousine, and when he alighted from it he was cheered as though he were a movie idol. People mobbed the dapper little man, begging him to take their money.

Once a man in a crowd shouted that Ponzi was "the greatest Italian of them all." He modestly shrugged off such an estimate. "What about Columbus, who discovered America?" he asked.

A voice shrieked, "But you invented money!"

There were, however, some cool heads still in Boston. Richard Grozier, son of the publisher of the Boston *Post*, was convinced that Ponzi was a racketeer. He told his reporters to get the goods on him. Meanwhile, federal postal authorities had launched an intensive undercover inquiry. The entire issue of postal-reply coupons over the past six years accounted for less than $1,000,000—and Ponzi had accumulated $10,000,000 in a few months. Ponzi didn't bat an eyelash when confronted by the *Post* with this evidence. "I've just used this postal-coupon idea as a blind," he confessed blandly. "I didn't want the Wall Street boys to get even a hint of what my real scheme is. And so long as my depositors get back their investments with profit, I don't have to account to anybody!"

To scotch rumors that he was a swindler, Ponzi offered to refund money to any depositor. Some who had invested their life savings did get cold feet. To take care of them, Ponzi rented a second office and for several days he calmly handed out cash to the tune of $500,000 a day. When the skeptical saw fellow investors walk out of the School Street office with twice as much money as they had deposited, the run dwindled to a trickle. New cash poured in. After the *Post*'s exposure, Ponzi managed to collect more than $5,000,000 of additional investments!

The authorities were now convinced that Ponzi was hoodwinking his investors with the oldest trick in the art of swindling: paying earlier investors with funds taken in from recent ones. On August 11, 1920, the Montreal police department identified Ponzi as the Zrossi Bank clerk who had served a three-year prison sentence for forgery. Two days later U.S. federal agents seized Ponzi's holdings and placed him under arrest. A mob of his victims stormed the School Street office in hysteria, shrieking, "Kill him!"

During less than a year of business, Ponzi had tricked forty thousand investors into handing over more than $15,000,000. No one could estimate his liabilities, but it was certain that only a few of the investors would be lucky enough to receive twenty-five cents on the dollar.

Indicted on eighty-six counts by the federal government, Ponzi pleaded guilty and was sentenced to five years. From jail he sent out Christmas greetings to his thousands of creditors. He expressed the wish that the "recent miscarriage of your investment would not mar the spirit of the Christmas season," and asked them to look forward to the day when, stepping from prison a free man, he would help them to recover their losses. Even in his cell Ponzi received letters from admirers enclosing money which they begged him to invest for them.

He was released after serving three and a half years of his sentence. Then the state of Massachusetts indicted him for grand larceny. After some delay—three trials and an appeal—he went to prison for seven years. In February 1934 he came out. At South Station the police held back a furious crowd of his creditors, who even now shrieked hysterically for the money they had lost fourteen years before. The following morning two U.S. marshals arrested him for deportation proceedings; he had never taken out U.S. citizenship. In October 1934 Ponzi was shipped back to Italy—in steerage quarters. But his incredible story was not yet over.

In Rome, Ponzi turned his versatile talents to politics and succeeded so well in ingratiating himself with the Fascist Blackshirts that he was sent to Rio de Janeiro as business manager for Mussolini's Lai Airlines. At sixty he had regained his youthful charm and exuberance. But this bubble also broke. When Mussolini fell, Ponzi was turned out. For a time after the war he eked out a living as a translator. But things changed from bad to worse. At last, blind in one eye and partially paralyzed, he was committed to a charity ward in Rio. There he died in January 1949, at the age of sixty-six. He left $75, barely enough to pay for his burial.

Acknowledgments

FOUR MONTHS IN A HAUNTED HOUSE, by Harlan Jacobs, cond. from *Harper's Magazine*, © 1962, Harper & Row, Publishers, Incorporated.

HOW WE TRAPPED CAPONE, by Frank J. Wilson, as told to Howard Whitman, cond. from *Collier's*, © 1947, The Crowell-Collier Publishing Co.

COUNSEL ASSIGNED, by Mary Raymond Shipman Andrews, cond. from *The Counsel Assigned*, © 1940, Paul Shipman Andrews, pub. by Charles Scribner's Sons.

THE MAN WHO SOLD THE EIFFEL TOWER, by James F. Johnson as told to Floyd Miller, cond. from the book, © 1961, James F. Johnson and Floyd Miller, pub. by Doubleday & Co., Inc.

THE STATE OF TENNESSEE VERSUS UNCLE JOE, by T. H. Alexander, cond. from *The Memphis Commercial Appeal*, © 1939, Memphis Commercial Appeal.

SECRETS OF A SOVIET ASSASSIN, by Isaac Don Levine, cond. from *The Mind of an Assassin*, © 1959, Isaac Don Levine, pub. by Farrar, Straus and Cudahy, Inc.

THE DREYFUS AFFAIR, by Nicholas Halasz, cond. from *Captain Dreyfus: The Story of a Mass Hysteria*, © 1955; Nicholas Halasz, pub. Simon and Schuster, Inc.

BOND OF REUNION, by Carl Carmer, cond. from *The Saturday Review of Literature*, © 1942, Saturday Review Co., Inc.

THE AMAZING MR. MEANS, by J. Edgar Hoover with Courtney Ryley Cooper, cond. from *The American Magazine*, © 1936, The Crowell Pub. Co.

ONE ALASKA NIGHT, by Barrett Willoughby, cond. from *Alaska Holiday*, © 1936, 1937, 1939, 1940, Barrett Willoughby, pub. by Little, Brown & Co.

THE CAPTURE OF ADOLF EICHMANN, by Bela W. von Block, cond. from *See*, © 1960, West Park Pub. Corp.

THE ABRAHAM LINCOLN MURDER MYSTERY, by Theodore Roscoe, cond. from *The Web of Conspiracy*, © 1959, Theodore Roscoe, pub. by Prentice-Hall, Inc.

WHY THE CHOIR WAS LATE, by George H. Edeal, reprinted from *Life*, © 1950, Time Inc.

THE LETTER THE BIRDS WROTE, by John William Rogers, from Dallas *Daily Times Herald*, © 1951, The Daily Times Herald.

THE KILLER, THE MOTHER AND THE BOY, by Ernest Havemann, cond. from *McCall's*, © 1956, McCall Corporation.

GHOST DOG OF SUNNYBANK, by Albert Payson Terhune, cond. from *The Book of Sunnybank*, © 1962, Anice Terhune, pub. by Harper & Row, Publishers, Incorporated.

CELEBRATED SCAMP, by Alva Johnston, cond. from *The Legendary Mizners*, © 1953, Evelyn Johnston, pub. by Farrar, Straus & Cudahy, Inc.

BAKER STREET EPISODE, by Ellery Husted, cond. from *The Baker Street*